D0371767

# The Last Putt

Books by Neil Hayes

*When the Game Stands Tall: The Story of the De La Salle Spartans and Football's Longest Winning Streak*

*The Last Putt: Two Teams, One Dream, and a Freshman Named Tiger*

Books by Brian Murphy

*San Francisco Giants: 50 Years*

*The Last Putt: Two Teams, One Dream, and a Freshman Named Tiger*

# The Last Putt

*Two Teams, One Dream, and
a Freshman Named Tiger*

NEIL HAYES & BRIAN MURPHY

HOUGHTON MIFFLIN HARCOURT
BOSTON   NEW YORK
2010

Copyright © 2010 by Neil Hayes and Brian Murphy

ALL RIGHTS RESERVED

For information about permission to reproduce selections from this book,
write to Permissions, Houghton Mifflin Harcourt Publishing Company,
215 Park Avenue South, New York, New York 10003.

www.hmhbooks.com

*Library of Congress Cataloging-in-Publication Data*
Hayes, Neil, date.
The last putt : two teams, one dream, and a freshman named Tiger /
Neil Hayes and Brian Murphy.
p. cm.
ISBN 978-0-618-84004-5
1. Golf. 2. College sports—United States. 3. Oklahoma State University—Golf.
4. Stanford University—Golf. 5. Woods, Tiger. I. Murphy, Brian. II. Title.
GV965.H34 2010
796.352092—dc22    2009035211

Book design by Brian Moore

Printed in the United States of America

DOC 10 9 8 7 6 5 4 3 2 1

To Marlys Gee for her counsel. For Charlee, Nick, and Riley, as always. Most of all, to Dad.

—N.H.


For my Mom and Dad, and for Candace and Declan . . . for inspirations past, present, and future.

—B.M.

# Contents

# The Last Putt

# Prologue

*Scarlet Course, Ohio State University*
*Columbus, Ohio*
*May 31, 1995*

CAR DOORS SLAMMED, golf spikes crunched, and heads turned as he walked onto the driving range on a late-spring morning at the Scarlet Course on the campus of Ohio State University. The dew had yet to evaporate, the sun barely peeking over the midwestern horizon, but already there was heat in the air.

He was skinny, only 160 pounds at six feet, and a bit gawky, but everyone looked. How could they not? Freshman or not, Tiger Woods had arrived at the NCAA Championships.

Just one month earlier, Tiger Woods had dominated the headlines at Augusta National, making the cut at the Masters in his first appearance at a major championship. As the winner of four consecutive USGA championships, he was a history maker. As the multiethnic star in an overwhelmingly white sport, he was a media fascination, with *Sports Illustrated,* the *New York Times*, and *Golf Digest* all clamoring for his time. To have Tiger Woods playing in the NCAA Championships was the modern equivalent of LeBron James or Kobe Bryant playing in college basketball's Final Four.

The Scarlet Course was the college playground of Buckeye legend Jack Nicklaus, the greatest player ever, but the presence of golf's celebrated new prodigy gave this year's NCAA Championships an unprecedented visibility. This was clearly Tiger's lair. The ESPN cameras proved it. The rookie arrived with his Stanford teammates, wearing Cardinal red, and with the most hype of any college player ever. By extension, that made the 1995 NCAAs the most-hyped team championship ever.

The Cardinal were defending national champions, intent on becoming the first college team in a decade to repeat. They were rock stars in an otherwise understated sport.

The Cardinal arrived in Ohio from the elite grounds of Stanford University in the progressive Bay Area, from one of the nation's most academically exclusive campuses. Their avuncular coach, Wally Goodwin, who had rebuilt this sleeping giant into maybe the most celebrated college golf team in history, led them. They were anchored by seniors Notah Begay III and Casey Martin, the core of a team who had shocked the college golf world a year earlier with an NCAA championship — best friends and kindred spirits.

Begay, who spent part of his childhood on a reservation in New Mexico, was already the best full-blooded Native American golfer in NCAA history. Martin, who grew up in rainy Oregon, was noticeable because of a rare circulatory disorder that made it difficult for him to walk — let alone be part of a national championship team.

Stanford had the buzz and the story lines. The Cardinal had the title, Tiger, and every reason to believe their destiny was another championship.

But they also had an adversary.

As Stanford arrived that day in Columbus for the first round, another team warmed up on the practice range, proudly flying the black and orange of their school, unintimidated by the Cardinal mystique. The Oklahoma State Cowboys were a year removed from watching Stanford steal the 1994 NCAA championship the Cowboys thought was rightfully theirs. They took it hard. Slowly, that bitter disappointment was replaced by a newfound resolve. Everything they had done since then, every early-morning workout, every practice shot, every round, was aimed at one goal: restoring Oklahoma State's tradition by winning the NCAA championship.

Oklahoma State leapfrogged Stanford on its way to *Golf World*'s number-one team ranking heading into Columbus. It was where the Cowboys expected to be. They'd won six national championships in twenty-one years under legendary coach Mike Holder and led the nation in top ten, top three, and top two finishes at the NCAA Championships as well. Despite the cow-town reputation and severe weather of the Stillwater campus, Holder had transformed it into a place known for its unyielding standards of golf excellence.

Stanford, which held the number-one spot for the first part of the season and had been described as perhaps the greatest collection of collegiate golf talent ever assembled, was now number two. More important, the final ranking would be determined during the next four tension-filled days in Columbus.

This championship was personal for seniors and best friends Alan Bratton and Chris Tidland, who were in danger of forever becoming known as members of the first class under Holder to graduate without winning a team championship. This was personal for junior Trip Kuehne, the can't-miss Golden Boy who looked at Tiger Woods that morning on the driving range differently from any other player at the Scarlet Course. They had a history, these two.

But the NCAA Championships were far from an individual showdown.

Scoring in college golf is dependent on five players, not one. A team sends its five best onto the course, and upon completion, the four best scores are counted in an aggregate total. The best four-day aggregate score would win the 1995 NCAA championship. This scoring system remained virtually unchanged until 2009, when the NCAA instituted a match-play format. In this system, the top eight teams qualify for head-to-head matches. In 1995, however, it was aggregate stroke play. Every member of the Stanford and Oklahoma State teams arriving in Columbus carried the burden of playing not just for himself but for his teammates as well.

Only in college golf do teammates spend years sacrificing for a common goal while creating bonds that last a lifetime. Maybe that's why Arnold Palmer once said his failure to win the NCAA tournament, when he was at Wake Forest, was one of the biggest disappointments of his career.

The NCAA Championships had a rich history. Name a great individual player from the last fifty years — Palmer, Nicklaus, Watson, Mickelson — and he played in the NCAAs. The tournament's legacy reaches back even farther than that, to 1897, when Yale won the first team championship, beginning a string of Ivy League dominance that lasted until the 1930s. But college golf was different then. Back then, college players mostly remained amateurs after graduation, true to the "gentleman's code" of the game, a code that frowned on playing golf for money.

Then, the sport evolved. The PGA Tour took off in the 1950s and 1960s, and soon the best training ground for the big-money tour was college golf. From the great Wake Forest and Texas teams of the 1970s, with Curtis Strange and Jay Haas, Ben Crenshaw and Tom Kite, all the way to Phil Mickelson's Arizona State teams of the early 1990s, the NCAA championship had become an almost mandatory, if sometimes overlooked, rite of passage for the greatest players.

In the last decade, college golf became deeper than ever. Dynasties like Dave Williams's Houston Cougars — who won sixteen national titles from 1956 to 1985 — were from another era. Even Oklahoma State, which replaced Houston as the dominant program in college golf, was struggling to keep up. Talent was everywhere. Texas remained a perennial power. So were the Arizona schools. Florida, too. Jim Brown, the twenty-second-year Ohio State coach, called the teams gathered at his school's golf course in 1995 "the most competitive field I've ever seen."

But this championship was billed as the "Showdown at the Scarlet Course" for a reason. College golf doesn't always have a tried-and-true rivalry, like Michigan–Ohio State in football or Duke–North Carolina in basketball, just as professional golf hasn't always featured a classic head-to-head competition to rival Palmer versus Nicklaus, or Nicklaus versus Watson. More often, one of a group of top-flight teams or players emerges to compete for team and individual championships. This was not the case in 1995.

What a study in contrasts these two teams featured: If Holder was the *über*-intense, detail-heavy taskmaster, Goodwin was the laid-back elder statesman who trusted his players to handle their business. Oklahoma State was an agricultural public school in the Midwest with a pig farm on the outskirts of town. Stanford sparkled in the golden California sun, bragged of its academics and scholars, and excelled at the so-called country club sports of tennis and swimming.

The two teams had gone toe-to-toe during the fall and spring seasons, and if anything the results had exceeded the hype. Magazine covers, TV previews, newspaper stories all centered on the same story line. If Oklahoma State was a five-man team of grinders, the Stanford team were the headliners of the sport, featuring the greatest young talent in the game's history, all of which had earned the team a lavish spread, replete with plenty of photos, in a recent issue of *Golf Digest*. Oklahoma State noticed, and quietly burned.

The tug of war between Stanford and Oklahoma State became the theme of the 1994–95 season, and what would happen over the next four days at the Scarlet Course, between raindrops and lightning bolts, would confirm it.

The first hole at the Scarlet Course is a par 4, 435 yards. Waves of threesomes followed their tee shots on that first morning, nerves jangling, the national championships under way. No matter how many groups teed off, no matter how many brightly colored golf bags and shirts—the fire-engine red of Arizona, the burnt orange of Texas—disappeared down the fairway, for many observers, the tournament did not begin until Tiger Woods pushed his white tee into the green grass for Stanford. The freshman unleashed his ferocious swing, all sinew and speed, and the first-timers ringing the tee box would swear it made a sound different from every other player's. Their heads followed the majestic trajectory of Tiger's high, drawing tee shot, and then their eyes returned to the object of their curiosity as he replaced his club and shouldered his golf bag and strode up the fairway.

Four days later, when the tournament was over, when the championship was decided, and the Scarlet Course lay in the gloaming on the evening of Saturday, June 3, 1995, Stanford coach Goodwin would survey the scene.

"People will be talking about this tournament," he said, "for a long, long time."

# 1

# Tiger versus Trip

*Ponte Vedra Beach, Florida*
*August 28, 1994*

THE HAVEMEYER TROPHY, an ornate eighteen-carat-gold stee-ple cup, rested on the first tee box in front of Tiger Woods and Trip Kuehne at the famous TPC Sawgrass course, the setting for the ninety-fourth U.S. Amateur, the most prestigious tournament in amateur golf. It held the greatest names in the sport's history: Ouimet, Jones, Palmer, Nicklaus. By the end of the afternoon, after thirty-six holes, after two trips through Spanish moss and forests of pine trees, past dozing alligators and the infamous island green of the seventeenth hole, either Woods's or Kuehne's name would be engraved on it, ensuring a permanent place in golf history.

From Sawgrass, the twenty-two-year-old Kuehne, the oldest child in one of the country's most celebrated junior golf families, would return to the college town of Stillwater to begin his junior year at Oklahoma State. Tiger, just eighteen years old, was a month away from moving into the Stanford dorms in Palo Alto, California.

On a windless, cloudless Sunday, with an 8:15 A.M. start on the short par 4 that eases the player into Pete Dye's wicked recipe of railroad ties and precise shot making, of ubiquitous water hazards and sandy white bunkers, Trip and Tiger stood in the glare of the golf spotlight, on ESPN's national broadcast. In many ways, however, they were very much alone.

The U.S. Amateur is defined by attrition. A championship that began with 5,128 dreamers, at seventy-five different sites, had been winnowed to 312 players who earned the trip to Sawgrass's finale. From there, the elimination process was relentless, each day featuring the vanquished checking out of hotels, zipping up golf travel bags, and boarding airport shuttles. First, the field of 312 was thinned to 64 over thirty-six-hole stroke play. Then, the field of 64 was narrowed, and in a hurry. Wednesday saw eighteen-hole matches reduce the field to 32. By Thursday sundown, with two rounds of play, only 8 players remained. After Friday's play, there were only 4. And by Saturday evening, in a championship marked by bustle and buzz, by the hum of constant results, the flurry of golf resulted in just 2 players—Tiger and Trip—left in an otherwise empty locker room.

Tiger looked every bit the teenager. Skinny as a 4-iron, he wore a straw Panama hat to block the sun, a look that only seemed to emphasize his spindly physique. In an unremarkable combination of blue shorts, white socks, and white golf spikes, set off by a somewhat garish sky blue shirt with vertical stripes down its left side, Tiger may not have looked like a star, but he was. Just two months removed from graduation at Anaheim's Western High, he was already famous. His three consecutive victories in the U.S. Junior Amateur, in 1991, 1992, and 1993, at ages fifteen, sixteen, and seventeen, were the stuff of legend. Nobody, not Nicklaus, not Jones, had won three consecutive USGA titles, a feat made more remarkable by the capricious nature of match play. The accomplishment resulted in Tiger being a media sensation. *Sports Illustrated* chronicled his exploits for the country. And already, the summer of '94 had been a good one. Tiger won the Western Amateur in July in what was becoming known as a Tiger-esque win—soaked with drama. In the Western, Tiger defeated an Oklahoma State player named Chris Tidland over twenty holes. Tidland birdied the twentieth hole. Tiger eagled it.

The next logical step in Tiger's progression was to win a U.S. Amateur, not against gangly teenagers, but against grown men. Tiger, at barely 160 pounds, didn't look the part. But the resumé he toted to the first tee for the Amateur final spoke far louder than any teenage appearance. Moreover, he was trying to become the youngest winner of a U.S. Amateur. In 1909, a nineteen-year-old named Robert Gardner won the trophy. And in 1959, a nineteen-year-old Jack Nicklaus did, too. No eighteen-year-old ever had.

Four years older, Trip was bigger and stronger. He was ready for his close-up. In khaki shorts, white socks, and Nike golf shoes, topped off by a red, white, and blue striped shirt, Trip looked decidedly more mature. Not only that, but his golf resumé was beefy. Two months earlier, Trip had shot 65 at the NCAA Championships at his home course of Stonebridge in Texas to help land him third-team All-American honors. Playing well under pressure was Trip's life story. He made American Junior Golf Association All-American an unprecedented five times and was a two-time state high school champ in the competitive world of Texas golf, the same state that produced Ben Hogan, Byron Nelson, Tom Kite, Ben Crenshaw, and Justin Leonard.

On top of that, Trip was a star off the course, too. He carried a 3.85 grade-point average with a psychology major and business minor, and there was already talk of Trip forgoing a PGA Tour career to enter the world of business. He eyed the MBA program at Oklahoma State, and his combination of good looks, great golf, and excellent academics earned Trip the nickname "Golden Boy."

Trip and Tiger weren't strangers, either. Four years earlier, they had been partners on Team USA's Canon Cup squad, a junior version of the Ryder Cup. They had even won an alternate-shot match together. And Tiger was pals with Trip's younger siblings, brother Hank and sister Kelli. Hank and Tiger were only three months apart in age, and Kelli was just two years younger than Tiger. Kelli, in fact, won the U.S. Girls Junior Amateur earlier that summer, and it was suggested that no family had ever won two USGA championships in the same summer. The Kuehnes, who had combined for ten AJGA titles as siblings, including Hank, had that chance.

Their fathers also forged the link between Tiger and Trip. On the tee box that morning in Sawgrass were Earl Woods and Ernie

Kuehne, who had known each other after serving on the AJGA board of directors. Each man was the force in his son's life, making sure financial and emotional support never ran dry. The best equipment, the best instruction, travel logistics . . . there was no hurdle Earl or Ernie wouldn't clear to keep their children competing on a national stage.

Ernie Kuehne once said of his family: "The Kuehnes may not always win, but nobody's going to out-tough us. Nobody's going to doubt our resolve on the first tee." If the Kuehne family mantra could be boiled down to two sentences, it would be those.

Ernie had taken the same approach to his career. From humble origins growing up on a cotton farm in Texas, Ernie parlayed a law degree into a small business empire and made for his family a life of privilege. The Kuehnes had two homes, one in the prestigious Highland Park neighborhood of Dallas and the other on the eighteenth hole at Stonebridge Country Club in nearby McKinney. Ernie bought the Highland Park home so his kids could attend Dallas's best public high schools. And the Stonebridge home was bought so the kids could have playing privileges at the country club, where their championship mettle would be forged. Hank Haney called Stonebridge home, and Ernie made sure the famous swing coach would school his children. For a man who played virtually no golf, Ernie Kuehne had a precise idea of how to produce golf champions under his roof.

That extended to Ernie's role at Sawgrass that day—he was Trip's caddie. It was, perhaps, a mixed blessing. Ernie Kuehne arrived at the first tee with a very precise idea of what his son must do to upset the budding legend of Tiger Woods. Ernie had an opinion about everything, it seemed.

Tiger's caddie was a man named Jay Brunza, and Brunza's role in Tiger's growth was representative of Earl Woods's level of dedication to his son's career. Earl was a retired lieutenant colonel in the U.S. Army and former Green Beret who had done two tours of duty in Vietnam. Earl was an athlete—he'd played college baseball at Kansas State as a catcher. Earl was a groundbreaker, too—he was the first African American ballplayer in the Big Eight Conference. Both of those facts served him well in his role as Tiger's father. He was an older parent, having fathered Tiger in his second marriage at age forty-three, just in time to coincide with his discovery of golf at age forty-two, a discovery that he pursued with the passion of a newcomer. He had a job as a contracts administrator at McDonnell Douglas in Huntington Beach, California, but his real job, it seemed, was chaperoning and nurturing his prodigy of a son. The Woods family took out loans to make sure no opportunity was missed. Their travel itinerary was impressive, including international tournaments in Europe and Asia. Part of Earl's job was to surround Tiger with the best possible people, including individual swing coaches and, in perhaps the most revolutionary move, a clinical psychologist from the U.S. Navy who was a family friend. Brunza worked with Tiger as early as age thirteen and used hypnosis in his training.

Tiger was reaching for his 3-wood when USGA official Kendra Graham introduced the first tee shot to be struck by "Tiger Woods, of Cypress, California." When he pulled it into the left rough, followed by Trip piping his drive down the middle of the fairway, they were off.

If Ernie Kuehne noticed anything about Tiger's game, it was that he was a slow starter. On Saturday evening, as they discussed strategy, Ernie told his son that instant intensity was paramount. Trip followed suit. He made birdie on the par-5 second hole and was 1 up. On the short par-4 fourth, Tiger missed a putt to halve the hole and slapped his ball away with his putter, miffed. He was 2 down. By the ninth hole, a par 5 with some trouble lurking, Trip stood tall. He was 80 yards short of the green in two and hit a wedge to 18 inches for birdie. Trip was on fire and 3 up on Tiger, who was yet to blossom, after nine.

Trip wasn't content, nor was he afraid of Tiger. Trip had lived a gilded life, mingling with the rich, famous, and powerful since early childhood. Tom Cruise lived two doors down for two years. The governor lived a couple of blocks away. Trip wasn't intimidated by Tiger or by the circumstances. At the par-5 eleventh, Tiger missed a 4-foot putt and fell 4 down. Trip's compact, powerful golf swing was dialed, and he smoked his drive on twelve over 300 yards. He hit a pitching wedge and used Pete Dye's slopes to his advantage, his ball trickling ever closer to the hole. Birdie, and Trip was 6 up on Tiger.

Seven birdies in the first thirteen holes meant Trip had fulfilled Ernie's wish. He'd punched Tiger, figuratively, in the mouth and set a tone for the morning eighteen that most had not seen coming. Tiger had plenty of comebacks on his ledger already, but being 6 down to a pedigreed champion like Trip Kuehne was not anybody's idea of a good time.

But at the fourteenth hole, a confounding par 4 with water left and trees right, Trip made his first mistake of the day. Even with momentum on his side, he hit a poor drive and failed to reach the green in regulation. Tiger stayed steady, and when Trip made his first bogey of the day, his lead slipped from 6 up to 5 up.

Trip and Tiger arrived at the sixteenth hole, one of Sawgrass's most famous. It's a par 5 that tests the placement of the drive—owing to a forest on the left—and the decision on the approach, owing to water surrounding the back and right sides of the green. Sixteen was the sort of hole that defined rounds, sometimes even more so than its famous neighbor, the island par-3 seventeenth.

Definition was forthcoming: Tiger sprayed his drive terribly, to the left, so far off line it even soared over the towering trees. Tiger was in jail. Incredibly, he still had big ideas. From his precarious spot, he tried to carve a 3-wood through the trees—a dicey idea, most present agreed. His ball cracked off a tree branch, falling as if dropped down an elevator shaft. It was still in play, though, resting beneath the branches. Observers couldn't help but wonder if Tiger had just been blessed with fortune. His second shot could have easily splashed into Sawgrass's waters but for that tree branch. He might have been farther from the hole in two than Trip was in one, but at least he was still alive—and still had a chance for a miracle.

Tiger pulled 3-wood from 250 yards out and, believing all the while, landed his ball on the sixteenth green. It was a gutsy shot, and Woods was 12 feet from birdie. Trip played the hole by the book: Drive in the fairway, lay up 100 yards short, a wedge to the green, and a two-putt for par. The problem was, Tiger was feeling something. He struck his birdie try and raised his putter early, calling his shot as it tracked toward the hole. Bingo, a birdie. Tiger was 4 down and had cheated death. The Kuehnes wouldn't have believed what they had just seen had it been anybody else but Tiger.

At eighteen, a par 4 with water all the way down the left side, Tiger found himself in an awkward lie after his second shot. He was in a greenside bunker, with an angle so poor one leg was outside. Still, he dug it out to 3 feet from the hole and made the par that would keep him at 4 down after the morning eighteen.

Earlier in the round, ESPN's Brent Musberger had wondered aloud on-air, "Maybe the only thing that could stop Trip Kuehne right now is lunch."

Instead, Trip Kuehne went to lunch confident, but knowing the match wasn't over. Tiger Woods knew, too. As Tiger went to shower and change clothes in the Sawgrass clubhouse, he would revisit in his mind a scene from earlier that morning, when he had been alone with Earl before the match. Tiger's father leaned in and whispered to his son, "Let the legend grow."

It wasn't until two nights before the final at Sawgrass that Trip Kuehne allowed himself to look ahead. As he studied the U.S. Amateur championship bracket posted outside the clubhouse before his Friday quarterfinal, he saw the unavoidable. He and Oklahoma State teammate Kris Cox were on a collision course. Getting to the Amateur final would be taxing enough, but having to defeat your best friend in the semifinals to do it was a wrinkle for which neither had prepared.

So, after dispatching their quarterfinal opponents on Friday, Trip and Kris felt equal parts excitement and dread when they high-fived in anticipation of their matchup the next day. They were excited to be in the final four of the U.S. Amateur. Each year the two finalists of the U.S. Amateur earned the chance to play at the Masters, every competitive golfer's dream.

While Tiger Woods remained the focus of the media as he arrived for the semifinals, Trip and Kris knew their less publicized match would be like nothing they'd ever experienced, and not just because of the setting or what was at stake. In one week, the duo would be back on campus at Oklahoma State, inseparable as ever. But first, they would have to square off as competitors for a chance to win the greatest title in amateur golf.

Kris and Trip had known each other since they were twelve years old. Both were highly recruited. Trip won six AJGA tournaments and had led Highland Park High to three Texas team titles while winning two individual championships and finishing second once. Many considered him the number-one golf recruit in the country. Kris's gaudy junior resumé included two Louisiana state high school championships and low amateur honors at the Louisiana Open in 1991.

If Trip's dad was the guiding force in his career, Kris's mom, Valerie, and his grandfather were the guiding forces in his. Oree Marsalis was a beloved teacher of the game in Shreveport, Louisiana, where he tutored future PGA Tour star Hal Sutton and coached the Centenary men's golf team into his eighties. He passed on his love of the game not only to his entire family, but especially to his grandson, Kris, for whom he dispensed simple advice, his grandson's own personal Harvey Penick.

Oree's three daughters were all competitive amateur players. Kris's mother, Valerie, was the oldest and inherited Oree's gift for coaching. She could observe a swing or a grip and tweak it to make a player better. Her life would be comprehensively involved in the game, from coaching two state high school championship teams in Louisiana to serving on USGA committees and as tournament director for a women's event in her home state.

Once they arrived in Florida for the Amateur, Kris and Trip spent every evening together, relaxing over dinner with Valerie and Ernie.

They were both playing their best golf in the biggest tournament of their careers, yet the pressure associated with playing in the U.S. Amateur had been the farthest thing from their minds. They were having too much fun hanging out together away from the course to worry about what was at stake on it.

Now, all they had to do was look at each other to know that the most pressure-packed round of their careers would also be the most awkward. This wasn't going to be easy. The Coxes and the Kuehnes had been rooting for each other for almost ten years, and now here they were, with a berth in the finals of the coveted U.S. Amateur as a prize, and only one of them could win.

Instead of Trip *and* Kris it had suddenly become Trip *or* Kris.

It wouldn't have been so bad if a berth in the Masters weren't on the line. Both considered the tournament on the fabled Bobby Jones–founded course in Augusta, Georgia, to be golf's Valhalla.

Trip, Kris, Valerie, and Ernie all felt the tension at the restaurant the night before the match. Kris and Trip did their best to lighten the mood. When their parents were away from the table, they conspired with the waitress, who brought them shot glasses filled with iced tea. When their parents returned and saw their sons throwing back shots of brown liquid, they were in shock. Trip and Kris laughed, breaking the tension, at least temporarily.

If it were only that easy on the golf course, when the match unfolded and there was nowhere to hide from the ESPN cameras that followed them around the course and broadcast their images on national television. They were anxious and played too quickly, spraying shots and missing short putts.

Trip, looking every bit the Golden Boy in khaki shorts and a white polo buttoned at the collar, held a 1-up lead walking to the famous seventeenth tee box. The gallery around the short par-3 island hole was swelling, as fans migrated over after watching Tiger close out his semifinal on the fifteenth hole.

The seventeenth hole was among the most unique and famous in golf. Controversial, with its island green that offered no bailout, the hole was often criticized by players who felt it unfair. Fans, meanwhile, loved the little 132-yard heart stopper for its do-or-die drama, its standalone status as the Scariest Hole in the Game.

Trip went with an 8-iron but hit it strong, the ball landing fortuitously on the causeway behind the green. The crowd gasped at his fortune, but he'd left the door open for Kris, whose clutch tee shot landed 6 feet from the hole, drawing appreciative cheers.

Trip hit a bump-and-run wedge onto the collar and watched the ball roll to within 5 feet of the hole. Kris's birdie putt to win the hole was full of possibility, but when it slid 4 feet past, the groan from the crowd mimicked his own internal disappointment.

That disappointment mounted when Trip holed his putt for par. Trip knew he could have won the match right there if Cox missed again, but instead he did something that is rarely seen, even in the gentlemanly world of amateur golf. Trip knew he'd gotten lucky when his ball stayed dry after hitting the causeway. The last thing he wanted was to win a U.S. Amateur semifinal match and earn a berth into the Masters after his best friend missed a 4-foot putt on a hole where luck had been his ally. Instead, he conceded the relatively lengthy putt to his buddy, staying 1 up as they left the island green.

Kris plodded toward the eighteenth tee box with his shoulders slumped and his head down. Trip met him there, high-fiving his Oklahoma State teammate and giving him an encouraging slap on the behind.

When his 40-foot, against-the-grain birdie putt on eighteen died 4 feet from the hole, Kris knew it was over. Trip waved politely to the crowd after his long putt from the fringe stopped 18 inches from the cup, all but ensuring victory.

Kris conceded the biggest match of his life to his best friend. The two embraced in the middle of the green before taking a step back and high-fiving.

When Kris's greenside interview with Jerry Pate was winding down, and Pate was about to turn his attention to Trip, who waited patiently nearby, Kris leaned in closer: "Go Cowboys at Augusta. And tomorrow!"

In the lunch break of the U.S. Amateur final, Tiger remembered the morning words from his father to "let the legend grow." Trip Kuehne, 4 up on Tiger and eighteen holes from the championship, heard advice from his own father about that legend.

"He's going to make a run at you," Ernie told his son. "We're going to have to have enough in the tank to withstand it."

The first clue that maybe something would be different in the afternoon eighteen was Tiger's change of wardrobe. While Trip lunched with Ernie, Tiger showered and changed clothes. Now wearing a peach-and-white-striped shirt to go with his Panama hat, Tiger still lost the par-5 second hole with a wayward drive and was 5 down almost instantly. He steadied with a dynamite par save on the third and hit an approach to 12 inches on the fourth. His birdie got him back to 4 down. But then, more wobbles. Tiger drove it left on the sixth, and his second shot hit a palm frond. He lost the hole and was 5 down again.

Five down to Trip Kuehne with twelve holes left meant it was time for something to change.

Tiger effected a bit of change, at last, with a long, running 35-foot putt on the par-4 seventh to win the hole. Out came a fist pump, and Tiger was 4 down.

On the par-3 eighth, Trip's lag putt was 24 inches from the cup, but no concession was forthcoming from Tiger. While Rosburg joked that Woods might have "lockjaw," a common golf barb for a player who does not concede short putts, it was a smart move: By not conceding a 3-footer to Buddy Alexander in the round of sixteen, Tiger had stayed alive when Alexander missed. Trip would make his putt on the eighth and, under the pressure of holding this lead, seemed to be staying firm.

They came to the par-5 ninth, Kuehne still 4 up. Woods was loose off the tee, his game unsteady. He'd been tight, barking at Brunza. In the morning eighteen, after Tiger had missed a birdie try at the seventeenth, he'd snapped, "Nice fucking read." After the eighth, when both made par, Woods turned to his caddie. "This guy's good," Woods said, nearly disconsolate. "He's not going to choke."

With ten holes to play, the U.S. Amateur trophy was nearly in the grasp of Trip Kuehne.

As he watched his tee shot on the ninth hole of the 1994 U.S. Amateur dive left, and then watched Kuehne send another picture-perfect drive, his sixteenth fairway in twenty-one holes, things looked bleak for Tiger.

And then, as so often happened in Tiger's career, things began to change.

Trip's first significant crack came from that pretty fairway lie. He had some doubt as to club choice and switched from a 3-wood to a 4-iron for his lay-up. Almost predictably, he yanked the 4-iron left, into a fairway bunker, behind an oak tree. Up in the tower, TV analyst Steve Melnyk wondered aloud about Kuehne's hesitation.

Woods, meanwhile, came to his ball and found fate on his side again. His lie was good, and he could lay up short of the green, and then pitch on en route to a par. Kuehne's second shot left him in despair, and after a skulled third shot over the green, he would make bogey. Despite a ragged game off the tee—Woods had hit just eleven of twenty-one fairways—and despite just one birdie on the afternoon front nine, Tiger was 3 down and still breathing.

That's when Trip started hearing voices. He didn't know if the man in the gallery was shouting or if, in his trancelike state, he just happened to pick up his lone voice from the crowd, but he could hear the man clearly.

"Tiger," the man said, calling out Trip's dwindling lead, "it's three."

If the harrowing climes of a make-or-break deficit at a U.S. Amateur would intimidate nearly anyone, Tiger was not among them. His comfort level on a golf course was fashioned famously early, when he won a junior world championship at the age of eight. Many of the precocious details are familiar by now: He shot 48 for a nine-hole score—at age three. He signed an autograph for an admirer—in block-print letters, TIGER WOODS—at age five. He had two holes in one—at age six.

And then there was the penchant for the dramatic. Tiger's teenage years were wonder years of comebacks, stories of adversities overcome that almost defied belief. Close observers of the junior golf scene like the Kuehnes who witnessed these miracles didn't know what to think: Why did so many competitors shrink at the most intense moments against Tiger? Was Tiger the luckiest player in the history of golf? Was he the best? Or was he both?

If there was an event that started a string of Tiger magic that alters between fascinating and eerie, it would be the 1991 U.S. Junior Amateur, at Orlando's Bay Hill. Tiger, just fifteen, made it through match play to the final against a kid named Brad Zwetschke of Kankakee, Illinois. Almost immediately, Tiger fell 3 down after six holes. In an eighteen-hole match, it looked grim. But part of Tiger's growing legend even then was the mental strength that Earl deemed so critical to his training, and Tiger didn't stop gunning. He fought back and took a 1-up lead on Zwetschke on the eighteenth tee, seemingly ready to win his first USGA title.

Incredibly, Tiger snapped his drive way left—out of bounds—and would lose the hole. He would reveal later that his nerves overcame him. "It's just the pressure," he would say. "I never dreamed the pressure would be this great."

And then, just when Zwetschke had the momentum back, he missed a 4-footer to halve the nineteenth hole. Tiger would survive, and Brad Zwetschke would become the first name on a lengthy list of the stunned and the vanquished, in that order. The *New York Times* would call Tiger the next day for a follow-up story on the youngest U.S. junior champion ever, and the fifteen-year-old calmly told them, "I want to become the Michael Jordan of golf . . . I'd like to be the best ever."

Next up in Tiger's run: the 1992 U.S. Junior Amateur at Wollaston Golf Club, at the foot of the Blue Hills, in Milton, Massachusetts. A seventeen-year-old named Mark Wilson from Menomonee Falls, Wisconsin, made the final, only to find Tiger, sixteen, waiting for him. No player had ever won two USGA Junior Amateurs, but Tiger played as if intent on history. None of Tiger's matches had yet reached the seventeenth hole. He closed out one match on eleven, another on twelve.

Not yet had Woods's aura grown to the point where it crushed every opponent before a match, so a confident Wilson was doing well to go 2 up through thirteen. But a Wilson bogey on fourteen and a Tiger birdie on sixteen made it all square, and the gallery of more than a thousand trampled toward the seventeenth tee.

At seventeen, both players handled the heat, Tiger hitting to 6 feet;

Wilson even better, to 5 feet. Tiger's birdie elicited one roar from the crowd, but Wilson's birdie elicited an even louder one, so loud it drowned out Wilson's own primal scream.

Wilson did hear one thing, though. As Tiger walked past him toward the eighteenth tee box, he heard Tiger say into his ear, through the din, "Nice putt." The extraneous compliment caught Wilson off guard. In this crucible of pressure, he was amazed Tiger was concerned with etiquette. With the compliment, in a way, it felt as if Tiger was reclaiming the momentum.

At eighteen, as so many had against Tiger, Wilson, overcome with nerves, chunked a bunker shot and made double bogey. Tiger's tap-in for bogey was good, and now the U.S. Junior had its first-ever repeat champion. Tiger celebrated with tears, bent at the knees, and disappeared into a hug from Earl Woods on the green.

One summer later, national press coverage of Tiger hyped his attempt at a "three-peat," though Tiger would dampen the enthusiasm before the 1993 U.S. Junior Amateur at Portland's Waverley Country Club by revealing he had spent most of the summer battling mononucleosis and had been in bed for two weeks.

It wouldn't matter. His semifinal win over much-hyped Ted Oh drew forty-five hundred fans, a crowd the USGA estimated was the biggest in Junior history.

Watching with great interest in the gallery were three men named Randy Lein, Dwaine Knight, and Wally Goodwin. Lein was the head golf coach at Arizona State; Knight, the head golf coach at UNLV; and Goodwin, the head golf coach at Stanford. Tiger publicly said his choice was down to those three, but a Stanford junior and Oregon native Casey Martin was in attendance, too, and he had a pretty good idea the Cardinal had a chance to land Tiger. "I think," Casey told reporters with a smile, "we can make room for him."

Tiger was one win away from a third consecutive U.S. Junior, a mark some thought so difficult it would never be accomplished again. Earl likened it to Joe DiMaggio's fifty-six-game hit streak. Waiting in the final was a sixteen-year-old boy from Silver Lake, Ohio, named Ryan Armour. Armour already had a history with Tiger, who had thumped Armour, 8 and 6, in the quarterfinals of the

Junior the year before. But Armour would say that he was intimidated last year, and that he mentally quit early in the match. He vowed it would be different this year and earned his spot by defeating ninety-four-pound, fourteen-year-old Charles Howell of Augusta, Georgia, in the semis.

The stage duly set, Armour did not shrink. On the fifteenth green, in an all-square match, his 40-foot birdie try rattled the golf course when it fell. It would rattle more when Tiger did the unthinkable, missing a 4-foot par putt to lose the sixteenth hole and fall 2 down, with two to play.

Armour was dormie on the greatest junior player in the history of the game, and he told himself as he walked to the seventeenth tee, *Two pars and the national title is yours.*

Tiger faced elimination on the seventeenth hole. Armour was steady and on the green in regulation. Tiger hit a 9-iron to the 432-yard par 4 and stuck it 8 feet. Eight feet can be a long way when match-play existence rides on it, and Tiger knew this. He whispered to his caddie: "Got to be like Nicklaus. Got to will this in the hole."

Alluding to Nicklaus at a moment of crisis was not coincidental. For a boy who'd grown up with the Golden Bear's career accomplishments tacked to his bedroom wall, it was comforting to imitate the great Nicklaus. Playing like his hero at the most important juncture of his golf career to date was almost like wrapping himself in a cocoon. He drew back his blade and buried the putt for the birdie that won the seventeenth hole. He was 1 down with one hole to play.

Eighteen was a 578-yard par 5, and with honors, Tiger bombed his drive over 300 yards, to the light rough. Armour, playing smart and sensible, knowing that par might still win him a U.S. Junior and a place in Tiger-slaying history, pulled an iron out of his bag for the safe play.

When Tiger saw the iron, his face hardened. He realized Armour was just trying to make par. He thought to himself: *You think I can't birdie this hole? Let me show you what I've got.*

Tiger's 3-iron to the green leaked, though, and found a bunker some 40 yards short of the green. The idea of an up-and-down birdie from there was unlikely, and Armour was in control when he found the green in regulation. Tiger's predicament was dire. He had a front right pin to deal with and a ball in a bunker that would be difficult to get close. One break: He had enough room to put spin on the ball, and to put a good swing on it.

As Tiger's golf ball left the bunker, Armour was watching and wondering if it even would find the green. It did, stopping 10 feet from the hole.

*How good is that?* Armour wondered to himself, incredulous.

Armour did his job, lagging to tap-in range, and made par. Now, it was all on Tiger. He needed the 10-footer to force extra holes, and when the ball fell into the cup, the frenzied gallery knew what it was witnessing, just as Brad Zwetschke and Mark Wilson had known before. The Waverley gallery cheered so loudly it drowned out Tiger, who was roaring, himself.

The nineteenth hole, which was the par-4 first, played out predictably. Armour, wounded, lost his focus and made bogey. Tiger's two-putt for par was the capper, and the only thing left was for Earl to charge onto the green and embrace his son. "I'm so proud of you," Earl sobbed, over and over, as he hugged his seventeen-year-old boy. Tiger's only response, over and over, whispered in his dad's ear: "I did it . . . I did it."

Afterward, Earl observed that time stops in moments like those. Tiger, standing next to him, would call it the most amazing comeback of his career.

For Armour, it was "the biggest heartbreak I've ever experienced. It was mine. I had it in my hands, but he was teasing me. I don't think many people could have done what Tiger did, professional, amateur, junior amateur, whatever.

"It was like he was following a script."

Not everybody believed the heroics were all because of Tiger's skill. Some on the junior golf circuit moaned about good breaks Tiger would get, or fortunate bounces. Brunza, the caddie and psychologist, called Tiger's comebacks "the gift of a champion." Whatever the reason—the subliminal tapes Tiger had listened to since age six, the training Earl had given him to overcome outside distractions, or the killer instinct for which his mother, Tida, took credit ("Go after them, kill them," Tida remembered saying to Tiger as a child; "after that, sportsmanship") — Tiger did things others could not.

Twelve months later, at Sawgrass, he would need to again. While Trip Kuehne and Kris Cox were heading on a collision course to the semifinals, Tiger wasn't even a lock to make it that far.

In the round of sixteen at the U.S. Amateur, Tiger's match against 1986 U.S. Amateur champ Buddy Alexander was slipping away. Alexander wasn't a teenage kid looking for an excuse to buckle at Tiger's aura. He was a forty-one-year-old man who was the golf coach at the University of Florida, and in the first eight holes, he threw a haymaker at Tiger and was 4 up. Just ten holes remained, but Alexander, like so many of Tiger's match-play foes before him, was unable to twist the knife into Tiger's figurative carcass.

When Alexander missed a short putt to go 4 up on the thirteenth hole, Earl walked by a reporter and did not miss the significance of the moment. "This isn't over yet," Earl said. "Tiger will make another run."

It wasn't so much Tiger's run as Buddy's fall. Bogeys on fourteen, fifteen, sixteen, and seventeen, plus a smothered tee shot into the water on eighteen, sealed Alexander's fate, and Tiger would advance.

ESPN broadcast the semifinals of the 1994 U.S. Amateur to a national audience and welcomed viewers with shots of the Jacksonville skyline ("which will welcome the Jaguars next year," noted Musberger). But the story wasn't the imminent arrival of the NFL to the north Florida coast. The story was Tiger, whom Musberger called the "wunderkind" in ESPN's opening package. His opponent, a Kent State University player named Eric Frishette, was no such wunderkind, just a nice player from the Midwest who had some past amateur glory, losing to eventual champion David Berganio Jr. in the 1991 U.S. Amateur Public Links. The everyman appeal of Frishette — he worked on the maintenance crew at Pine Hill Golf Club near Columbus — caused ESPN analyst Melnyk to overreach in his prediction. "On paper, Tiger is the prohibitive favorite," Melnyk said. "But I don't think that will be the case. This Frishette kid is maybe a little feistier than Tiger . . . I think he has a lot more to gain, personally, than Woods."

No such thing would take place. Though Tiger admitted to tossing and turning on Friday night, feeling huge nerves and thinking of a possible invitation to Augusta National, his dispatching of Frishette was clinical, 5 and 3.

While Earl Woods watched approvingly, listening to jazz music on a pair of headphones, Tiger did his post-match interview with ESPN's Bob Rosburg, a Stanford alum. Rosburg asked Tiger why he chose Stanford as his school, given that Stanford was not a traditional golf power.

"One night, I was just lying in my bed thinking, and my mindset is, there's more to life than just golf," Tiger said. "From then on, I knew what the decision was going to be."

Said Rosburg, "Well, an awful lot of Stanford people and coach Wally Goodwin are happy you made that choice."

Back in the booth, Musberger took note of the unfolding scene.

"The story of the year in golf is Nick Price," Musberger said of the Zimbabwean who won the British Open and PGA Championship that summer. "But if Tiger wins here tomorrow, it could be a major happening."

With only nine holes left in their championship match, Ernie and Trip started to wonder how many breaks Tiger was going to get. They watched Tiger bomb his drive wildly right on ten—only to find a lie with a clear shot to the green. He cashed in, though, and smoked a 4-iron to 24 feet. Trip, affected by the ninth hole's turn of events, hit a poor drive and second shot, and he needed a nice flop to get to 8 feet for par. It began to feel different out there. Kuehne all of a sudden needed the putt, and it felt as if he were the one trailing. He missed, and the lead was now 2 up.

"Tiger, now it's two," came the voice from the gallery.

At eleven, Tiger used the momentum to crush his drive to the middle of the fairway. Trip's consecutive bogeys were awakening memories of Alexander's back-nine collapse, and when his second shot on the par-5 eleventh went into a greenside bunker, and when he failed to get it out to the green with his third, Tiger's two-putt birdie meant he'd won three consecutive holes—and closed to 1 down.

By fourteen, the Kuehnes were turning incredulous. They watched Tiger again soar his drive right—way right. If there's any justice, they thought, he should be in jail. Instead, Tiger's ball hit a USGA cart, of all things, and left him a plausible shot to the green. Granted, Woods always made good on his opportunities—often showing mind-blowing imagination and shot-making skills from trees and lies that would shake the faith of anyone else—but still, the Kuehnes wondered: *When will the fates catch up to this kid?*

Moreover, Tiger was playing at a snail's pace. Long reads of putts, lengthy deliberations of club choice—he was slow, and it annoyed Ernie Kuehne. He thought about protesting to rules officials but held off. In the ESPN booth, Musberger noticed the pace: "By the time he finishes this round," Musberger joked at the thirteenth hole, "he may no longer be the youngest winner in U.S. Amateur history."

After the big break of a lie on fourteen, Tiger did what he always seemed to do. He cashed in. He choked down on a 6-iron and punch-cut a shot that somehow navigated the trees, and his golf ball ran onto the green in another display of cold-blooded, demoralizing shot making. Trip had crushed his drive, reached the green in two, and even at that needed to make a 4-foot knee knocker to halve the hole.

At fifteen, more of the same: Tiger pulled his tee shot left, into the woods. He didn't look or feel stressed, though. A trademark of his game to that point in his life was wildness off the tee, and Earl Woods coached his son to feel comfortable in those situations, to use them as escape opportunities. "I grew up in the trees," Tiger would say. So, he executed a creative punch hook that flew 100 yards and then ran the final 55 to the green for a par that would halve the hole.

The afternoon definitely had a different vibe from the morning.

Once again, sixteen and seventeen would be the stage for the thrilling, unscripted theater—or was it scripted? as Ryan Armour once wondered—so familiar to Tiger's game.

Trip couldn't feel good about a 1-up lead coming to sixteen, where Tiger had such good mojo from the morning round. Sure enough, another bit of gold came Woods's way after a drive into the right rough. His second shot was loose and headed for trouble when it hit a tree limb short of the green and fell into a nice lie. Tiger had a play from there. He seized it and hit a cold-blooded chip to 4 feet. Kuehne's birdie try from off the green lipped out. They were all square.

The greatest players in the game have said they start thinking about seventeen when they tee off—on the first hole. It's as if the hole has crawled inside the head of the world's best with a flashlight, illuminating all the worst fears that plague the fragile mind of a golfer.

With the U.S. Amateur on the line, Tiger Woods was unsure of what club to hit.

The flagstick was daunting—back right, only three paces from a thin collar of rough, which gave way to wooden railroad ties . . . and then the water. The safe play was to the fat of the green, left and center. But that would leave a lengthy putt and almost surely eliminate birdie. Tiger took what seemed like forever over the tee shot. He had pulled a 9-iron and a pitching wedge. The best young player in the game could not make up his mind. He tested the wind. He stared at the hole, as if wishing it would come closer or give him an answer.

The Kuehnes fidgeted on the tee box. The pace was excruciating.

Tiger chose the 9-iron and was preoccupied with his pre-shot routine when he felt the wind change. He backed away from his ball and decided to change clubs again.

Armed now with a pitching wedge, Tiger Woods wanted to play the most important hole of his life aggressively, true to his nature. He wanted to make a full swing, hit the ball hard.

His tee shot soared dangerously toward the back right of the green, toward the flagstick. The problem was immediate: At that trajectory, and with so little room behind the pin location, Woods's ball was surely headed for a watery grave.

In the few seconds it took for Tiger's ball to approach the green, the Kuehnes knew he'd miscalculated. The green would never hold this tee shot. Tiger's luck had run out. The momentum was theirs.

Before Trip and Ernie could even complete the thought of taking back the match, the golf ball landed on the green, hopped sideways toward the water, and . . . somehow . . . stopped. Just one pace from the water, but on dry land. On the tee box, Tiger betrayed no emotion, even as the crowd's gasp turned into a roar.

The Kuehnes were flabbergasted, even if they didn't show it. Ernie Kuehne felt helpless and handed Trip his pitching wedge as the crowd buzzed.

Kuehne played the hole more traditionally, sticking to the game plan he'd followed all afternoon. He hit to the fat of the green, leaving a 50-foot putt. He nearly jarred it, too. A 3 on the seventeenth at Sawgrass was normally cause for relief, if not celebration. But not for Trip Kuehne on August 28, 1994. Not yet. Tiger Woods still had to attempt his birdie putt.

It was a doozy, too. Tiger's right foot backed up against the wooden railroad tie, and his ball lay in such a spot that Tiger's putter would have to brush through the collar of rough before making contact. And then there was the break—a significant right-to-left action that meant bogey was still in the equation, too.

There was even a question as to whether Woods should chip it or putt it. With so many questions hovering, and with so much pressure looming, the buzzing cicadas were the only things making a sound.

Tiger went with his putter, and the ball tracked on its break as if preordained. Maybe it was. It slid right in for birdie.

Tiger's reaction was a roaring, knee-bending, cathartic fist pump. The image was so indelible, the *New York Times* would splash it on A1 of the next day's newspapers.

He was 1 up, with one to play.

Eighteen was a fait accompli. Trip made bogey and conceded a par putt to Tiger.

Earl Woods, who had set Tiger in a high chair to watch him swing a golf club in a Southern California garage eighteen years earlier, had just witnessed the greatest comeback in U.S. Amateur history. He came onto the green for an emotional embrace with the youngest winner ever.

At first, Earl laughed, the laugh of a proud father and a disbelieving fan at the same time. Soon, he was crying.

"I love you," Tiger whispered in his father's ear.

"I love you, too," Earl said, his voice breaking.

While that father-son embrace played out, Trip and Ernie Kuehne waited patiently a few paces away to congratulate the player who had crushed their dreams. It was one final obligation for the Golden Boy who thought he did everything right and now had to stare at a runner-up medal that would nearly define his golf career.

Finally, Tiger and Earl separated. Tiger wiped his eyes.

"I played as good as I could," Trip said in his Texas twang. He had one hand on Earl's shoulder, another on Tiger's shoulder. "Y'all did, too. Way to go."

He walked away, leaving the champion with his dad, alone at the scene of victory.

In the TV booth above the eighteenth green, ESPN's Musberger wondered aloud: "Could Tiger Woods," he closed the broadcast, "be the next superstar in golf?"

# 2

# The Freshman

*Albuquerque, New Mexico*
*September 16–17, 1994*

THREE WEEKS LATER, the next superstar in golf was a bellhop.
Tiger Woods may have been the youngest U.S. Amateur champion in history, he may have just executed the greatest comeback in U.S. Amateur history, and he may have received a personal letter from President Bill Clinton congratulating him, but to the Stanford golf team, who were riding high from their national championship win just three months earlier at the close of the 1994 season, Tiger Woods was a freshman. He needed to be hazed. Notah Begay, the charismatic Native American senior who was Stanford's most mischievous and talented player, and its leader, approached Tiger during the team's first week of practice on campus, in mid-September.

Stanford's season was set to start on September 16 at the Tucker Invitational, in Notah's hometown of Albuquerque. Notah threw his arm around Tiger in front of the team.

"Tiger," he said, "you're going to be the strongest freshman in the country."

Tiger knew he was making history as a player, but he was still embarrassed by the praise. After all, a freshman is a freshman, and he knew to respect the seniors. He looked at the ground a bit sheepishly and thanked Begay for the compliment.

"Because," Begay continued, flashing his devilish grin, "you're going to carry all of our bags this year on road trips. Congratulations, freshman."

As the team laughed a razzing laugh, Tiger realized Notah wasn't kidding. He laid out the ground rules. From clubhouse to van, from van to airline check-in, from baggage claim to van, from van to hotel, from hotel to van, and from van to golf course—Tiger Woods would be the national champion of bag schlepping. He knew he couldn't fight it. He was the new guy. And there were four seniors who weren't going to let him forget it.

Begay's brash show in front of the team served two purposes, by his estimation: One, it kept alive the age-old tradition of hazing a newcomer, in any sport. Two, it was meant to remind Tiger that, as big as he was on the national stage (*New York Times* front page, *Good Morning America,* the *Today* show), he was still just a baby around the Stanford team. That the Cardinal surprised everyone by winning the '94 team title added ballast to Notah's power play. The best Tiger could do as a Stanford freshman was simply match what the '94 team had done months earlier. Already, the map was laid out.

In truth, Notah and the rest of the seniors knew that if Tiger fought back and rejected the assignment, they might not have much leverage. Tiger Woods, after all, was considered by most to be the most famous recruit in the history of high school sports. He had a little leverage himself. Already there was a different air around the Stanford team with Tiger arriving only that week. The media requests were piling in, and even Stanford's seniors felt the kid's aura. They were impressed by his combination of quiet humility off the course and the utter devastation of his competitive streak on the course.

Stanford officials were scurrying around their athletic department offices, trying to make sure they were prepared for the media onslaught. The school had dealt with major athletic stars in the recent past. John Elway was a Stanford product. So was Olympic superstar swimmer Janet Evans. So was John McEnroe. But they all agreed none of them was bigger than Tiger. Wally Goodwin, the Stanford golf coach, tried to warn them of the attention Tiger would get. School hadn't started yet, and they were beginning to get the sense. Tiger was their biggest star ever.

Back on the practice range with the team, Tiger stood with Begay's arm around his shoulder while the team cracked up, laughing. They were ready to toss him their travel bags, but first, Tiger had an idea.

"OK," he said. "I get it. I'll do the job. But I have a proposal."

The seniors perked up their ears. Tiger wanted to negotiate?

"If I win a tournament, and beat the entire field, including you guys, my teammates," Tiger said, "I'm off the hook. I don't have to carry your bags."

Begay had been called out on a dare. Tiger's gambit was a brilliant one. It appealed to the sense of competitiveness in Stanford team members, not to mention appealing to their egos. They didn't want to be seen as backing down from a challenge on the golf course, especially from a freshman. Notah pondered it. He knew Tiger was awesome, the best player he'd ever seen. But he also figured the combination of classes, travel, and distractions meant Tiger would have a little bit of an adjustment period. He knew Tiger would win an event eventually, perhaps as soon as the late fall or early spring. That still gave him four or five solid road trips of schlepping.

"You've got yourself a deal," Notah said. "You beat us, and you're off the hook."

Nearly every college golf recruit in the history of the sport arrived on campus in a cloak of anonymity, his presence usually noted only by his golf coach, his teammates, and maybe his dorm roommate, who might say something like "Oh, hey, I didn't know we had a golf team." Though players like Jack Nicklaus at Ohio State and Phil Mickelson at Arizona State had achieved junior golf fame when they arrived at college, it was still on a niche level. College golf, unlike the popular sports such as football and basketball, didn't have a face on it or much fan interest, if any.

There were many appealing aspects to Tiger's story, historic and groundbreaking aspects, and many of them were known by the casual sports fan by the time Tiger arrived in Palo Alto. By now, they are familiar in his sport's lore.

His father was a former Green Beret who settled into a post-army life in the Orange County, California, suburb of Cypress. When Earl and his second wife, Kultida, a Thai whom Earl had met and courted during an army stint in Thailand, had a baby on December 30, 1975, Earl was forty-three and intent on becoming a better father to this new boy, Eldrick, than he had been as an absent military father to his three kids from his first marriage. So, when Earl hit golf balls in the garage of their modest, one-story home in a mostly faceless street in Cypress, he brought his diapered baby out to watch him.

Notably, Earl didn't call the boy Eldrick. From the get-go, he wanted to nickname the boy "Tiger," in honor of a South Vietnamese lieutenant colonel named Vuong Dang Phong, who Earl said had saved his life on more than one occasion. Earl used to call Phong "Tiger," and he wanted to remember his long-lost war buddy with his son's nickname. So, there sat baby Tiger, in the high chair, at six months, watching Earl hit golf ball after golf ball into a net. Earl wasn't a bad player. In just one year of play, he'd established a handicap of 12. He loved the game, and so it became a ritual for Earl and wide-eyed baby Tiger in the garage. Four months passed, and one day during a break, baby Tiger came down off the high chair, picked up Earl's putter, did a small waggle with his diapered rear end, and made what Earl described as a nearly perfect pass at the ball. Tiger's daddy was flabbergasted. He ran, screaming, into the house, telling his wife they had a genius on their hands.

It was at that moment, Earl would say, when he thought the Man Upstairs had big plans for his baby Tiger.

What followed was a parade of amazing accomplishments: Tiger hit a bucket of balls at a driving range at eighteen months. Tiger could play an entire golf hole at age two. Tiger broke 50 on a par-3 nine-hole course at the age of three. His proud mother wanted to brag to the world about her boy and phoned a Los Angeles TV station to tell her baby's story. Sportscaster Jim Hill came out with a camera crew and did a feature on two-year-old Tiger playing a golf hole. A producer from *The Mike Douglas Show* saw it and thought Tiger too precious to be ignored. In a now famous bit of video, he upstaged guests Bob Hope and Jimmy Stewart by participating in a putting contest—only to pick up his ball, march it to 6 inches from the cup, put it down, and tap it in. Hope roared with laughter, as did the audience. A star was born.

The legend would only grow. When other kids used crayons to draw animals and houses, a young Tiger used crayons to draw the trajectories of different irons used to hit golf shots. He could identify a reverse pivot on a golfer when he was five years old. Earl wanted to nurture his creative side, and the first music he played for baby Tiger was jazz, to let him hear what Earl thought was the most creative form of music. Earl got him a swing coach at the age of four, a man named Rudy Duran at Heartwell Golf Park in Long Beach. The TV show *That's Incredible!* booked Tiger at age five, and he hit whiffle golf balls into the crowd.

An incident at *That's Incredible!* served to highlight another aspect of the Tiger Story. At the taping, they saw a ten-year-old girl who was a weightlifting phenomenon. Earl made sure to point out the girl to Tiger. He told him: "That girl is as good at what she does as you are at what you do. There are many special people in this world." It was an early lesson in humility, and one of many Earl and Tida wanted to impart to young Tiger in the mental training of their only child.

First and foremost, they always said, Tiger's bearing as a person meant the most to his parents. As supremely talented as he was at golf, Earl repeatedly told reporters that Tiger was not raised to be a good golfer, but to be a "good person." An "upright citizen" was another of Earl's go-to phrases in describing his desires for his son. "If he wants to be a fireman in Umpty Ump, Tennessee, that's fine, as long as he's an upright citizen," Earl said. Tida's emphasis on homework was equally blanketing. "No homework, no practice," she would tell Tiger, instilling in him early a sense of discipline that he would carry with him for the rest of his life. The early lean toward hitting the books would also play a role in the Woods family's early attraction to the heady academic climes of Stanford, perhaps the most academically prestigious university on the West Coast.

That said, the other part of Tiger's mental training wasn't so warm and fuzzy. Earl and Tida wanted to raise a ruthless competitor, too. For Earl, the concept was a connection to his training as a Green Beret, instilling the understanding that sometimes in the world, you become the hunter, so you don't become the hunted. Or, as Tida said sometimes to Tiger of his foes on the golf course, "Kill them, Tiger." They played subliminal tapes for him at age six, to craft his mind and expand its potential. So Tiger heard these words piped into his ear: *My decisions are strong! I do it with all my heart! I focus and I give it my all! My will moves mountains! I believe in me! I will my own destiny! I am firm in my resolve! I fulfill my resolutions powerfully!*

Heady stuff for a six-year-old, but Earl and Tida felt they had a powerful being in their home and wanted to maximize all the boy could be. In competition, that meant Tiger would be ferocious, unmerciful. Earl's goal was simple: He wanted it so that Tiger *never* met anybody mentally tougher than him. He wanted Tiger to find a "dark side," or what he called a "coldness," in competition. He wanted his boy to have the heart of an assassin, and he said as much.

Earl tested Tiger's concentration by playing mind games when they played golf: A cough during young Tiger's backswing. A jingling of coins as he lined up a putt. A pumping of a golf cart brake; a tear of a Velcro glove . . . Earl would enact all of these when Tiger was trying to pull off a golf shot, and he wouldn't apologize, either.

What Earl and Tida knew would make all the mental training effective was the backdrop of it all: unconditional love. "If you treat your child with admiration and respect," Earl would say, "a miracle will occur." Earl had a routine before every one of Tiger's youth competitions. He would tell him, "Son, I want you to know this: No matter how you do today, I love you very much." And he'd send him off to play golf.

When Tiger was in his first important international competition at age six, Earl told Tiger that he loved him and to go have fun. After Tiger roped his tee shot on the first tee, Earl asked him, "What were you thinking of when you were over the ball?" Answered Tiger, "Where I wanted my ball to go, Daddy." To Earl, it was a perfect answer. He knew the boy was a winner.

If Earl had a mantra for Tiger, it was the phrase "Care and share." He told Tiger that's how he should approach his life and his dealings with others. It led to Tiger's passion for giving youth clinics, especially for underprivileged kids, at major amateur tournaments in the summertime. If Tiger ever were to doubt his commitment to golf, Earl told him, that wasn't a concern. If he went after his dreams and goals and failed, that wasn't a concern, either.

"No matter what happens in life," Earl told him, "we are your parachute. You will land softly."

The unconditional parental support started at the very beginning, with Tiger's given name. Tida came up with the name Eldrick in an effort to make sure that the first letter, *E*, came from Earl, and the last letter, *K*, came from Kultida. By surrounding the name with *E* and *K*, the parents were giving Tiger in nomenclature what they tried to give him in life: the feeling that they would always surround him, always take care of him.

It helped that he had a natural passion for golf. He told a reporter once at a young age that it was like a drug for him; he always needed more. He found inspiration in the greatest player who ever lived, Jack Nicklaus. The famous cutout from *Golf Digest* magazine charting Nicklaus's career accomplishments—Tiger's road map—hung on the ten-year-old's wall next to a *Star Wars* poster. Validation and inspiration came just five years later, when Tiger was fifteen and had the honor of serving as a warm-up act for a Nicklaus clinic at Bel-Air Country Club. Nicklaus watched, and when he stood in front of the crowd to begin his clinic, the Golden Bear nodded toward Tiger. "Tiger," Nicklaus said, "when I grow up, I want to have a swing as pretty as yours."

The swing didn't come out of nowhere. He worked and he worked, and he even took on a new swing coach at age ten, a man named John Anselmo at Meadowlark Golf Club in Huntington Beach. Earl and Tida took Tiger to Anselmo because he was one of Orange County's best swing coaches. The parents never cut corners in training young Tiger, and Earl estimated he floated five mortgages to cover the costs to travel to various youth tournaments. Tiger's foundation with Earl led him to trust most everything his daddy told him, so when Earl told him, "There are no shortcuts in life, son. You have to pay your dues if you're going to be the best," Tiger took it to heart. He practiced, and he practiced. He hit chip shots in the living room at their Cypress home, testing himself by chipping over Tida's glass coffee table, trying to get his golf ball to stop before it hit Tida's crystal on the other side. To Tiger, it was the perfect motivation to execute a flop shot. "If I hit her crystal," he said, "she'd chase me down and kill me, so I make sure I don't hit it."

Imbued with that strength, young Tiger saw the accomplishments pour in, in outrageous amounts. He won the Optimist International Junior Golf championship at ages eight, nine, twelve, thirteen, and fourteen. The Woodses treated the Junior Worlds as a major, so that Tiger was already comfortable with the idea of winning a major at age eight. At age eleven, he went undefeated in over thirty Southern California junior tournaments. At age thirteen, he qualified for the nationally prestigious Insurance Youth Golf Classic, a landmark tournament for junior players known as the "Big I." He was the youngest player in the field for the event at Texarkana, Arkansas, and told reporters he didn't expect to make the cut. He made the cut and, for the honor, got to play with a pro. The pro turned out to be John Daly, Arkansas's 1986 and 1987 Player of the Year, who found himself 3 shots back of Tiger at the turn. Daly, twenty-three, turned to a friend between holes and said, "I can't let a thirteen-year-old beat me." Daly had to birdie three of the last four holes to shoot 70 to Tiger's 72. Tiger would win the "Big I" the next year at age fourteen—the youngest ever to win it. That same summer, in 1990, he made the semifinals of the U.S. Junior Amateur at Lake Merced in Daly City, California—the youngest ever to reach the U.S. Junior semis. At age sixteen, he became the youngest ever to play in a PGA Tour event, when he got a sponsor's exemption to play in the 1992 L.A. Open at Riviera. He missed the cut but heard shouts of "You the Kid!" and enjoyed front-page reports in the *Los Angeles Times* and a lush spread in *Sports Illustrated*.

The L.A. Open appearance brought to light another aspect of the Tiger Story: his ethnicity.

It wasn't just that Tiger Woods had a poetic name, or that Tiger Woods was destroying the parameters of what a junior golfer could accomplish; it was that Tiger Woods was *black,* too. At least that's what nearly every report, story, feature, or TV piece on young Tiger pointed out. True enough, his father was half black. But his father also had one-quarter Chinese blood and one-quarter Native American. Tida was half Thai, and one-quarter Chinese and one-quarter Caucasian. In reality, Tiger's ethnicity included bloodlines found in the continents of Asia, Africa, Europe, and North America. But he was described as black by most every writer who chose to pen his story and by the outside world, too. Earl, too, used the terminology. He often told reporters that Tiger was the "first black intuitive golfer ever raised in the United States."

Being 25 percent black in the United States, Earl taught Tiger, meant that you'd be thought of as black by the white world. The description angered Tida, as she viewed every reference to Tiger being black as disrespectful to her heritage. Tiger knew as much and always checked the box marked "Asian" when asked for his ethnicity. But Earl knew whereof he spoke: He'd often had to eat at different restaurants and stay at different hotels from his white teammates at Kansas State. Tiger felt the sting, too. At the Navy Golf Course in Los Alamitos, near the Woods family home, Earl often played with Jay Brunza, the navy captain who was Tiger's sports psychologist. At age ten, Tiger was a popular addition to the Saturday morning fourballs, but not to everybody's view. Pro shop workers reported that some members objected to Tiger playing at the golf course and sometimes used disparaging language about Tiger's skin color in their objections. Once, he was told to stop hitting golf balls at the driving range because a neighbor complained that a "nigger" was hitting balls into his backyard.

At the L.A. Open, death threats were reported before Tiger's appearance. Each of the threats used the word *nigger* in them.

Tiger's answer to racists was, like so many of his life views, mature beyond his years. He never lashed back and instead lived by the credo that "racism is the racist's problem, not mine." If he felt somebody staring at him at a country club, his response was grounded in competition: He'd stare back, until the person felt uncomfortable and looked away. If Earl and Tida were raising their boy the way they wanted, he would kill racial hatred the same way he killed opponents on the golf course: by being better than anybody else.

In 1989, when he was thirteen, colleges began to take notice. There was no Internet to track junior golfers, and the AJGA, now a de facto farm system for the PGA Tour, hadn't yet reached its monolithic state in the world of junior golf. So, word of mouth was sometimes still an effective way to recruit somebody.

An influential Southern California teaching pro named Tom Sargent watched Tiger tear up the Yorba Linda Junior Invitational and sent a letter to two college coaches: UNLV's Dwaine Knight and Stanford's Wally Goodwin. He apprised Knight and Goodwin of the thirteen-year-old and his talents. Goodwin immediately wrote Tiger a letter dated March 28, 1989.

"Dear Tiger: Here at Stanford, I'm finding that it is never too early to get word out to you exceptional young men."

The contact from Stanford resonated in the Woods household on many levels. They always valued academics, and to establish a relationship with a university as prestigious as Stanford—the school had one of the most selective admissions policies in the country—jibed with their goals for Tiger. Stanford also held a reputation as a place where athletes could go to compete on a championship level. The baseball team won national championships in 1987 and 1988. The men's swim team won the national championship in 1987; the women's, in 1989. The women's tennis team won its fourth consecutive national title in the spring of 1989. Tiger's letter from Goodwin came from a place where athletics meshed with academics as at no other school in the nation. If providing the best of the best was the plan for Tiger, Stanford was about as natural a fit as any school his parents could imagine.

Plus, it was in California, a seven-hour drive from their Orange County home. Tiger may have been only in seventh grade, but the arrival of the letter from Goodwin put Stanford ahead, way ahead, in the race for Tiger's college affections. He responded to Goodwin's note with a letter of his own, a handwritten, cursive, error-free document that would become known only as "The Letter" around the Stanford campus. It read:

April 23, 1989
Dear Coach Goodwin,

Thank you for your recent letter expressing Stanford's interest in me as a future student and golfer. At first it was hard for me to understand why a university like Stanford was interested in a thirteen-year-old seventh grader. But after talking with my father I have come to better understand and appreciate the honor you have given me. I further appreciate Mr. Sargent's interest in my future development by recommending me to you.

I became interested in Stanford's academics while watching the Olympics and Debi Thomas. My goal is to obtain a quality business education. Your guidelines will be most helpful in preparing me for college life. My GPA this year is 3.86 and I plan to keep it there or higher when I enter high school.

I am working on an exercise program to increase my strength. My April USGA handicap is 1 and I plan to play in SCPGA and maybe some AJGA tournaments this summer. My goal is to win the Junior World in July for the fourth time and to become the first player to win each age bracket. Ultimately I would like to be a PGA professional. Next February I plan to go to Thailand and play in the Thai Open as an amateur.

I've heard a lot about your golf course and I would like to play it with my dad some time in the future.

Hope to hear from you soon.
Sincerely,
Tiger Woods 5-5/100

Even when he was just five foot five and weighed just one hundred pounds, Tiger would tell a reporter later that year he was 90 percent certain he would attend Stanford. When Goodwin was contacted, he echoed the affection: "If I'm still alive," he joked, "I will attempt to get him."

Goodwin kept alive the lifeline. The next year, he was leafing through *Sports Illustrated* and saw the "Faces in the Crowd" feature, the page that spotlighted significant amateur athletes from around the country. The fourteen-year-old Tiger was cited for winning the "Big I" and reaching the U.S. Junior semis. Goodwin had an idea. His wife, Nancy, had also been featured in "Faces," as a Masters swimmer. He cut out Nancy's photo and Tiger's photo and pasted them together on a piece of paper. He sent it off to Tiger with the inscription "Aren't these two of the best smiles you've ever seen?"

In the summer of 1990, Tiger and his parents traveled to France for an international junior event called the Southern California/French Junior Cup in Paris. There, Tiger and Earl sought out and approached a Frenchman named Christian Cevaer, who attended Stanford and played golf. Cevaer won the 1989 Pac-10 individual championship and represented part of a renaissance in Stanford golf under Goodwin, who had been hired in 1987. They asked Cevaer all about Stanford, and Cevaer came away with the impression that Tiger was all but ticketed to be a Cardinal.

The certainty of Tiger graduating from Western High in Anaheim in June of 1994, then enrolling in Stanford in the fall of 1994, began to gain momentum with each passing month and year. Tiger left his options open by declaring midway through his junior year in high school that it was down to three schools: UNLV, Arizona State, and Stanford. National golf powers like Oklahoma State, Texas, and Florida were off the list, as they feared. Oklahoma State coach Mike Holder had done his due diligence, watched Tiger on practice ranges since he was thirteen, and tried to keep alive the Hail Mary pass of a hope that Tiger would be a Cowboy. But he was a California kid and wanted to go to college at a place within a day's drive of home. Arizona State made the list because of its golf pedigree. The Sun Devils won the 1990 NCAA title and had graduated Mickelson as a three-time NCAA individual champion in 1992. UNLV produced 1991 NCAA individual champ Warren Schutte, and Knight was named National Coach of the Year that same year. Plus, Vegas featured the added attraction of Tiger's high school girl-friend—she was set to enroll at UNLV.

Stanford's inclusion on the list needed little explanation. Earl, Tida, and Tiger knew Stanford wasn't the best place for his golf career. He'd study less at UNLV or Arizona State and play at a school with better golf facilities. But they were serious when they said they wanted Tiger to be the best person he could become, and that Stanford was the best fit for that goal. He liked the peaceful feel of the campus. He would call it a "utopia," where Tiger would happily get his "butt whipped," in his words, academically. He liked the challenge and felt an attraction to a school where he'd be surrounded by the best—whether the best pianist, the best swimmer, or the best golfer. "Without a good mind," he'd say, "what are you?" Further, Earl and Tida knew Tiger was so self-assured, he wouldn't feel jealous or overmatched if he met kids who were smarter than he was.

The mutual attraction was so strong, it began to have a ripple effect on campus. Goodwin's team was on the rise. He'd bumped up the program with Cevaer, then landed two recruits in the spring of 1990 who would redefine the team's expectations: a New Mexico product named Notah Begay, and an Oregon product named Casey Martin. In their freshman year, they helped Stanford finish tied for fifteenth at NCAAs, their best finish since a tie for ninth in 1985. In their sophomore years, they finished tied for ninth as a team and started thinking they might have the goods to make a run for the national championship. One problem: Begay and Martin were set to graduate in June of 1994. Tiger would arrive in the fall of '94. They would never play together.

Thus was born an idea they called the "Great Experiment."

The "experiment" was this: Begay and Martin would redshirt the academic year of 1992–93. They'd use the time to catch up on their studies and work on their games, and then come back for their junior years in 1993–94 . . . and their senior years, in 1994–95. If the experiment went well, Begay's and Martin's games would be peaking in their senior years, and they'd be adding the greatest junior player in history to their team that very same year. The experiment contained explosive potential: a national championship.

It also contained a small gamble. What if Tiger changed his mind about committing to Stanford?

The team could help matters along when they hosted Tiger in the fall of '93 on his recruiting trip. Tiger already knew Begay fairly well. They'd bonded at some junior golf tournaments as two non-whites in an overwhelmingly white sport. Goodwin wanted Tiger to get another view of Stanford, so he had him stay with a nervous freshman named Conrad Ray. Ray was a junior golfer of some repute in Minnesota, but he wasn't in Tiger's universe when it came to accomplishments. He was a nervous wreck when Tiger was assigned to his room in Branner Hall for the weekend—especially because all he had to offer Tiger was a futon on the floor. The previous week, at his UNLV recruiting trip, Tiger had slept on a feather bed at the Mirage.

On the Friday night of Tiger's visit, the entire team took him to Chili's on El Camino Real, the main drag that runs along the Stanford campus. Over the meal, the veterans on the team submitted Tiger to a grilling. They asked him every question imaginable and were quite serious about it, too. Steve Burdick was a junior and one of the best ball strikers on the team. He'd known Tiger since they flew together to the 1989 "Big I" as qualifiers from the Sacramento site. Back then, Burdick was fifteen and Tiger was thirteen, scrawny and wearing thick glasses. Burdick wondered, *Who is this kid?* When they got to Arkansas for the "Big I" and played a practice round, Burdick found out. When Burdick finished twenty-fifth, and Tiger finished second, Burdick found out some more. Now, Burdick had the advantage. He was an established player at Stanford, a third-team All-American from the previous year. He'd turned down offers from Cal, USC, UCLA, and Pacific to attend his dream school and now had a chance to ask Tiger some questions.

"What else," Burdick asked him, "do you do besides play golf, Tiger?"

Tiger didn't blink.

"Eat," he said, "and sleep."

They waited for him to laugh, but he didn't. *My goodness,* Burdick thought. *He's serious.* At least Tiger was consistent. In junior high, he once told a reporter that a girl had asked him out on a date. He answered her: "Nope. Too much golf."

The team and the recruit retired to the room of Will Yanagisawa, a junior who'd transferred to Stanford from UC Irvine. There, they engaged in a time-honored tradition: They watched the movie *Caddyshack.*

On Saturday morning, they met on the practice range. Begay was forever trying new things to improve his game and had a practice club called the Medicus, a dual-hinge training aid designed to let you know when you swing incorrectly. The thing was nasty, and Begay was struggling with its intricacies. Tiger asked if he could take a few rips with it. He took it out of Begay's hands and, without any warm-up swings, ripped five consecutive high draws traveling 185 yards—without any break in the shaft. The Stanford players laughed in disbelief. Begay hadn't even gotten the ball off the ground.

It came time for Tiger to fly home, and the team gathered at the Stanford clubhouse. Shortly before Tiger left for the airport, Begay called him over. He wanted a one-on-one conversation, in Goodwin's office. They shut the door.

"Look," Begay told him, "we're going to be a great team whether or not you come to Stanford. We're going to contend for the national title with or without you. You need to do what's best for you."

They emerged from the room, and Begay thought two things: One, *I hope Tiger respects me and the school for our honesty.* Two, *Coach Goodwin would kill me if he knew what I just said.*

In November of 1993, Tida called Goodwin.

"You coming down to the house for a visit, Coach?" she asked.

"I hadn't planned on it," Goodwin said.

"You better get down here!" she said.

Goodwin booked a flight to Los Angeles and then drove to Cypress, a town of forty-five thousand on the northern border of Orange and Los Angeles counties. Cypress was like so many Orange

County towns, virtually indistinguishable from the next town over. In Orange County, you can be driving down a street in Huntington Beach and, without any obvious physical line of demarcation, suddenly be in Cypress.

Goodwin found it difficult to navigate. He had the address, but driving up and down the streets he got lost. Up one street . . . down another . . . he couldn't find the house of Tiger Woods.

Finally, Goodwin figured out that the house addresses were stenciled on the curbs in front of each home. He found the Woods family home—an unglamorous suburban home built on an unglamorous suburban street—and knocked on the door.

Tiger answered.

"Hey, Dad," he yelled, "Coach is here!"

From the back of the house, Earl shouted: "Entertain him for a few minutes! I'll be out in a few."

Goodwin knew that Earl was a night owl who liked to nap in the daytime, so he entered and chatted with Tiger. A few minutes later, Earl showed up and took out a couple of glasses.

"What are you drinking, Coach?" Earl asked.

"Oh, I'd love a ginger ale," Goodwin said.

"Oh," Earl said, "because I'm drinking Jack Daniel's."

Goodwin didn't want to offend his host. "I'll have one, too, then," he said.

Tida pulled into the driveway with dinner—a takeout pizza.

Goodwin joined the family at a table in the living room and they began to eat. Goodwin noticed that Tiger was on edge.

"Coach," he said, "I've got something to tell you."

Tiger reached down below the table and pulled out a UNLV baseball cap. He put it on his head. "Sorry, Coach," he said.

Goodwin didn't miss a beat.

"Tiger, I'm older," said Goodwin, sixty-six at the time, "but I'm not so stupid as to think you'd invite me down here to dinner to tell me you're going to Las Vegas."

"Oh, sorry, Coach," Tiger said, removing the UNLV cap. He reached down below the table and pulled out another cap.

It was an Arizona State cap.

"Come on now," Goodwin said, not finding this as amusing.

Tiger broke up laughing. He took off the ASU cap and put on a Stanford cap, flashing that grin that had captured Goodwin's eye in *Sports Illustrated*. Hugs all around.

He signed his letter of intent at 8:30 A.M. on November 10, 1993, sporting a 3.70 GPA and the best junior golf game in the world.

"When you're lucky enough to sign the best junior player who's ever lived, you have a star in your midst," Goodwin told reporters. "He's not only a great player, but a great kid. He seems motivated to help us attain our goal of a national championship. He's a team guy.

"And it's going to be a powerful team."

To warm up for his freshman year, Tiger played a summer of golf in 1994 that Goodwin called "probably the greatest summer an amateur ever had."

The stirring achievements included skipping U.S. Open qualifying. Tiger's game was good enough to make him a probable qualifier for the '94 Open at Oakmont, but he passed. The reason: Western High graduation was set for the same week as the Open. Tiger didn't want to miss his high school graduation.

He did, however, finish up his high school career by setting a California Interscholastic Federation and course record at La Cumbre Country Club in Santa Barbara with a 66 to win the Southern Section individual title for the third time in four years. High school golf was an interesting thing for Tiger. On the junior circuit, he had always played as an individual, so playing for Western High was a new sensation. He was seen as a great teammate, but curiously, Tiger would not always play his best golf in the team setting; the league championship match his sophomore year was an example. Tiger needed only to two-putt the eighteenth green to win the league title for Western, but he ran his lag putt 5 feet past. He missed the comebacker. Shockingly, he then missed the tap-in for a four-putt. He walked off the green, still thinking his team had won it all. Instead, Tiger's four-putt cost them the league title.

As an individual, however, there weren't any stories like that. Tiger was a machine, especially in that summer of '94. The list of wins was dizzying.

He blitzed the field in match play at the Pacific Northwest Amateur at Royal Oaks Country Club in Vancouver, Washington, closing out Oregon golfer Ted Snavely, 11 and 10, in the thirty-six-hole final. Tiger called it the best round of his life. Snavely didn't disagree. Snavely didn't win a hole until the twenty-third and said out loud, "At least I didn't get shut out." Casey Martin, a Stanford teammate-to-be, just weeks removed from winning the team national championship, watched from the gallery. "He'll make," Martin said with a smile, "a good fifth man for us."

At the Southern California Amateur at Hacienda Golf Club in La Habra Heights, California, he shot an SCGA and course record 62 to win, including a bit of Tiger serendipity. He hit a wild tee shot on the fifth hole that bounced off the cart path and back toward the fairway. He hit an approach to 40 feet and drained it for a birdie.

Tiger beat longtime Southern California friend and rival Chris Riley, 2 and 1, at the Western Amateur, considered "the Masters of amateur golf," at Point O'Woods in Benton Harbor, Michigan. But the story was the match he played against Oklahoma State's Chris Tidland in the quarterfinals. Tiger was 4 up through twelve, a lock to advance to the semifinals. But Tidland birdied thirteen, and fourteen, and fifteen, and sixteen to square the match. Tidland then birdied seventeen, and so did Tiger. Tiger was about to birdie eighteen when Tidland chipped in for birdie, extending the match. Tidland was safely on the nineteenth hole in regulation and two-putted for par. Tiger was wild off the tee, long with his second shot, and flopped a third shot to 40 feet. He had to make it to extend the match. He did. "I had this funny feeling that I saw the line of my putt," Tiger would say. "I just stood over it and said: 'Hit it and it will go in.'" Tidland wasn't swayed. He birdied the twentieth hole. Tiger, by canning a 20-footer, made eagle. Tiger won, 1 up. Tidland had gone 7 under in the final eight holes—and lost.

Tiger's summer closed, of course, with the U.S. Amateur at Sawgrass.

• • •

When Tiger accepted his scholarship to Stanford, Earl Woods told Wally Goodwin he wouldn't be around much. He was letting Tiger grow up on his own, he said. He compared raising Tiger to a snowball. "It gains size and speed on its own," Earl said, "once it starts moving."

So eighteen-year-old Tiger Woods drove his Toyota Supra from Orange County to Palo Alto in September of 1994 and pulled up to Larkin, his freshman dorm. Nametags were laid out on a table, and roommate assignments were forthcoming. Tiger was paired with a boy from Virginia who didn't know much about golf. Most everyone in Larkin knew who Tiger was. The U.S. Amateur win was only a month old and had been covered by the evening news on all the major networks. Some of his dorm mates, especially the sports fans, didn't want to appear to be fawning over the celebrity, but they were pleasantly surprised to find Tiger to be a modest, good-humored student, a regular guy.

He liked to watch *Monday Night Football* on the dorm's common TV and was always up for piling some fellow freshmen into his car for food runs to Fresh Choice, an all-you-can-eat restaurant on El Camino Real, where the teenagers stuffed their faces with dinner rolls. His car, like most eighteen-year-olds' cars, was a mess, with CD cases everywhere. But Tiger would clear the CDs off the seat and pop in R. Kelly's latest. Yes, the kid who could hit bump-and-run shots found nothing wrong with R. Kelly's "Bump and Grind."

Yet, Tiger wasn't an entirely typical freshman. Often, he'd rise at 6:00 A.M., grab his golf clubs, and head out for a morning practice. This was unlike many of his dorm mates, who slept well past 6:00 A.M. His work ethic never wavered.

And he had access to things other freshmen didn't. One thing Tiger did miss about being at college was his conversations with his father, in which they'd talk about everything in life, matters serious and nonserious. Because he was Tiger, however, he was welcomed in the office of Stanford football coach Bill Walsh. "The Genius" won three Super Bowls as a coach and had returned to Stanford in 1992 to coach again. Their friendship was a casual one. When he would walk into the football offices, Tiger would breeze right past

Walsh's secretary, who understood Tiger had carte blanche. He'd plop down in a chair in Walsh's office, and his Stanford "father figure" would entertain conversations on sports and on winning and on discipline with the golf world's shining star. Tiger would come to love those conversations and treasured them. He would later form a similar friendship with Walsh's successor, Tyrone Willingham, and with Stanford's provost, future Secretary of State Condoleezza Rice.

Classwork was fulfilling for Tiger. In his freshman quarter he enrolled in calculus, Portuguese culture, and what Stanford called your freshman "CIV" class: "Cultures, Ideas, and Values," a requirement for graduation. He walked into his first CIV discussion group and saw a handful of athletes in the classroom. He figured it would be an easy class, with "dumb jocks" filling up seats. The discussion began, and Tiger was blown away. Many of the athletes engaged in and led the discussion, pushing it forward with an impressive vocabulary and intelligence. *Whoa,* he thought to himself, laughing. *I need a thesaurus to keep up with these guys!* He loved this about Stanford. One student in his dorm tore down and rebuilt his own computer. Another was into dissecting DNA. "I'm just a face in the crowd here," he'd say, perhaps not noting that it was *Sports Illustrated*'s "Faces in the Crowd" that had attracted Goodwin's eye four years earlier. The studies meant he'd be tired on the golf course sometimes, but that was OK with Tiger. In some ways, he enjoyed college life more than college golf.

Certainly, he enjoyed the anonymity and rhythm of on-campus life to the times he'd have to swing by the athletic department and deal with what he saw as a necessary evil: feeding the media beast.

When Goodwin warned the Stanford sports information department that they wouldn't know what hit them, he was right. He was also incomplete. Goodwin, too, wouldn't know what hit him. He was overwhelmed. They all were. An average of fifty-one calls per day came in, all requests for something related to Tiger—an autograph, a speaking engagement, a photo, an interview. The coach could spend five consecutive hours on the phone, dealing with matters related to Tiger, and still be way behind on his messages to return calls. Goodwin needed help and made a move.

He taught a golf class on campus and met a field hockey player named Sara Hallock. Hallock was a good athlete from the San Diego area, and Goodwin encouraged her to go out for the Stanford women's golf team. It would prove to be a fruitful move for Hallock, who competed on the LPGA Tour years later, after she married, under the name Sara Sanders. At Stanford, though, Goodwin asked Hallock if she'd join his staff for the 1994–95 golf season, to help him handle the never-ending requests and logistics. Hallock agreed. Shoot, why not? She would draw a salary, get to work with the defending national champion men's golf team, and have a front-row seat for the Tiger Phenomenon.

The sports information department had to take similar measures. Gary Migdol, Stanford's sports information director, stepped in and told his staff he'd handle all of Tiger's requests. Migdol knew the tidal wave of demands called for a tight, focused approach. Already the onslaught had begun. In Tiger's first two weeks on campus, over seventy-five interview requests came in. Migdol would whittle them down and leave the answer up to Tiger. Every other freshman he'd ever dealt with looked to Migdol for answers. Not Tiger. He weighed the requests on his own, considered the benefits and drawbacks of each, and gave Migdol a yea or a nay.

The early list of requests was almost comical. Migdol reduced the first two weeks to nineteen requests, ranging from *People* magazine wanting to name Tiger one of their "Most Intriguing People of 1994" to *Libération* newspaper in France wanting a feature, to the March of Dimes, which wanted to honor Tiger as "Bay Area Collegiate Golfer of the Year," even though he hadn't struck a golf ball in collegiate competition in the Bay Area.

While Tiger might say yes to *Golf Digest*, he said no to Letterman and Leno, to the *Today* show and *Good Morning America*. As a youth, he had appeared on *Today* and *GMA*, but now that he was at Stanford, he viewed his time differently. Mostly, he told Migdol, he wanted to hang out with his teammates and his dorm mates and have a cheeseburger in peace like a normal college kid. In fact, Tiger had to leave Stanford one week into school to fly to France as part of Team USA in the World Amateur Team Golf Championship. His chaperone there was U.S. team captain C. Grant Spaeth, a Bay Area attorney who was the former president of the United States Golf Association and himself a former national champion golfer at Stanford, part of the 1953 title winners. Spaeth was protective of Tiger and scheduled a major press conference early in the week, to get the demands out of the way. The French press seized on the more human aspects of Tiger: that he didn't like French food ("all those sauces," he said, crinkling his nose) and ate every meal in France at McDonald's. Spaeth took note of Tiger's calm as a person and was also one happy captain when Tiger teamed with forty-six-year-old Allen Doyle to help lead the Americans to a win in Versailles before jetting back to California to resume his freshman year.

Almost as an afterthought, there was the golf, too. On the driving range, Tiger's teammates were continually fascinated by his talent and quickly began to hold him in awe. They would gawk at the perfect, tiny divots he'd leave after hitting a bucket of balls. He exuded so much confidence, they'd sometimes roll their eyes when Tiger would calmly tell them that he expected to be the best player who ever lived. Burdick scoffed at him, but when he was alone in his room, thinking about it, he found himself envious of Tiger's poise and belief.

He was always friendly and engaging with his teammates. They liked to have chipping and putting contests for a few bucks, and sometimes Tiger would get so caught up in socializing, he'd find himself four holes down. "Whoops," he'd say, flip a mental switch, and win the next five holes.

One day after a practice round, the team was eating lunch on the back patio by the eighteenth green at Stanford Golf Course. Tiger walked past them with his golf bag over his shoulder.

"What's the matter, Tiger, didn't hit it well today?" one of them said.

"No," Tiger said. "I hit it so well, I need to go to the range and groove it."

The seniors teased Tiger for what seemed like a cocky statement. Most players headed to the range after bad ball-striking days. Tiger headed to the range to prolong a good day, to make that day's near-perfect swing all the more retrievable the next time out. "Oh," they heckled, "you gotta go *groove* it." It became a goofy rallying cry—"you gotta go *groove* it"—but in reality, they admired his work ethic and demands for perfection.

When Casey Martin and Notah Begay took Tiger out to Sharon Heights, a private golf course in nearby Menlo Park, they wanted to see what the kid had. Tiger put on a ball-striking display, calling every shot before he hit it. He hit every green, and Martin thought Tiger would have shot 60, but Sharon Heights had just aerated the greens, and they were unputtable.

Martin and Begay got back into their car after the practice round, looked at each other, and said, "What was *that*?"

Once, Casey Martin and Tiger were playing a practice round in New Mexico when a massive storm rolled in. The temperature dropped to 45 degrees, and the wind blew, hard. Most players thought of quitting. On the tenth hole, Tiger was 240 yards out. He roasted a 4-iron that never got more than 10 feet high and flew right to the front of the green, rolling to 10 feet.

"How'd you do that?" Martin asked him.

"Put it back in my stance," Tiger said.

Martin called home to his parents in Eugene, Oregon.

"I don't know, Dad," Martin said, "he's just different."

When the Stanford team flew to New Mexico's Championship Golf Course for the season-opening Tucker Invitational, Tiger fulfilled his duty. He carried the bags.

He also had to attend a press conference, called in his honor just to sate the many media requests. Burdick couldn't believe it. He was a senior, and he'd never seen a press conference at a college golf tournament—much less a season-opening tournament in Albuquerque, of all places. Even the famously laid-back Bay Area newspapers acted on the Tiger Phenomenon; the *San Jose Mercury News* sent a reporter to New Mexico. Truly, it was a different world.

Begay and Martin would not make the trip. They were suspended for one tournament for a minor rules infraction, self-reported by Goodwin to the NCAA. The previous spring, Begay and Martin had played a round at the exclusive San Francisco Golf Club as guests of two Stanford alums and financial titans, George Roberts and Charles Schwab. After the round, Roberts and Schwab bought the boys soup in the clubhouse. This was an NCAA infraction. Nobody present knew it, but when Goodwin found out about the soup, he reported it.

The defending national champions were without their biggest senior stars, leaving all the more room for Tiger to steal the spot-light—a position in which Tiger always felt comfortable.

In front of galleries four deep, Tiger opened his college career with a day's best 68. One round into his NCAA life, and he had the lead. His afternoon round was more ordinary, an even-par 72. Still, his 140 was 2 strokes better than Alan Bratton of Oklahoma State's 142 when the teams left the golf course after the first day.

His team wasn't so fortunate. Goodwin, perhaps distracted by the klieg lights and by Tiger Mania, turned in a scorecard from senior Yanagisawa that wasn't signed. Yanagisawa's 78 had to be thrown out, replaced by Conrad Ray's 83. Stanford lost 5 strokes as a team because of it, and instead of trailing leader Oklahoma State by 12 strokes, the Cardinal trailed by 17.

If Tiger had proved anything in his eighteen years on Earth to that point, it was that he was a magnificent front-runner. Given a 2-stroke lead on the final eighteen, he wasn't about to blow it. Not with a chance to send an early shot across the college landscape that the greatest junior player ever was here, and players had better take cover. Tiger's 68 did the trick, giving him a three-day total of 8-under 208. Bratton was second after a final-round 69, 3 shots back at 5 under.

Tiger Woods had gone wire to wire in his first college tournament. He was gracious and calm afterward, complimenting and thanking the gallery for its attendance. Bratton, one of the best players in the country, knew the freshman was no joke. "I played a pretty good tournament," Bratton said, "but Tiger was better."

Stanford, without Begay and Martin, and after the scorecard incident, limped home in eighth place, but the Cardinal knew that wasn't representative of how deep and talented their team would be with Begay and Martin back in the fold. The Tucker was won by Oklahoma State, which cleared Texas by 10 strokes. It was an important early strike for Mike Holder's Cowboys, who had their eye on Stanford as defending champs.

"There are a lot of good teams in college golf," Holder said, "and ours is one of 'em."

Stanford's was one of 'em, too. Especially with this freshman. There was just one thing: They'd all have to carry their own bags now.

# 3

## Iron Mike

*Columbus, Ohio*
*September 24–25, 1994*


AT FORTY-SIX YEARS OLD, Mike Holder was the unquestioned dean of college golf, as recognizable in his sport as Bobby Knight was in the world of college basketball and Joe Paterno in college football. His focus was so acute, his intensity so singular, he was oblivious to the whispers that followed him from the parking lot to the clubhouse to the practice range at the Scarlet Course, site of the early-season Ping Preview tournament in late September of 1994, whispers that defined a legacy that towered over his sport like a monument.

Whether he was scouting or coaching, everybody on the course knew the man with the expressionless face and orange wraparound sunglasses, resting beneath a thick mop of reddish blond hair. His was the most familiar pose in college golf. "Look, it's Mike Holder," they would say, the respect discernible in their voices, the news spreading through the gallery. When he was recruiting at American Junior Golf Association events, people followed him just to see which player he had come to see. It was a great compliment for a junior player to know that Holder was watching. Galleries parted when he passed through, which also spoke to his natural ability to intimidate.

He put people off, made them feel uncomfortable. It had always been that way. You might find yourself getting to know college golf's mystery man at one tournament only to have him walk past without a word or a look of recognition two weeks later. Just because he was scouting a potential recruit on the practice range didn't mean he wanted to engage in friendly conversation with the recruit's parents. He was often referred to as arrogant, aloof, or worse.

Holder didn't worry about what other people thought of him.

He was the embodiment of Oklahoma tough. To him, golf wasn't a country club sport. He was disciplined, demanding, and determined to push players to their limits both mentally and physically. He made them qualify in the rawest weather, made grueling early-morning workouts mandatory, and considered character building the most important part of his job, which wasn't always the most popular approach in a sport where athletes were often coddled as in no other.

At different stages of his career Holder made players run laps for hitting balls out of bounds and do pushups for three-putting greens. He loved Oklahoma State's other dominant sport—wrestling—and impromptu greenside matches between player and coach were not uncommon. He had once angrily and, he believed, justifiably bloodied Bob Tway's nose in a wrestling match moments before Tway was to tee off in the first round of a tournament.

His players learned about excellence from being around him. He strove to operate with integrity and did everything to the best of his ability. Mostly, he did things his way. If his players preferred some other way, he would refer to the major north-south highway that splits the state. "I-Thirty-five," he would say slowly, looking his target right in the eye, his accent so purely Oklahoma it could double as a voice-over for the state department of tourism, "goes both ways."

No wonder other college golf coaches referred to him, behind his back, as the "Great Iron Fist of the Midwest."

He preached the basic tenets: Be on time, go to class, tell the truth, give 100 percent, play one shot at a time, conduct yourself with class, stay physically fit, and never make excuses. Any player in need of discipline could expect to run steps inside the football stadium at sunrise.

Everything he did was designed to make his players better. He dared them to be great, in the classroom and on the course, in everything they did. If you were going to play for Mike Holder, being average was not an option.

All this contributed to Holder's status as his sport's most controversial and dominant figure and, by far, the least understood.

Holder was the John Wayne of college golf, but to define him as one-dimensional failed to acknowledge his complexity. He was also perhaps the greatest innovator college golf had ever seen. He ran his program as if it were a Fortune 500 corporation and he the CEO. He had won six national championships, ten fewer than legendary former University of Houston coach Dave Williams, the dynasty builder who dominated college golf for thirty-six years. But Holder's overall contribution to the sport was perhaps greater.

Williams reinvented the game and became known as the "Father of College Golf." Holder reinvented it again and again, in ways dramatic and subtle, forcing those who wished to compete with him to adopt his model and methods. Although the first intercollegiate golf tournament was held in 1897, and although no coach will likely win more titles than Williams, Holder was, in many ways, college golf's first modern coach.

He was the first to take the same microscopic approach to his sport that is common in football and basketball, single-handedly ending an era when golf coaches simply "drove the van," or shuttled players from tournament to tournament. As his teams continued to win, opposing coaches, albeit reluctantly and sometimes even unknowingly, would do as Holder did, and soon what seemed like a radical idea would become a standard practice.

At a time when most college coaches did their recruiting by phone or simply welcomed players who arrived on their doorstep, Holder became a fixture at American Junior Golf Association events, always making sure he was the first coach to arrive in the morning and the last to leave at night. He spent ten weeks each summer scouring the nation and beyond for the best talent and forced others to do the same.

The equipment kept improving. So did instruction. Holder was convinced his athletes had to improve as well, and that meant they had to be in better physical condition. He made demanding, thrice-weekly 6:30 A.M. aerobics sessions mandatory.

Opposing coaches criticized him and his workouts while competing for recruits. "If you go to OSU you'll have to do aerobics," they would say. But within a few short years virtually every top program had adopted a conditioning program.

Holder didn't ask his players to do anything he didn't do himself. He worked out right along with them, never missing a session, pushing the instructor to push his players—and himself—to their limits and beyond. On days when there were no aerobics, he and his stepping machine waged epic battles. Holder was a workout fiend, and the stepping machine was his torture device of choice. It was man versus machine in a daily pitched battle of wills. Holder wasn't going to quit. As long as the electricity held out, the machine wasn't going to quit either.

The sport had experienced a major transformation during the two-plus decades Holder coached the Cowboys. Much of it was because of him. When Holder started coaching, coaches rarely watched their teams compete in tournaments. On the contrary, fearing their presence might disrupt their players, they often left the grounds altogether, sometimes even getting together with other coaches to play a different course. Holder remained close to the action. He began lingering near the par 3s to offer advice on club selection during the early 1980s and had recently started walking entire rounds with players in an attempt to steady their nerves and keep them focused, prompting other coaches to do the same.

He had also learned at a young age that above and beyond everything else he did as a coach, the one thing that separated him from his peers was his ability to raise the money his program needed to thrive. He needed the money to schedule events outside the Midwest, which allowed his teams to hone their skills on the best courses against the best competition. He needed it to fund his ever-growing recruiting budget, to upgrade his facilities, and to purchase the latest technology. Most of all, he needed it to make his greatest vision, the one thing that could elevate Oklahoma State's golf program to a level only he envisioned, a reality.

He had set out to build the nation's most dominant college golf program, and he achieved it. Not even his detractors could deny that. His teams won 135 of the 295 tournaments they entered during his twenty-one years at OSU for a 45.8 winning percentage. They finished second in 73 more of those tournaments, which meant Holder's teams finished in the top two in 70.5 percent of the tournaments they entered. In nineteen of those twenty-one years, his teams won the Big Eight Conference championship and finished either second or tied for second in the two years they failed to win. He coached seventy-six All-Americans, including twenty-nine first-team selections. More than a dozen of his former players, such as Tway, Bob May, Scott Verplank, and David and Danny Edwards, were competing on the PGA Tour. Numerous others were playing on mini-tours and overseas.

But these gaudy statistics, while helpful in recruiting, were not what drove Holder. Winning national championships was his singular goal.

He measured his success and failure at the NCAA tournament. During his tenure, his Cowboys led the nation in top-ten, top-five, top-three, top-two, and first-place finishes at the NCAA Championships. Only twice did his teams finish outside the top four at the NCAA tournament. In thirteen of the fourteen years between 1975 and 1988, his teams finished either first or second. No current coach had won more than his six national championships.

This 1994–95 team, he knew, on this same course eight months from now, had the opportunity to make it seven. Given their talent, it was almost an obligation.

His five returning players had all won All-American honors the year before. Seniors Alan Bratton, from College Station, Texas, and Chris Tidland, from Placentia, California, were best friends and the backbone of his 1994–95 team. Bratton was named national co–

Player of the Year after finishing runner-up to Justin Leonard of Texas at the 1994 NCAA tournament. He had expected little of Tidland, who he doubted had the skills to compete at the elite level. But Tidland had surprised him by blossoming into a first-team All-American in 1993 and honorable mention the following year. The most experienced player on the roster, Tidland finished in the top twenty in twenty-five of the forty-five tournaments he entered and proved his taste for a good fight when he took Tiger Woods to the twentieth hole of an epic Western Amateur match that summer, a match won when Tidland birdied the twentieth and Tiger eagled it.

Junior Kris Cox was another first-team All-American from Lafayette, Louisiana, and one of Holder's more consistent players. Cox's 72.15 scoring average the previous season was second only to Bratton's 71.28.

Trip Kuehne's transfer from Arizona State to Oklahoma State completed Holder's team in ways he could not have predicted. Trip was an outstanding student and player and would have been an asset to any team, but it was his personality as much as his game that made him such an ideal fit. Bratton and Tidland were inseparable at home and on the road, always talking about the game, always working on their swings. Kuehne's friendship with Cox balanced out the foursome; sophomore Leif Westerberg served as the easygoing fifth wheel.

Holder had been billed the "Most Feared Man in College Golf" in a *Golf Digest* article published in 1991 that was as damaging as it was accurate. He had been known to chew out players for their behavior on the course—even if those players competed for other teams. When his teams played poorly, he was prone to tantrums, which became known throughout college golf. His legendary scuffle with Tway spoke to Holder's demanding standards and the lengths to which he'd go to uphold them. At one tournament without a practice range, Holder was the only coach with the foresight to bring practice balls and a shag bag, balls he dutifully retrieved for each of his five players during warm-ups. It was hard labor, but Holder was willing to give his players an advantage as he fetched one hundred golf balls five times over each day. Tway had the nerve to complain. He didn't like that the balls were dirty. Enraged by Tway's sense of entitlement, Holder jumped him and the grappling began.

He had mellowed significantly through the years. If he hadn't toned down his hot-tempered ways, he would have driven himself out of coaching, but the reality didn't change people's perceptions, and his reputation began working against him. Rival coaches were promoting the idea that he was too strict and too demanding. Playing golf for Mike Holder was no fun, they claimed. Wasn't college supposed to be fun?

Now, there was turbulence in Holder's world. In the 1991–92 season, Oklahoma State did not win a single regular-season tournament for the first time in history. Worse, the Cowboys had their streak of eight consecutive conference titles snapped.

Holder had been forced to make some concessions after his team finished twelfth at the 1993 NCAA Championships in Nicholasville, Kentucky. Even more embarrassing to Holder, they never contended and wouldn't even have made the fifteen-team cut if several other teams had not collapsed. The college landscape was changing.

College programs were producing more quality players than ever before. That unprecedented depth affected Holder's teams' dominance. Moreover, schools were allocating more resources to college golf. Coaches were getting better, and schools such as Arizona State, Arizona, Florida, Texas, and Stanford threatened Oklahoma State's place atop the throne.

Holder had to arrive at the course even earlier and stay even later to be the first to arrive and the last to leave at junior tournaments. He noticed the tournaments were now crowded with other coaches competing for the nation's top players. Some wondered if the Cowboys dynasty was in decline.

Holder adapted and evolved, as he always had.

He'd never liked transfers to his program. They violated one of Holder's credos: "Finish what you started." But his assistant coach, Bruce Heppler, convinced him to make an exception for Kuehne, who had initially spurned OSU for Arizona State but wanted to join his younger brother, Hank, who had decided to attend college in Stillwater.

More changes: Holder had recruited foreign players before, but never sight unseen. But he knew that the best player in Sweden was better than the thirtieth-best player in the United States, so when he heard about Leif Westerberg, a product of the Swedish junior golf program, Holder offered a scholarship immediately. Westerberg made good on the offer, making honorable mention All-American as a true freshman.

Despite the relative woes of the current team, Holder was as proud of them for what they accomplished in the classroom as for what they did on the course. He knew they worked hard at the game, but it was gratifying to know that all five of his starters were also named to the Big Eight's All-Academic team.

The problem was, for whatever reason, the 1994–95 team had yet to scratch the surface of its potential.

Kuehne joined the team before the 1993–94 season and made an immediate impact, finishing third in scoring average and being named third-team All-American. Westerberg solidified the five spot, and Bratton, Tidland, and Cox continued to mature. Holder was convinced, just as his players were convinced, that they were the best team in the country. Nobody could tell them otherwise after they won eight of the sixteen tournaments they entered during the 1993–94 season and finished no lower than fifth in the others. Holder was confident he had the nation's best team heading into Stonebridge for the 1994 NCAA Championships.

Nobody who knew college golf would have picked Stanford to win that tournament. But when the smoke cleared, it was the Cardinal who flew home with the championship trophy. They weren't the best team in the country that season, but they had turned in the best aggregate score after four rounds at the NCAAs. Such was the fickle nature of college golf. If there was one thing Holder learned from firsthand experience during his twenty-one years of coaching college golf, it was that the best team didn't always win.

Now media members drawn to the long-overlooked sport because of the presence of one of the game's greatest prodigies, media members who didn't understand the college game the way he did, were calling Stanford one of the greatest golf teams ever assembled. Stanford was formidable. No question. They had replaced their worst player from their national championship team with by far the greatest young talent Holder had ever seen. But not even the presence of Tiger Woods, whose rare skill Holder had been admiring for six years, could convince Holder that Stanford was the better team.

Mike Holder felt at home at the Scarlet Course.

How could he not? The famed Alister MacKenzie layout in Columbus, Ohio, had hosted eight NCAA Championships, more than any other course, and Holder's Cowboys had won two national titles by navigating its traditional, tree-lined fairways and notoriously slick and canted greens.

But as Holder arrived at the Scarlet Course, where the national championships would be decided in the spring of the 1994–95 season, his storied program was a mere sidebar.

Tiger was the talk of the Scarlet Course as the Oklahoma State Cowboys teed off for the first round of the Ping Preview in the fall of 1994. Additional marshals were hired to handle the larger-than-normal crowds in Columbus, drawn to the event by golf's great prodigy.

Nobody had to tell Holder about Tiger Woods. With the exception of Earl Woods, few had seen Woods play more golf than Holder had.

Woods was thirteen and playing in the U.S. Junior Amateur when Holder saw him for the first time. Holder had heard a lot about this kid with the strange first name, so he watched him for a couple of holes just to see what this "Tiger" had. It wasn't the prudent way for Holder to spend his time. Woods wasn't even in high school yet, and Holder needed to sign recruits for the upcoming season. But he couldn't help himself. Holder followed him for the entire tournament, mesmerized.

He had never seen anybody doing the things this kid was doing. He hit the ball high, far, and long like Jack Nicklaus, especially his long irons. He had an unbelievable short game. He would later tell people that Woods was the best golfer he'd ever seen.

Holder didn't want anybody to misunderstand him. He wasn't calling Tiger the best *junior* golfer he'd ever seen. Holder had been coaching or playing collegiate golf for nearly a quarter-century, and he genuinely believed that this kid was the best *player* he had ever seen. Period.

He found himself looking forward to tournaments when he knew Tiger was competing because it meant he could watch him play. He admired the kid's white-hot desire to win. Holder realized early on that Woods was a once-in-a-lifetime, maybe once-in-a-millennium, player and watched him every chance he could.

Every college golf coach in the country knew that Earl wanted his son to attend college near their Southern California home, but Holder had to at least try to recruit the best player he'd ever seen.

His assistant, Bruce Heppler, had been an assistant at UNLV before coming to Stillwater before the 1992 season and, like Holder, had watched Tiger play numerous times when he should have been watching others. Heppler even developed a relationship with Earl. On July 1, 1993, the first day coaches were allowed to contact recruits, Heppler called Earl on Oklahoma State's behalf.

"You're in the wrong place," Earl had told him. "My boy is never going to go to school that far away. I want him close enough to come home on weekends. That's our number-one priority. He's going to play on the West Coast."

Holder had figured as much. At least Earl hadn't wasted Holder's time.

Holder knew Woods wouldn't have any problem adjusting to college golf. Heck, he was convinced Tiger could compete successfully on the PGA Tour right now. The freshman had played in seven tour events and not yet made the cut, but Holder knew that with Tiger, it was all about focus. If he focused on those events, the results would have been radically different.

If Tiger wouldn't come to Stillwater to go to school, Holder would have to find a way to beat him. He couldn't impact what Woods accomplished as an individual, but he wasn't concerned about that, anyway. To Holder, team titles were the most important.

Bratton was again paired with Woods in the first round of the Preview. The field featured the top fifteen teams from the 1994 NCAA Championships plus three at-large teams. The Preview consisted of three rounds, morning and afternoon rounds on Saturday followed by a final round on Sunday. Bratton had seen Tiger for the first time in 1989 playing the "Big I" in Arkansas. Justin Leonard, age seventeen, won. Tiger, age thirteen, finished second. Bratton was impressed with the kid's swing, and especially his clubhead speed.

Bratton was a senior in high school when he asked Holder how long Tiger was off the tee. "Longer than anybody on tour," Holder replied matter-of-factly. Then his future coach told him what he had told everybody else—that Woods was the best golfer he'd ever seen.

It was hard to believe at first. But in the four years since, Bratton learned that Holder didn't exaggerate. Tiger was every bit the player Holder claimed. He could hit his 2-iron as far as Bratton could hit his driver. Tiger gave away shots and still dominated. That's how he explained Tiger's ability to Leif Westerberg, the sophomore from Sweden who, until the Tucker Invitational, had never seen Woods play.

"But you were the Player of the Year, Alan," Westerberg had replied in his Swedish accent, unable to fathom that anybody could be far superior to the older teammate he so admired. "How could he be better than you?"

"Just watch," Bratton replied flatly, his eyes never leaving Woods.

Alan knew he had the skills and experience to compete against and defeat Tiger, but he was honest enough with himself to realize that the ceiling on his ability was lower than Tiger's. But he was less concerned about future potential than about seizing the moment. Bratton finished the morning round with a sparkling 70. Woods was at even-par 72. When all the first-round scores had been posted, and players were eating lunch and preparing for their afternoon rounds, Stanford and Oklahoma State, the first- and second-ranked teams in the country, were tied for fourth place in the team competition behind Oklahoma, Arkansas, and Georgia Tech.

Prior to the Preview, Bratton had shot 80 only once in his entire college career. That was way back during the second tournament of his freshman year. But in the afternoon round at the Scarlet Course, he was playing as poorly as he ever had. It was raining, and his feet were killing him. The golf shoes Nike sent as part of its sponsorship deal with Oklahoma State didn't fit. He kicked his shoes off after every shot, walked to his ball in his socks, and put his shoes back on again before hitting the next shot. He wished he could blame what would become the second 80 of his career on his sore feet, but he came undone with a triple bogey on the eighth hole before his feet started bothering him.

Woods shot a second-round 71 and lamented being 1 under after the first two rounds to reporters afterward. "I didn't play good," he said. "I didn't grab the ball. I didn't hit the ball solid. I didn't chip well. I didn't putt well. Other than that, everything went great."

Casey Martin, back in the fold after the soup suspension, shot a brilliant 67 in the afternoon and finished the first two rounds at 2 under par for Stanford, and Notah Begay, also back in the fold, went 69-76 to sit at a tidy 1 over. Stanford's other seniors, Will Yanagisawa and Steve Burdick, were 4 and 5 over, respectively. It added up to a thirty-six-hole lead for Stanford, atop the eighteen-team field.

Tidland turned in Oklahoma State's best two-round total with a 1-over 145. Kuehne was 4-over 148, Bratton 6-over 150, Cox 8-over, and Westerberg 10 north of par.

The Cowboys were 17 long strokes behind Stanford.

Mike Holder wanted to play golf. He had never considered coaching it.

Holder was one semester away from his master's degree in business when Labron Harris, Oklahoma State's first and only golf coach, retired in 1973. He might have already been on the PGA Tour if he hadn't been advised to attend graduate school in part to avoid the draft.

Harris was a big, bald bear of a man as generous with his time as he was frugal with a dollar. Harris was a teacher first. His subject was golf, and Lakeside Memorial Golf Course, a wide-open layout he had designed himself, was his classroom.

Harris had never gripped a club when he was invited to play on a sand greens course while attending Southwestern Oklahoma State College in 1930. He was twenty-one. He borrowed clubs and teed up on cow chips. Within a few years he was one of the best players in the state. He was contemplating turning pro after winning the Oklahoma and Arkansas Amateurs in 1945 when he was approached by the basketball coach and athletic director Henry Iba, of the school that was then known as Oklahoma A&M. The iconic coach had just led the Cowboys to back-to-back national titles when university regents approved the hiring of coaches for several so-called minor sports. Iba was aware of Harris's success as a player and asked him to coach the school's first-ever golf team before the 1946–47 season. At least that's the official version. Other accounts have Harris approaching Iba about starting a team after two elite players enrolled after World War II.

Regardless, OSU's first golf team finished fifth at the NCAA Championships. By the time his twenty-seven-year coaching career ended at the mandatory retirement age of sixty-five, Harris's teams had produced twenty-four conference championships, a national title in 1963, twenty top-five finishes at the NCAA tournament, two NCAA individual champions—Earl Moeller in 1953 and Grier Jones in 1967—and thirty-one All-Americans. One of those All-Americans was Mike Holder.

It was Harris who saw the coaching ability in his former pupil that Holder didn't see in himself. He was the one who recommended that Holder apply to be his successor. Holder thought it was a crazy idea. He only had to fulfill the last remaining requirements for his master's degree, and get his game in shape, and he could realize his dream of playing professionally.

His would be an unlikely path. Holder grew up in the small Texas and Oklahoma towns where his father's job in the oil fields took them. Bernice Buford Holder, a tough, freckled man nicknamed

"Speck," instilled in him a work ethic and first showed him how to grip a club and keep his left arm straight during a backyard lesson that sparked a lifelong obsession.

He didn't realize it then, but golf was a perfect outlet for a shy, determined, and increasingly competitive only child who several times found himself the new kid in a small town. As a teenager, he was a certified loner and a mystery to his classmates. His intensity, focus, and single-mindedness put people off, as they would throughout his life.

Holder didn't know there was such a thing as college golf until he visited Oklahoma State's home course and stared at the All-American plaques inside the clubhouse. He had heard about All-Americans in football but didn't realize such an honor existed in golf.

Harris offered him a chance to walk on and a $500 scholarship, and that was only if he was willing to study agronomy. Oklahoma had offered between a half and a full scholarship, but Mike chose Oklahoma State, where he went on to a career that satisfied everybody but himself.

He was never the best player on the team. Grier Jones, who won an NCAA individual title in 1967 and PGA Tour Rookie of the Year honors one year later, and Mark Hayes, who would go on to be a three-time PGA Tour winner, were better. Still, Holder had won the Oklahoma State Amateur title in 1968 and was the Big Eight Conference medalist in 1970. Twice he was named honorable mention All-American before being named to the third team during his senior year. That made him Harris's first three-time All-American.

Despite his playing credentials, he couldn't understand why school administrators would consider hiring a twenty-four-year-old with no coaching experience to replace a legend. To Holder, it made no sense, but at Harris's urging, he agreed to interview.

Holder was stunned when they offered him the job. When they told him it paid $6,500 per year, he realized why. The other finalists couldn't afford to take it.

Holder had been too busy finishing his graduate degree to work on his game. He needed to practice if he was to make it as a professional. Coaching the golf team for one year meant he would get paid, however little, to get his game in shape for the PGA Tour, he reasoned. When OSU officials offered to let him teach a business class, upping his salary to $9,000 per year, Holder accepted. He had responsibilities and needed a salary.

He was married now, after all. He had met his future bride, Robbie Yeates, a country girl from Jasper, Texas, at the All-American Intercollegiate Invitational in Houston during his sophomore year. No college golf event rivaled Dave Williams's tournament for pageantry. There were thirty "Golf Queens" in attendance, one for every team. Yeates had been assigned to OSU and was smitten with the shy, slender Holder. She sought him out when the Cowboys returned the following year. They were engaged by Thanksgiving and married in the following August.

The couple had no health insurance when daughter Michele was born. Holder won a Calcutta to pay the hospital bill.

Harris had recruited Tom Jones of Tulsa. Harris and Holder were giving lessons in Brazil during the summer of 1973 when they met Mario Gonzalez, winner of the 1947 Spanish Amateur, and his nineteen-year-old son, Jaime, who was the Brazil Amateur Open champion in 1969 and 1972. Jones and Gonzalez would form the nucleus for Holder's first recruiting class. He later added Lindy Miller, who had broken many of Ben Crenshaw's high school records in Texas and was the most coveted junior player in the nation. Landing Miller from deep in the heart of Williams's recruiting territory was his first major recruiting coup. As a result, Holder's inaugural team not only finished a surprising fifth at the NCAA Championships in San Diego but also formed a young foundation that the rookie coach felt could compete for national titles for the next several years.

Holder played professionally that summer. He used the money he won by being the top pro in the 1974 Colorado Open to pay back his parents for a down payment on a house he and Robbie had bought earlier that summer. The encouraging performance suggested that he could earn a living playing professional golf, but other factors were conspiring to keep him in Stillwater.

One was a conversation Holder had with the man who hired

him. Athletic director Floyd Gass told the first-year coach that his budget would be slashed after the season so more money could be funneled to the football program. Holder told Gass that he couldn't compete for national titles with less than the $27,000 then allocated to the golf program.

"That's OK," the former OSU football coach told him matter-of-factly. "We're not interested in winning national championships in golf."

Coaching was supposed to have been temporary, a way to get his game in shape before heading out on the PGA Tour, but Gass's words stoked Holder in a way he could not have predicted. His boss may not have been interested in competing for national championships, but to Holder that was exactly what he had been hired to do. He was determined to deliver them whether Gass wanted them or not.

His desire to play on tour was replaced by the mission of turning OSU's program into the greatest in the country.

Although he was not an accomplished player himself, Williams built a dynasty at Houston by raising money and recruiting the best junior players in the country. It was said that the toughest competition Williams's players faced at Houston was midweek qualifying to determine which five would represent Houston in the upcoming tournament. Rivals were only half kidding when they said Houston had the best three teams in the country—the five guys who qualified for that week's tournament and the ten who failed. Fred Couples, Steve Elkington, John Mahaffey, Bill Rogers, Fuzzy Zoeller, Billy Ray Brown, Keith Fergus, Bruce Lietzke, and Homero Blancas were among the eighty pro golfers that Williams's program produced.

Williams had made Harris's career accomplishments shrink in comparison to his own. The Houston coach dominated the rivalry with Oklahoma State while building a dynasty unequaled in the history of college golf. As if falling off an assembly line, championships fell to Williams. Now the young protégé of an old rival was studying his every move. He would couple Harris's ability to develop players with Williams's recruiting salesmanship. He would promote his program and raise the money necessary for it to thrive. He was determined to accomplish what his mentor couldn't: help the Cowboys replace Houston as the number-one program in the land.

Oklahoma State finished second as Wake Forest won its second straight national championship after the 1974–75 season. With Curtis Strange and Jay Haas in their lineup, the Demon Deacons were heavy favorites to win their third straight NCAA championship the following year.

Holder had recruited David Edwards because his older brother, Danny, had been a star at OSU, not because he thought he would develop into a top-tier player himself. David Edwards quickly proved him wrong, and his first-round 69 at the 1976 NCAA Championships in Albuquerque helped give Oklahoma State a lead they would not relinquish. When the smiling Gonzalez tapped in on the eighteenth green, it was official. Oklahoma State, without a senior in the lineup, was the national champion by 7 strokes. Houston was third.

In just his third season as Oklahoma State's head coach, Holder had already won as many national titles as Harris had claimed in twenty-seven.

But Holder was growing increasingly frustrated with the continuing movement to commit more resources to football and less to nonrevenue sports, frustrated enough to accept a job at Oral Roberts before changing his mind. Arkansas athletic director Frank Broyles interviewed Holder, and other schools would inquire through the years, but initially accepting the Oral Roberts post was as close as he ever came to leaving his alma mater.

The 1976 national championship coupled with the interest in Holder from other schools awakened OSU officials to his value. They approved upgrading Holder's position and awarding him a raise and a three-year contract. Holder signed only after regents agreed to explore the possibility of developing a golf course on university-owned land west of Stillwater.

The university's willingness to consider his golf course plan was critical. Tom Doozan, a member of Holder's first team, had designed a scale model of a golf course in a landscape architecture class during Holder's rookie season as a coach in 1973. For years the OSU golf team had been based out of Lakeside Memorial. Later, Stillwater Country Club had become its home course, the spacious backyard of a booster serving as the program's unofficial driving range.

Doozan's model convinced Holder that he would have to build a championship-caliber golf course strictly for the recruitment and development of his players if Oklahoma State was to supplant Houston as the nation's top golf school.

He understood the arrogance and absurdity of his plan, especially given the dilapidated state of the university's other sports facilities. The school didn't have the money to upgrade facilities for revenue-producing sports, let alone sink millions into a golf course for a program that didn't produce significant revenues. Holder vowed to raise the money himself, but even this was problematic. The last thing university officials wanted was their golf coach soliciting donors for a low-priority project such as a university golf course when they might want to ask those same donors for money to help refurbish the football stadium or the basketball arena.

From that point forward, Holder's bold plan for a golf course would never be far from his mind.

Holder's legend grew as the championships accumulated. His Cowboys claimed their third national title in five years with a 4-stroke victory over Brigham Young at the Scarlet Course in 1980. His fourth and the program's fifth came in 1983, when his team was led by brash freshman Scott Verplank, who finished tied for second place in the individual standings, only after losing a sudden-death playoff to Arizona State's Jim Carter.

Verplank won the individual title in 1986, Brian Watts in 1987, and E. J. Pfister in 1988, giving Holder back-to-back-to-back medalists. Holder's fifth NCAA title came in dominating fashion with a 16-stroke victory over Wake Forest in 1987. It was only fitting that the 1987 NCAA tournament was held at the fabled Scarlet Course in Columbus, Ohio. It was Dave Williams's last.

The Houston legend was retiring after thirty-six years that saw his program produce sixteen national championships, fourteen conference titles, and 340 total wins. Seven of his players had claimed NCAA individual titles, and forty-one were named All-Americans.

OSU rallied for a 7-stroke win in 1991. The Cowboys trailed by 3 strokes before the final round and by 2 at the turn before blistering the back nine during what Holder called the greatest clutch performance in the program's now rich history. The victory had prevented Bob May and Kevin Wentworth from becoming the first class under Holder to graduate without winning a national championship—a burden that would later haunt Bratton and Tidland as the 1994–95 season dawned.

As unlikely and ultimately satisfying as Holder's sixth national title was, he now knew that winning national championships would not be his sole legacy. He was about to do what most thought impossible.

He was about to build a golf course in Stillwater, Oklahoma, the likes of which college golf had never seen.

Oklahoma State officials did not want Mike Holder to build a golf course. The OSU athletic department had much more pressing needs, namely, upgrading the football and basketball facilities to compete with deep-pocketed Big Eight rivals such as Oklahoma, Nebraska, and Texas. That was the first priority. Building a golf course that would serve only a small portion of the student population was not a priority at all.

Lakeside Golf Course had been designed by Labron Harris, Holder's mentor, and built with volunteer labor. It had been the program's home course when Holder was competing for the Cowboys, and its board of directors didn't want Holder to build a public course that might draw players away from the city-owned facility.

Stillwater Country Club had replaced Lakeside as the Cowboys' home course in 1983. Stillwater Country Club members who allowed Holder's team to use their course didn't want him building a private facility that would compete with their club for members.

Few believed Stillwater could support a third golf course—public or private—let alone the championship-caliber course Holder proposed.

Holder didn't disagree with any of it. He had a master's degree in business and enough country sense to know that it would be a tough sell.

He also understood that college golf was changing in the early 1980s. More and more programs were becoming competitive on a national level. Recruiting was becoming more difficult than ever, and other coaches frequently mentioned Stillwater's remote location and hostile weather in an attempt to discourage potential recruits. Holder didn't want facilities to be strike three.

Opposition to his plan, no matter how well reasoned, only strengthened his resolve.

Holder had been scouting sites since school officials agreed to explore the possibility of building a golf course on university-owned land. That was back in 1977, as part of the contract extension he signed.

In 1980, he discovered a remote lake nestled among blackjack and pin oak trees seven miles west of Stillwater. The 110-acre lake was small enough to design holes around and big enough to use for irrigation. The land surrounding it had natural elevation changes uncommon in central Oklahoma.

He later learned that OSU owned much of the land. He convinced a prominent local cardiologist and longtime friend of OSU golf to purchase an adjoining 160-acre parcel. A generous donation from another booster allowed Holder to begin making plans.

Tom Fazio had just finished designing the new Golf Club of Oklahoma near Tulsa. Holder toured the course and admired the layout. The topography was similar to that of the land he had acquired. Holder contacted Fazio, who designed routing plans for a 7,046-yard, par-72 course that would follow the natural contours of the land Holder had chosen.

Now all he had to do was raise the money.

School officials were having little luck soliciting donations to improve the football and basketball facilities in the early 1980s. The last thing they wanted to do was compete with Holder for what little money was available.

They granted him approval to begin fundraising in 1983 but put every obstacle in his path. School officials had the most difficulty soliciting donations of $30,000 or more, so it was stipulated that Holder could not receive donations of $30,000 or less. They refused to give him a list of potential donors or to solicit donors on his behalf.

Holder would have to raise the money on his own. In the past, he'd proved to be a successful fundraiser. Holder put his program on firm financial footing in the 1970s, when Oklahoma's oil economy was booming, by raising the money necessary to endow seven scholarships. Raising the estimated $2.5 to $4 million to build a championship-caliber course would be the ultimate challenge, especially since, unbeknownst to him, the region was on the brink of an oil bust that would become a defining economic event in the region.

Holder persevered. He built a growing list of wealthy and influential friends, including Ping founder Karsten Solheim and OSU grad T. Boone Pickens, the billionaire oil magnate and hedge fund manager.

Solheim was no longer crafting revolutionary "heel-toe" weighted putters in his garage in 1976. Ping, the company he named after the sound the former General Electric engineer heard when his metal putter hit the ball, had become well known for its putters. His cavity-backed irons designed for extra forgiveness had yet to gain a toehold in the market. Gary Hart was hired to build Ping's PGA Tour program by convincing professional players to use the company's new Ping Eye irons. It wasn't easy. Established players were bound by sponsorship deals with more established club manufacturers, and fringe players were reluctant to try products that weren't time-tested.

Largely spurned by the pros, Hart decided to focus on college players who would have time to grow accustomed to the clubs before they began earning their living on tour.

He first approached Houston and Wake Forest, only to find out both programs were bound to more traditional club manufacturers. His next stop was Oklahoma State. Holder was noncommittal but open-minded.

It wasn't long before Holder became convinced that the cavity-backed irons were superior and insisted that his players at least try them. Within a few years, Oklahoma State's entire team was using the perimeter-weighted irons, giving Ping instant credibility within the college golf community.

By the time the 1980s were over, Ping Eye irons were the number-one seller in golf history.

It was the same way with standup golf bags. Hart sent Holder several of the lightweight bags a few years later. Oklahoma State players at first spurned what they called "old man bags." Eventually, however, they discovered that the standup bag kept their clubs drier when it was raining or when there was heavy dew on the course. It wasn't long before Holder's entire team was using the new bags. At first other players snickered when they saw the Cowboys shouldering bags with kickstands attached, but within a few years virtually every college team in the country was using them. It wasn't long before sales of standup bags soared, making Ping millions.

Ping's association with Oklahoma State had proved to be invaluable, and Karsten, and later his son, John, showed his appreciation by becoming one of OSU golf's biggest benefactors. John Solheim's son, John, was on the Cowboys' roster during the 1993–94 season, and younger brother Andrew was a freshman in 1994–95.

Pickens, meanwhile, was a major ally with profoundly deep pockets. Holder met Pickens through Jerry Walsh, a successful businessman in the region. Walsh took golf lessons from Labron Harris whenever he visited his sister in Stillwater and befriended Holder when he was named Harris's successor.

Harris hadn't been a fundraiser but hosted a pro-am to raise money to host the 1972 NCAA Championships at Stillwater Country Club. Holder made the Cowboy Pro-Am an annual event, and Walsh convinced his two best friends, Pickens and oil-drilling contractor Sherman Smith, to come to the Pro-Am and donate money to the program. The Pro-Am became more successful and lucrative every year, not only allowing Holder to supplement his meager budget, but eventually creating a sizable surplus.

Holder saved every penny. He had complained for years about

the university not giving him enough funds to compete for national titles, only to realize it was the best thing that could have happened. It forced him to raise money himself and would later result in him accomplishing what many thought impossible.

Walsh arranged for Holder to meet with Pickens so he could ask him to become one of eighteen donors willing to pledge $150,000 toward the new golf course. One hundred and fifty grand would buy the donor the right to have a hole dedicated in his honor. Pickens thought Holder's plan was too bold, but he had to admire his pluck. He eventually agreed to pledge $150,000, a sum he never expected to pay, because it was contingent upon Holder first finding donors for the other seventeen holes.

It took Holder almost a decade to find the other donors, during which time he learned that the key to raising a large sum of money was credibility. He considered himself a steward of the donors' money. OSU continued to win, which meant donors could see positive results from their contributions. University officials were soliciting contributions to improve other athletic facilities, but they didn't have any of their own money at stake. Holder wasn't asking anybody to do anything he wasn't prepared to do himself. He pledged $75,000 of his own money and later upped his personal contribution to $150,000.

Several people suggested he finance the deal. He refused. It all went back to what he had been taught by his parents: If you're going to buy something, pay for it in cash. He didn't know if the course would be able to operate debt-free, let alone if he had to make interest payments every month. Besides, stockpiling donations until he had saved enough to build the course created a sense of urgency that prompted people to keep giving.

Holder had made a personal pitch to Karsten Solheim. His phone rang late one night several weeks later.

"I'm going to send you half a million dollars," Solheim told him.

The news excited and depressed Holder. It was a generous contribution, to be sure, but Holder had privately been hoping for even more, enough to allow him to move past the planning stages that were now eight years in the making.

Holder was as deflated as he had been throughout the long, arduous process after opening a package from Solheim a few weeks later. The check Solheim had sent was for $100,000, $400,000 less than promised. It wouldn't be enough for Holder to break ground.

When Holder's wife, Robbie, saw the disappointment on her husband's face, she snatched the check from his hand. "No, dummy, it's for a million," she said, examining it. "You missed a zero."

Solheim's contribution meant Holder had $4 million in the bank when he called Fazio in 1991. Fazio had become one of the nation's most sought-after golf course architects in the eight years since he had sketched the original routing plans for a course that Holder had decided would be named Karsten Creek. Demand for Fazio-designed courses was high. Holder wasn't sure if the architect would take time away from more lucrative projects. He wasn't even sure if he could still afford him.

On the strength of the terms of their original handshake agreement almost a decade earlier, Fazio agreed to build the course. Ground was finally broken in May 1992.

Chris Tidland and Alan Bratton were redshirt freshmen then, and for two confirmed range rats, the opportunity to witness the construction of a golf course was bliss. They skipped class and tagged along with Fazio when he surveyed the property. They cleared brush and planted multicolored flags that outlined tee boxes, fairways, and greens.

Trip Kuehne and Leif Westerberg hadn't had time to unpack when they arrived for the 1993–94 school year before Holder had them laying sod on the eighteenth fairway. Holder wanted his players to experience building a golf course from the ground up. He thought actually helping to build the course would give them a sense of ownership. A little hard work, Holder knew, wouldn't hurt them, either.

Trucks loaded with zoysia grass arrived full and left empty as OSU golfers worked under a brutally hot Oklahoma sun. Holder told Westerberg to go home at lunchtime. His newest recruit had arrived straight from Sweden and hadn't had time to acclimate himself to the heat of an Oklahoma summer. Westerberg refused to leave. If his new teammates were expected to keep working, then he would do the same, he told Holder, and he did, finishing the day with a severe sunburn that would be the source of his new teammates' amusement for the entirety of his Oklahoma State career.

The course was scheduled to open in the fall of 1993. Holder planned for all the donors to gather on their respective holes, where a plaque mounted on native rock would memorialize their contributions. The donor would then be the first person to play his respective hole.

Weather forecasts called for rain as the opening approached. Holder didn't want donors traveling to Stillwater only to have the event rained out, so he postponed it—until the following spring.

The course would only benefit from being allowed to mature for several months. Holder wouldn't allow anybody on the course in the meantime. The donors would be the first to play the holes, that much Holder knew, which meant Chris, Alan, Trip, Leif, and other OSU players were like kids locked out of a candy store.

When Karsten Creek did open in May of 1994, it did so to rave reviews. Holder's vision and Fazio's design resulted in a course that was as visually stunning as it was demanding. The use of natural landmarks such as the creek itself, the lake, and exposed native rock gave the secluded course an only-in-Oklahoma feel. The course was so wooded, only the three holes that bordered the lake were visible from other holes. The seven homes Holder sold around the property to raise capital were on one-acre lots, so it took considerable effort to see them from the course, and his players could practice in solitude.

Only OSU golfers and former Oklahoma State players knew a path hidden behind some trees. It led to a practice facility that included a driving range with seven tee boxes, so players could practice in any wind direction. Chutes carved out of the dense forest were the exact width of U.S. Open fairways. The short-game practice area included two greens of different grass types, allowing players to prepare for various surfaces. A third green was in Holder's future plans, as was a clubhouse that would include a locker room, pro shop, and restaurant. He also wanted to build an indoor practice facility that would finally render criticism of Oklahoma's imperfect weather moot.

*Golf Digest* named Holder's vision the "Best New Public Course" in the country. If there was one complaint, it was that the golf course was too difficult. Many college programs prefer their home courses to be easily playable, to build confidence for the rigors ahead. Holder went the opposite route. He wanted his course to be such a stern test that any other course Oklahoma State players might play would be a welcome relief. The result was a challenging but straightforward course—but a golf course far too tough for the average weekend player.

Karsten Creek was a public course with greens fees high enough to prevent it from competing with Lakeside Memorial. Holder sold select memberships but not enough to threaten Stillwater Country Club.

The course would be as meticulously maintained as any private track, and with only approximately ten thousand rounds played annually it would not be subject to the wear and tear of a typical municipal course. Was it a private course? A public course? It was both and it was neither. It was Oklahoma State's course, Holder's course, and his players would soon discover that attempting to conquer Karsten Creek was a humbling experience.

If Holder was seething about his team's poor play on Saturday afternoon at the 1994 Ping Preview, Sunday's final round at the Scarlet Course offered no relief. Starting the day 17 strokes behind Stanford was bad enough, but now, just as his team started to gain traction and make up ground, rain halted play, not once, but twice.

The Cowboys had passed Texas Christian and Georgia Tech to move into second place behind Stanford in the team standings, but it didn't count. Weather forced tournament officials to cancel the final round, erasing Oklahoma State's momentum and giving Stanford the team title in the rain-shortened, thirty-six-hole event.

In their first showdown with both rosters intact, Stanford landed the first blow. It was a senior for the Cardinal, Martin, who led the way by finishing tied for second with UNLV's Chris Riley, just

2 strokes behind medalist Stewart Cink of Georgia Tech. Stanford's depth shone with their starting five in full force, as Tiger was only 1 stroke behind Casey in the final standings.

For Holder's Cowboys, only Chris Tidland finished in the top twenty, tied for twelfth with a solid 1-over 145. Even at that, Stanford's Begay was right with him, also tied for twelfth.

Begay's influence on the rivalry transcended the scorecard. An incident during Kuehne's second-round play with Begay would gnaw at the Cowboys. It happened on the tenth hole, when Begay's approach landed above a greenside bunker.

Trip thought Begay had addressed his ball before backing away and watching the ball roll down into the bunker. Begay disagreed. Instead of taking a penalty stroke, Begay blasted a brilliant bunker shot to within 3 feet and buried his par putt.

Trip was furious, and his game unraveled. He sometimes struggled to maintain his composure on the course. Now he was spraying the ball everywhere.

When Holder learned of what angered Trip, he offered him some perspective: "What goes around comes around," he told Trip.

He meant it, too. More often than not in life—and especially in golf, Holder had learned and believed—that seemed to be the case, even if the results of the 1994 Ping Preview were not to the coach's liking.

The trip to Columbus for the Preview hadn't started well, either. Stillwater is equidistant from Oklahoma City and Tulsa. The team flew out of either airport, depending on which offered the most convenient flight time. Holder had dropped the team off at the Tulsa airport when Heppler, standing at the ticket counter, realized their flight to Ohio departed from Oklahoma City.

"Have you ever seen the Grim Reaper?" Heppler asked the airline representative.

He had been Holder's assistant for four years and knew how his boss would react to the mistake. He would smolder, his anger as visible as heat waves off asphalt. He would be, everybody knew, a miserable traveling companion.

"Well, he's in long-term parking right now," Heppler explained to the confused attendant behind the ticket counter. "We need to figure out a way to get us from Tulsa to Columbus because—trust me here—you don't want to meet him."

Now, because of the rain delays, they were in danger of missing their flight home as they packed their clubs into the back of the rental van and headed to the airport.

They barely made their 4:20 flight, and as the landing gear lifted into the belly of the plane, Oklahoma State players were acutely aware of where they stood. The first two tournaments of the season had done nothing to decide which team was superior. The Stanford–Oklahoma State rivalry, which had been simmering since the NCAA Championships the year before, was officially on.

# 4

## Wally's World

*Birmingham, Alabama*
*October 25, 1994*

IT WAS GOOD to be Wally Goodwin. He was the coach of the
reigning national champions, his team was off to a dynamite start
to the fall season, and he had the world's most talented freshman
in Cardinal colors.

All of it seemed to barely faze Goodwin, who'd seen a lot in his
sixty-seven years and deduced over that time that most of it was
not worth worrying over. Goodwin's persona was from another,
more modest era in the country's history, and born of his childhood in his native, quiet, pre–World War II–era Cincinnati, along
with stretches of time on a family ranch in northern Wyoming. Not
much in the way of chest thumping or drill sergeant tactics from
silver-haired, blue-eyed Wally Goodwin. Those were traded in for
a voice so soft and whispery, it seemed invented to read bedtime
stories to grandkids; and a manner so unassuming and easy, he
seemed typecast to be everybody's favorite teacher in a small midwestern town. Some might see Goodwin's style as avuncular, and
others joked that Goodwin's slightly daffy affability led to an M.O.
that was equal parts golf coach and absent-minded professor.

As he headed down to Alabama in late October, however, Wally's world was headed for some turbulence. As usual, it would center on Tiger.

So far, everything about the Tiger Phenomenon was working. The kid won his first college start, finished fourth at the Ping Preview to anchor Stanford's team win at the site of next spring's national championships, then left for Europe for the international team event, leading the United States to its win. Tiger and Wally were both feeling good. In an attempt to shelter Tiger and fulfill his wish of living "the normal college life" he requested, the athletic department set up weekly sessions with the media for Woods only, held in the same room Stanford used for big events, like Bill Walsh press conferences. He'd come to the Arrillaga Sports Center, accompanied by Goodwin, and sit at a circular table with the various reporters who had filed requests that week. Tiger would look sleepy, like a typical college freshman. Week after week, his answers were nailed down to a steady, if dull, monotone. Goodwin was his bright-eyed, benevolent guardian, making sure all went well.

Then, it was back to classes and to the golf course for Goodwin and Woods. Next up on the schedule in late October of 1994 was a road trip down to Alabama, a long way both physically and spiritually from Stanford's diverse Palo Alto campus.

The Jerry Pate was a prestigious event with heavyweight golf teams, including the number-two-ranked Oklahoma State Cowboys, who served as a neat foil for Goodwin's top-rated Cardinal. Also due at the Pate were number-three-ranked UNLV and number-five-ranked Florida. Top-ten school Georgia Tech, with star senior Stewart Cink, was due at the Pate, as was Stanford's Pac-10 rival, Arizona, making for a banner event in college golf.

The Jerry Pate Intercollegiate was also notable for something else — its site.

The Pate was played at Shoal Creek Country Club, a place whose very name evoked charged emotions in the 1990s. There was history at Shoal Creek, and it wasn't good. The golf course had been set to hold the 1990 PGA Championship until it was reported that the club had no black members. Making matters worse for its public image, club president Hall Thompson gave an interview in which he said that Shoal Creek had no black members because Birmingham society did not operate that way. Hall also said he wouldn't be pressured to admit a member solely for the sake of public relations.

This flew in the face of the PGA Tour's announced policy that no tournaments would be held at golf courses that discriminated, and it offended many American sports fans, to boot. Though the PGA Championship was a tournament under the purview of the Professional Golfers of America, a different body from the PGA Tour, the public pressure in 1990 to change Shoal Creek's membership was enormous. Embarrassed by the outcry, Thompson said his statements were taken out of context and offered an apology and a statement saying the club did not discriminate in its admissions policy. More to the point, Shoal Creek buckled and admitted an honorary black member, Louis J. Willie, the president of Booker T. Washington Insurance Company, just days prior to the championship. The PGA Championship went on as scheduled and was won by Australia's Wayne Grady, though its lasting effects went well beyond Grady's triumph.

Four years later, as Stanford arrived for the Pate Intercollegiate, Willie remained the only black member at the club.

As a result of all these cultural strands, the very words *Shoal Creek* were code for the unspoken but understood problem in golf: The game historically lacked minority participation and, even in the late twentieth century, featured many more all-white clubs than most golfers would know or want to know.

Now here came Wally Goodwin and his Stanford Cardinal, barreling down to Shoal Creek with the most diverse team in college golf history. Stanford's top senior player was a Native American. The star of last year's NCAA Championship final round was the son of Japanese immigrants. And its freshman wunderkind, though mostly of Asian descent, with some Caucasian, black, and Native American blood in his history, was considered a symbol of black golfers in a white sport. Surely, something had to give. Though a dozen top teams were invited, including 1994 national runner-up Texas, all pre-tournament attention centered on Tiger Woods playing Shoal Creek. The Stanford players treated the whole situation with the insouciance of college kids. They jokingly called the golf course "Soul Creek."

At Sunday's practice round, a dozen reporters gathered around the freshman and poked and prodded him for thoughts on the sociological significance of the moment. Woods tried to deflect some of the tension by pointing out he had been only fourteen years old when Hall Thompson tried to take his stand, and that playing golf was hard enough without worrying about civil rights. Eventually, reporters got him to talk about 1990 and Shoal Creek.

"I thought it was a sad situation," Woods said. "It's not supposed to be like that in the nineties. Isn't this America? Aren't we supposed to be one big melting pot?

"Then again, it woke everybody up that this kind of stuff still happens."

Woods's quotes gave reporters all they needed for a pre-tournament story, and that seemed to be the end of the issue. Tiger spoke, Tiger addressed the issue, and now Stanford and Tiger would go about trying to win the tournament. Goodwin hadn't coached Tiger on the topic, instead relying on the eighteen-year-old's innate maturity, and on the theory that his team was there to play golf, and that's all they would worry about.

Besides, Goodwin knew his team was jelling. The jet lag from a team trip to Japan had subsided, and Tiger was back in the fold. It all played out beautifully over 7,145 yards on the thirty-six-hole first day. Tiger shot 71-68 for a 5-under total of 139. Yanagisawa shot an even-par 72 followed by a 4-under 68. Begay followed suit with a 69-73, 2 under for the tournament. Stanford was rolling again and had a 10-shot lead on Auburn, its closest pursuer. Tuesday's eighteen-hole finale would almost certainly see another team title, and the only other question of import was whether or not Tiger would make up a 3-shot deficit to Auburn's Ian Steel for the individual title. What could go wrong?

Goodwin found out when he got back to his hotel room and flipped on his television that night.

A local civil rights activist named Ronald Jackson was on the screen, and he had a message for Tiger.

"We ask that you withdraw from and not participate in any golf tournament where African Americans and other minorities are not accorded . . . membership in club facilities because of their race, color, sex, religion, or national origin," Jackson said.

Jackson even contacted Goodwin at the hotel and wanted to hold a joint press conference addressing civil rights, golf, and Tiger's role. Outside of his brief comments in Sunday's practice rounds, Tiger hadn't come close to addressing such charged issues in such a formal setting. Goodwin didn't want to force Tiger into an uncomfortable position. The coach also wondered why the activist didn't address Begay or Yanagisawa playing an all-white club, but such was life with Tiger on your team. By dint of the kid's otherworldly talent, focus, drive, and achievement, because his father was mostly of African descent, and because the sport and the South had historical baggage that far outweighed the Jerry Pate Intercollegiate, Tiger was in the spotlight again.

Jackson called for a protest at Shoal Creek the next morning. Activists would gather at the front gate and demonstrate against Shoal Creek, and against the idea of Tiger playing there. Goodwin sat on his hotel bed, troubled and unsure of how best to handle this unexpected turn.

He hadn't anticipated this, nor did he want it. His usual easy manner gave way to stress. He feared for Tiger and remembered his own basic law from all his years coaching youths: Not only was he responsible for their play in the sport, but he was also ultimately responsible for their safety.

Wally Goodwin needed a plan, and he needed one quickly.

When Goodwin arrived at Stanford in the fall of 1987, he didn't need a plan so much as he needed a place to stay.

Famously casual about most everything in his life, Goodwin accepted the job on the Farm over the phone and flew west without much of an idea of where he would live, what he would drive, or what he was going to eat for dinner that night.

He'd been golf coach at Northwestern when Stanford athletic director Andy Geiger called and asked him to come rescue a floundering program. They had a history: Goodwin had interviewed for the Stanford job in 1981 but didn't get it, leading to Goodwin being snatched up for the same job at Northwestern by Northwestern's young athletic director, Doug Single. Northwestern was a natural apprenticeship for the Stanford job, as Goodwin dealt with academic restrictions that would foreshadow his biggest hurdles in Palo Alto—convincing the admissions committee that the players he wanted were good enough for Stanford's high standards.

Goodwin loved it on the North Side of Chicago. He and his wife, Nan, made a comfortable home in Evanston, the kind of leafy college community that fit Goodwin's friendly midwestern persona. They lived two blocks from the Northwestern football stadium and felt at home.

But when Stanford called, Goodwin understood the deal. Stanford was unique and not to be taken lightly. He had history in California from his time coaching sports at the prestigious Robert Louis Stevenson prep school on the Monterey Peninsula and saw the prestige of the Stanford job as a perfect coda to a lifetime spent coaching. Plus, Goodwin felt a loyalty to the idea that Stanford had once considered him. If it sounds like an outdated code of ethics, nobody close to Goodwin would question it—a lot about Goodwin came from ideas more common to an older generation.

"Sportsmanship, decorum, academics" was how Goodwin described what he expected of his players, a philosophy that would have sounded hokey if it wasn't exactly how Goodwin lived his life. Goodwin's history wasn't a complicated one, not a tale of a hardscrabble childhood filled with an obsessive desire for greatness, or a life of dreams denied that fueled a hungry champion.

Wally Goodwin was born in Cincinnati in 1927 to Ralph Goodwin, a stockbroker whose family had deep roots in Ohio, and his wife, Ann, a national-class badminton player and accomplished amateur golfer. Ann's trophies cluttered up the Goodwin family home, and her athletic success led Ralph to joke that he should change his name to "Mr. Ann Goodwin." Ralph, too, excelled at badminton, and the Goodwins were known to dominate the badminton world of Ohio and Indiana, fostering in young Wally a love of sports and a lifelong desire to compete.

The family had some money, and Goodwin's grandfather made a significant purchase of a ranch in northern Wyoming in the early 1900s. Young Wally often spent his summers there. The Rafter Y Ranch was a tourist business, replete with guest cabins, helping shape Goodwin's hospitable nature. Even though the ranch didn't require Goodwin to wrestle steer or lead cattle drives, it did seep into his bones and help create within him the air of an outdoorsman. His players at Stanford would call him the "Cowboy" and idealize his time on the ranch as part of his personality, short on hype and bluster and long on hard work and good moral conduct.

If Goodwin sometimes veered into old-school style, so be it. Perhaps the most famous photo of Stanford's 1994–95 college golf team—a shot of Woods, Begay, Martin, Will Yanagisawa, and Steve Burdick—still hangs on the wall in the Stanford golf office. It's notable for the now famous autographs on it, and for the fairly cheesy outfits sported by the team: white polo golf shirts and fire-engine-red pants. Sure, Stanford's school colors are red and white, but the joke is that Tiger, Notah, Casey, and the boys looked more like Avis rent-a-car employees than defending national champs. Goodwin thought they looked sharp.

Goodwin's modest style belied his privileged background: prep school in the tony town of Pomfret, Connecticut, where he captained three sports, and eventually a swimming career at the prestigious University of Virginia. Goodwin did his patriotic duty and enlisted in the navy in 1945 when he graduated from high school. In a bit of foreshadowing, he was stationed in San Francisco for a time before his discharge in 1946. In his late twenties, he reconnected with a pretty young girl he'd known at Pomfret through mutual friends, making Nancy Booth his wife in 1954. It was a nice life he was leading, but there was little to indicate this was a national-championship-caliber coach in the making. There were no mantras repeated, or pyramids of success in his desk drawer, or tomes read on motivational tactics. He was Wally Goodwin, American, husband, father of two boys, and sportsman, who wanted not much more than to coach high school sports one day, preferably basketball and baseball.

There was some golf in his background. He even made a go of it on the PGA Tour in 1959, taking leave of Nancy and the kids to see, briefly, how good he could be. He had about $7,500 worth of stock given to him by his father, and he used some of it to drive a brown station wagon down to Florida and play the tour as an amateur. He'd won some amateur tournaments in New England and was still young enough—thirty-two—to see what would come of it. It wasn't glamorous, though. Goodwin spent many nights sleeping in the station wagon. His golf experiment ended after a few months, when he realized he wasn't going to be the next Arnold Palmer, and because he finally got a job offer that sounded great to him: to be the director of athletics at the Fountain Valley School in Colorado Springs.

Mountain living, fresh air, coaching sports with youths . . . it all fit Wally Goodwin.

Thus began a parade of coaching jobs throughout the 1960s— Fountain Valley in Colorado Springs, Hudson High in Ohio, and Robert Louis Stevenson on the Monterey Peninsula—where Goodwin shaped young men playing basketball and baseball. It was not a high-profile life, but it was a happy life, and it remained so until 1978, when Ralph Goodwin died and Goodwin promised his mother he'd come back to the ranch to help out. He and his family left California.

Eventually, coaching called Goodwin again. Stetson University in Florida offered a basketball job in 1978, maybe the sport closest to Wally's heart. Goodwin took the gig and coached until 1981—when he was called for an interview to coach Stanford golf.

Stanford? Golf? Wally Goodwin?

"Out of the clear blue sky," Goodwin said of the Stanford interview. Because of the physical proximity of RLS to Stanford—only ninety miles separated the schools—he'd made contacts at Stanford, often calling the campus to find young Stanford graduates who were interested in coming down to the Del Monte Forest to become assistant coaches in various sports. A young Stanford assistant athletic director, Single, liked Goodwin and called him to interview. Goodwin was honored. Who wouldn't interview for the chance to work at Stanford?

The campus itself, situated about thirty-five miles south of San Francisco, was a little slice of heaven even to Goodwin's well-traveled eyes, and the eyes of many others, too. Nicknamed "The Farm" from its nineteenth-century rural origins, Stanford had grown into one of the country's most prestigious universities. Only one of ten applicants was able to crack the admissions code, and the sixty-five hundred undergraduates, taught by a faculty laden with Nobel laureates, pursued excellence amid bike paths that crossed through groves of eucalyptus trees; they walked in the shade of long corridors and quadrangles of Spanish-style architecture splashed by the California sun, passing Rodin originals resting in campus gardens.

"Unencumbered by ivy" is how the powers at Stanford bragged about the school's rise to challenge the Yale-Harvard-Princeton triumvirate for the best students in the country.

Unlike the Ivy League schools with which they competed for the nation's top scholars, the Farm had athletic facilities that housed national champions in swimming, tennis, volleyball—you name it. John McEnroe played tennis there. John Elway played football. Pablo Morales swam there. And, yes, the golf mattered, too.

The foundation of Stanford's golf tradition came from the land itself—Stanford's nationally rated private campus golf course, a George Thomas and William Bell–designed gem that opened on January 1, 1930, a product of America's golden age of golf course design. Stanford Golf Course was one of the best golf courses in a Bay Area filled with excellent, world-renowned tracks: eighteen traditional, tree-lined holes tucked against the campus's western edge, where Stanford's property began to creep against the golden foothills of the Portola Valley. Over those hills lay the Pacific Ocean, which offered the gentle relief of soothing and picturesque fog to a sunny and warm day on the Stanford Golf Course.

It was about as perfect a place as Wally Goodwin or anybody else could imagine, so when the interview offer came, Wally and Nan came west to talk.

He didn't get the job.

He did get a job because of the interview, though. Single left Stanford to become the athletic director at Northwestern, and the first man he called to coach golf at the Evanston, Illinois, campus was Goodwin. So, in the fall of 1981, Wally and Nan moved to his fifth coaching job in twenty years, and to their fifth new home in that same span. Northwestern was almost a mini-Stanford in its emphasis on academics. Goodwin wouldn't win any national championships coaching golf at a snowbound Big Ten school, but he could recruit good-character kids and try to teach them the lessons of life: sportsmanship, decorum, academics . . . the usual Goodwin stuff.

And then, in 1987, as if the job was meant to be his, Stanford called again. Things had not gone well on the Farm since Goodwin didn't get the job the first time around, and this time assistant A.D. Alan Cummings was calling on behalf of A.D. Andy Geiger. This time, there wasn't even an interview. This time, Goodwin got the job offer over the phone.

Goodwin flew to California with the hope of wrapping things up quickly and exchanging Wildcat purple for Cardinal red. But when he got to Palo Alto, he wavered. Nan went house hunting and returned in tears, telling her husband they couldn't afford even a garage in the Bay Area's outrageous real estate market. They went to dinner that night at a popular Palo Alto restaurant, the Fish Market, a local staple on the main thoroughfare, El Camino Real. Goodwin surprised himself by beginning to think it wasn't the right job. He was conflicted about his commitment to Northwestern, but he also knew somewhere in his gut that Stanford was a beautiful place for him to coach "Wally Kids"—good students, focused athletes who aimed high and were self-starters. With Wally and Nan that night at dinner was a family friend named Don Texdahl, who owned a sporting goods store.

"Wally," Texdahl asked, "are you going to take the job?"

"I don't think so," Goodwin admitted.

"Wally!" Texdahl barked at his friend. "You have one more job in you. Take it!"

Wally Goodwin was nothing if not easygoing. His friend's words were enough. He went to a pay phone outside the Fish Market and called Cummings.

"It seemed like a job I could tackle" was how Goodwin explained a career change and cross-country move at the age of sixty.

When Goodwin entered the 1930s-built clubhouse on his first day, he found a modest setting and a depressing lack of organization. The coach's office was a room just steps from the eighteenth green, one of the prettier settings in college golf. The eighteenth tee box is on a hilltop from which the player can see all the way to the San Francisco skyline. But inside Goodwin's new office, there was little in the way of grandeur. He looked on the walls for historic photographs; he found none. Alumni contacts, school records . . . none of this stuff was around. Goodwin thus had his first mission: to restore history and pride to the program.

And there was some meaty history at Stanford. Using Stanford Golf Course as its base to develop quality players, Stanford's golf program was a shining light as far back as the Depression. Both Lawson Little and Charlie Seaver were Stanford, class of '34, and brought prestige to the program. Seaver was a Walker Cup player (and father of baseball Hall of Famer Tom Seaver), and Little, by double-dipping the U.S. and British Amateurs in both 1934 and 1935, won what *Time* magazine called the "Little Slam," becoming Stanford's most famous athlete since the great Ernie Nevers played football for Glenn "Pop" Warner in the 1920s.

Golf was valued at the campus, and any talented player on the West Coast who was interested in pursuing academics and a college golf career found his way to the Farm. As a result, national championships followed in 1938, 1939, 1941, and 1942. With the Monterey Peninsula, the world-famous golf haven, just an hour's drive from Stanford, and with the San Francisco area's excellent golf courses like Olympic Club, Harding Park, and Lake Merced, all traditional 1920s designs, just up the road, golf was part of the Stanford culture. It was still a few years before San Jose State would build its own golf program and recruit Ken Venturi, so Stanford was the preferred destination for golfers and students in the prewar Bay Area.

The program had its own landmark names, too, like future USGA president Frank "Sandy" Tatum, who was the 1942 individual champion, and his teammate Raymond "Bud" Brownell, who set the course record at Stanford with a 63, which stood for more than sixty years. Brownell was killed in action in the Pacific during World War II and is one of the program's most legendary figures for his heroism.

National championships in 1946—anchored by Bob Rosburg, who called the 1994 U.S. Amateur at Sawgrass for ESPN—and 1953, featuring another future USGA president in C. Grant Spaeth, meant Stanford's golf fraternity was tight and productive and had six national titles by the time TV began to alter the face of golf forever.

Times were changing. College sports as a financial boon were becoming bigger and bigger on the national landscape in postwar America, and amateur golf was losing its luster in favor of the growth of the PGA Tour. When Arnold Palmer turned professional golf into a TV-friendly sport, talented young players began to devalue Stanford as a golf destination. The school always prided itself on academics, and players who wanted a golf program to emphasize golf over school began to flock elsewhere. Stanford's golf program began a long, slow decline on the national scene while schools like Oklahoma State rose to take its place.

Make no mistake; there was still some glory. The team often made the thirty-team NCAA Championship field, even if it never finished in the top five. And the legacy included future Hall of Famer Tom Watson, who finished fifth at the 1970 NCAA Championships. But Watson, an excellent player, didn't go to Stanford for athletic reasons. His father, Ray, was a Stanford alum and had his heart set on sending his son to the Farm.

The player Mike Peck won back-to-back Pac-10 individual titles in 1977 and 1978, but Stanford golf was not dominating. The school's athletic department produced some notables—Jim Plunkett won the Heisman Trophy in 1970, and John Ralston took two Stanford football teams to Rose Bowls—but the golf was inconsistent. The

Cardinal won the conference team title in 1970, with Watson, and also in 1974 and 1977, but by the time Goodwin arrived, there had been a team drought of significant proportions. The last coach to gain notice had been Bruce Summerhays, who was Pac-10 Coach of the Year in 1978. The Pac-10 golf scene was now defined by the programs at USC, which produced 1982 Masters champion Craig Stadler and 1987 U.S. Open champion Scott Simpson, and at UCLA, which produced future U.S. Open champion Corey Pavin and PGA Tour mainstay Duffy Waldorf. In 1981, Arizona State won the Pac-10 title behind future tour regular Dan Forsman, and in the spring of 1987, Arizona won its first Pac-10 title with the conference individual champion, Larry Silveira.

In other words, Goodwin was not walking into a job where the country's best golfers would be knocking at his door. Not only were the L.A. and Arizona schools drawing all the talent, but Stanford was making an even steeper rise into the upper crust of the elite schools in the country academically, which would pose a problem for recruiting. Throughout the 1980s, when the college admissions game grew exponentially tougher and high schoolers began taking SAT prep classes and Advanced Placement courses, Stanford's already stringent admissions policies tightened. That meant an even smaller recruiting pool for Goodwin.

Perhaps the case of Phil Mickelson's recruitment told it best. Out of San Diego's University High in 1988, Mickelson was the hottest golf recruit in the United States. He visited Stanford early in Goodwin's tenure, saw the beautiful campus, appreciated the California lifestyle, toured the classic Stanford Golf Course, but ultimately told Goodwin the truth.

According to the story, Mickelson told Goodwin: "I love it here, Wally. But I don't know that I want to study that hard while I'm playing golf."

"OK," Goodwin said. "Stanford's probably not the place for you."

Mickelson enrolled at Arizona State and would go on to win three NCAA titles as an individual.

Goodwin knew the deal. He had to recruit students who would pass muster with admissions, and it wasn't easy. Even good students like future U.S. Amateur champion Jeff Quinney and future Ryder Cup star Luke Donald would eventually be victims of Stanford's admissions department. Moreover, Goodwin wanted to find "Wally Kids": players whose character he admired, players who weren't selfish, players who were good athletes in sports other than golf.

Perhaps because of his varied coaching background, Goodwin seemed to rate players higher if they excelled at other sports. He would famously recruit Notah Begay after seeing him play only high school basketball. Players often joked that Goodwin was almost too obsessed with a player's all-around character and personality. Once, he bragged about a recruit named Conrad Ray from Minnesota. Understand, every player who ever played for Wally can do a spot-on impression of his Reagan-esque intonation: "Boys, you should see this young man from Minnesota. Stout of build . . . three-point-nine student . . . wonderful football player who is tough in the trenches . . . and plays the cello like a dream . . ."

"Yeah, Coach," his players would nearly yell at him, while stifling laughter, "but can he *play golf?*"

"Oh, yes!" Goodwin would say. "Sure! I nearly forgot. Yes, he can play golf, too."

Enunciating his philosophy of recruiting and coaching golf, Goodwin saw an individual game as more of a team game. Again, it was his baseball and basketball background at work. "It's totally different from coaching basketball and football," he would say. "In other sports, you play against somebody. In golf, you play with somebody. And most important: Number one, we are a team. If you're not a team guy, you're not for me."

Teaching the team aspect was perhaps Goodwin's toughest task. Junior players were used to seeing their individual names on leaderboards. Goodwin wanted them to get used to seeing the team— Stanford—as more important.

Walking the golf course in blue jeans and white golf shoes, Wally Goodwin was an original. You could take the boy out of the ranch, it seemed, but not the ranch out of the boy. Players nicknamed him "Red"—not for Stanford's colors, but as a joking reference to Goodwin as "Coach Redneck," which was another of his nicknames.

Goodwin had his limits as a golf coach. If you were looking for a swing coach, he wasn't the players' first choice. Players would joke that if Goodwin offered you a swing tip, it most likely appeared in that month's *Golf Digest*. He did have some swing theories from his playing days, and he believed in a theory he liked to call "chopping wood." Sometimes, he would offer the "chop wood" tip to Tiger Woods, but it wasn't welcome advice—and perhaps one reason, along with Goodwin's frustration at the workload involved with handling Tiger's off-the-course demands, why some close to the Stanford team thought Goodwin and Tiger never truly got on the same page during his freshman year. Tiger's swing coach was Butch Harmon, the world-famous instructor who guided Greg Norman to number one in the world. He didn't need Wally Goodwin to tell him to chop wood.

But if you were looking for somebody to encourage you, or convince you that you were capable of doing something you might doubt, then Wally was your guy. He was a lifter of chins, not a driving range taskmaster. Players liked his attitude, for the most part, and how he trusted them to be self-sufficient. He wouldn't walk eighteen holes with you to analyze your swing, but he would remind you to be "relentless"—a favorite Goodwin word—and to attack your task with enthusiasm.

With that unique character came quirks, too. For one, Goodwin was famously frugal. Stanford would sometimes see other teams at tournaments with nicer gear, or newer equipment, or better resources. But Goodwin, a product of the Depression, wasn't into extravagance. He'd pinch a penny, and it frustrated his players at times. On one road trip through Texas, Goodwin took the Stanford team to eat at Denny's, since it was near the team hotel. When the Stanford team heard that Mike Holder took Oklahoma State to a Ruth's Chris Steak House, they shook their heads.

In Tiger's freshman year, the team took a road trip to Southern California to play in USC's Southwestern Intercollegiate at North Ranch Country Club in Westlake Village. The team was in town a day early, and the players figured Goodwin would have them go to practice at North Ranch. Goodwin, however, didn't want to bother the country club a day early. He said they'd practice somewhere else. The players couldn't believe it. Here they were, the defending national champions, with Tiger Woods in tow. They thought Goodwin would call the country club, say, "I've got the defending national champs, plus Tiger Woods," and they'd cruise out to North Ranch. Instead, Goodwin took them to a public golf course, where the team hit range balls off mats. The seniors looked at Tiger, who was bewildered, as if to say, "Sorry, but this is how Coach is sometimes."

At his core, however, Goodwin was about spreading good vibes. His first year at Stanford, the Pac-10 Championships were hosted by Cal and held in Orinda, California, across the bay from Stanford. Goodwin was patrolling the grounds, as usual, when an innocent young woman who was raising money for Cal's golf program approached him. She had no idea who Goodwin was.

"Would you like to buy a membership in the Cal booster program?" she asked the head coach of Cal's mortal archrival.

Goodwin thought it was too rich to be true. Plus, he liked helping people.

"Sure thing, young lady," Goodwin said, digging into his wallet and donating to the enemy.

"Thank you," she said, and merrily went on her way.

Goodwin laughed. After all, he was wearing a Cardinal red ball cap with a white S on it. He got a kick out of receiving Cal Booster Club notices for years afterward.

That was one of the few light moments in Goodwin's first season of 1987–88, though. As a whole, he didn't see many "Wally Kids" when he took over the program. Instead, he saw players who were underachieving and nowhere near what he thought Stanford deserved as players. Goodwin saw his job as getting the team organized and making them respectable, improving the sorry state in which he'd found the program.

As such, one of his first acts was to declare the 1987–88 roster wide-open for tryouts.

As in, totally open.

No privileges for scholarship players. No favors to anybody. Play your way to Wally's top twelve, and you were in. After the bloodletting of the open tryout, one player found himself on the outside, missing a spot. He'd been a scholarship player the year before. He was stunned. "You do know," he told Goodwin, "that I got paid to play here last year, don't you?" Goodwin was unimpressed. The tryout was the tryout, and he wouldn't budge.

He had a roster, though. That at least put him ahead of the game in one respect, since he arrived on campus to find no schedule or budget. Worse, an assistant athletic director swung by Wally's office to tell him, "Oh, and in about ten days, you have a tournament down at LSU."

Goodwin chose his top five and headed to the Bayou. He drove the van to the golf course and arrived at the same time as the golf team from Memphis State. Goodwin knew the coach at Memphis, and when the coaches and teams piled out of the vans, Goodwin, being the polite man he was raised to be, moved to introduce his new players to the coach.

One problem: Goodwin barely knew who they were. He could feel his heart pounding and flop sweat forming as he half guessed his way through the introductions. As if a precursor to Goodwin's future success at the school, he nailed all five names under pressure.

Things wouldn't go so well when the LSU coach, Buddy Alexander, asked Goodwin to write down his roster before a quick press conference. Goodwin accidentally wrote down "Northwestern University" on his team roster and handed it to Alexander, who noted the honest mistake at the opening ceremony with a smile. It was a vivid illustration of how rushed Goodwin's indoctrination was at Stanford. As might be expected, Stanford played terribly at the tournament, and Goodwin knew his next step was to impart the golf philosophy that controlled his coaching.

For a man with a football-basketball-baseball background, Goodwin did have a controlling golf philosophy, and it could be boiled down thus: Golf is about scoring. Scoring has its biggest momentum swings in the short game. Thus, you will practice the short game more than anything else.

The second corollary of Goodwin's philosophy was another basic premise: You will hit the driver fourteen times per round off the tee. You will hit the driver more than you hit your irons, three through nine. Therefore, you will practice the driver more than you will your irons.

He put it into practice with something he called WallyGolf. True to its founder, WallyGolf was unique. In WallyGolf, you hit your tee shot. If your second shot hits the green, you have to take it *off* the green.

"So what you're trying to do is hit the ball off the fairway grass just in front of the green," Wally told his players.

And here was the kicker: Your score started to count only when you were chipping and putting.

For highly trained junior golfers, some of whom were prima donnas who believed they knew more than Goodwin, WallyGolf seemed eccentric and, well, maybe stupid. But Goodwin forced it on them, and sure enough, scores . . . got . . . lower.

Now, Goodwin needed to find the right players to implement his team-first, character-heavy, academic-ready guidelines—not to mention players who wouldn't mind playing WallyGolf. He knew he had a trump card in the lure of Stanford as a world-class university, but he also knew Stanford's exclusivity would limit playing of the trump card. It would take a special type of recruit to begin Stanford's long climb back to its gloried golf roots, but if Goodwin had a skill above all others, it was his recruiting vision. Gather enough good seeds—self-motivated players who were dying to play at Stanford—and a good garden will grow, he thought.

The first seed would come from a place Goodwin knew well, the elite campus of Robert Louis Stevenson prep school in Pebble Beach.

Christian Cevaer was a French boy who grew up in Tahiti where his father, Yves, was a bank manager. Young Cevaer took to golf in the South Pacific, where he was taught by a Tahitian named Exalt Hapo, who'd been certified as a teacher by the PGA in the United States. Hapo would teach Cevaer the intricacies of the golf swing, and the importance of dreaming big, by showing videotapes of U.S. PGA Tour events. Cevaer would watch the exploits of the likes of Ben Crenshaw and notice that the commentators would always mention the schools of the tour players, like Crenshaw's affiliation with the University of Texas. Thus was planted the idea in Cevaer's brain of attaining a golf scholarship to a U.S. college, a plan that was put into action when a Cevaer family friend recommended Robert Louis Stevenson School in Pebble Beach as a good place for a boarding-school education and a chance to play high-level golf.

He enrolled at RLS as a fourteen-year-old and immediately fell in love with Spyglass Hill, the golf course RLS used as a practice and playing facility. The Monterey Peninsula has always been considered among the finest spots on the globe for golf, world-famous Pebble Beach and Cypress Point being the obvious reasons, but for some connoisseurs, Spyglass's rigorous test, a track that winds downhill and out to the ocean, then twists back uphill and into the Del Monte Forest, may be the finest of them all. Cevaer would only improve his already skilled game at such a difficult training ground, and from there he dreamed of playing U.S. college golf. His first choice was Stanford.

The only problem was that the coach who was recruiting Cevaer most intently was a coach who used to work at RLS—Northwestern coach Wally Goodwin.

Cevaer had to laugh, ruefully. Here he was, a boy from French Polynesia, and the one coach recruiting him was from Ice Country.

Maybe it was the golf gods who then broke the news to Cevaer in the fall of 1987, as he began his senior year at RLS: Goodwin was now the head coach at Stanford.

His motivation through the roof, Cevaer aced his classes, played good golf, and earned an acceptance to Stanford, with a half scholarship, to boot.

Goodwin would call Cevaer one of his most important recruits, a good apple who played well and was a team player. Moreover, Stanford offered Cevaer the opportunity to play immediately, a factor Goodwin communicated to Cevaer when he explained his project at Stanford, to raise the program to the place where it "deserved" to be. Emboldened, Cevaer won the Pac-10 individual title as a freshman in the spring of 1989 with a four-day total of 289, leading Stanford to a third-place finish, its best at Pac-10s in five years.

At the awards ceremony, Washington coach Bill Tindall took stock of Goodwin's work in progress. Cevaer was on board, and already Goodwin was hard at work recruiting two players who would have a monumental effect on Stanford after the following school year—a kid from New Mexico named Notah Begay, and a kid from Oregon named Casey Martin.

"Watch out, folks," Tindall told the crowd, "because here comes Stanford golf."

To think that one day Wally Goodwin would take Stanford to the top of the NCAA golf world was a reach. Golf-mill factories like Oklahoma State, Texas, Arizona, and Arizona State offered a richer tradition, better facilities, easier admissions policies, and a larger pool of talent. And Goodwin didn't arrive at Stanford thinking it was his mandate to win a national championship. The administration never pressured him that way. Goodwin had seen a lot in life, and if he wanted his teams to be known for anything, it wasn't how many tournaments they'd won.

"It was never a goal of mine," he would say, "to win a national championship. My goal was to play as well as you can and see what happens . . . and sure, at a place like Stanford, if you're lucky enough to get some talent, you probably have a chance to go someplace in the NCAAs."

Begay and Martin, who arrived in the fall of 1990, were unquestionably part of the talent. Not as well known were some of the others who would craft an unforgettable chapter in Stanford golf history.

Brad Lanning was from Sarasota, Florida, and while he was a good AJGA player, he wasn't a nationally coveted recruit. But the golf gods move in mysterious ways, and he found himself in the final hole of an AJGA event at Pinehurst No. 2. If he finished in the top ten, he would qualify for a number of key events that summer. But Lanning was on the borderline when he came to number eighteen, and nerves got the best of him. He pumped his drive right into the trees and knew his goose was cooked. He began walking toward the woods when an observer said to him, "Hey, there's a ball in the middle of the fairway."

It was Lanning's ball. It had kicked out of the trees and into the fairway, and he made par from there. The par landed him in the top ten and qualified him for the big summer events. At one of those events, a match-play tournament at Innisbrook, Lanning was paired against a French boy who went to high school in California —Christian Cevaer. Wally Goodwin was in the gallery, watching Cevaer, when he noticed the manner and game of Lanning. From that observation alone, he took an interest in Lanning, stayed in contact, and eventually offered Lanning a scholarship.

Lanning would marvel that a fortunate kick at Pinehurst punched his ticket to Stanford.

Another Goodwin recruiting story: Steve Burdick was a top junior player in the Sacramento area, from a town called Rocklin, which at that time was most famous as the location of Sierra College, where the San Francisco 49ers held training camp. Burdick was a good student and a devout Christian who walked the walk and wouldn't cause any trouble for any school that recruited him. Inspired by his father, Gary, who was an excellent amateur player, Burdick played golf from a very young age. While he was outstanding, he favored baseball and dreamed of playing college baseball—down in the Bay Area, at Stanford.

Eventually, though, Burdick got too good at golf. He played well at Northern California junior tournaments, including qualifying at Sacramento in 1989 for the "Big I" in Arkansas. He would fly there with the other qualifier from Sacramento—a thirteen-year-old with Coke-bottle-thick glasses named Tiger Woods.

Burdick qualified for the 1990 U.S. Junior Amateur at Lake Merced in Daly City, California, an event chock-full of future teammates. Notah Begay qualified for that event, and Tiger became the youngest semifinalist in U.S. Junior Amateur history when he made it to the final four at age fourteen. Burdick qualified for match play but lost in nineteen holes in his first-round match to a boy from Westlake Village, California, named Jerry Chang. Burdick and Chang would become teammates at Stanford.

At Lake Merced, Burdick met a Stanford coach who wanted to recruit him. It wasn't the baseball coach. It was the golf coach. Burdick's grades and SAT scores were good enough, and he would fulfill his Stanford dream and accept a 70 percent scholarship to the Farm in the fall of his senior year at Rocklin High—in a different sport.

Will Yanagisawa was an unlikely piece of the puzzle of Goodwin's greatest team.

Yanagisawa's youth golf career was nominal. If Tiger Woods made his first golf swing at ten months, Yanagisawa didn't make his until he was ten years old. His parents were Japanese émigrés who ran a golf shop in Long Beach. One of the regular customers was a retired engineer and good recreational player named Mark Hitt, who was in his late sixties. Hitt mentored the young Yanagisawa and gave him lessons at the shop, while Will's parents manned the cash register and repaired golf clubs. Hitt's strategy was to tell the boy that the short game was everything. The longest club they hit in the first year of lessons at the shop was a sand wedge into a net. The rest was chipping and putting, as Hitt told Yanagisawa it was the lifeblood of golf. For a year, he didn't hit anything over 70 yards.

Yanagisawa attended Long Beach's Polytechnic High School, diverse enough to produce the likes of Calvin Broadus—better known by his name as a recording artist, Snoop Dogg—and the actress Cameron Diaz, both of whom were at Poly at the same time as Yanagisawa. At Poly, Yanagisawa was just another high school golfer, not good enough to get any scholarship offers, especially not to his ultimate dream school up the coast, Stanford. He couldn't even qualify academically for Stanford. But he loved the game, and he knew the University of Arizona was one of the best golf schools in the country. Encouraged by his parents, he drove to Tucson and tried to walk on to the team. It didn't go well. He played poorly in tryouts and realized his dream was dead. He'd already been accepted academically at UC Irvine, so he got back into his car and drove from Tucson to Irvine—and walked on to the golf team at UC Irvine.

UC Irvine, suffice it to say, was not a golf factory. But Yanagisawa thought it was a program on the rise, and it had good access to private Orange County golf courses for practice. The Irvine experiment went well for Yanagisawa. The Anteaters made the NCAA Championship field in Yanagisawa's sophomore year for the first time in school history. And then, just like that, over the summer, Yanagisawa was told the athletic department was looking to cut budgets, and golf might be the first to go.

Downcast, he talked to his father about his future. He still had an abiding passion for the game and wanted to be the best he could be. He knew what that meant: He wanted to try to transfer to Stanford, to test himself academically and athletically. But Yanagisawa lacked confidence. He thought Stanford wouldn't take him. His father told him: You have to try. You have to knock on that door and see what happens.

He phoned Goodwin, whom he knew casually from tournaments at which Stanford and Irvine both played. Goodwin asked for Yanagisawa's GPA and test scores, then dropped the hammer: "I don't think I can help you."

"I just wanted to try," Yanagisawa said.

"Well," Goodwin told him, "it's a tough school to get into."

Goodwin went home that night and didn't feel right. In talking to Yanagisawa, he heard an earnest voice of a good kid whom Goodwin liked. He was a good player and an effort-first player who fit Goodwin's game plan for recruiting. The more he thought about it, the more he liked the idea of adding Yanagisawa to a team that had Begay, Martin, Lanning, and Burdick. Will Yanagisawa, the coach began to realize, fit his style. The next day, Goodwin went back to campus and called Yanagisawa.

"I want to try and help you," he told him.

Yanagisawa was over the moon. Whatever Goodwin wanted, he'd do. He'd have to retake the SAT, and he'd have to hope Goodwin could make his case to the admissions office. Goodwin went to admissions believing more and more that Yanagisawa was the right guy for Stanford. Admissions resisted. Goodwin would say later that he went to his knees in the office, telling the admissions department, "If you accept this kid, we can win the national championship." Goodwin didn't know why he said it. It wasn't necessarily true. But he believed in Yanagisawa's story of perseverance. Admissions, unmoved, waited for test scores. They were good enough.

In January of 1993, Will Yanagisawa enrolled at Stanford.

Thus assembled, the 1993–94 Stanford team arrived at the 1994 NCAA Championships at Stonebridge Ranch Country Club in McKinney, Texas.

Stanford came with two labels. One, they were "Next Year's Team." Tiger was due to arrive in the fall, when Burdick, Yanagisawa, Martin, and Begay would be seniors.

And two, they were the team with no chance.

The Ping Preview, held every year in the fall at the site of the spring national championships, was an unmitigated disaster for Stanford. Goodwin couldn't make the trip, so he deputized Casey Martin's father, King, to coach the team that week. It didn't go so well: Stanford finished dead last in the field. Stonebridge became a sick joke for the team all year. They would joke about how they didn't want to qualify for NCAAs in the spring, for fear of returning to the place they laughingly called "Stonehenge."

Sure enough, they made it back, but with little fanfare. Most observers tabbed Texas as a home state favorite, especially with top gun Justin Leonard in his senior year. The other favorite was, of course, Oklahoma State. Alan Bratton was one of the best players in the country, vying with Leonard for National Player of the Year honors. Plus, Cowboy Trip Kuehne's family had a home on the eighteenth hole at Stonebridge. Stonebridge itself figured to work against the Cardinal for other reasons, too. Pete Dye designed wide-open fairways, but he also designed the course to play into some ferocious Texas winds, the course's only defense. Midwestern schools like Texas and Oklahoma State fared better in wind than the schools from the West Coast. The Cardinal just wanted to play well and leave a good thought for the summer before gathering in the fall with Tiger on the team.

But everything changed in the second round, when Stanford started the day in eighth place, 13 strokes behind first-round leader Arkansas. The wind was down, way down, and scoring conditions were ripe. And when Notah Begay made a 60-foot putt on his eighteenth hole, he raised his arm in triumph and walked in a wide circle, pumping his fist. His eyes gleamed behind a pair of tinted Oakley shades, and in a Cardinal red polo shirt, Begay picked up the ball for his 62nd and final stroke.

Begay's 62 (10 under par) startled the field, not to mention tying the NCAA Championship record for lowest round in history (with UNLV's Robert Gamez from 1989) and setting the NCAA Championship record for most under par in history. Gamez's 62 came at a par 70. Phil Mickelson in 1992 and Oklahoma's Jim Begwin in 1984 shot 9 under par as prior record holders.

Suddenly, Stanford was in it. When Casey Martin turned in a 70, and when Steve Burdick turned in a 70, and when Yanagisawa shot 71, all in the second round, not only did Stanford set a school record—by 6 strokes—for one-day scoring, but the Cardinal took the halfway lead at the 1994 NCAA Championships. It was almost too funny to be believed. Stanford? Next Year's Team? At Stonehenge, of all places?

Texas coach Jimmy Clayton tried to needle Goodwin before the final two rounds. "Wind's coming today, Wally! Watch out!" he said on the driving range. Goodwin laughed and felt the air. No wind. Trip Kuehne couldn't believe it. He knew how it was supposed to howl at Stonebridge. "The members are hating this," Kuehne said. "The only day they have ever seen with no wind like this, they had snow on the ground."

At the close of fifty-four holes, things tightened. Stanford and Georgia Tech were tied for the lead, with Florida and Oklahoma State 2 shots back. Texas, surprisingly, was 6 shots back but still alive. Interviewed before the round by ESPN, Goodwin played it as low-key as ever. Asked if he gave his team a pep talk, he answered: "No, I don't think those things change kids. I've treated these guys the way I've treated all my teams through the years. It's your game, you go play it."

*It's your game, you go play it.* If there was ever a credo for Goodwin's style of coaching at Stanford, there it was.

And then, just as Begay's bolt on Thursday had stunned the field, little Will Yanagisawa, all five foot five of him, began to march his way around Stonebridge. He felt great. For some reason, he was hitting the ball big during the final round, a club, sometimes a club and a half, longer than usual. It could have been the adrenaline, but he drove it through the green on the downhill tenth hole, a short par 4. He got home for birdie there. He hadn't really stopped to calculate it, but heading to the par-5 sixteenth hole, he was 6 under par. Will Yanagisawa, the walk-on at UC Irvine who was told by Goodwin he couldn't get into Stanford, was clinching the national championship for the Cardinal.

Oklahoma State never made a move. Texas did but wound up blowing up on the eighteenth hole. Yanagisawa was giving Stanford the cushion it needed, and he felt so good after his drive at the 535-yard par-5 sixteenth, he pulled 3-wood and made a mighty pass at it. His golf ball rocketed toward the green, bounced up to the uphill green, and settled 35 feet from the cup. When he got to the green, he was in such a state of concentration, he barely noticed Goodwin watching from a bluff near the seventeenth tee.

"Hey, you little squirt!" he yelled down to Yanagisawa, waving, with a laugh in his voice. "Don't leave that putt short!"

Yanagisawa chuckled at the sight of Wally, as relaxed as ever, calling him a "little squirt" in the final holes of the NCAA Championship. He studied his line, and when he got up to look for Goodwin again, Goodwin was gone. Just like that. A little coaching advice, and back to seventeen for Goodwin. Yanagisawa smiled. *Coach is a beauty,* he said to himself.

And then he made the 35-footer for eagle.

Goodwin didn't know until Yanagisawa got to seventeen tee and his scoring standard had a red 8.

"Hey," Goodwin said, "you made it!"

By then, Stanford had a 4-shot lead over Texas. Incredible, but true: If Stanford's players navigated seventeen and eighteen standing upright, and kept breathing, they'd be national champions—at "Stonehenge" and without Tiger Woods.

Seventeen was a long par 3 with water right, but none of the Stanford players got wet. Eighteen, also with a water hazard lining the right side of the fairway, had given the team trouble earlier in the championship, but the momentum was too strong to stop now. Lanning was the first to come home, and he made par on eighteen to finish with a final-round 73. He walked behind the green to the scoring tent and then eagerly awaited his parade of teammates.

Casey Martin was next. Martin's championship rounds were a revelation. After shooting 80 in the first round, he posted rounds of 2-under 70 and 4-under 68. When he hit his tee shot safely to the left side of the fairway on eighteen, away from the water, then hit a conservative approach, he would three-putt for bogey. Still, his 72 was excellent, and it meant he'd been 6 under for the fifty-four holes after his opening-round downer.

Yanagisawa was next, and now Martin and Lanning were behind the green, barely able to contain their enthusiasm. They'd done the figuring, and Stanford was going to win the national championship, as long as somebody didn't make a snowman on the final hole. Like his teammates, Yanagisawa took a safe route down the left side of the fairway off the tee, but his second shot from 175 yards, an 8-iron, sailed long and left of the green, owing to his extra adrenaline that day. He was left with a dicey bunker shot. Not only was his stance difficult, but if he bladed it, it could fly over the green and into the water hazard.

But Yanagisawa remembered practicing similar shots at Stanford, almost exactly the same distance and lie. He told himself he was on the practice range at Stanford and carved a bunker shot to 7 feet. It was a gorgeous golf shot. Nobody was surprised when Yanagisawa buried the 7-footer for his otherworldly 64 and shouted, "Yes!" when it fell. Lanning and Martin slapped five, and then slapped five with Yanagisawa when he walked to the scorer's trailer.

Burdick was next, but it wasn't his day. He was en route to shooting 80, but he still couldn't stop smiling. He'd made his contribution with 70-70-71 in the first three rounds, so this was his day to have his score tossed. He still loved the fact that he was about to be a national champion.

And then came Notah Begay. His tee shot hit the middle of the fairway, and when his approach found dry land, he turned to the ESPN camera walking alongside him. He flashed his index finger, and said: "Number one, baby."

For purposes of the record book, if Begay made his 20-foot birdie try, Stanford would set the all-time NCAA Championship scoring record. Begay's birdie try stopped inches short, and with his tap-in par, Stanford became the 1994 national champions with 1,129 strokes, 23 under par, tying Arizona's record from 1992.

Seven years earlier, Goodwin had walked into a coach's office with old furniture and no historical records. Now, he delivered the school its first NCAA golf championship since 1953 and its seventh overall.

The players were unusually composed afterward. No shouting, no screaming. There were a lot of satisfied smiles and earnest hand-shakes, and some warm hugs, too, from parents and relatives. Notah Begay's parents were there. So were Casey Martin's, and Burdick's, too. Goodwin was proud of his team's demeanor. In victory, they were humble, just as he expected them to be.

Begay would comment afterward that he was scared all day of Oklahoma State, figuring the Cowboys would put together a final-round run, which he felt was the trademark of Mike Holder–coached teams. They never did. College golf is such a chaotic sport, with wild swings of fortune all over the course, that Begay said he felt nervous when he heard word of Texas making a run, but then felt a warm comfort and reassurance when he heard of Yanagisawa's epic final round. Not bad, Begay said, for a team that thought about tanking it at Regionals so they wouldn't have to return to the scene of their fall meltdown.

When it came time for Stanford to accept the trophy, Goodwin tried to put the golf team in the larger context of Stanford's athletic tradition.

"People probably don't realize this," Goodwin said, "but this is the fourth national championship Stanford has won this year." He was right—the men's and women's swimming teams had won national crowns in '94, as had the men's water polo team.

The veteran coach looked at the trophy. He was pleasantly surprised. "Next Year's Team," of all things, had become "This Year's Team."

"I've had a lot of kicks in life," he said, "but this is the greatest."

Casey Martin disappeared for a moment, to check on the viability of the water hazard near eighteen. The team wanted to give Coach Goodwin a celebratory toss in the drink.

"Oh, no they won't," Goodwin said. "They're going to respect me today. I'm older. They won't throw me in that creek."

And they didn't. Goodwin stayed dry, and so did the national championship trophy. It would need to be in good shape, and in a prominent place at school, for when Tiger Woods arrived on campus in three short months.

Five months after Stonebridge, Tiger was playing for Stanford, and Goodwin's sweet satisfaction from that national championship had turned into the headache at Shoal Creek.

Civil rights activists were planning a protest of Tiger Woods playing at Shoal Creek. The activists were asking Tiger not to play. Goodwin didn't know if it would be a big protest or a small protest, a safe protest or an unsafe protest. He was worried and needed a plan to protect his player.

Goodwin phoned the tournament organizers on Monday night. The best idea they came up with was to announce a change in starting time, in an effort to get Stanford and Tiger safely through the gates and onto the golf course without interference. Tournament organizers told local news stations to announce a 10:00 A.M. start time on Tuesday, instead of the normally scheduled 8:00 A.M. Goodwin figured it was the best he could do. He was still worried all Monday night and Tuesday morning when the team drove to Shoal Creek.

It worked.

There were no protesters present when the Stanford team drove through the gates and safely made it out to the golf course. In fact, the protest fizzled nearly entirely. Just three activists picketed the gates during play, and Stanford and Tiger were unfazed—so unfazed, in fact, that they continued their attack on Shoal Creek.

Tiger was paired with Auburn's Steel and faced a 3-shot deficit to start the day. He'd erased it by the turn. Steel was unnerved by the gallery following Tiger, which included several of Shoal Creek's African American caddies. The caddies vocally cheered on Woods. Steel would admit, after shooting 73, that he couldn't block out the distractions of the crowd.

Tiger could. He came to the seventeenth hole thinking he had a good grip on the individual title—only to get word that his teammate, Yanagisawa, was on fire and en route to a 4-under 68. That would put Yanagisawa at 8 under. Coming to seventeen, Tiger was also at 8 under. Worse, Tiger got some bad information, believing Yanagisawa birdied seventeen to go to 9 under. He felt some heat and responded. The par-5 seventeenth was 539 yards of risk-reward, with a water hazard surrounding a green that was almost an island. Tiger went for it—and was pin-high in two, 50 feet from the pin. He hit an expert lag putt and tapped in for birdie.

To eighteen, a 443-yard par 4 that required a tee shot to a narrow fairway, and then a downhill approach to a spacious green, possibly bringing a three-putt into the equation. Tiger piped his drive and then hit a good second shot that found a dip in the green. As Tiger's group approached the green, a fan watching from a nearby home in the trees shouted, "Go, Tiger Woods!" The encouragement would have been easier to take if Tiger didn't then face an uphill putt out of the gorge in the green, and a left-to-right breaker once it reached the shelf.

He buried it for a 67 and raised his putter toward the house in acknowledgment when it fell.

Tiger Woods had won his second college tournament in just his third start, and more important to Goodwin, he'd navigated Shoal Creek safely and without incident. Stanford destroyed the elite field, too. At 18 under par—with Tiger and Yanagisawa combining to shoot 18 under together—the closest team to Stanford was Auburn. They were 27 strokes back. It was a blowout.

Reporters covering the event tried to get Tiger to comment on the significance of a multiethnic kid—most called him "black"—winning at a golf club famous for its role in golf's racially checkered past. Tiger wouldn't bite.

"The significance to me is our team won," Tiger said. "And I also happen to be the individual champion. That's what we came to do. We play to win."

An interested observer was the same guy who saw Tiger play the "Big I" as a thirteen-year-old: John Daly, who was at Shoal Creek to help coach Arkansas during his sabbatical from the PGA Tour. Daly had gone on to win the 1991 PGA Championship, but Tiger was still wowing him the same way he had as a kid who almost beat him in the summer of 1989, when he was barely a teenager.

"It's not only Tiger, it's the whole team," Daly said of Stanford. "They've got everything. Stanford is better with the short game than any team I've seen."

As Tiger walked off the golf course, a fan who had followed his round approached him.

"You're a great player," the fan said. "I'm proud of you. You're superb."

The fan was Hall Thompson, founder of Shoal Creek.

Goodwin, meanwhile, gathered his troops to fly back to California. They were leaving "Soul Creek," and they were leaving as the best college golf team in the land.

# 5

# The Burden of Expectation

*Hilton Head, South Carolina*
*November 11–13, 1994*

EXPECTATIONS WEIGHED HEAVILY on Chris Tidland and Alan Bratton when they arrived in Hilton Head, South Carolina, for the last tournament of the fall season. College golf's calendar calls for an intermission over the winter holidays, when teams can assess strengths and weaknesses before launching their final run at springtime's national championships. For Oklahoma State, and especially for Bratton and Tidland, the news was disturbingly mixed.

The seniors were playing good golf. The problem was, Stanford and its superstar freshman were playing even better. This dated back to September, when Bratton was the best player not named Tiger in the field at the Tucker Invitational in New Mexico. The Cowboys had won that team title but since then watched Stanford clip them at the Ping Preview in Columbus, and at the Jerry Pate at Shoal Creek, two significant and loaded fields.

Bratton and Tidland were doing their jobs, carrying the team. When OSU won the Red River Classic at Dallas Athletic Club, it did so on the strength of Bratton's second-place finish and Tidland's tie for fourth. When Stanford and Tiger blitzed Shoal Creek, Bratton was hanging around again, tied for third, and Tidland was competitive, too, tying for eighth.

Now the fall season was coming to a close, meaning it was time for strategy and reflection. Unfortunately for Holder's team, OSU had done nothing to prove the pundits wrong: As good as the Cowboys were, Stanford seemed to be that much better. That's why the fall's closing tournament at Hilton Head, the Golf World Intercollegiate, provided an important chance to change some momentum and perceptions.

For Bratton and Tidland, it almost felt like a last chance.

Their journey started in 1990. Tidland and Bratton became best friends soon after their parents dropped them off at school, mostly because they shared common goals—to win an NCAA championship and play on the PGA Tour. For them, playing golf for Oklahoma State was akin to playing football at Notre Dame, yet they both felt like outsiders among college golf's elite. Although Tidland had spent much of his childhood playing and practicing at Alta Vista Country Club, and both had worked with club pros on and off throughout their young careers, both had more of a muni golf course mentality. They cast themselves as underdogs from the moment they arrived on campus.

Both achieved individual accolades during distinguished college careers. Both won All-American honors. Bratton even was named the 1994 NCAA co–Player of the Year. But the Oklahoma State golf program was ultimately about team success, and the program was struggling as never before. The team's two seniors were acutely aware that the decline coincided with their arrival in Stillwater.

Both were drawn to the program because of its tradition, but as they surveyed the palmetto-lined fairways and rolling dunes of Arthur Hills Golf Course, they felt as if they were being crushed by the weight of it. Trip Kuehne, Kris Cox, and fifth man Leif Westerberg felt it as well, but Bratton and Tidland were under as much pressure as any two players in Oklahoma State history. For them, the expectations were suffocating.

It had been that way since the previous spring, when Bratton,

Tidland, and their teammates sat in the parking lot at Stonebridge Ranch Country Club in McKinney, Texas, and watched Stanford celebrate a national championship that they believed was rightfully theirs. At that moment, each of the five realized they were failing to live up to the tradition of greatness Holder had built, the same tradition that had made them want to play for Oklahoma State in the first place.

Many thought the 1994 NCAA Championships would be a coronation for the Cowboys. They won eight of the sixteen tournaments they entered during the regular season and had finished no lower than fifth in the others. They were convinced they were the best team in the country heading to Stonebridge, a course that Oklahoma State players knew intimately. Trip Kuehne's family, in fact, owned a house along the eighteenth fairway, which gave Trip and his teammates insider's knowledge of the layout. Kuehne's mother even made a banner, featuring Oklahoma State Cowboys mascot Pistol Pete swinging a golf club above the words *OSU Golf.* The orange banner hung from the back of the house, a reminder to fans and participants that Oklahoma State was, as always, lurking.

Nobody anticipated what happened next.

The expansive fairways of Pete Dye's layout found their defense in the prevailing winds of Texas. But perfect weather conditions during the week of the NCAAs left Stonebridge vulnerable, and scoring opportunities meant the championship was as wide-open as the fairways. Scores plummeted, led by Begay's 62, which put Stanford—not Oklahoma State or Texas—as the halfway leader. Holder said it looked as if players were putting into cups the size of Stonebridge's ponds.

Oklahoma State got a blast of good news when Kuehne shot 65 in the third round, the lowest round ever by a Cowboy in NCAA championship play, and his team moved 2 shots off the lead, positioned to win the championship heading into the final round. That's when things fell apart. While Stanford continued blistering the course, led by Yanagisawa's 64, the Cowboys flat-lined. Not one of Holder's players was under par at the turn, by which time the championship was all but decided. Oklahoma State finished at 12 under for the tournament, their final score of 1,140 tying a school record for lowest score in an NCAA tournament. Big deal, they thought. It wasn't enough to win the championship in a go-low week, leading to the team-wide sulk in the Stonebridge parking lot.

Bratton played brilliantly, as he had all year. His 12-under 276, the lowest four-round total in the Mike Holder era, while the stuff of a champion, was still 5 strokes off the pace set by Texas's Leonard, whose 17-under 271 set an NCAA record and won him the individual title. Bratton didn't know it then, but it would later be announced that he and Leonard would share the 1994 NCAA Player of the Year honors.

Despite Bratton's individual success, he still felt empty as he watched tournament officials hand Stanford the team trophy on Stonebridge's eighteenth green. His second-place finish earned him a smaller replica of the trophy that Stanford received, but accepting it brought no satisfaction.

It wasn't the trophy he had come to collect.

Tidland, meanwhile, was mired in his own private hell after turning in the most disappointing performance of his college career. His junior year started well, when he posted his first collegiate win. But a late-season slump was ill timed and unfortunate, and it left him playing his worst golf when his teammates needed him most.

"Justin Leonard had seven birdies on the front nine," Holder told Tidland, referring to Leonard's second round. "That's more than you have in the entire tournament."

It was all so frustrating for Tidland. His time at OSU was otherwise an unqualified success. Despite a lack of AJGA credentials, and despite Holder's initial skepticism about awarding Tidland a scholarship, he'd long ago proved that he was worthy of that scholarship. In fact, he exceeded everyone's expectations by developing into one of college golf's top players. He had done everything— except prove he could play his best when the lights were brightest. His tie for sixty-seventh place, at 11 over par, was painful evidence at Stonebridge.

He was convinced he had cost his team the national championship. If he had not fallen apart, if he had just played decently, he was sure, Oklahoma State would have won.

Nobody took the loss harder than Tidland and Bratton. They had spent countless hours thumbing through Oklahoma State media guides, studying a history and tradition they knew they had thus far been unable to uphold.

The five Oklahoma State players remained in the parking lot, like victims unable to leave the scene of a crime. Around them, other teams packed up their vans and headed to the airport. They all knew that Stanford's fifth man, Brad Lanning, was graduating and would be replaced by the best player any of them had ever seen, Tiger Woods. Had this been this band of Cowboys' last, best chance to win a national championship?

Bratton and Tidland had been part of a lot of "firsts" at Oklahoma State. Unfortunately, they weren't the "firsts" they wanted. As freshmen, they were part of the first OSU golf team coached by Holder to finish a season without a tournament team title. That was also the year they failed to win the Big Eight Conference championship for the first time in eight years.

As sophomores they finished twelfth at the NCAA tournament, which was OSU's worst finish since 1947. That failure prompted a preseason meeting in which coach Mike Holder let it be known that the results of the previous two years were unacceptable.

Stonebridge felt like their best chance to avoid being forever known as the first class under Holder to graduate without winning an NCAA team title.

The only solace: They knew it wouldn't be their last chance.

Returning the Cowboys to their former glory meant beating Stanford. That much was obvious. Those billing the 1994–95 Stanford team as one of the greatest collections of talent in college golf history rankled Oklahoma State players, who still thought they were superior all around—despite Tiger's immense talent. Holder drilled his players not to watch the scoreboard, not to be distracted by what their opponents were doing or by friends and family watching from the gallery. Holder told them over and over, what seemed like a thousand times, "Only worry about yourself."

Try as they might to focus only on themselves, Stanford loomed as the Golf World Intercollegiate Tournament got under way at Hilton Head.

Which was precisely why the dramatic ending on the oceanfront golf course in South Carolina was so satisfying.

Alan Bratton and Chris Tidland didn't know it, not while honing their golf games growing up two thousand miles apart—Bratton on a battered university course in College Station, Texas; Tidland running from his front door to the first tee in his golf course community in Southern California—but they shared the same dream.

Each was obsessed with becoming the best player he could be. Neither could imagine dedicating his life to anything other than competitive golf. Each wanted to make the sport his profession and was willing to wear the numbers off his irons on the driving range if that's what it took.

In the minds of each, there was no better place to improve than at Mike Holder's PGA Tour prep school in Stillwater, Oklahoma.

Again and again they were told they were making a mistake. Why go to Oklahoma State, where you might never crack the starting lineup? Why play for joyless taskmaster Mike Holder? Why spend four years in desolate Stillwater, Oklahoma, when Malibu, California, and Austin, Texas, beckoned?

Rival college coaches told Bratton he was making a mistake by accepting a scholarship to Oklahoma State. He was a classic late bloomer, exploding onto the recruiting scene after most of the top recruits in his recruiting class had been identified. It was another case of negative recruiting, and with every word rival coaches used to convince him he was making a mistake, that he would be in over his head in Holder's program, the more determined he became to succeed—if only because of their promise of failure.

It was different for Tidland. Even his parents were skeptical of his college choice. Why go to Stillwater? The Oklahoma town may as well have been on Mars to Deni and Steve Tidland, who were both native Californians. They couldn't understand why their son wouldn't stay closer to home. Why play for a coach who expressed little interest in him and doubted his ability to succeed at such a high level? Why not accept a scholarship from a coach begging him to attend instead of one pushing him away?

Tidland didn't have a fast answer to those questions, but it did not lessen his resolve. He wanted to play on the PGA Tour and was convinced he could learn more under Holder—even if he never qualified for a varsity tournament—than he could learn as the number-one player at the handful of schools that had courted him.

Tidland and Bratton had dissimilar backgrounds, but a closer look revealed they were very much the same.

Bratton's introduction to golf came when he was five years old. It left him with a concussion and five stitches on his forehead near his hairline. His brother Tony, five years his elder, was swinging his father's clubs in the backyard of the family home in Knoxville, Tennessee, when Bratton crept too close to Tony's backswing.

The accident didn't dampen Bratton's enthusiasm for the game. After he and his family moved back to Texas, he was often found swinging his father's oversized clubs in the backyard, and he first got an invitation to play from his friend Steve Tatum, who was two years older.

Tatum's father played a lot of golf, and Tatum had played numerous times. Bratton's dad, Gerald, on the other hand, played once a month if he could find the time. Bratton had never picked up a club outside his backyard, yet from the moment Tatum and Bratton teed off at the ragged Texas A&M course, it was clear that Bratton was the superior player. The hand-eye coordination that allowed him to excel in youth baseball and football served him well on the golf course, but it was more than that. It didn't matter if he was blasting a ball out of the sand, hitting a fairway wood, or chipping close to the green; he had an innate ability to know how hard to hit the ball. He was a natural.

Tatum had expected to win, expected to tutor his young friend in how the game was played. But when their balls found the hole on the eighteenth green, Bratton was the winner by a wide margin.

After three lessons, the local pro recognized Bratton's talent. "Keep bringing him out and pay for his balls," he told Bratton's mother, Lyle Myrta. "I won't charge you anything else."

Bratton improved rapidly during the summer between his seventh- and eighth-grade years. Much to the dismay of his father, who had played baseball in high school and for a year in college, and to the disappointment of his mother, who always envisioned her son as a football player, Bratton lost interest in those sports. His friends thought he was crazy, but what Bratton loved about golf was that nobody could beat the game. Until he made eighteen consecutive holes in one, he knew, he could always do better.

It wasn't long before his mother was dropping him off at the Texas A&M course every morning. She worked as an office manager across the street, and because Gerald was a faculty member, Bratton could play eighteen holes for $4. He was often matched up against college kids, who weren't about to let this skinny, quietly determined preteen with a grim resolve beat them, although he often did.

"I'm going to get a golf scholarship," Bratton told his mother when he was in junior high.

"That's great, honey," Lyle Myrta told her son. "Where would you like to go?"

"Oklahoma State," Bratton told her. "But I'm not good enough."

Two thousand miles away in Placentia, California, Chris Tidland had come to the same conclusion.

Like his future teammate Kris Cox, Tidland was introduced to the game by his grandfather, Wilfred Henry "Spider" Tidland. Spider worked as a pipe fitter for an oil company in Torrance, California, for thirty-eight years and was a good high school athlete before serving in the coast guard in World War II. He especially liked golf, at which he excelled in his later years. Not even the arthritis that ravaged his knees robbed him of his graceful swing.

He had tried to teach his son, Chris's father, and his oldest grandson, Chris's oldest brother, Brett, to play, but their impulsive personalities were ill suited to the sport. Brett, who was six years older than Chris, was a standout soccer player, as was Chris. Steve Tidland, Chris and Brett's father, was a banker who so enjoyed officiating at youth soccer games that he became a successful high school, and later professional, soccer referee.

It was Spider who taught Chris how to hit plastic golf balls in his backyard when Chris was eight. It was Spider who took him to local golf courses. It was Spider who recognized how much Chris enjoyed the sport, how his patient, thoughtful nature, which more resembled his daughter-in-law's than his son's and oldest grandson's, gave him the perfect temperament for the game. It was Spider who bought him a set of sawed-off clubs at a pawnshop.

Tidland was small for his age. His chubby cheeks, curly, dirty-blond hair, and impish smile made him appear even younger than he was. He became a conversation piece at the municipal courses around his home, as much for his appearance as for his ability.

The Tidlands moved into a new house in the neighboring community of Placentia. That it bordered the first fairway of Alta Vista Country Club was more of an irony than a selling point. For Tidland it changed everything. From that day forward his life was simple. Steve built a gate so his son would have easier access to the course. He spent so much time there that Steve and Deni, who were determined to raise a well-rounded child, wondered if the move had been such a good idea after all.

Tidland was using crutches after surgery to correct a circulatory problem in his knee when he tried out for his high school golf team. First-year coach John Winek held his crutches while Tidland took a few easy swings. His swing looked more promising than his appearance. Still, Winek had no idea he was looking at a future Southern California Player of the Year.

Five-foot Chris Tidland became a curiosity during his freshman year. He used a 3-wood off the tee on a par-3, 150-yard hole while opponents were using irons. More often than not, however, Tidland's ball landed closer to the flag.

"Remember that little kid?" opponents, holding their hands out to Tidland's approximate height, would tell teammates after a round. "He shot two under."

Thanks largely to Tidland, the still-new golf program at Valencia High ran its unbeaten streak to thirty-seven straight dual-meet victories during his sophomore year, but it was a growth spurt the following summer that changed Tidland's game. His long game improved after he shot up eight inches between his sophomore and junior seasons. His newfound length combined with his chipping and putting proficiency made him an elite player.

Only recently have team and individual "state champions" been crowned in California. In 1989, the state was divided into ten geographical sections, each of which held sectional championships. Tidland had qualified for the 1989 Southern Section tournament, but neither he nor Deni understood that it was the single biggest event of Southern California's high school golf season.

Palm Springs is only a ninety-minute drive from the Tidlands' north Orange County home. Deni and Chris planned to leave at five thirty in the morning but overslept. Still, they would have easily made the tee time had Deni not gotten lost in Palm Springs. By the time they reached Canyon Country Club, it was only minutes away from Tidland's scheduled tee time. A frantic Winek was pacing the parking lot. Tidland scrambled out of the car, grabbed his clubs, changed his shoes, ran to the first tee, and promptly birdied the first hole.

He was 2 under before two late bogeys dropped him to even par and forced a one-hole playoff. Tidland birdied the 390-yard par-4 first hole for the second time that day to capture the prestigious Southern Section title.

Chris and Deni called Steve afterward to tell him of the victory. Steve wanted to know what his son had won. Deni and Chris said they didn't know but that it must have been important because several reporters interviewed him afterward. It wasn't until the next day, when they read about Tidland winning the California Interscholastic Federation Southern Section Championship in the *Los Angeles Times* and *Orange County Register,* that they realized the significance of what Chris had accomplished.

Tidland had made a name for himself in Southern California. Despite missing the cut for the first-ever CIF State Tournament as a senior, his high school credentials were so impressive, the *L.A. Times* would name him High School Player of the Decade for the 1980s.

Outside of the *L.A. Times* circulation area, however, he was a virtual unknown. Not much about Tidland's game stood out. He didn't shoot incredibly low scores but ground out victories against opponents unable to match his consistency. That, combined with the fact that Tidland did not play in AJGA tournaments, which served as the chief recruiting ground for major college golf coaches, meant his pool of big-name college golf schools was limited.

At first, Tidland assumed he would go to USC, where his dad had gone to graduate school. The family always cheered for the Trojans when they played crosstown rival UCLA. The problem was, USC expressed little interest. It was the same with UCLA.

Pepperdine, Fresno State, Illinois, Miami, and UC Irvine were the schools that most actively recruited Tidland. He was even talking to Stanford coach Wally Goodwin until Goodwin gave his last available scholarship to a Native American prodigy from New Mexico named Notah Begay.

Pepperdine's campus is nestled in the Santa Monica Mountains and offers stunning Pacific views. Steve hoped Tidland would stay close to home and accept a scholarship to Pepperdine, where the coach was aggressively recruiting him.

"Wouldn't it be nice to go there?" Steve said after driving Tidland back from his campus visit.

"Forget it, Dad," Tidland responded matter-of-factly. "I'm going to a golf school."

At the time, Oklahoma State was the most visible golf program in the nation. Anyone who followed college golf was besieged with news of the Cowboys' massive success. Scott Verplank stunned the golfing world and became a household name overnight when he won the Western Open as a collegian in 1985. Verplank would win the NCAA title while wearing Oklahoma State colors the following year. Bob Tway, a three-time first-team All-American who joined the PGA Tour in 1985, won four tournaments the following year, including the 1986 PGA Championship, and was named PGA Player of the Year. All told, former Oklahoma State players won twenty PGA Tour events in the 1980s while Holder's team continued to dominate.

Tidland knew he wanted to play college golf and knew where he wanted to play it. He had known ever since he had seen Bob May's bright orange golf bag.

Bob May grew up in La Habra, where the Tidlands lived before they moved to neighboring Placentia. May used to pick up range balls in exchange for free tokens. His father, who owned a gas station, drove Bob one hour each way to get lessons from the legendary Eddie Merrins at Bel-Air Country Club every Sunday morning. May dominated the region in junior and high school golf, qualified for the Los Angeles Open when he was sixteen, and accepted a scholarship to Oklahoma State, where he would go on to be a three-time All-American and lead the Cowboys to the 1991 national championship. Yes, Tidland knew about Bob May.

Tidland was practicing at Alta Vista but taking lessons from Tom Sargent at Mesa Verde Country Club in Costa Mesa. Sargent also instructed May. That's how Tidland met him for the first time. Tidland was a sophomore in high school. May was a redshirt freshman in college. Tidland sat and watched Sargent give May a lesson. That's when he first saw that bright orange golf bag with *Oklahoma State* stamped on the side. Sargent introduced them. May asked Tidland where he wanted to go to school.

"Oklahoma State," Tidland said.

"Practice hard," May replied knowingly.

Two thousand miles away, in College Station, Texas, Alan Bratton was just as determined to play for the Cowboys.

Bratton and Tidland had been on similar paths to this point. Like Tidland, Bratton had established himself as the top junior player in his region, even winning the Central Texas Junior Golf League championship. The problem was, outside that region, Bratton, like Tidland, was an unknown.

Bratton finished second in a Houston Golf Association event and won the sixteen-to-eighteen-year-old division at the Pan American

Junior Golf Classic during the summer before his junior year of high school. That's when everything changed, when he first became aware of the world of elite golf that existed beyond central Texas. Before that, he didn't know that AJGA stood for American Junior Golf Association. Before the summer was over, he had joined Notah Begay, Matt Gogel, David Duval, and future teammates Trip Kuehne and Kris Cox as a national finalist in the Insurance Youth Golf Classic, the "Big I," the biggest youth event in the nation, and had qualified for the Optimist International Junior Golf tournament in San Diego.

After firing a 70 to share the lead after the first round at the AJGA Fairways Oaks Junior Classic in Abilene, Bratton was wrapping up a practice session on the driving range when he spotted Mike Holder out of the corner of his eye. There wasn't anybody who competed in AJGA events who didn't know about college golf's preeminent coach. Bratton realized that Holder was watching him through his wraparound sunglasses.

Bratton was ready to put his clubs away for the day before thinking better of it. He pulled them out again and hit shot after shot, using club after club, going through his whole bag. He made a game of hitting fades and draws, hitting the ball high and low. He put on a show until Holder left the range area as silently as he had appeared.

Bratton finished fourth in the event but was still largely unknown outside of central Texas. He discovered as much at the Texas 4A State High School Tournament in Austin the following week, where his name was spelled *Allen* on the scoreboard at Morris Williams Golf Course.

Bratton birdied the first two holes and was 5 under after ten holes. By the time he walked off the eighteenth green—his first-round score of 2 under giving him a 3-stroke lead over Matt Aycock of Rockport Fulton and Harrison Frazar of Highland Park—tournament officials had corrected their spelling error. A voice was heard from the crowd milling around the clubhouse when his name was posted atop the leaderboard: "Who the hell is Alan Bratton?"

Lake Highlands and Highland Park high schools were located in exclusive Dallas suburbs and had the preeminent golf programs in the state, featuring star junior players from wealthy families who benefited from the finest equipment and instruction that money could buy. Highland Park was led by Frazar, who played out of Royal Oaks Country Club with best friend Justin Leonard, and Trip Kuehne, considered the can't-miss star of a remarkably talented group of Dallas-area junior players.

Bratton, who played for a team that had never qualified for the state tournament and played out of Texas A&M's unglamorous municipal course, had never heard of Lake Highlands, Highland Park, Trip Kuehne, Harrison Frazar, or Justin Leonard. Leonard had never heard of Bratton either. He didn't need to. Leonard would go on to win his second straight 5A state title.

Again, Bratton fought the familiar and unwelcome feeling of inferiority in the 4A tournament. He had played against country club kids before. He knew competitive golf was more their world than his, and he never quite felt as if he belonged. He often felt a nagging dread on the practice range. The one thing that gave him hope and confidence was that even though his game wasn't as pretty, and his clubs were less expensive, he could score. Bratton knew he could do one thing as well as anybody: put the ball in the hole.

Later that night, Alan's coach Danny Hayes was checking into his hotel when he overheard the same question posed earlier in the day: "Who in the hell is Alan Bratton, anyway?" one woman asked another in the lobby. Their hands dripped with diamonds.

Bratton had been playing near-flawless golf for more than a month, a trend that continued into the back nine of the second day of the thirty-six-hole 4A state finals. There were no on-course scoreboards, and coaches weren't allowed to speak with players during play. Add to the mix Bratton's perpetual scowl on the golf course, and nobody—Bratton included—seemed to know he was surprising the field, 1 shot back of Highland Park's Trip Kuehne with two holes to play. Bratton had an inkling things were going well and told himself, *If I birdie the final two holes, I'll be a state champion.*

He made a 12-foot birdie on seventeen to pull into a tie with Kuehne, still not knowing for sure where he stood. By the time he reached the eighteenth green in regulation, he noticed Highland Park fans staring him down as he lined up his birdie putt. It was tracking perfectly toward the cup until it broke away at the last minute, prompting muffled applause from several Highland Park fans. Bratton's heart sank. He was sure that he had just lost the tournament. Then he saw his coach's smiling face. It reassured him. He tapped in for par, knowing that the Texas 4A state individual championship had yet to be decided.

In the one-hole playoff between future Cowboy teammates, Trip ran his 6-foot par putt past the hole, and Bratton knew all he had to do was make the 3-footer for a title he was afraid to even dream he could win.

When his ball rattled into the cup, making him the 4A state medalist, everybody in the field knew who A&M Consolidated junior Alan Bratton was—even if the Texas high school golf establishment forever exacerbated its snub by misspelling his name *Allen* in the record books.

A letter from Holder was waiting for Bratton when he arrived at home. The win did more than confirm the talent Holder saw on the practice range. It sent Bratton's confidence soaring, convincing him he was the equal of contemporaries who honed their skills on manicured courses behind the gates of exclusive country clubs, while he was forced to manufacture shots from imperfect lies on his shabby home course.

The win did even more than that. It won over Gerald Bratton, too.

His father had always taken a pragmatic approach to his son's career. He knew how fleeting it could be to have a dream of playing major college golf before graduating to the PGA Tour. He knew serious golfers were only as good as their last round, and that even the most impressive victories could be followed by career-altering defeats. Gerald always hoped his son would develop into the elite player he was working so hard to become. But he also wanted to prepare his son for the more realistic alternative, demanding he maintain high grades and pursue other interests—even while receiving congratulatory notes from colleagues trying to curry favor with the new dean of the veterinary school after his son's milestone victories.

Gerald Bratton hoped his son was capable of greatness, but he wasn't convinced of it. That's why he had been hesitant to finance his son on the AJGA circuit. Beating Kuehne and joining a list of Texas high school champions that included Tom Kite, Ben Crenshaw, Blaine McCallister, Jeff Maggert, Bob Estes, Jaxon Brigman, and Justin Leonard cemented Bratton's talent in his father's eyes. From that point on, when Bratton wanted to compete in elite junior tournaments outside the Lone Star State or even outside the Southwest, Gerald found a way to pay for it.

In the coming weeks and months Bratton would do everything within his power to prove that he was worthy of the scholarship offer that Holder had extended, putting together an amazing string of performances at high-caliber AJGA events. It was all so good, until his senior year ended in disappointment.

When he was a junior, it seemed as if every putt he struck found the bottom of the cup. His senior year, they all seemed to lip out or stop short. The season should have been fun. A&M Consolidated earned long-overdue respect and qualified for the state tournament for the first time in twenty years. As a bonus, Consolidated finished a surprising third. What wasn't so fun was Bratton's failure to defend his state crown, finishing fourth, as Kuehne, now a junior at Highland Park, avenged his defeat. Kuehne's individual title helped lead Highland Park to consecutive team championships and set the stage for Kuehne to win the state title again in his senior year.

As for Bratton, he'd won a Texas individual title and proved he was among the elite junior players in the country, named to the AJGA All-American squad for the second straight year. His coach and parents watched proudly as he signed his scholarship offer to Oklahoma State during a brief ceremony. By rights, he should have felt worthy of the honor, as worthy as any recruit in America, but doubt lingered. After all, he was going to school at a place where resumés like his were the norm.

· · ·

Tidland had also placed Oklahoma State on top of his list of favorite colleges. There was just one problem: Mike Holder had never heard of him.

Bob May was the first person to tell Holder about Tidland's desire to be a Cowboy. May even recommended that Holder recruit him. But when Holder checked Tidland's junior record, he found a blank slate. In the world of elite junior golf, Chris Tidland hadn't accomplished anything of significance, at least as far as Holder was concerned.

Holder knew you didn't have to be a junior golf superstar to develop into a top-tier college player. In his own playing days, even Holder did not compete nationally before he arrived in Stillwater.

Still, when Tidland first called Holder to inquire about playing for the Cowboys, Holder replied with a noncommittal letter signed in orange ink.

> Thank you for your telephone call. You seem to have a sincere interest in Oklahoma State University and a strong desire to be a good player. Those are qualities that would certainly enhance your chances for success at our university.
>
> Over the next few months, I suggest that we continue to communicate and perhaps an opportunity to be part of our golf program will develop.
>
> Good luck in 1990 and keep up the good work in the classroom.
>
> Sincerely,
> Mike Holder

It was bad enough Tidland was determined to go to Oklahoma State, too far from home, at least by his parents' reckoning. Worse, the coach didn't want him. Or at least that was the impression they got from Holder. They wanted their son to go to a school where he would be embraced. Holder, meanwhile, kept pushing him away.

Tidland was practicing at Alta Vista one day when Holder called. Deni answered. Holder was frank. He wasn't looking for some laid-back, Southern California, country club kid. Deni responded angrily. Holder made it sound as if they lived in Beverly Hills. Alta Vista was a country club, true enough, but it was one of the least pretentious and least expensive country clubs in Southern California at the time. Steve and Deni worked hard to support the family. Tidland didn't travel around the country playing in junior tournaments because they couldn't take the time off work and because they couldn't afford the travel expenses, and here was Holder, making it sound like they belonged to Hollywood's elite.

Deni told Chris that Oklahoma State was a lost cause when he got home that night. "The coach doesn't want you," she told her son, and it was true. Holder had said as much on the phone, encouraging her to persuade Chris to attend a lesser program. She told Chris she was sorry, but there was no way Holder was going to call back. His Oklahoma State dream was dead.

Undeterred, Chris would leave more messages, and to everyone's surprise, Holder did call back. Tidland was practicing at Alta Vista at the time. Holder tried again. Same thing. That made an impression on a coach who still hit more range balls than his players. Every time Holder called the Tidlands' home he got the same response: Chris wasn't home. He was practicing.

Tidland was serious about his dream to become a professional golfer and one day play on the PGA Tour. He knew academics were important. His parents instilled that in him. But while some people study accounting or history to prepare for a career as an accountant or a professor, Tidland wanted to major in golf, and there was no more prestigious school than Oklahoma State. He was determined to go to OSU, even after Holder told him the only scholarship he had available was promised to somebody else. If Tidland wanted to come, Holder said, he'd have to walk on and earn his scholarship.

There was no way his parents would let him commit without visiting the campus first, and they couldn't take the time off work to take him to Stillwater themselves. They enlisted the help of Chris's Uncle George. Together, he and Chris flew to Oklahoma City and made the one-hour drive to Stillwater. Tidland met Holder and they played nine holes. Holder wasn't any more impressed with

Tidland's game in person than he had been on the videotape Tidland had sent him.

*This kid better be able to chip and putt or he's not going to beat anybody,* Holder thought to himself.

He still thought it best that Tidland attend another school and encouraged him to do so. But Tidland was persistent, as was Bob May, who kept recommending Tidland to his coach. The kid was a hard worker and determined to get better, Holder had to admit. He also liked Tidland's sincere answers to his questions, and there was something else. Holder felt a connection with Uncle George. The more time they spent together, the more Tidland's uncle reminded Holder of his own father, Speck, who had by then retired from the oil fields.

Holder finally relented. He had only one scholarship freshman coming in that year, and it might be beneficial for him to have another freshman to compete against, even if it wouldn't be much of a competition. They could live together in the dorm, Holder reasoned. He even gave Tidland a $1,000 scholarship, although it was against his better judgment. He figured the stubborn kid ought to get something for coming all the way from California.

Bratton was delighted to hear that another freshman was walking on and would share his residential suite. Bratton had been told he would be the only freshman in the 1990 recruiting class and would be living alone in the athletic dorm in a room designed for four. Comically, it was a room designed for basketball players.

They recognized each other right away. Bratton had never heard the name Chris Tidland but remembered they had played together at the Optimist International Junior Golf Tournament in San Diego two years before. Bratton remembered being amazed that someone as small as Tidland could hit the ball so far.

Steve and Deni took Tidland and his new roommate out for pizza and listened to them swap golf stories. They talked about what they witnessed as they drove back to their hotel after dropping their son and Bratton off at the dorm later that night. They had never before heard anyone talk about golf with the same passion as their son did. It was almost a relief to know there was someone else who shared his obsession with the game.

Steve and Deni felt uneasy during the drive back to Oklahoma City. The Oklahoma landscape, where trees grew bent over from the wind on a vast tabletop that stretched to the horizon, seemed like a foreign land. Holder had not endeared himself to Steve and Deni, which was not uncommon for a man who didn't always make the best first impressions. To them, he seemed as cold and unfeeling in person as he had been on the phone. They had spent two days in Oklahoma, and whenever someone learned they were from California, the Tidlands heard the same incredulous reply: "What are you doing *here*?" They couldn't help but wonder the same about their son.

The truth was, Tidland had never felt more at home. It wasn't long after Steve and Deni left that he and Bratton went to the practice range, only to come back to their room hours later to sit and contemplate what they might do to improve even more the next day. It became a daily ritual.

In the coming days, weeks, and months they would come to realize how much they had in common. They had the same sense of humor and the same single-minded determination to improve their games. Both came from athletic families but neither grew up in a golf family.

Perhaps their greatest bond was their own insecurity. As the weeks and months passed, sharing a suite designed for the tallest athletes on campus only contributed to their feeling small and inconsequential. The team they were joining was deep. The top four players returned in 1990 from a team that had won six regular-season tournaments, the Big Eight Conference championship, and the NCAA Central Regional before finishing fourth at the NCAA Championships. These Cowboys were an experienced team with national championship aspirations.

Bratton and Tidland offered little competition for Kevin Wentworth, a two-time first-team All-American and the star of the team.

They watched Wentworth hit the ball all over the course and still card a 70. The seventh and eighth players on the roster would occasionally post 65s. Bratton was scoring in the mid-70s—on a good day—and Tidland's scores were higher still.

They were together in the dorm room one night, talking golf and brainstorming for ideas that might help them close the gap, when it came to them. They didn't think Oklahoma State's top four players—Wentworth, Craig Hainline, Scott De Serrano, and May—worked as hard as they could. They knew they couldn't always control how well they played. But they could control how much they practiced. That night they made a vow to out-work every other player on the roster every day of the week. It was a pact that would bind them for the next four years.

That pact helped establish them as elite players in college golf during their first two seasons. The pair spent countless hours at Stillwater Country Club or at the driving range. Holder's tutelage, combined with their continued physical maturation, had them hitting the ball longer and straighter. Hours spent chipping and putting honed their short games. By the time the 1992–93 season dawned, Bratton and Tidland were redshirt sophomores who had credentials, Bratton by being named the Big Eight's Newcomer of the Year, Player of the Year, and a second-team All-American. Tidland had also exceeded Holder's wildest expectations during his first competitive season by being OSU's top finisher in five tournaments and second in four others en route to being named an honorable mention All-American.

Bratton and Tidland had proved they belonged at Oklahoma State and could compete against the best players in college golf. They also knew that what they accomplished wasn't good enough. Individual success was important, no question, but in Holder's program, team success was paramount.

That was the major lesson they learned during their first season in Stillwater. OSU won only two regular-season tournaments that year but captured Holder's seventeenth conference title in eighteen years. The bigger surprise came two weeks later, when a seemingly undermanned Oklahoma State team came from nowhere to win Holder's sixth, and by far most unlikely, national championship at Poppy Hills on the Monterey Peninsula in California.

The Cowboys trailed by 3 strokes at the start of the final round and were down 2 strokes at the turn before rallying for a 7-shot victory over runner-up North Carolina. Oklahoma State's Craig Hainline shot a final-round 72 and finished in a tie for fourth with two-time defending NCAA individual champion Phil Mickelson of Arizona State. Holder, who always preached that national titles are won and lost on the final day, called it the greatest clutch performance he'd ever witnessed.

The unexpected victory kept another tradition alive. "We would have been the first class to go through the program without winning an NCAA championship [in Holder's tenure]," May told reporters afterward about himself and Kevin Wentworth. "That was right in the back of our minds."

Avoiding that same fate was foremost in Bratton's and Tidland's minds as they prepared for their second national championship in the spring of 1993.

Holder always preached that the NCAA Championship was the easiest tournament to win because so many of the participants choked. He had seen it year after year. What he had rarely seen was his own team choke.

Oklahoma State entered the 1992–93 season ranked second in the nation behind defending national champion Arizona in the *Golf World* preseason poll but won only two team titles all season. More surprisingly, for the first time in Holder's tenure, Oklahoma State completed a season without an individual winner. Mind, they were still a powerhouse. The Cowboys were always deep and posted thirty-two top-ten finishes in fifteen tournaments. Despite not having an individual titlist all year, OSU was ranked number one in the country in one of college golf's two national polls heading into the NCAA Championships. Arizona was number one in the other.

The Champions Golf Club course in Nicholasville, Kentucky, just outside Lexington, was set up fairly for the 1993 NCAA Championships. Conditions were ideal; everything seemed good. And yet, for the Cowboys, who came to Kentucky hoping to claim the program's eighth national title, it was a disaster from the start.

As a team they were a more than respectable 3 over through the first eleven holes of the first round. Then, disaster. The Cowboys posted three bogeys on thirteen and a triple bogey on fourteen. The infamous eighteenth hole in Nicholasville is nicknamed "Waterloo," a 425-yard par 4 that features the twin evils of brutal rough left and water right. OSU surrendered, marking two bogeys, a double bogey, and a triple bogey at Waterloo. Oklahoma State had not finished out of the top five at the NCAA Championships in Holder's nineteen years as coach, but despite a 1-under 71 from Bratton, the Cowboys finished the first round 13 over, 17 strokes behind first-round leader North Carolina and in twenty-first place. Because the field is trimmed from thirty teams to fifteen after the second round, Bratton, Tidland, and their teammates needed a strong second day to avoid another dubious distinction—becoming the first Oklahoma State team to miss the cut at the NCAA tournament.

Bratton wasn't surprised to see Holder as he approached the par-3 ninth hole. Holder often lingered at par-3 holes to offer advice on club selection to his players.

"Five-iron to the middle of the green, right?" Bratton asked in a low whisper.

Holder rarely let his players know where the team stood when they were on the course. Knowing how well or poorly the team was doing would only distract them, which is why Bratton was stunned when, instead of affirming his club selection, a disgusted Holder said, "Unless you knock this in the hole you're not helping us one bit."

He stood, mouth agape, as Holder strode off.

Bratton missed the green but got up and down for par and eventually finished with a second-day 76. Tidland turned in a 73, as did Bill Hoefle and Brandon Knight. Cox, the Big Eight Newcomer of the Year, shot a 75, which meant Bratton's second-round score was the highest and would not count. Oklahoma State played better in the second round but was still 19 strokes over par. Barring a miracle, everybody knew, that would put them well over the cut line.

It was the most interminable wait any of the Oklahoma State players ever experienced. It took five hours for the final teams in the thirty-team field to post their scores.

Meantime, there was no escaping Holder's wrath.

He didn't yell. He didn't have to yell to make his words bite. Everybody who played at Oklahoma State was aware of the team's history. Holder was seething when he dressed them down near the eighteenth green when the last Oklahoma State player had finished his round.

"I'm going to get a phone call from Coach Harris and I'm going to have to explain this," he said, measuring his words, referring to his coaching mentor. "I'm going to tell him this is the worst team I've ever had. Anybody who had anything to do with it will never play for me again."

When the tongue-lashing ended, the players retreated for a somber meal, only to receive a second helping of stinging criticism as they stood near the team van later that afternoon.

The unthinkable—Oklahoma State missing the cut—gave way to the unimaginable. As dusk began to settle over the rolling hills of central Kentucky, as the final players struggled home, scores were checked and rechecked before it became official: Oklahoma, Oklahoma State, and defending national champion Arizona had finished in a three-way tie for the final spots in the fifteen-team field. Holder couldn't believe it. Neither could Bratton or Tidland. They assumed they would miss the cut. Hanging around to make sure had been a mere formality. Holder had even packed the van before the final scores and subsequent three-team playoff were announced.

Now they were back in it.

"Forget about what I said," a reenergized Holder told his players as they prepared for the playoff's shotgun start, which pitted one player from each team on each of the first five holes. "We're going to whip these guys in the playoff. The worst mistake this field ever made was letting us back in this tournament."

Bratton was dispatched to the par-3 second hole, which is where Holder had been coaching his players, making club recommendations throughout the tournament. Players had been alternating between a 5- and a 6-iron throughout the first two rounds, depending on their length off the tee. Bratton was always more effective when he swung the club easily, which is why Holder recommended he use a 5-iron. Bratton did and was so jacked up about OSU's second chance that his tee shot bounced off the back of the rock-hard green and caromed well past.

Dejected and deflated, Bratton sat behind the green and listened to the tournament official responsible for his hole announce his score over his walkie-talkie: "Bratton, five," the official said. The next score that crackled through the receiver depressed him further. Tidland, with Holder watching, three-putted from 30 feet for bogey.

Tidland and Bratton were a combined 3 over, enough to doom any team in a playoff. They were convinced they had blown the playoff when radio reports began arriving from the other holes. All three players on number three, including Kris Cox, made par. Bill Hoefle and his Oklahoma counterpart parred the fifth hole, and Arizona's Ted Purdy bogeyed. That was good news.

Finally came the report from the fourth hole, where Pepperdine's Jason Gore bogeyed and Oklahoma State's Knight rolled in a 15-foot birdie putt, which made it official.

Oklahoma and Oklahoma State had secured the final two spots in the fifteen-team field in the unprecedented playoff. The defending champions from Arizona—not Oklahoma State—would pack their clubs in the van and head for the airport after making history of their own. It was the first time a defending NCAA champion had missed the cut in thirty-eight years.

Holder tried to convince his players before the third round that the 27 strokes separating them from first place weren't impossible to make up. Given how Oklahoma State had played during the first two rounds, and considering how they had backed into the third round via a playoff, he wasn't very convincing.

Oklahoma State players weren't halfway through their third round when a series of thunderstorms suspended play for six hours. Finally, tournament officials postponed the completion of the round until Saturday morning. Saturday turned into an endless slog. The Cowboys hit so many balls into the lake that bordered the eighth hole that the water level actually rose, or so went the joke in the clubhouse. Tidland shot a 2-under 70 in the fourth round, which was the Cowboys' best round of the tournament, but there was no salvaging the worst performance by a Holder team in his two decades as coach. Their twelfth-place finish was stunning considering the Cowboys' success on college golf's biggest stage. Oklahoma State finished fifth at the NCAA Championships in 1974 when Holder was a rookie coach. Since then, they had won six national titles and had been runners-up eight times. They had finished third once and fourth on three other occasions.

Tidland had Oklahoma State's best four-round total, tied for twenty-eighth. Bratton finished tied for thirty-fourth; Cox, tied for fifty-sixth. The record book soon confirmed that it was the worst showing since the Cowboys had placed twenty-second in 1967.

Bratton and Tidland would soon be named first- and second-team All-Americans, which were startling accomplishments, especially for Tidland, given their doubts and fears when they arrived as freshmen. The individual recognition did little to lift their spirits. While they had accomplished so much, they had accomplished nothing at all in Holder's currency.

"We're going to do things differently next year," Holder told his players matter-of-factly on an otherwise silent trip back to Stillwater. "This isn't Oklahoma State golf. Things are going to be different next year."

*Golf World* magazine published a list of the top fifty players in college golf in the September 30 issue of 1994. Now a senior, Bratton made the list, as did Kris Cox, Trip Kuehne, and even Leif Westerberg. Stanford's Notah Begay, Casey Martin, Will Yanagisawa, and, yes, Tiger Woods were mentioned. Chris Tidland, also now a senior, had been a first-team All-American in 1993 and an honorable mention All-American in 1992 and 1994. He had twenty-five top-twenty finishes heading into his senior year. He had finished third, tied for twelfth, tied for fourth, and tied for eighth in the first four tournaments of the fall season heading into the Golf World Intercollegiate at Palmetto Dunes.

Tidland did not make the list. The omission stung.

He had clearly established himself as one of college golf's better players, yet here he was, on the outside looking in. The *Golf World* staff weighted its rankings heavily on the results of the 1994 NCAA tournament, where Tidland finished sixty-seventh. That was the only explanation Tidland and Bratton could conjure. Tidland even had a solid summer, finishing third in the Oklahoma Open and ninth in the prestigious Northeast Amateur and giving Tiger Woods all he could handle in that epic quarterfinal match at the Western Amateur in Benton Harbor, Michigan.

Growing up in Orange County, Tidland knew about the Tiger legend, although Tiger, three years younger, often competed in a different age group.

They didn't meet until the summer before Tidland's freshman year at Oklahoma State, when the Southern California Golf Association sent a team that included Tidland and Tiger to France to compete, the same trip on which Tiger and Earl talked to Christian Cevaer about attending Stanford. They even played together during an alternate-shot competition. Tidland couldn't believe it when Tiger paused on the tee box to ask Tidland which side of the fairway he would prefer to hit his second shot from: the right or the left?

"When it's my turn," Tidland told him, "I'm just going to try to hit it *in* the fairway."

A lot of the junior golfers in Southern California who had heard of Tiger but never played with him didn't believe the hype. He couldn't be as good as everybody said he was. Tidland had played with him enough to know he was special. Any lingering doubt was erased the moment those words came out of his mouth. Tidland was three years older than Tiger, but Tidland realized the kid was thinking about the game at a much deeper level.

Later that summer, the two played together during the stroke-play portion of the prestigious Western Amateur before being matched up again in match play. The mood between the two had been casual, but in the quarterfinal match, Tidland started too casually. He was 4 down with six to play.

Over a thousand fans were on hand to watch Tiger, and to Tidland it seemed as if teammates Bo Van Pelt and Kris Cox, in the gallery, were the only ones rooting for him. That began to change on the thirteenth hole, when Tidland caught fire, making the first of six straight birdies to force a playoff.

The friendly conversation stopped when Tidland started to make his run. He didn't want to lose. Tiger wanted to end the match. The competition turned tense, and some in the gallery even began to root for Tidland, who appeared to be on the verge of a stunning come-from-behind victory before Tiger sank that absurd 40-foot, par-saving putt on the first playoff hole. On the twentieth hole, Tiger buried an 18-foot downhill eagle putt that had everyone buzzing, to win 1 up.

Bratton was also in the quarterfinals of the Western in the summer of '94. Hearing the cheers resonating from the thriller between his best friend and Tiger, he desperately tried to put his own opponent away to be part of the excited gallery following Tiger and Tidland. By the time Bratton won his match, the Tiger-Tidland playoff was over. Bratton had to learn about it secondhand. When he learned the details, he approached Tiger.

"You made a forty-footer?" he asked Woods, incredulous.

Afterward, Tidland was philosophical.

"When you're playing with someone like Tiger, you expect him to make those putts," he explained. "That's a great way to lose. What can you do? It doesn't get any better than that."

Tiger went on to win the tournament, beating UNLV's Chris Riley 2 and 1 before catching a redeye from Chicago to Los Angeles, where he qualified for the U.S. Amateur at Sawgrass. Everybody knew what happened there.

• • •

Months later, the college golf season was under way, and even though the fall season was coming to a close, their memorable Western Amateur match was still fresh in their minds when Tiger and Tidland teed off on the rolling dunes of the Arthur Hills Golf Course for the first round of the Golf World Intercollegiate on a cool, breezy morning in Hilton Head, South Carolina.

Tidland had a lot to prove, or so he told himself. So did his Oklahoma State teammates, who would go head-to-head with Stanford once again. Oklahoma State players and Stanford players had laughed and joked with each other on the practice range the day before, as they always did. They had competed against each other for years during junior and amateur tournaments, and the members of both teams genuinely liked each other, but there had been an undercurrent of tension since Stanford walked away with the national championship in June. That underlying tension was present at the Golf World Intercollegiate.

After thirty-six holes, Tidland was tied with Stanford's Steve Burdick, 2 shots behind Woods in the individual standings. OSU trailed Stanford by 3 shots in the team competition heading into the third and final round.

For those final eighteen holes, Tiger and Tidland were paired for the first time since their epic match at the Western Amateur the previous summer.

Holder always told his players to ignore the scoreboard. Their job was to negotiate the course in the fewest strokes possible, regardless of where they stood in the individual standings, where the team stood, or how well or poorly they were playing, which made what happened on the eighteenth fairway so surprising.

Tiger wasn't going to win the tournament. That was evident early in the round. He was playing poorly and was unable to control his drives en route to what would be a shocking final round of 80. Tidland and Georgia Tech's Stewart Cink, meanwhile, were still competing for individual honors when Tidland teed off on eighteen.

Holder gave Tidland a scoreboard update moments after his tee shot stopped rolling in the fairway. Holder told him he would have to birdie the 516-yard, par-5 eighteenth hole to force a playoff with

Cink. Tidland digested this surprising information before asking where Oklahoma State stood in the team standings.

"Don't worry about that," Holder told him. "We've got that handled."

Holder knew that Tidland had succumbed to pressure at the NCAA tournament in each of the past three years and thought the best way to help a player who had a history of not playing well under pressure was to put some pressure on him. He knew how much not appearing in the *Golf World* rankings stung Tidland, and he knew how much winning the tournament would mean to him. More important, he knew that his team couldn't afford for Tidland to collapse at nationals for a second straight year.

Holder had asked Bratton, Kuehne, and Cox, who were watching from a mound behind the eighteenth green, if Tidland would want to know where he stood in the individual standings. They all agreed he would, especially in this case. Knowing that he needed a birdie to force a playoff might impact his club and shot selection. What Holder didn't tell Tidland was that the Cowboys didn't have the team competition "handled" at all. Oklahoma State needed a birdie to beat Stanford for first place in the team competition.

Holder wanted to put some pressure on Tidland, all right, but he didn't want to put so much on him that he would be crushed by it.

Tidland's third shot was on the fringe, 20 feet from the pin. He was taking off his glove and walking toward the green when Holder approached him with yet another update. Cink had bogeyed the last hole, which meant that making the birdie putt would hand Tidland the second tournament title of his career and his first since he won the Ping/Tulsa Invitational the previous season. Tidland came through. He rolled in the birdie putt for a final-round 68.

It was a bonanza. What Tidland didn't know until later was that the putt also provided the winning margin of victory over Stanford in the team competition—by 1 thin stroke.

Tidland had proved beyond any doubt that he deserved to be ranked, if not in the top ten, then at the very least among college golf's top fifty players. And Oklahoma State had ended the fall season by defeating Stanford for the second time in three head-to-head competitions.

As satisfying as that was for Tidland and Bratton, and as satisfying as avenging his loss to Tiger in the Western Amateur had been for Tidland, they both knew the victory would ring hollow if they couldn't duplicate it when it mattered most.

# 6

## Notah and Casey

*Mid-November 1994 to*
*Mid-February 1995*

IN THE HISTORY of organized sports, there have been more intimidating team names than "Team Spam."

Team Spam was the Stanford golf team's intramural basketball team, a hodgepodge of gunners and trash talkers, players with occasional flashes of talent and players who featured amusing displays of no talent.

Amazingly enough, Tiger Woods was guilty of the latter. Despite being the greatest junior golfer ever, Tiger was a 25-handicapper on the hardwood. Though an enthusiastic participant, he'd often be needled for a game line of zero points and zero rebounds, and for his signature move near the bucket—an air ball from two feet.

Making fun of Tiger's skills was all part of the levity for Team Spam, so named because team member Conrad Ray's father worked for Hormel, the company that produces the famous canned, precooked meat product. Ray's father donated Spam T-shirts, and the team wore them in their IM games during the wintertime of 1994–95. It was, really, just a silly team name, as if to emphasize how unthreatening their team was in the weeknight games at Stanford's on-campus Arrillaga Sports Center.

Actually, there were some players. Notah Begay had been on two state championship basketball teams at Albuquerque Academy in New Mexico, and he played like it. Steve Burdick was an all-around athlete who didn't embarrass himself on the court. And Casey Martin, despite a disabled right leg, hung around on the perimeter occasionally to exhibit his specialty—conscience-free shooting from the twenty- to twenty-five-foot range. When Martin's leg got too painful, he'd retreat to the sidelines to "coach" the team. "Coaching" the team meant heckling student officials during the game, exhorting his teammates to shoot more, and giving his extra-special free throw advice when a teammate was on the charity stripe: "Flex your knees! Follow through! These are *tap-ins!*"

With the college golf season on hiatus from the fall to the spring—Stanford's appearance at Hilton Head in November was the team's final tournament until a February date in Hawaii started the spring season—the team used the downtime to hang out together, enjoy each other, and have some laughs playing basketball.

For Notah Begay and Casey Martin, the time was especially precious.

The two fifth-year seniors were entering their final stretch together, after arriving on the Stanford campus jointly in the fall of 1990 toting wildly different background stories—and a common desire to make something of their time at a university they considered it a privilege to attend. Notah and Casey, Casey and Notah . . . their names were almost interchangeable around the Stanford golf offices; they were close compadres who viewed the world differently but would defend each other to the end, unlikely friends who embraced different value systems but shared a bond in lifting Wally Goodwin's program to the deliriously happy air of a national championship, finding a lasting friendship along the way.

The spring of 1995 was a sentimental time for Begay and Martin, as graduation would cast them out into the world, and out of the safe cocoon of Stanford and the golf team. It would be a sentimental time for Goodwin, too, who considered Begay and Martin to be his two most important recruits ever, and the two most unusual.

If Goodwin's controlling philosophy in recruiting was to find players who moved him in some way, he was never more moved than by the stories of these two players who persevered despite obstacles, who succeeded when there were plenty of reasons not to. In many ways, Begay and Martin were more meaningful to the Stanford program than Tiger Woods himself. After all, when Tiger arrived on campus, he had the pressure of doing something Begay and Martin already had done—winning a national team championship.

A national championship wasn't what Goodwin had in mind when he first heard the story of Notah Begay. He merely wanted to learn more about an intriguing young player from Albuquerque who boasted 100 percent Native American blood—half Navajo, half Pueblo. To say it was odd to recruit a Native American golfer from New Mexico was an understatement. Only one Native American had ever won an event in the history of the PGA Tour, and that was Rod Curl in 1974. Curl was a Wintu Indian from Redding, California, and he won the Colonial National Invitational in Fort Worth, clipping the great Jack Nicklaus by 1 stroke. Other than that, Native Americans and organized golf, especially college golf, were not a common mix. Begay knew that growing up in New Mexico, witnessing the hardships of Native American life in the United States. There was precious little time for golf, he observed, when living on a reservation that he at times likened to living in the Third World.

But Begay came from a family of athletes. His father, also named Notah, was an ex-Marine who played some college basketball and made time for golf as an adult. When Begay got good enough in golf, and when Goodwin heard he had a chance to recruit him, he flew to New Mexico in the winter of 1990, to watch Begay play basketball. Goodwin loved basketball and felt he could assess an athlete's mind from watching him play. It was a cold night in Albuquerque when Goodwin got there, but when he entered the gym he felt the familiar heat of a prep basketball game under bright lights. He saw Begay, only five foot ten, hustling on both ends, his mullet soaked with sweat, making his free throws and playing the team game. Within five minutes Goodwin knew he had his man. It wasn't just Begay's inspiring story of overcoming an underprivileged background; it was that he was a "Wally Kid," all heart and determination and fire. Goodwin had never seen him play golf, but he told himself, *I've got to have him on my team* and offered Begay a scholarship fifteen minutes after the game, standing outside the locker room, with Begay's extended family all around, congratulating the kid on a high school basketball game well played.

Goodwin had seen Martin play golf. It was the summer of 1989 at the Junior Worlds at Torrey Pines, a benchmark tournament that would make or break junior golfers. It helped make Tiger Woods, who had won it five times in different age groups by the time he was fourteen.

For Casey Martin, the 1989 Junior Worlds changed his career. He played brilliantly and wound up as the top junior American, second in the world, in his age group. He was about to enter his senior year at South Eugene High, and recruiters would come calling. There was just one problem: Martin had a disabled right leg. Born without a deep venous system, he had a rare ailment called Klippel-Trenaunay-Weber Syndrome, which meant blood could be pumped down to his leg but had trouble being pumped back up. Blood would collect in his leg, and his leg would swell, and the pain was extraordinary. It affected his ability to walk and threatened his leg long-term.

And now here he came at Torrey Pines, limping down the fairway. Goodwin stood with a handful of other college golf coaches, mesmerized by Martin's courage.

"Wally, what do you want with Casey Martin?" one of the coaches said. "With that leg, he's just not going to make it."

"I don't care if Casey Martin plays golf at Stanford or not," Goodwin said. "But I want him on my team."

The other coach raised his brow.

"His heart is the biggest I've ever seen," Goodwin said. "He fits me."

Goodwin would always go back to the recruiting questions he asked himself: *Do I want this player to be around my other players? Do I think this player has a big heart? Do I want to be around this player?*

For Casey Martin and Notah Begay, Wally Goodwin wasn't sure he'd ever answered yes more emphatically to those questions. There was something ineffable about these two. He had to have them at Stanford.

When Stanford announced the signing of Begay and Martin on May 2, 1990, Goodwin cited Begay's proud family heritage and hardscrabble upbringing. He cited Martin's never-ending desire to fight his body's pain and called him "the most outstanding youngster I've ever met."

"They're both fighters," Goodwin said. To Goodwin, no quality was ever more important.

Moreover, they made good on their promise. In their freshman year, Begay and Martin teamed with Christian Cevaer to bring Stanford a tie for fifteenth place as a team at the 1991 NCAA Championships at Poppy Hills, the first time the Cardinal made the cut as a team since 1985. Martin parlayed a clutch final-round 69 to tie for sixteenth as an individual, and the Casey-Notah era was off to a good start. Martin earned honorable mention All-American honors. Things got even better in their sophomore year, when Cevaer was a senior and won the Pac-10 individual title to lead Stanford to a conference championship—the school's first in eighteen years. This was the year Steve Burdick and Brad Lanning joined the starting five, and Stanford powered to a ninth-place team finish at the 1992 NCAA Championships in Albuquerque, the first time they'd made back-to-back cuts as a team at NCAAs since 1977 and 1978. The star turn came from the hometown boy himself—Begay had a rollicking third round of 64, which set an all-time Stanford record for a single-round score. Begay was named third-team All-American.

Now things were really humming around Stanford golf, and with the near certainty that Tiger Woods—then finishing up his sophomore year at Anaheim's Western High—would arrive in the fall of 1994, Begay and Martin embarked on their "Great Experiment," redshirting a year to wait for Tiger in order to form what might be the greatest college golf team of all time. That they'd jump the gun and win the national championship in 1994 made it all the richer.

Their careers were storybook stuff, and now they were writing the grand finale of a final chapter.

Goodwin sometimes thought about the two of them during their senior year. To get a player with a story like Notah Begay's, and to get a player with a story like Casey Martin's, in the same year? He'd been around long enough to know it never happened.

And now, in the winter of 1995, the last chance to bond was dawning for Begay and Martin. One was a clean-cut devout Christian from a nuclear family in the leafy Northwest, the other a Native American and self-professed nonpracticing Catholic who wore hoop earrings and came from a broken family in the arid Southwest. They were unlikely friends, and now their time together was coming to an end. Begay sometimes used the poetic language of his native people to express himself, and he thought of life's journey as a "long walk." He was proud, he would think, to take this long walk together with Martin.

From the day he was born, September 14, 1972, in Albuquerque, New Mexico, Notah Begay III was raised to be in touch with his Native American bloodline.

His mother, Laura Ansera, was a Native American of Pueblo descent, half San Felipe and half Isleta. His father, Notah, was a Navajo. They would divorce early in Begay's life, but each would watch with wonder as their boy barreled through life differently from other kids, always more competitive, always more confident, always making an impact. At age six, young Notah accompanied his mother to a ceremony in a Pueblo kiva, or gathering place. As the story goes, young Begay slept in his mother's lap until the ceremonial elders came and began to dance, and Begay then stirred, rose, and danced alongside the elders. He was the only audience member to do so, and when the elders rewarded him with corn and watermelon, it only encouraged his dancing. His mother would marvel at the boy's fearlessness.

Later that year, young Begay's father was headed off for a three-mile run. His son wanted to come along. The father knew it was too much for a six-year-old and told him he couldn't go with him.

The son cried and cried, but it wasn't just the normal wail of a six-year-old, the father noticed; it was the cry of a boy yearning to push himself physically, to accompany his father on his run. Begay's father agreed to take him and cut it to a mile and a half, expecting to carry his son halfway. He warned him: You'd better keep up. I won't take you if you don't keep up.

Six-year-old Notah Begay never stopped running the entire time.

Begay's parents would figure their son was simply wired differently from others, and early in his life they would decide that Begay deserved a chance to make something of his passion and energy. They valued his gifts and wanted to maximize them, so they came to a bold joint decision: They would try to send Notah to the prestigious Albuquerque Academy for his sixth-grade year. The academy was New Mexico's most exclusive school, a gorgeous 312-acre college preparatory private school with demanding academics—and demanding tuition, too. In the fall of 1983, when Notah would enter sixth grade, the academy charged $12,000 a year, which was far more than the Begays could afford for school.

But their determination was fierce, and through the academy's financial aid program, and through sacrifice on other fronts, Laura and Notah made it work for their son. It wouldn't always be easy. There were times checks bounced, and times the financial aid office would pester them with calls for delinquent payments. Begay's counselor at school tried to serve as a buffer between the family and the financial aid office, but even he, an ally, would sometimes call Begay's father and say: "I'm running out of time . . . they're on my case, Notah. We have to have the money." Begay's parents would then find some way to come through. Always, the school and Begay's parents found common ground to make sure he stayed in school. It was important to all involved—after all, Begay was aiming to become the first full-blooded Native American to attend the academy from sixth through twelfth grade.

To attend a school like the academy asked a lot of Begay, his parents knew. Until the age of eleven, all he knew was the "Indian" world. He'd spent time living on the reservation and even for a

Tiger Woods celebrates after an improbable birdie on the seventeenth hole that propelled him past Trip Kuehne in the 1994 U.S. Amateur. *Getty/Michael O'Bryon*

Tiger Woods as a freshman at Stanford

*Rod Searcey, Stanford Athletics*

Tiger Woods was arguably Stanford's highest-profile recruit ever.

*Rod Searcey, Stanford Athletics*

Tiger Woods tried to live the life of an average freshman.

*Getty / John M. Burgess*

Notah Begay's second-round 62 launched Stanford to the 1994 NCAA Championship. *Stanford University*

Stanford coach Wally Goodwin was awed by Casey Martin's ability to play in pain.

*AP Images / Jamie Sabau*

Will Yanagisawa honed his game in the back of his parents' golf shop in Long Beach, California.

*Rod Searcey, Stanford Athletics*

Teammates felt that Steve Burdick was the best ball striker on the team.

*Rod Searcey, Stanford Athletics*

Jerry Chang replaced Steve Burdick at the 1995 NCAAs.

*Rod Searcey, Stanford Athletics*

Wally Goodwin made recruiting quality individuals his priority.

*Rod Searcey, Stanford Athletics*

Wally Goodwin thought his players looked stylish in their Cardinal red sweatpants. *Rod Searcey, Stanford Athletics*

Trip Kuehne was the perfect addition to Mike Holder's team.

*Oklahoma State University*

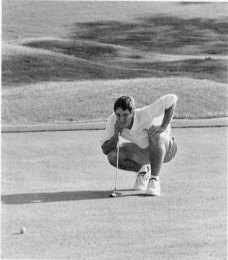

Alan Bratton's gutsy, grind-it-out style personified Oklahoma State.

*Oklahoma State University*

Chris Tidland developed into one of the most decorated golfers in Oklahoma State history. *Oklahoma State University*

Kris Cox's grandfather and mother nurtured his love of the game.

*Oklahoma State University*

Mike Holder offered Sweden's Leif Westerberg a scholarship sight unseen.

*Oklahoma State University*

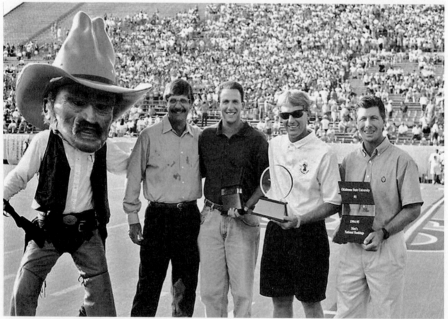

Oklahoma State mascot Pistol Pete, *Golf Week*'s Ron Balicki, Bruce Heppler, Mike Holder, and Jim Armstrong pose with awards won by the Cowboys in 1995.

*Oklahoma State University*

Stanford and Oklahoma State players were friends as well as rivals.

*Getty / David Liam Kyle*

Oklahoma State players celebrate at the 1995 NCAA tournament.

*AP Images / Jamie Sabau*

Relief mixed with euphoria after the Cowboys won Mike Holder's seventh national championship. *Oklahoma State University*

Trip Kuehne lost the 1994 U.S. Amateur but helped his brother, Hank, win in 1998. *Getty / Andy Lyons*

stretch watched as his mother used food stamps. He spoke Navajo, too. In fact, his grandfather, also named Notah Begay, was a "code talker" for the U.S. military in World War II, part of the elite team of Marines in the Pacific Theater who used their language to create a code that was credited with helping to win the war and save hundreds of American combat soldiers' lives. So immersed in the Native American world, Begay was making a major transition by joining the world of the rich white kids of Albuquerque at the academy. His father knew his son would have to juggle what he called the "white man's world" and the "Indian world," and it wouldn't be easy.

Begay's solution to the tension was to hurl himself into sports and competition, full-bore. It was in his blood.

Even though his grandfather, raised in a remote, rural area of New Mexico called Manuelito, didn't get past the ninth grade, he was an excellent football and basketball player at a school called the Albuquerque Indian School, a place the federal government sent youths from the reservation. His son, Notah Jr., was an All-State end in football at Cathedral High in Gallup, New Mexico, and, at six foot one, was one of the tallest and best players on his high school basketball team, good enough to earn a scholarship to play ball at a small Catholic college called St. Joseph's.

Soccer and basketball were among Notah III's favorites, but the sport that enraptured him was golf. At age six, he tailed along as his father played a recreational round of golf in a Thursday night league for duffers at the University of New Mexico. Begay's father was not a good player—he often wondered how being so good at other sports translated so poorly to the difficult world of golf—but he enjoyed the camaraderie and the occasional can of beer after the match with the boys. Sometimes "Little Note," as they called him, tagged along. That part was great, having his son along. What was not so great was six-year-old Begay running out of the golf cart to play in any sand trap he could find. Pressed for a baby-sitting solution, Begay's father gave his son a cut-down golf club to swing and keep him occupied. Little Begay had the golf bug.

He began showing up at Albuquerque's public golf course, Ladera, to putt and chip and hit buckets of balls. He was so eager to hit the ball, he'd sometimes run out onto the driving range to pick up loose range balls to hit—while other players were hitting balls. This caught the eye of Ladera's head pro, Don Zamora, who loved the kid's passion, but he had to call his father to warn him about the safety risks. It was about then the Begay family realized they had a golfer on their hands.

He'd do anything to keep practicing, including washing golf carts in exchange for driving-range tokens. By eight he was playing competitively and catching the eye of Zamora and a local teaching pro, Leo Van Wart, who began to nurture and encourage Begay's love of the game.

Zamora asked permission to drive Begay to a weeklong golf camp in Roswell, to take advantage of the boy's natural talent with focused lessons. His father would know it was going well when, after the first day or two, his son phoned home with a quiver in his voice, homesick. Then the boy stopped calling home the next two days. The transformation was made. He was sold on golf.

Zamora would sell Begay any club he wanted at a discount price and give him all the time he needed to pay it off. Begay treasured golf clubs and cleaned his constantly. He learned tricks of the trade, like soaking them in Coca-Cola to make them extra-shiny. When he was ten years old and won the New Mexico State Juniors eleven-and-under tournament, he'd gotten all the taste and motivation he'd need.

Van Wart became his swing coach and was unorthodox. He'd test Begay's mind, tell him to never stop asking questions. He stressed short game, short game, short game and made Begay putt through "gates" of tees on the putting green. That wasn't unusual. Dave Pelz, the national short-game guru, was famous for having his students putt through a "gate" of two tees. Van Wart, though, had Begay putting through three, four, even five "gates," to truly test his putter's accuracy. The emphasis on the short game meant Van Wart didn't spend as much time on the golf swing, and the result of his teaching was not what anybody would call a classic golf swing. In fact, if anything defined Begay's swing, other than its effectiveness, it was its ungainliness. It was less a golf swing than a lashing action. Steve Burdick, who would be Begay's teammate at Stanford, first saw Begay swing a golf club at an America's Cup junior event. Burdick's only thought: *Wow. That's a horrible swing. How can that guy be any good?*

If you were looking for a swing out of Ben Hogan's *Five Lessons,* watching Begay wasn't the thing. Instead, he concentrated on three swing thoughts: One, his posture—making sure his alignment was good and his back was at the correct angle. Two, his grip. And three, where he wanted to hit the ball. Then all he'd do was try to hit the ball. Like its proprietor, Notah Begay's golf swing was an original. Years later, he'd proudly call it a blue-collar golf swing, to match his background.

Begay wanted to be different and didn't want to just play golf—he wanted to beat people. He'd come by before school and hit golf balls in the early morning. In the New Mexico winter, when nobody else was on the practice green, Begay would sometimes wear five layers of sweaters to still get his work in. He told friends that he could never hit enough wedges close, could never chip too many balls close. He'd strap on orange foam Walkman headphones and tune to the local pop-music radio stations to pass the time on the range.

Playing at Ladera was good for his training. Like most good city munis, Ladera had a steady money game going among its regulars. Begay was a regular, and even though he was a youngster, he'd play for a few dollars in the skins games. As at most good city munis, Ladera's regulars included players who could go low, so Begay had to learn early to score to keep his money. There was no mucking around: You had better go out and make birdies, or you were paying up.

From Zamora's friendly financing plan, Begay landed a set of beryllium-copper Ping Eye2 irons, and he took those golf clubs at age fourteen into his first real competitions of note—four regional junior tournaments, one in Denver, one in Tucson, one in San Diego, and one at home in Albuquerque. He won three of them.

By now, Begay was entering his freshman year at the academy, and he had a problem. His mother got a job in Santa Fe, working for the government. His dad got a job in Arizona, working for the Navajo Nation. Begay would have to move away from Albuquerque, at least for the summer.

Enter the benefactors in Begay's life: the Zamoras. Don Zamora took Begay into his family's home in Albuquerque, to allow Begay to spend the summer there. This would allow Begay to continue to hold his job at the golf course and have a daily ride to Ladera, too. There wasn't a ton of room at the Zamora household, and Begay had to share a bed with their son, Len, but so be it. The Zamoras cared about Begay and wanted to encourage his talents on the golf course.

The next summer, the same problem arose, but worse. Begay's father would go to Arizona for work, and this time it would involve the entire sophomore year of Begay's high school life. Begay had nowhere to go, and worse, he'd have to leave the academy. Nobody wanted this to happen. Begay loved the challenge of competing against the best and the brightest at the academy and feared losing the opportunity.

Enter the second set of benefactors in his life: assistant pro Mike Yrene and his wife, Deborah Bunting. They had no children but knew how important it was for Begay to stay in Albuquerque. They took Begay in, telling him they had an interest in his education and golf career and wanted to help make his dreams come true. They drove him to school and to the golf course, and Begay's academics and golf continued to flourish. These were important life lessons for Begay, learning that helping out is a noble thing.

When Begay's father returned from Arizona, he wanted to eliminate the problem of transportation to the golf course for his son and bought a home on the fourteenth fairway at Ladera. It was more than he could afford, so there was little in the way of furniture in the house, and no phone or heat, either. Well, there was some heat. Begay's father invested in solar panels, but they could heat only part of the house at a time. That meant that sometimes in the wintertime they'd have to take cold showers. They also slept in the same bed to stay warm—Begay, his father, and his younger brother, Clint.

Begay knew that most academy kids weren't living in homes with no phones and little heat, or sharing beds with their family members. He knew he was different, and he looked different, and this produced in him some sense of not belonging, or feeling he had to prove himself. The result was the competitive fire that produced his athletic career. He'd go to golf tournaments, surrounded by Caucasian kids who wore polo shirts and had short haircuts. Begay wore jeans and hoop earrings and had a mullet. This dissonance was something Begay felt since entering the academy in the sixth grade.

When his father drove him to the academy for his entrance exam, he drove a 1969 Chevy truck that was dinged and scratched up. It occasionally backfired, too. Little Note noticed how it stood out in the parking lot, amid the Cadillacs. He mentioned it again to his father when he got another ride in the '69 Chevy. Finally, one day driving to school in the Chevy again, Begay told his father: "Look, Dad, you work hard and you need to get to work. So why don't you just drop me off a few blocks short of school? I can walk."

His father knew the deal.

"Look, I know you're embarrassed by my car, but this is who we are," he told his son. "We can't change who we are. By sending you to this school, we are giving you the opportunity to, in your life, maybe change that down the road.

"But when you do, please don't ever forget where you came from."

The class distinction was further on display when Begay's father drove to pick up his son from academy golf practice. The team practiced at tony Albuquerque Country Club, and when the '69 Chevy truck pulled up to the gates, a security guard stopped it. The guard wanted to know what business a car like that had on the manicured grounds of Albuquerque C.C.

"I'm here to pick up my son, Notah Begay," his father said.

Security radioed to the clubhouse. After a wait, the word came through. There was a Notah Begay inside the gates. It was OK for the truck to come through. The Begays would laugh when, after a few practice pickups, the guard would just wave through the '69 Chevy, without even stopping him.

Begay felt the best way to belong amid the rich kids was to beat them, and it produced in him a competitive edge—some would call it extreme confidence, others would say cockiness. He did beat them, though. He won the New Mexico state high school golf title as a junior—and a senior.

His success extended to the soccer pitch, where he was All-State. And to the basketball court, where twice he started on the academy's state championship teams. He would later say that when he got to Stanford, a campus full of champions, he already knew what winning felt like. He wouldn't accept anything else.

There was the matter of college. At the academy one day, one of the rich kids, a great student, was bragging. He asked Begay, "Where are you going to college?"

Begay was flustered. He didn't have an answer, so he turned the tables. "Where are you going?" he said.

"Stanford," the kid said, haughty.

"Yeah, me, too," Begay said. The rich kid eyed him suspiciously. Begay said it just to tick the kid off.

The truth was, he dreamed of going to Stanford, which seemed a far-off paradise on the golden coast of California, galaxies away from New Mexico. Once again, a benefactor would step in.

John Fields was the golf coach at the University of New Mexico, and he knew all about Begay. He wanted him on his golf team, which Fields intended to build into a power. But living in Albuquerque, and knowing Begay as a teenager, he also knew how much Begay always wanted to push himself, and that Stanford would be an ideal testing ground, athletically, academically, and socially, for the kid he liked so much. Instead of hoarding Begay all to himself—Colorado and some Division II schools had also sent some letters—Fields picked up the phone and called Wally Goodwin.

"Wally, do you know about Notah Begay?" he asked Goodwin.

Goodwin said he didn't. After all, Begay didn't travel to many

AJGA events, and his name wasn't well known outside the Southwest.

"I think you should know about him," Fields said, beginning the recruitment of Notah Begay to Stanford.

Begay would always regard Fields's phone call to Goodwin as an act of altruism and was blown away by his selflessness. As it became more apparent that Stanford was interested and this might actually happen, the Begays asked Fields why he made the call. In effect, he was weakening his own team and strengthening an NCAA rival. But Fields told them he thought it important that Begay push himself. He'd breeze, academically, through UNM. At Stanford, he'd be challenged on all levels. The Begays could never thank Fields enough for his thoughts. As Begay learned from the Zamoras, and from Mike Yrene and his wife, and now from Fields, it was sometimes important to think about someone other than yourself.

Once Goodwin investigated Begay's story, he fell in love with him as a recruit. He flew down to New Mexico to watch him play basketball and had his instant revelation that a competitor like Begay had to be on his golf team. After the basketball game, Goodwin met all of Begay's relatives—aunts, uncles, and grandparents. He got a tour of the reservation. Begay, always the jokester, would tease Goodwin years later about his ranching roots, and that day on the reservation. "It was better than Thanksgiving, Coach," Begay said. "We had cowboys and Indians!"

Goodwin and Begay had mutual interests. Begay wanted the dream of Stanford; Goodwin wanted Begay's skill and desire on his golf team. Goodwin would offer Begay a scholarship but had to get his test scores first. It all went well until Begay's SAT scores returned. He scored 1100. Stanford wanted him to score 1200. Problem.

Or, maybe not. Begay approached the issue as he would a golf match, as if he were 3 down at the turn. He attacked.

The varsity soccer coach at the academy was also the head of the English department. Begay went to him and asked for help improving his verbal score on the SAT. The teacher asked him to come to school at 6:30 A.M. for private tutorial sessions: grammar lessons, sentence structure, and vocabulary exercises. He gave Begay flash

cards to carry around in his pocket to test himself, different vocabulary words like *diffident* and *ubiquitous*. He took the SAT again
and raised his verbal score by 150 points.

Notah Begay was accepted at Stanford. And, as it happened, that
rich kid who bragged about going to Stanford? He didn't get in.

Melinda Martin knew something was wrong with her second son,
Casey, the minute he entered the world on June 2, 1972, in Eugene,
Oregon.

The nurses noticed a huge birthmark on Martin's right leg, all
the way to his buttocks. Doctors didn't know what to make of it,
but Melinda and her husband, King, knew at ten months, when
Martin started to walk, that their baby was not right. He'd scream
in the middle of the night, a scream so profound, they knew it went
beyond colic. He'd bring his knees to his chest and howl, and the
Martins, sick with worry, would rush him to the emergency room.
In his infancy, doctors guessed that he had a stomach ailment and
tried to treat it. Nothing worked. The baby Casey would howl again,
and the Martins would rush him again to the hospital.

On one trip to the emergency room, after the baby Martin received a barium enema, a nurse noticed him lying on the gurney.
She touched his birthmark and had a thought that the baby's problem could be related to his leg, not his stomach. Thus began the
quest to figure out what was wrong with baby Casey Martin's leg.
Doctor after doctor tried to figure it out, and it went this way until
Martin was five years old. A pediatric surgeon from Seattle moved
to Eugene and took a look at Martin. He thought he knew what the
problem was.

The surgeon knew of a very rare ailment called Klippel-Trenaunay-
Weber Syndrome, in which the patient is born without a deep venous system. The doctor performed a venogram and confirmed the
diagnosis, but for a disease that had no cure, either. For the rest of
his life, Martin would deal with a right leg in which blood was not
pumped back and would swell, causing pain that ranged from dull
and throbbing to sharp and crackling. The doctor told the Martins that their boy's right leg would swell with blood, which they

would have to regularly aspirate to alleviate the pain. He would be prescribed a stocking to wear on the leg to keep the swelling down. Other than that, the doctors told them, he would lead a normal life. The Martins would come to call his ailment "KT," for short.

When the Martins weren't sure how to raise a young boy in so much pain, one doctor gave them advice they took to heart: Let the pain dictate what young Casey could and could not do.

Unfazed, Martin plunged into childhood. He loved sports, as did the whole family. King and Melinda were University of Oregon graduates and imbued in their boys a love of Ducks sporting events. Martin went nuts for Ducks football and basketball at a young age.

He also looked up to his brother, Cameron, who was two years older, and athletic. They played H-O-R-S-E in the driveway, and Martin developed a love for the art of burying baskets from long range. He played youth soccer and made a nice place for himself at the goalie position, where he didn't have to run and where he could learn to kick left-footed. He didn't play Little League, because the stop-and-start nature of baseball put too much strain on the leg, but one day, driving home from work, King noticed the neighborhood boys playing tackle football in the mud, including Cameron. That wasn't a problem, until he saw his young son, Casey, playing quarterback. King nearly drove his car into a tree.

He tried to stay calm and waited for Cameron and Casey to get home. When they did, he sidled up to Casey in the kitchen.

"What'd you do today, Casey?" he asked.

"Played football," Casey answered.

"Pal," King said, "do you think it's a smart idea to play tackle football?"

"Oh, it's OK," Casey answered, earnest. "The boys made me the automatic quarterback for both teams, and they weren't allowed to tackle me."

King was touched by the natural goodness of the neighborhood boys, and by the fact that Cam was so caring in protecting his little brother. The Martins would come to learn that Casey had three parents—Melinda and King, and his sheltering older brother, Cam, too. The unconditional love meant Martin didn't think of himself as being any different from the other boys. He had no limitations in his mind.

King Martin, too, was an athlete, and when he made a little bit of money in his job as a financial adviser, he joined the prestigious Eugene Country Club, ranked in the top hundred golf courses in the country. He took his two sons out to the club, and by age five, Casey Martin was swinging a cut-down golf club. At age six, he was playing regularly. By age eight, he was competing in peewee tournaments.

Golf was a godsend. It allowed Martin to compete and be an athlete, as was his natural inclination, yet it didn't create the crippling pain other sports did. He could play golf with his KT, and, better than that, he was good. The club pros at Eugene C.C. told the Martins when Casey was young that he had a natural talent, and he started racking up trophies in the peewee tournaments. The combination of success at the sport and love for the game meant Martin would not be deterred, even when the KT acted up. Doctors would sometimes splint his right leg after they drained it, but Martin would go play golf anyway. It was not unusual to see Martin hobbling down the fairway at Eugene C.C., limping with a splint on his right leg, chasing his golf ball from tee to green.

The breakthrough came when Martin was fourteen years old and qualified for the "Big I." He knew then he could play on a national level, and if his ultimate dream of becoming a shooting guard for his beloved University of Oregon Ducks would never come true, he might one day play college golf. He knew it could be done—Cam was a good golfer, too, and earned a scholarship to play at UNLV. Watching his brother accomplish it, Martin knew he could do it, too.

All the while, he battled the KT. He would never make excuses or talk to anybody about the pain, but doctors and his family knew it was excruciating. Nighttime was the worst. He would unwrap the stocking, and the swelling would come, sure and steady and agonizing. Doctors suggested that occasional surgeries to clean out the leg might help, and he had one by the end of his eighth-grade year. It was a Sisyphean task. They'd clean up his leg and drain it, and the KT would go right back to work, swelling his leg and causing him pain that would rack him. His mother would sometimes weep, wondering if her son's leg would need to be amputated, something the doctors never ruled out.

By the time he was in high school at South Eugene High, he'd won seventeen Oregon Golf Association tournaments in age groups from ten to fourteen. He was a medalist at the Oregon state high school championships his junior year, and then he had the monumentally good tournament at Torrey Pines, finishing as top American in the Junior Worlds and searing himself into Wally Goodwin's heart forever. Stanford would make a run at Martin.

Surprisingly, Stanford wasn't the only school. The Martins thought schools would be scared off by the precarious situation with his right leg, but UCLA wanted Martin. So did Washington, Oregon, and UNLV. Some schools were more aggressive than others, but none more so than Goodwin and Stanford. A risk taker in recruiting, Goodwin didn't hesitate in courting Martin. It was as if Goodwin felt it was destiny that Casey Martin would become a Cardinal. If ever there was a "Wally Kid," it was Martin.

His schoolwork was all As, until his first B came in the spring of his senior year, a stumble Martin would admit was brought on by senior-itis. Melinda and King never had to push him to study, either. Home from school, he'd go to his room and hit the books. He was a parent's dream that way. Plus, much to Melinda's delight, Martin was an accomplished pianist, too. She wanted him to play piano at the age of seven, but Martin didn't want to. She begged, and he made a savvy deal: If she paid him $50, and if she let him play music from the radio instead of classical, he'd do it. She agreed, and Martin filled their home with the sweet sounds of his piano skills, only he'd play songs by Billy Joel and Journey instead of Beethoven and Brahms.

And he walked the walk. Martin came from a deeply Christian home and embraced his faith wholeheartedly, remembering asking the Lord into his heart as early as when he was eight years old. Honoring Christ meant no drinking or partying or straying from his morals and ideals. He was as clean as they come, and Goodwin wanted his influence on his team, extending a scholarship offer to him as soon as he could in Martin's senior year.

From Martin's perspective, Stanford's appeal was a slam dunk. While he liked and respected the other Pac-10 schools recruiting him, and while UNLV offered the promise of a golf program on the rise, excellent facilities, and an emphasis on the sport, he knew his KT worked against any dream of becoming a professional golfer. Stanford provided the chance to earn a degree that would last longer than a golf career contingent on a faltering right leg. He thought to himself that if he wanted to become a pro golfer, he'd go to UNLV. But if he wanted to make the most of a college education, Stanford was the far smarter choice.

He scored a respectable number on his SAT, but he was light-heartedly embarrassed by it and would say that at Stanford, it was hard to find anybody who had a lower score. Realistic above all else, he knew that the admissions department looked favorably upon his story as a disabled athlete, and he knew it helped his application's acceptance. Goodwin made sure of it. He marveled at Martin's mental toughness, calling him extraordinary. In Martin, Goodwin would say that he saw "an eternal happiness, and from it a light that was shed on all who came in contact with him." Safe to say, the coach liked his recruit.

His parents were blown away, too. From the moment Melinda Martin saw something wrong with her infant son when he was born, to the painful mystery of his suffering, to the diagnosis of the KT, to his childhood and adolescence spent fighting off physical adversity, she was amazed at who he was now, a scholarship golfer at Stanford. King felt the same way. Melinda and Casey drove to Stanford to drop him off, and King followed a day later, so Casey could have a car on campus and King could drive Melinda back to Eugene. King found himself alone driving into the Stanford campus just as a tape of music featuring Christian trumpeter Phil Driscoll filled his car stereo. The timing was exquisite, the music soaring, as he drove onto the campus and admired its openness, its golden California beauty, and here it was, taking in his son, his disabled son who never put a limit on himself, now a scholarship athlete. King Martin was overwhelmed with emotion.

Goodwin wanted both Martin and Begay, but he had only one scholarship to give in 1990. He explained as much to Begay and Martin, and Begay offered a solution: Give the scholarship to Martin. Begay said he'd get by on financial aid and loans for one year and wanted to sacrifice so that he and Martin could be on the same team, together.

There was another reason why he offered up the scholarship to Martin. Begay was so deeply confident of his own skills, and so certain of his own successful and lucrative future as a professional golfer, that he figured getting by on loans his freshman year was only a temporary blip.

And so Stanford was introduced to Begay, who may have owned more self-confidence, pound for pound, than any other golfer in Stanford history.

He hit the Stanford Golf Course with Martin and fellow freshman Mark Freeland, and he'd do ridiculous things, hit wild shots. The second hole at Stanford is a par 4, dogleg left. Martin, Begay, and Freeland would hit their tee shots and have about 180 yards in. Martin and Freeland pulled 5-irons. Begay would pull a 9-iron and hit it with a 50-yard draw. Later, he'd have 135 yards in, and Begay would pull a 5-iron and open it up, trying to hit a soft fade. In a bunker? Begay would try to carve 3-irons out, seeing how much loft he could get on his shots.

"What are you doing?" they'd ask Begay.

"I'm getting ready to win a major," Begay would say. "I need all sorts of variety in my shot making if I'm going to be the best in the world."

*Wow,* they'd think. *This guy has some serious self-belief.*

Begay always spoke in the future tense, always seemed on the way somewhere. His name in Navajo translates to "almost there," and it seemed as if that was how Begay lived his golf life, as if he hadn't yet reached his destination and wouldn't stop until he got there. The Stanford players noticed that while Begay respected the leadership and game of Christian Cevaer, who'd won the Pac-10 individual title in 1989 and was the team's best player, Begay had the attitude that one day soon, he'd be better than Cevaer.

At the first Stanford tournament of their freshman year, the Coca-Cola Classic at New Mexico State, Martin and Begay were sitting on a bench near the first tee with some Stanford parents. Goodwin was monitoring starting times and looked at his watch. "Notah," he said, "you're up."

Begay stood and walked toward the first tee. But he turned around and winked at the rest.

"Showtime," he said, smiling.

If some opposing players found him difficult and cocky, the Stanford players loved him for his intensity and competitiveness, how he always thought about the game in unconventional ways, just as he had learned from Van Wart at Ladera. Once, at Stanford, he was playing in a foursome and hit a tee shot wayward, into the trees, in jail.

"I love that," Begay said.

A member of his foursome raised his brow. "You love that?" he said.

"Yes, I love it," Begay said. "I love to hit my ball into trouble, because I love to hit my ball *out* of trouble. I love creating solutions to problems."

Who was this guy? He was the player who walked up to Goodwin at the Pac-10 championships one year, pointed to Arizona State's All-American, Phil Mickelson, and told his coach, "I'm going to give that guy something to remember me by."

His 64 at the 1992 NCAAs, a school record, helped seal the growing legend of Notah Begay and his unique and sharp edge. On the eighteenth hole, he'd missed a putt he wanted for 63. He let loose with a profanity. In the scorer's tent, an NCAA rules official told Begay he was thinking about assessing him a 2-stroke penalty for his behavior. Begay seethed. The rules official dithered.

"Well!" Begay howled. "Are you going to give it to me, or not? I've got to sign my card!"

The rules official nearly DQed him on the spot. Begay held firm, furious. It was a stare-down. The 64 at NCAAs was almost out of the books as soon as it was finished.

The rules official backed down. No penalty stroke. Begay signed his card. He had a 64 at NCAAs on his resumé forever.

"Instigator" . . . "rogue" . . . "troublemaker" . . . "smart-ass" . . . all the words his teammates and dorm mates came up with for Begay rang true. He had a lust for life and partied heartily at the fraternity he pledged with Martin, Sigma Chi. His teammates found that out at Hilton Head in the fall of 1994, when he got behind the wheel of the rental car coming back from dinner. Begay jerked the wheel sharply to the side and took his terrified passengers on an impromptu off-road trek through the sand dunes of South Carolina, while he cackled mightily. When Begay was an upperclassman, freshmen had to watch out. He'd haze them in rousing style, lining 2-irons at Conrad Ray as Ray hid behind the 100-yard marker on the Stanford driving range. Nobody on the team would forget that Begay smoked one low liner that — *clang!* — bounced off the 100-yard marker protecting Ray. He'd have been a dead man without the sign.

On the road, he was a constant source of entertainment. In the fall of 1994, when the team went to Japan, the boys headed out to the Roppongi district, Tokyo's center of nightlife. Begay told Burdick, the nondrinking Christian, to keep an eye on him, make sure he didn't get into any mischief. Burdick agreed. After a few hours of clubs and bars, the team was headed back to the hotel. Burdick tapped Begay on the shoulder, to let him know they were leaving.

"You go on without me," Begay said. "I'm fine."

The boys went to sleep . . . and Begay didn't come home all night.

When the sun rose, he walked into their room.

"Where were you?" they asked.

Begay laughed. The only thing he remembered was waking up on a park bench in the Roppongi district, with no money and no Japanese language skills. With only the business card of the hotel, he convinced a cabdriver to take him back. That would be classic Notah, the same guy who was part of a fraternity prank at San

Francisco's St. Francis Hotel, where a group of Sigma Chis got into the hotel's famous glass elevator—and stripped nude. Part of the prank required photographic proof, and sure enough, it was Begay who stopped the elevator, ran out naked to frame the elevator full of *au naturel* Sigma Chis with a camera, and shot the photo. A couple approaching the elevator got more of Notah Begay than they bargained for.

With all this madness came varied moods, too. Stanford's players would learn that Begay's passions ran both ways, and in the fall of 1993 the team went to Colorado for a tournament. Overnight, a foot of snow fell unexpectedly, and when the team awoke, they went outside and began happily chucking snowballs at each other. Begay was sleeping on a rollaway bed and stayed asleep while the team frolicked. Burdick heaved one into the room for fun.

"If anybody throws another snowball," Begay roared from the rollaway, "I'll kill them!"

Burdick didn't need another prompting. He drilled Begay with another snowball.

Begay threw off his sheets and came barreling out of bed in his boxer shorts. His facial expression and charge were later likened to those of a raging bull, as he picked up Burdick and heaved him into a snowbank, pounding his head with snow over and over, shouting, "Snow in the morning is not fun! Snow in the morning is not fun!"

Add to all of it Begay's serious side, and his inquisitive side, forming the most dynamic personality on the 1994–95 Stanford golf team. There was nothing Begay wouldn't try to improve his golf game. Most significantly, in 1993, a physics professor from Stanford visited the team with a new theory: ambidextrous putting. The theory was, if a golfer assesses the break on a putt, he is best served by developing the ability to putt both left- and right-handed, to let the break of the putt work for him. In sum, if the putt breaks left-to-right, the golfer is better served by putting left-handed. If the putt breaks right-to-left, the golfer is better served by putting right-handed.

The bottom line: It's better, the theory went, to have a putt break into you than away from you.

Begay believed it, bigtime. In an effort to always save a stroke whenever he could, he analyzed the theory and accepted it. He would spend his entire redshirt year, 1992–93, learning to putt both left- and right-handed. And that wasn't all. He so badly wanted to incorporate this theory, he began training the left side of his body. He began to eat left-handed. He began to write left-handed. He opened his car door with the key left-handed. When people scoffed at the theory, Begay would shake his head. He couldn't understand why so many people fell so easily to skepticism. He loved that in golf, as an individual, you could put your own stamp on your game and play it in your own style.

In perhaps the direst example of Begay's commitment, he was driving with teammate and friend Freeland through Arizona one summer. A gigantic summer thunderstorm descended on them as they drove near Flagstaff, and visibility grew poor.

"Get the eye patch!" Begay shouted at Freeland.

As part of his training, Begay carried an eye patch he would wear over his right eye, to strengthen his left eye. Now, in a wild summer monsoon, with a windshield hard to see through, he wanted to test the left eye.

"I'm not giving you the eye patch!" Freeland said.

"Give me the eye patch!" Begay insisted.

There was no turning back Begay. He donned the eye patch, and Freeland turned a shade of green in the passenger seat. They were on a two-lane road, in an old Camaro, and Begay was driving one-eyed. Freeland was one of Begay's best friends, so he resigned himself to the situation. *If this is how I go out,* he said to himself, *this is how I go out.*

Begay navigated the storm.

To Begay's mind, being the best wasn't a matter of convenience. It was something for which he burned. Begay's father once explained to Notah's teammate Will Yanagisawa the many conflicts between different Native American tribes. "The one thing that can unify them," he told Yanagisawa, "is Notah." Yanagisawa considered this when he looked at Begay and understood the pressure, and Begay's complex personality, a little more.

He placed importance in his heritage and wore earrings in both ears, as many Native Americans did. He also dabbed clay under his eyes before playing in tournaments, a gesture from his culture that he said was giving thanks to Mother Nature for providing the beautiful Earth on which they played. He would eventually stop doing this, when he deduced that the media were making too much of it and perhaps pigeonholing him into a stereotype. Such a development would be distressing to Begay, who didn't want the media to take his family's entire heritage and describe it with a few pat phrases or symbols. He carried, as a Native American, a great task on his shoulders, as a symbol of hope for a people who found hope in short supply.

It all came together—Begay's pride, his cockiness, his talent, his sense of the moment—in that 62 at the 1994 NCAAs, essentially the round that won Stanford the national championship. Four birdies came on left-handed putts; six birdies came on right-handed putts. The round was off-the-charts good, and it resonated in Stanford lore. Begay's father was at the par-5 sixteenth watching his son when a marshal asked how Begay was playing.

"He's eight under," the father said, proudly.

"Wow, that's funny," the marshal said. "Some kid from Georgia Tech just finished at nine under."

True story. Georgia Tech's Mikko Rantanen shot a course-record 63 a few groups ahead of Begay. When Begay chipped in for birdie on sixteen to get to 9 under, word spread that one more birdie would get the record. It came down to a 50-footer on eighteen, a putt that started left, broke right, went straight for a while, and then broke a little left again. The gallery shot to their feet tracking the ball, so Begay's father, seated on the grass, never saw the putt fall. He had to hear the crowd react and then see his son with his fist in the air.

Begay loved being the one in the spotlight, and yet he felt a deep pride and joy when Yanagisawa sealed the deal with a final-round

64 at Stonebridge. When Begay thought about Yanagisawa's journey, from the failed walk-on at Arizona, to the nearly disbanded UC Irvine program, to his unlikely transfer to Stanford, and about his parents leaving Japan to make a life in America, Begay thought it was appropriate that Yanagisawa shoot the final-round 64. To Begay, it reemphasized how diverse the Stanford team was and, by extension, the campus, and how much they all meant to each other.

Begay was the last player on the course that day in 1994, the one who sealed the national title by making par on eighteen. At Stonebridge, the tee shot on eighteen is safe down the left side, but a tee shot there sacrifices yardage. The more aggressive play is to take it out right, flirting with a water hazard, to give yourself the better second shot into the green. When Begay got to the eighteenth tee, Stanford had a 4-shot lead. Goodwin was on the tee box, and he told Begay, "The title is ours; just hit a nice, safe tee shot down the left side and bring it home."

He teed it up and let it rip—taking his tee shot aggressively down the right side of the fairway, flirting with water, and drawing it to a gorgeous spot in the fairway.

He turned to Goodwin and winked.

If Notah Begay's Stanford career was about pushing edges and testing himself and others, Casey Martin's Stanford career was quieter and more inward. Not that Martin was quiet. He was someone who could light up a room with his jokes and entertain with his quick-paced speech and easy manner. But as close as Martin grew with Begay over the years, he didn't have Begay's outward fire. Martin's journey at Stanford was about fighting off the pain and limitations of KT and finding solace in his important relationship with his faith.

Perhaps the Begay-Martin dynamic could be best summed up by the times spent on the driving range, when Begay would ask Martin about his religious beliefs and have him explain his faith.

"I understand you believe that," Begay would say, before flashing his mischievous grin. "But *why* do you believe that?"

Martin was OK with Begay's needle. He loved Begay and would

sometimes marvel that the two were so close, yet held such differ-ent worldviews. In his most private moments, Begay would admit that part of the reason he was so fond of Martin was his amaze-ment at and admiration for Martin's traditional, tight-knit family. Begay knew there was love in his family; he just hadn't had it served in such a nuclear manner as King, Melinda, Cameron, and Casey Martin had up in Eugene, Oregon. Ever since they met on the re-cruiting trip, Begay wanted to be close to Martin, in part to have some of that family togetherness rub off on him.

Martin, meanwhile, loved his Stanford experience. He enjoyed how Goodwin ran matters, letting the players lead self-sufficient existences. Some college programs held weekly qualifiers, making players prove themselves over and over. Martin loved that he had to qualify only once in four years. Goodwin trusted his starting five, and they reciprocated.

From the moment he moved into Rinconada freshman dorm, his classmates liked Martin. They found him to be funny and engag-ing, and if anybody wanted to know why he walked with a limp, or showed a stocking on his leg when he wore short pants, he had no problem telling them about the KT, about how it worked, how he was able to play golf, and then move on with the conversation. To Martin, it was no big deal to talk about it. So, for his dorm mates, it was no big deal that he had it. If Casey Martin was anything, it was comfortable in his own skin.

His playful nature showed as much. He once phoned the room of a college rival, pretending to be a reporter, asking questions that were more and more absurd until he broke out laughing. And a common gag was one he and Begay would work on airplane flights for road trips.

On the jetway as they boarded, Martin would make sure to say, loud enough for fellow passengers to hear: "Oh, man. I am not feel-ing well. I knew I shouldn't have had that burrito." Begay would say, "Why don't you sit in an aisle seat, just to make sure?" As passen-gers showed their unease onboard, Begay would milk it and call the flight attendant over, asking for extra airsickness bags, then walk them up to Martin, who would loudly thank him.

When the team went to Japan, and Tiger missed the trip because he was playing in the World Amateur Team Championships in France, Goodwin brought along Conrad Ray, who was a stout young man. An equipment mix-up meant Ray's rain pants for the tournament were something close to XXXXL, which brought much hilarity among the teammates. After a round, when Ray was showering in his hotel room, Martin and Burdick dashed into his room, picked up his rain pants, held them up, and stepped inside them, abreast, for quite the visual when Ray came out of the bathroom. Martin and Burdick fell about the room, laughing.

His easy, conversational style and his clean-cut good looks made him popular with the girls, too. Yanagisawa would marvel at Martin's ability to go on dates with the prettiest girls at Stanford. He'd marvel equally at Martin's blasé attitude toward it all.

Inevitably, Yanagisawa would say to Martin on the practice range that he was wildly impressed with his most recent date.

"Yeah, I had to let her go," Martin would say. "It wasn't going to work out."

Yanagisawa and his teammates were dumbfounded.

Begay, of course, would jump on this part of Martin's personality. When Martin did dare ask Begay about all his female conquests, Begay turned up the heat. He would describe, in graphic detail, things that awaited Martin one day. Martin, naive about it all, would absorb it in equal parts ignorance and awe. He was laughingly likened around the team to the bespectacled teenager in Van Halen's "Hot for Teacher" video, blown away by the mere notion of sexuality.

In truth, even though he loved playing golf for Stanford, and though he loved having a few laughs at the fraternity, Martin was spending his college years searching his soul and exploring his faith. He rushed Sigma Chi, and the outgoing part of his personality loved the parties and the laughter. But somewhere inside, he felt the hedonistic lifestyle was betraying a larger calling in his life. Through Athletes in Action, an on-campus spiritual group of athletes who studied the Bible, Martin became friends with Stanford football players Steve Stenstrom, the quarterback, and Justin

Armour, the wide receiver. They bonded over their Christianity, and it was a huge moment in Martin's Stanford career when he decided to move out of Sigma Chi and rent a house in nearby Woodside with Armour and Stenstrom.

He didn't want to say so for fear of its sounding shallow, but it helped that football stars like Stenstrom and Armour were passionate about Christianity, too. For most of his life, Martin had found that the hard-core Christians were not the "cool" kids at school. That football stars found it cool to be Christians, too, made it all the better for Martin to dive headlong into his faith. Somehow, he felt validated. His times talking about the Bible with Stenstrom and Armour around the Woodside home would be among the happiest times of his life.

Martin even saw the Lord's work in dealing with his KT. He would tell reporters, "I don't feel sorry for myself, and I look at this as an opportunity. I believe the Lord has given this to me so that I can stand out and be a witness for him."

And, of course, Begay would pounce on this angle, too.

Practice rounds at the Stanford Golf Course were battlegrounds of personality as well. Begay laughingly called himself a "nonpracticing Catholic." Tiger, taken under Begay's wing as a freshman, would say that he was a "nonpracticing Buddhist." So, Begay reasoned, Tiger and Begay should take on the two good Christian boys, Martin and Burdick.

"The holy wars!" Begay would call them, cracking up.

It always made for a good time. Begay would try to raise the stakes of the match higher than Martin wanted, and when Martin talked him to a more reasonable dollar amount, Begay would tank the first few holes, just so he could get multiple press bets going, and really start playing for some dollars, to get his juices flowing, just like back at Ladera.

Despite all their differences — add politics to the list, too, with Begay leaning left and Martin leaning right — Casey and Notah always sought adventure together. Sometimes they felt too invincible. Begay and Martin talked for a year about rafting the creek near the

Stanford Golf Course during the winter rains. Finally, in the winter of 1994, a big storm came, and the creek was raging. Begay and Martin, along with two other teammates, got an old two-man raft and jumped in. It was a disaster from the outset, the creek's current undermining their attempts at steering. The raft crashed into a fallen tree and flipped up, and all four went spilling into the waters. Martin was shot thirty feet down the river. Begay remembered thinking only one thing: "Casey's leg ... Casey's leg ..."

Fortunately, they made it ashore, with a pledge: No more rafting.

All the while, the golf was good for Martin. In addition to all the Stanford success, he was carving out a name for himself, enough to make him think that maybe, just maybe, he could make a run at professional golf after school was over. When he left South Eugene High, that was not a strong consideration. But his ability to adapt to the KT was remarkable, as was his competitive streak. He posted highlight performances, such as taking Mickelson to the nineteenth hole of the 1991 U.S. Amateur before losing. And his performance at the 1993 Oregon State Amateur at Pumpkin Ridge was an epic one.

Wanting badly to win the '93 title, since his brother, Cam, had won it in '92, Martin played beautifully, all the way to the semifinals. In the semis, he met an excellent player from Oregon State named Birk Nelson. Three down after eleven holes, Martin was feeling out of it and, worse, was hearing way too many loud cheers from Nelson's mother, who was walking with the match. Partially because he wanted Nelson's mom to stop exhorting, but mostly because he wanted to win, Martin went birdie-birdie-eagle-birdie-birdie on holes twelve through sixteen, not only to advance to the finals, but to quiet the Nelsons once and for all. In the thirty-six-hole final, he had to birdie the thirty-sixth hole to stay alive, then won the State Amateur on the thirty-seventh hole.

Winning it in thirty-seven holes was one thing. Walking thirty-seven holes with KT was another.

Martin continued to take the stiff-upper-lip approach to his leg disability, but by his junior year, it was worrying Goodwin. He began to insist to Martin that he take a golf cart and could get special dispensation from the NCAA to do so. Martin would have none of it. They battled over it, but Martin continued to walk.

Finally, in the spring of 1994, it came to a head. Stanford was playing at Arizona State's home course, a Pete Dye design that featured steep-faced bunkers and sharp angles. It was searingly hot, and Martin was tiring. He hit a bunker shot, then tried to scurry out of one of those steep-faced bunkers, when his leg gave way. He tumbled to the turf and could barely crawl. Goodwin saw it and rushed to get Martin a cart.

When they got back to Stanford, Goodwin called Martin into his office. He told Martin it was mandatory that he ride in a cart the rest of the year. Martin fought him on it. Goodwin brought down the hammer.

"Either you use a cart," Goodwin said, "or you don't play on my team."

The word *team* resonated with Martin. He realized, at that moment, that he was not being a team player. *Here I am,* he thought, *and my team needs me, and I'm crawling down the middle of a fairway. Not exactly team play,* he thought to himself. He relented, and when Stanford won the 1994 national championship, Martin took a cart around Stonebridge.

Begay wouldn't say much to Martin about it, but he watched his battle with KT up close and personal, and over their years together, Begay found himself more and more emotional about Martin's courage. It dawned on Begay that Martin never complained about the leg, not once. He couldn't believe the grace with which Martin handled it, and Begay found himself, as they grew closer to graduation, ever more inspired by Martin's unapologetic, headlong dive into life. He was so glad that they redshirted together in 1992–93, to make sure they were all one unit for the arrival of Tiger Woods. Begay would laugh about their redshirt plan and how it coincided with Tiger: "Hey, we're Stanford kids," he said, "we plan for our future."

That it was he and Martin made it all the more special. At times, Begay felt almost embarrassed by his good health, because Martin did so much more to compete. In the end, Begay would know that of all the people he'd met in his life, he hadn't met many personal heroes bigger than Casey Martin.

And now it was the winter of 1995, and the IM basketball games would end, and they'd all head out into the chilly Palo Alto night, making their way across campus, or to an eatery for a late-night food run, to share a few more stories. Neither Martin nor Begay touched his golf clubs from Thanksgiving through the New Year. Goodwin didn't pressure them to. That was part of his plan, to keep the players focused on school, and IM hoops, leading balanced lives.

But soon February would come. The first road trip of the spring season was to Hawaii. Oklahoma State would be there. The Stanford players felt good about their team after the fall season, but the loss to the Cowboys at Hilton Head stung just a little. It would be good to get to Hawaii to reestablish dominance, and to begin their final season together, to shoot for that second national championship together, to begin the final, memorable steps of their long walk together.

# 7

# Hank Kuehne Has a Secret

*Stillwater, Oklahoma*
*February 4, 1995*

OKLAHOMA STATE'S SPRING season began with a BMW speeding down a gravel road. Hank Kuehne, Trip Kuehne's immensely talented younger brother, was behind the wheel.

Hank, the middle son of America's premier amateur golfing family, often described himself as the black sheep of the Kuehne clan. He wasn't like his intensely driven older brother, who embodied the all-around excellence of an astronaut, or his precocious little sister, the mentally toughest competitor as well as the best all-around golfer in the clan. Hank had a brilliant mind and was a gifted athlete but was decidedly less focused than his siblings and rarely lived up to expectations on the course or in the classroom.

Trip was the golden child, the "Can't Miss Kid," the responsible one who achieved spectacular success at almost everything he did with stunning ease. He was as comfortable around his father Ernie's powerful friends as he was with kids his own age. He was a gifted student and athlete who never gave his parents any trouble. Trip was a shining example of what you could be if you did things the Kuehne way.

Kelli was the most disciplined and determined—and the most

like Ernie—of the three. Her goal was to "hit the ball like a man and walk like a lady." When she was diagnosed with diabetes at age ten, she decided she would control the disease instead of letting it control her. "Little Princess, what's the best part of your game?" Earl Woods asked her at a golf banquet when Kelli was thirteen. "My mind," she snapped back, giving Earl Woods a story he would repeat for years.

Hank was a free spirit, an eminently likable character who inspired comparisons to Huckleberry Finn. He made people gawk at the driving range with his ability to bomb the ball off the tee. Family friend Tiger Woods acknowledged that Hank consistently hit longer drives than he did. Hank had once bested two-time national long-drive champ Art Sellinger by 15 yards in an exhibition.

He was as well known for his length as he was for his looseness off the tee. Once, he hit two shots out of bounds to the left and two out of bounds to the right on the same hole. When he did hit the middle of the fairway, one family friend often joked, he might just venture into the rough in search of snakes.

Trip was three years older than Hank, and if you combined his career with Kelli's—she was only a junior at Highland Park High—they'd won a combined five individual high school state championships and were named first-team All-Americans by the American Junior Golf Association an astonishing nine times. Hank never won an individual state title or made first-team AJGA. But everybody agreed that he had the most potential.

Trip and Kelli always brought home straight As, but for Hank school had always been a struggle. Even when he worked hard, he didn't always get good marks. He was barely able to read, a fact he was too ashamed to admit. Writing an English paper was torture.

He beat himself up over it, asking, *Why am I so stupid?*

Unrealized potential may have best defined Hank Kuehne. It drove Ernie Kuehne, the unquestioned head of the Kuehne family, to distraction.

Ernie tried to instill in his children the same ferocious competitiveness that allowed him to rise from a poor cotton farm in central Texas to become one of Dallas's most successful and wealthiest attorneys. He was a hard-charging, type A personality who dominated the room.

He had a simple philosophy when it came to parenting. He gave his children direct feedback. He told them when they did something well. He told them when they did something poorly. All the while, he made sure they knew his love was unconditional.

They picked the sport and he provided them with the opportunity to become the best. The Kuehne kids had the best equipment and the best instruction and were exposed to the best competition, regardless of cost. In return Ernie demanded supreme effort, that they not make "asses of themselves" on the course.

Lack of preparation upset him most. It was the trial attorney in him. Preparation was everything. Ernie paid for Trip to play the course that would host the regional tournament during his sophomore year in high school—twenty times. Ernie wanted Trip to know every blade of grass and grain of sand before playing in the tournament that would decide whether he qualified for the state tournament. Trip arose every Saturday and Sunday for two months and drove to Denton, Texas, to play fifty-four holes on that golf course. Ernie even picked up the tab when Highland Park's entire golf team traveled to play the course where the state tournament would be held during the spring of Trip's sophomore year, a tournament where Trip was nipped by future teammate Alan Bratton in a playoff for the individual title.

Ernie gave his children opportunities and they seized them. Soon the trophies they were bringing home began to crowd the family den, but as long as the preparation and tenacity were there, as long as they conducted themselves with class on the course, he didn't care if they finished first or last.

"You're never as good as your best round or as bad as your worst" was Ernie's oft-repeated mantra. "What you shot is not who you are. If it is, you're in big trouble as a person."

Ernie was always in the background, a dominating figure, plotting strategy, advising his children how best to attack a course and with what clubs to attack it. He preferred the textbook approach to golf: driver to the middle of the fairway, short iron to the fat part of the green, putt for birdie. Easy.

Hank wasn't easy. He wasn't a walking, talking endorsement of the Kuehne way as Trip and Kelli were. He did things his way, and although he tried to please everybody, most of all his father, he wouldn't forsake his independence to achieve that goal.

Trip and Kelli liked to practice. Hank liked to play. Trip and Kelli were grinders, just like their old man. They adopted Ernie's fairways-to-greens philosophy, while Hank preferred a more scenic and circuitous route. Trip and Kelli embraced par; Hank, birdies and bogeys, double bogeys and eagles.

Hank would rather hit his ball out of a tree even if taking a penalty stroke was the logical alternative. He was a creative shot maker with the raw ability to make recovery shots that others would deem impossible. When Hank got into trouble on the course, crowds would gather to see what he would do next.

Even his sometime caddy Kevin Casas would get excited when he saw Hank pondering an outrageous rescue shot. Forgetting Ernie's pre-round instructions on how to best chaperone Hank around the course to avoid such situations, Casas would look over both shoulders. If Ernie was nowhere to be seen, he would hand Hank the club of his choice. "Shit, I've got to see this" would replace the more sensible advice he had promised Ernie he would deliver.

He might hook a 2-iron dead left behind a tree and then, instead of chipping safely back into the fairway, hit a towering, impossible 7-iron over the tree to within 4 feet of the cup. Hank might then notice a young lovely in the gallery and miss a birdie putt. Ernie would stand behind the ropes grinding his teeth into a fine white powder.

Ernie quickly learned that he couldn't motivate Hank the same way he did Trip and Kelli. Trip and Kelli would use Ernie's criticism to fuel their determination. They might get angry at Ernie's biting analysis of their performance, stalk off the practice range, and pound a hundred balls to blow off steam. Hank was more sensitive to the criticism, more likely to let a bad shot turn into a triple bogey when he knew Ernie was seething about his club selection.

Hank couldn't be motivated by a kick in the pants, literally or metaphorically. Hank needed a hug. But when he was enveloped with positive energy, when he was being encouraged instead of criticized, Hank Kuehne could flat play golf.

What the Kuehne clan didn't realize was that Hank had a secret.

Mike Holder recruited Trip's younger brother because his talent intrigued him, as it did everybody else who had watched Hank come through the AJGA ranks. Holder knew Hank was intelligent and thought it strange that he was struggling during his first semester at Oklahoma State in the fall of 1994. It didn't make sense. Finally, at Ernie's urging, Holder had Hank seen by experts who diagnosed him with attention deficit disorder and dyslexia.

But the larger problem went largely unnoticed.

Hank Kuehne was an alcoholic.

He was thirteen the first time he got drunk. He had always felt the need to escape, and it intensified when his best friend committed suicide when they were both in junior high. His pronounced depression dissipated when he'd had a few drinks.

He stole booze from his parents and neighbors. He and some other kids got caught drinking at a junior golf tournament, but it was passed off as kids' stuff, boys being boys. In high school, he often left golf practice early to drink. Always physically mature for his age, Hank acquired a fake ID when he was fifteen.

He drank more and more. He drank until he passed out. He threw up for three days after one binge while his parents were in Hawaii. There were times when he would almost pass out when he bent over to tee up his ball.

Trip didn't drink until he was a senior in high school. Hank was a freshman at the time. They went to some of the same parties. Trip knew Hank drank, but he had no inkling his brother had a serious problem.

It was the same with Kelli. She adored Hank. Trip was five years older than Kelli and was her role model, her mentor, her idol. Hank was her partner in crime. Hank was popular and funny. She loved hanging out with him in high school and hated the fact that he wouldn't let her date his friends.

They partied together in garages and at the homes of friends whose parents were away, but not even Kelli, who knew Hank best of all, understood the grip alcohol had on him. Not even she knew that when the Kuehnes gathered for a family dinner each and every night, which Ernie insisted they do, Hank was often drunk after having spent the afternoon at a local bar.

Hank used gum and toothpaste to disguise his breath. He was always a natural storyteller, and his alibis always had enough truth in them to divert suspicion, so it wasn't hard to cover his tracks. He would say that he was staying over at a friend's house and then stay out drinking all night. He got into a bar fight during his senior year in high school. His head was rammed through a TV, opening a nasty cut on the back of his head. The bursa sac in his elbow burst when he was slammed into a brick wall. His teeth were pushed through his lower lip. He told his parents that he'd slipped while jogging in the rain.

It didn't take Holder long to realize that the personable, respectful young man who had visited Stillwater on a recruiting trip during his junior year in high school was not the same person who arrived on campus during the fall of 1994 to begin his freshman year.

Holder had only three primary rules: Tell the truth, go to class, and be on time. Hank broke them all. Infuriated, Holder tried everything to discipline Hank, including stern warnings, chewing him out in front of his teammates, and putting him through grueling workouts. Nothing worked. He attended class sporadically. Although he could never catch Hank in a lie, Holder knew his excuses were less than truthful.

Hank Kuehne, metaphorically, at least, spent his first semester at Oklahoma State giving Mike Holder his middle finger.

It's easy for an alcoholic to go unrecognized on a college campus, but Holder had his suspicions. Holder had his own definition of a drinking problem. Some people could drink ten beers and have no problem. Somebody else might have three beers and end up in some sort of trouble. That person, according to Holder's definition, anyway, had an alcohol problem.

Holder had educated himself about dependency and addiction. He recognized the telltale signs and ordered Hank to see an alcohol counselor on campus. He disagreed when the counselor concluded that Hank did not have a problem and was just a typical party-hearty college student.

When Hank continued to break team rules, Holder suspended him from the team. "Get your life in order," he told Hank. "Then we can start talking about the possibility of you rejoining the team."

Trip and Hank had always been close. Both considered winning a Texas high school team title together during Trip's senior and Hank's freshman year at Highland Park their greatest athletic accomplishment. They promised their grandmother they would do it before she died, and then they accomplished it, the two brothers embracing on the eighteenth green after the final scores were posted.

Hank having committed to Oklahoma State was a factor in Trip leaving Arizona State for Stillwater in the fall of 1994. They talked about accomplishing in college what they had accomplished in high school, but instead of winning a state title they talked enthusiastically about winning an NCAA championship.

They both fell into college life but ran in different circles. Trip was as busy as he had ever been in his life. He was working on his golf game while recovering from a shoulder injury he had suffered while still at Arizona State. Holder promised Trip nothing when he transferred. Trip spent hours hitting balls, determined to land a spot in the Cowboys' traveling five.

He was also taking a heavy load of academically challenging courses and spending most of his free time with his girlfriend or his teammate Cox. He saw Hank only three times during the first semester, and each time it was because his younger brother needed something or had been involved in a minor fender-bender.

Then there were the reports he heard about Hank from his teammates, all involving alcohol and all unflattering. "Hey, Trip, did you hear what your brother did?" became a question that made Trip wince. Trip, ever dutiful, ever the older brother, ever the embodiment of the Kuehne way, looked out for his kid brother, but going to Oklahoma State with Hank wasn't what he'd thought it would be. His little brother had become a royal pain in the ass.

Ernie suspected Hank was struggling with alcohol problems. He also knew Hank wasn't ready to seek help and he couldn't force him to do so. He had visited Stillwater a month after Hank started his fall semester. He would always remember the cold October day he headed back to Dallas, hoping, praying, that his middle child didn't kill himself or somebody else before he realized that rehab was his only option. He knew the day was coming, knew he had to let Hank fail so he could eventually succeed.

By the time Hank returned after winter break, his behavior was even worse. He was shutting out friends and family members, who were becoming increasingly concerned about his erratic behavior. What they didn't know, what nobody knew, not even Ernie, was that by then Hank was drinking a fifth of whiskey and a case of beer a day.

Trip reached out to his brother on the afternoon of February 3, 1995. Hank didn't answer his phone. Trip left a message inviting him to dinner later that night. Hank never called back.

Holder received a late-night phone call that same evening. Oklahoma State's director of academic services had driven past a grisly accident and thought one of the cars involved might belong to one of Holder's golfers.

Holder drove to the scene, hoping it wasn't true, his intuition telling him otherwise. He parked his car and strained to see through the flashing lights. Then he recognized Hank's red BMW crumpled in a ditch. The windows were shattered. The roof was caved in.

Holder felt a wave of nausea envelop him. It didn't look as if anybody could have gotten out of that car alive.

Ernie Kuehne grew up on a cotton farm in Otto, Texas, where his day started when the sun rose and ended when it was too dark to keep working. He was driving a tractor when he was six. When he was thirteen he harvested five hundred acres of cotton himself while his parents held down full-time jobs.

His father was a hard, tough man who valued education above

all else and was convinced that college was the best way to escape the life that he endured. He demanded academic excellence from his son, who delivered it dutifully. Between homework and school-work, there was little time for Ernie to pursue his passion: sports.

Sports broke the monotony of the numbing routine of farm work, school, and church. Ernie had athletic ability but most of all a competitive fire that burned to his core. He made the All-District teams in football and basketball and was a standout in track even though his father discouraged his participation. Sports were a dead end, he was told, a waste of time when he should be working.

His parents would attend home football games but that was it. That's when Ernie made a vow to himself: *When I'm a parent, I'll always be there for my kids.*

His father insisted that he choose a college based on academic excellence and not athletic opportunity. Ernie went to North Texas State, where he joined the track team without his father's knowl-edge, before giving up the sport for good when he realized the iden-tities of his fellow athletes on campus were too wrapped up in their chosen sport. What, Ernie wondered, would they do when their athletic careers were over?

He graduated from Baylor Law School with a goal that would consume him for most of the next decade: He was determined to be a millionaire by thirty.

He was employed as a corporate attorney after his marriage in 1968 to Pam Hill, the daughter of a high school football and basket-ball coach. He later started his own firm. He made connections. He had the foresight to anticipate lucrative legal arenas.

His ability as a litigator was equaled, if not surpassed, by his abil-ity as a businessman. He was a natural risk taker with an intellect that allowed him to quickly learn, master, and then exploit oppor-tunities in the business world.

In less than a decade he realized the dream he had dared to dream while sitting on a tractor in the dusty cotton fields: Ernie Kuehne, aged twenty-nine years, was a millionaire.

By the time his oldest son, Ernest William Kuehne III, whom he'd nicknamed "Trip," was ready to begin his athletic career, Ernie was in a position to do what his father hadn't done. He left work every afternoon at three to coach Trip's baseball, soccer, and football teams, just as he would later do for Hank and Kelli.

Ernie Kuehne was going to be there for his kids. They were going to have every opportunity he had been denied.

All three Kuehne kids were natural athletes and tenacious competitors. They were rich kids living in an exclusive neighborhood, but there was nothing about the Kuehne kids that would suggest they had been coddled.

The Kuehnes' lawn was the only one long enough to double as a football field. The Kuehne three took on all comers. Trip was the leader, the quarterback. Hank was rawboned, easygoing, and uncommonly athletic. Kelli, in pigtails, was determined to keep up with the older brothers whom she adored and quickly developed into the fiercest competitor of all.

There were a lot of athletic kids in the neighborhood, the gifted sons and daughters of former college athletes, but almost immediately a trend developed that would continue throughout their athletic careers: The Kuehnes rarely lost.

Trip played football, basketball, and baseball and ran track, and he was a natural at all of them. Ernie was the demanding coach; Trip, the star athlete. Their teams so dominated the highly competitive youth sports leagues that rule changes were adopted to promote parity. Hank played football and basketball, and Kelli won ice-skating competitions and excelled in soccer and tennis.

It was Trip who first ventured into golf when he entered the Dallas city tournament when he was eight. By the time he was eleven, he had won ten local tournaments, and local pros were marveling at his natural skill, predicting he would accomplish anything in the sport that he chose to. Eventually, Hank and Kelli followed their older brother onto the golf course.

Golf was the most difficult sport, the most challenging, and for that reason, to the Kuehne kids, it was also the most intriguing.

Ernie and Pam didn't demand that they play, but if they wanted to, and they did, they were provided with everything they needed to become the absolute best. Ernie shagged their balls on the practice range, paid their travel expenses, caddied for them in tournaments, and ensured they had the best equipment and teachers. He became a lightning rod in the local, then regional, and finally national junior golfing community, a force of nature not unlike Earl Woods.

He knew that golf was a different sport, that you couldn't win every time out no matter how good you were, but there was one thing that he wanted everyone to know whenever his kids teed it up: The Kuehnes came to play.

"Sometimes it just isn't OK to lose," he told them. "Sometimes you have to bow your neck, show some sac, and refuse to lose."

The Kuehne family's success was unique even in a community filled with overachievers. Ernie was the alpha-dog lawyer. Everybody knew not to mess with him or his clients. Pam was the shuttle-bus driver and team mom who always had an ice pack or a granola bar at the ready. Ernie was the driving force, the author and architect of the Kuehne way. She was the nurturer who told her children they did a great job even after her husband had told them the opposite.

To stand out both athletically and academically the way Trip did from the moment he stepped onto the Highland Park High School campus was not an easy thing to do. Even as a freshman in high school, Trip was mature beyond his years. He never earned less than an A in the classroom, always showed great composure on the golf course, and was a natural leader who put others at ease because they knew he had everything under control.

By the time he was a senior in high school, Trip had given up other sports to concentrate on golf. Giving up football was the toughest. Ernie didn't tell him he couldn't play football in high school but steered him away from his favorite sport without Trip realizing it. His rationale was simple. Trip had always been so good at everything he did that it was difficult for him to choose what he should do. Trip loved football, and although he was a gifted quarterback who was projected to be a standout in high school, what future did football offer to an athlete, however gifted, who was six feet, 185 pounds?

Golf would be the sport that would take Trip the furthest. There-fore, Ernie was convinced, that was the sport Trip should pursue.

The rise of Highland Park's golf program coincided with Trip's arrival as a freshman. Highland Park won its first state champion-ship when Trip was a sophomore. Highland Park, led by Trip and future PGA Tour pro Harrison Frazar and, later, Hank Kuehne, would win three straight team titles, and Trip won the individual title twice.

His success in high school, along with his dominance at the AJGA level, made Trip the Tiger Woods of Texas golf.

Trip loved the competition, the elements, the battle that went on within him when he played, and the camaraderie among players. Football was easy. Sports were easy. He had always been the best player in whatever sport he chose. Golf, on the other hand, was dif-ficult. Hitting balls on the driving range relieved whatever pressure and stress he happened to be feeling. He craved the solitude. Golf was an escape, an intellectual as well as an athletic pursuit. Most of all, golf was just a game.

The players he competed against in the AJGA and in high school, future major champions such as Justin Leonard, David Duval, Ti-ger Woods, and Phil Mickelson, all dreamed of playing on the PGA Tour. They dreamed of standing over a 6-foot putt, knowing that hundreds of thousands of dollars were on the line.

Their dream wasn't Trip's dream. He was one of the best junior golfers in the country, and everybody assumed the Can't Miss Kid would eventually turn pro, but few knew that Trip had dual passions. He loved golf, but he was also fascinated by the stock market.

Trip had grown up a huge Southern Methodist University fan. It was difficult for a Highland Park kid not to be. The school's campus was located in neighboring University Park, and Lance McIlhenny, a nineteen-year-old freshman from Highland Park, was named SMU's starting quarterback in the days leading up to SMU's stun-ning upset of Texas in 1980 that launched the "Pony Express" era.

By 1982, when Trip was ten, SMU's "Pony Express" backfield of Eric Dickerson and Craig James was riding roughshod over college football. SMU's basketball team was also among the best in the country that year, so when it was announced that Trip's fourth-grade class, which was learning about the stock market, would have a stock-picking contest, the winner receiving everything necessary to build his or her dream room, Trip was determined to win. He wanted to turn his room into a shrine honoring his beloved SMU Mustangs.

Each student was awarded imaginary money to buy stocks. Trip studied the business pages. He chose his stocks carefully. He won in a landslide.

From that moment forward, Trip read the sports page first and the business page second. He listened to the stock market report every day.

Every year, the Kuehnes went to New York during the first week of December. The golf clubs were left at home. They visited museums, attended Broadway plays, took carriage rides through Central Park, skated at Rockefeller Center, and watched the Christmas lights twinkle in Times Square.

Trip loved everything about New York and looked forward to the vacation every year, but it wasn't until he visited the New York Stock Exchange that Trip realized that golf wasn't the only thing he wanted to do with his life.

He wanted to work on Wall Street.

Trip grew up surrounded by the rich and powerful and became fascinated by the accumulation of wealth. He stood spellbound, knowing that millions of dollars were being won and lost in the frantic trades on the floor of the stock exchange. It was like a game. The more research you did, the harder you worked, the more you knew about a stock, or an industry, the more money you could make, the more wealth you could accumulate.

Trip followed the stock market as closely as he did the local golf scene. His interest in picking stocks was equaled by his interest in golf.

But it was his athletic ability that drew Mike Holder and other top college golf coaches to his living room. Justin Leonard had taken a recruiting trip to Stillwater and was unimpressed. He didn't fit in, he told Trip. Stillwater wasn't anything like Dallas, Leonard said. It was too small, too remote, too much of a cow town.

Kuehne was Holder's number-one recruit that year. He sat in Kuehne's home and told Trip how he had coached fifty-six All-Americans, how his teams had never finished lower than fourth at the NCAA Championships during his seventeen-year coaching career. He told him how he coached four individual NCAA champions and won five team titles, and how eleven of his former players were on the PGA Tour.

Most players were impressed by Holder's pitch. Trip Kuehne was the exception. He knew Holder was the best college golf coach in the country, and that Oklahoma State was the nation's best college golf program, but something was holding him back. The more Holder ticked off his accomplishments, the more Trip became convinced he didn't want to be a number. He didn't want to be another trophy on Holder's crowded shelf. He wanted to be treated like a person, not a commodity.

After whittling the finalists to UNLV and Arizona State, Trip chose the Sun Devils. He began to regret his college choice while playing in his first college tournament. Paired with an Oklahoma State player, Kuehne noticed how prepared his opponent and Holder seemed to be. That's when he began to realize he might have made a mistake.

While rooming with ASU All-American Phil Mickelson, Trip posted a 74.5 scoring average in thirteen tournaments as a true freshman at ASU in 1991, finishing in the top twenty four times and the top ten once. He started his sophomore year hot, placing in the top six at three consecutive tournaments. That's when his left arm started bothering him. What was later diagnosed as a rotator cuff injury would keep him out for the remainder of his sophomore season.

Before the injury, Trip was a blue-chip stock himself. Expectations for him were off the charts. Then it all went away.

It was a serious injury. Doctors weren't sure what was wrong. Some prescribed rest, others weightlifting and rehabilitation, still others surgery. Trip and Ernie weren't sure what to do. Suddenly, through no fault of his own, his stock was dropping. For a while, it appeared as if fate would intervene and perhaps the Can't Miss Kid could miss.

Ernie was convinced that Hank and Kelli were destined for life on tour. He wasn't so sure about Trip, even after he'd recovered from his injury. Trip was almost too smart to spend his life as a golfing nomad on the PGA Tour. Ernie thought Trip could make a grander statement by becoming a modern-day Bobby Jones, who dominated the sport in the 1920s as an amateur while running a business and raising a family.

Plus, things were changing at ASU. When Mickelson left Arizona State to make his professional debut at the 1992 U.S. Open at Pebble Beach, he took ASU coach Steve Loy with him. Loy was a big reason why Kuehne had committed to Arizona State. When Loy left to become Mickelson's agent, Trip wasn't so sure he wanted to remain in Tempe.

In the spring of 1993, Trip went to the NCAA Championships in Nicholasville, Kentucky. Even though injured and unable to play, Trip spent most of his time hanging out with his buddy Kris Cox and the Oklahoma State team.

Oklahoma State finished twelfth in the NCAAs that year. The previous lowest finish under Holder had been fifth, and that was when he was a rookie coach in 1974. Despite how poorly Oklahoma State played, Trip once again thought the Cowboys were the best-prepared team and Holder the best-prepared coach.

Hank Kuehne had already committed to Holder and OSU for the fall of 1994. Teaming with his little brother to win the Texas 4A high school team championship was one of Trip's greatest athletic thrills. How cool, he thought, would it be to win an NCAA championship together?

Trip was still undecided when he made the four-hour drive from Dallas to Stillwater, a town just as Leonard had described it. One difference: Trip felt as comfortable as Leonard had felt out of place. He was impressed by the championship-caliber golf course Holder was building on the outskirts of town.

He wrestled with his decision during the long drive back to Dallas. Should he transfer to Oklahoma State and play with Kris and his brother and compete for a national championship? He was half-way home when Trip made up his mind. He would go to Oklahoma State.

Trip, Ernie, and Holder met to discuss the possibility of Trip becoming only the second player to transfer to Oklahoma State during the Holder era.

"I'm not blown away by numbers," Trip told Holder. "I don't want to be your hundred and twenty-fifth All-American or your hundred and fifth academic All-American or on your fifteenth team to finish in the top five at the NCAA Championships. Numbers are numbers. They don't prepare you for life. I don't want to be another one of your unbelievable statistics. I want to be Trip Kuehne the person."

Later, Holder began to rattle off what his former players were currently doing. He knew whom and when they married, how many kids they had, what tour they were playing on, and where they worked and lived. Trip was satisfied.

"I don't have any money to give you," said Holder, who was fresh out of scholarships.

"This isn't about money," Ernie Kuehne said flatly. "This is about winning a national championship."

Mike Holder spotted Hank leaning against a police car, bloody and in shock, which alleviated his worst fear — that Hank had died in the accident.

Hank did not appear drunk to Holder, and he would later learn that Hank and his two friends had only one beer before leaving for the Tumbleweed, a honky-tonk on the outskirts of town that was popular with the under-twenty-one crowd because, unlike bars within city limits, it allowed eighteen-year-olds to enter but not drink.

Details about the accident began to filter in during what soon turned into an endless night for Holder, Trip, Hank, and the rest of the Kuehne family.

Hank was driving at least sixty-five miles per hour down the gravel road. He didn't see the stop sign. He didn't see the other car. The last thing he remembered was the Pearl Jam lyric "Can't find a better man" blaring from his car stereo at the moment of impact. The next thing he knew, bright lights were in his face. A camera crew from *Real Stories of the Highway Patrol* was traveling with one of the state troopers who arrived on the scene.

Hank was not yet intoxicated, although that had been his plan for the evening. His car contained an open whiskey bottle that belonged to one of his friends, which triggered his arrest.

He fractured four ribs on his left side and had glass shards in his eye, face, and back. The bursa sacs in his knee and elbow had ruptured. He had a concussion. Amazingly, his two friends suffered only cuts and bruises. The driver and two passengers in the other car were all hospitalized, but the injuries were mostly minor, thankfully, the most severe being a broken leg.

Trip's message light was blinking when he returned to his apartment later that night. He thought it might be from Hank, whom he had invited to go out to dinner with him and Cox earlier that afternoon. They had a quiet meal, knowing they had aerobics class early the next morning and would then board a private plane to Tucson for the Ping/Arizona Invitational at Randolph Park, which was the first tournament of the spring season.

Nothing prepared Trip for what he was about to hear.

The first message was from a state trooper. Hank had been in a car accident. The second message from the state trooper said Hank had been injured and would be taken to the hospital. The third message said Hank had been taken to Payne County Jail.

Trip's girlfriend's father was an Oklahoma judge. Trip woke him up with a phone call in the middle of the night. The judge made a few calls on Trip's behalf, only to call back with news Trip didn't want to hear: There was nothing anybody could do. Hank would spend the night in jail.

Trip showed up early to aerobics the next morning, exhausted after a sleepless night. Holder, looking just as tired, met him outside the aerobics studio, filling him in on the details from the night before.

Trip was distraught. He knew there was no way he could have or should have known that Hank's drinking was out of control, but that didn't prevent him feeling as if he should have known and intervened.

Holder told him to go home and get some sleep. There was nothing they could do until later that morning, when they could both go to the county jail to bail out Hank before driving to the airport.

Trip didn't want to go to Arizona. He didn't want to play golf. He was the oldest of the three Kuehne kids and felt a parental responsibility for Hank. He told Holder that he wasn't about to abandon his brother.

Holder wasn't surprised by Trip's reaction. He wanted Trip to play, not because it would increase Oklahoma State's chances of winning the tournament, but because Holder knew there was nothing Trip could do for Hank now. The best thing for Trip was to get out of town for a few days with four of the people to whom he was closest and get his mind off what had happened to his brother.

Ernie was more direct. Your life can't stop because of what Hank is going through, he told Trip. Nobody could take care of Hank now. He had to take care of himself.

It was only after Trip and Hank's teammates, redshirt freshman T. J. Nance and redshirt sophomore Bo Van Pelt, assured Trip they would spend night and day with Hank that Trip relented and agreed to travel with the team to Arizona. But first, he and Holder had to bail Hank out of jail.

The tears were streaming down Trip's face when he saw his bruised, battered, and humiliated brother. Hank was crying, too, when the two embraced.

"I love you, little brother," Trip told him. "Please get better."

"I love you, too," was Hank's reply. "I'll figure something out."

Holder had only recently begun using private planes to shuttle his team to a tournament or two every year. To him, it made sense. Using a private plane didn't cost much more than flying commercial, and they weren't bound by commercial flight schedules, which meant less time in airports and fewer missed classes.

Trip was as exhausted as he had ever been when he boarded the

Beechcraft King Air with the rest of Oklahoma State's golf team. No one talked about what had happened to Hank or grilled him for details of the accident.

"Is he OK?" Cox asked.

Trip nodded.

"If you want to talk about it," Cox said, "let me know."

The people sitting in the four captain's chairs or on the bench in the back of the cabin were Trip's support group. Nothing needed to be said. These were people Trip knew cared for him deeply and would do anything for him.

They were all there, all except for Holder, who would catch up with them later, if he came at all. He had a more important job to do, more important, even, than starting a spring season that he hoped would end with him coaching his seventh—and Oklahoma State's eighth—national championship team.

Somebody had to stay behind and take care of Hank.

The shadows were slowly retreating from the rocky outcroppings of the distant mountains when Trip teed off for the third round of the Ping/Arizona Invitational at Randolph Park in Tucson on a cool desert morning.

Trip had not been able to focus on golf all week, and this morning was no exception. He still wasn't sure he had made the right decision to come to Arizona. All he could think about was getting back to Stillwater, making sure his brother was OK, and preparing to do what everyone knew Hank must do—enter an alcohol rehabilitation facility.

Trip was rational enough to understand there was no way he could have known how bad Hank's problem was, but that didn't keep him from shouldering an overwhelming sense of responsibility. Had he spent more time with Hank during the first semester, he might have noticed how much his brother was drinking, prevented the accident, and convinced him to change his life.

Every member of the Kuehne family was wrestling with his or her own sense of responsibility. Ernie knew he had not always been the best father for Hank. He had held Hank up to the impossibly high standard set by Trip and later matched by Kelli, which wasn't fair to a middle child who was wired differently from his siblings.

Ernie finally learned that he couldn't prevent Hank from making mistakes on or off the course as he could with Trip and Kelli. Hank learned by making his own. Hank always had talent in abundance. But his golf game didn't take off until Ernie, who by then had been involved in the horseracing business for more than two decades, finally realized he had to let this thoroughbred run.

Pam felt culpable, as if there were something only a mother could have seen or known that might have changed the course Hank charted for himself.

Kelli felt both terrified and abandoned after being awakened by the late-night phone call informing Pam (Ernie was out of town on business) of Hank's accident. Kelli worried that Hank would suffer in jail, and she blamed herself. She was the one who had spent the most time partying with Hank and his friends.

Kelli also knew her oldest brother well enough to know the private hell he was putting himself through, which is why she wrote a letter and faxed it to the hotel where Trip and his Oklahoma State teammates were staying.

Trip received the message when he checked in. He quickly recognized the fat loops of his sister's handwriting and began to read.

"Who are you?" Kelli had written on top of the first page.

> Throughout my entire life I've been able to look up to you. I have more respect than words can allow for you and what you do.
>
> You will always be my hero . . .

The second page was less sentimental and more motivational.

> I still believe in you! Do your best! Remember, absolutely, positively . . .
>
> No Fear!
>
> I love you always and forever, good luck,
>
> Kelli.

Kelli's note meant the world to Trip. But no matter how many times he reread those words, he couldn't get his mind off Hank's troubles.

Trip's never-ending quest for perfection had driven him to become one of the top student-athletes in the country, regardless of sport. But it was his desire to be perfect on the golf course—to hit the perfect shot and play the flawless round—that contributed to his not winning a college tournament in three-plus years of collegiate competition.

Trip was analytical, unforgiving. He would be critical of himself for shooting a 68 if he felt it was an ugly 68. A few misplaced shots stuck with him longer than a dozen perfect shots hit during the same round. Even if he made up for an errant iron with a well-placed recovery, he would beat himself up for the mistake instead of congratulating himself for saving par.

The biggest difference between Hank and Trip wasn't that Trip's swing was more mechanical and Hank's more fluid. What Trip envied most about his brother was his ability to shrug off a bad shot the moment he hit it.

Since he had landed at the Ping/Arizona Invitational, the critical voice in Trip's head was silenced. His demons, as he called them, were mute.

It had been that way since the tournament began two days before. He was emotionally numb and physically robotic, which was perhaps the biggest reason why, when the second-round scores were posted, Trip Kuehne was 1 stroke out of the lead and in position to win his first collegiate tournament.

Stanford wasn't in the field. A Texas team that was consistently being overlooked during a season dominated by Stanford and Oklahoma State's blossoming rivalry was the biggest threat to Oklahoma State in the team standings. Not only that, but Oklahoma State players knew that the Longhorns, who had nearly won the NCAA tournament at Stonebridge the year before, were a legitimate threat to win the upcoming NCAA tournament.

Eleven players shot under par on the birdie-friendly course during the first round, including Trip, whose opening-round 68 put him 1 stroke behind leader Chris Couch of Florida.

Temperatures in the seventies and eighties were welcome to Trip and his teammates, whose games were thawing in the warmth of the desert. Staying sharp during an Oklahoma winter was a challenge. Coaches from warm-weather states frequently referenced Stillwater's harsh climate when trying to steer recruits away from Oklahoma State. Holder had a pat answer for the negative recruiting tactic: "If our weather is so bad," he told recruits, "why are we so good?"

They had all kept their games in shape during the three months since the fall season ended with Chris Tidland winning the individual title and the Cowboys winning the team title at Hilton Head.

The weather in Stillwater leading up to the Ping/Arizona Invitational had been especially bad. A winter storm dumped snow and ice on central Oklahoma, forcing the golf team to hit balls into a net in Gallagher-Iba Arena, which is where OSU's basketball and wrestling teams competed. Holder planned to add an indoor practice facility at Karsten Creek, but that project was still several years away. Meanwhile, Trip, Alan, Chris, Leif, and Kris made do watching their swings from a mirror on the wall as they pounded balls into a net.

Thankfully, the 6,828-yard, par-71 Randolph Park North course was more than accommodating, which helped Oklahoma State players shake off the rust. Bratton returned as the defending champion after turning in three under-par rounds, including a scorching 5-under 66, the previous year.

This time, Bratton followed up an even-par first round with a 1-over 72. Tidland balanced a first-round 76 with a second-round 68. Fifth man Westerberg had finished the fall season strong by tying for thirteenth place at Hilton Head. He was playing well in Tucson, too, following up a first-round 74 with a second-round 68.

Cox was also playing well. His 72-71 start in Arizona was good news, considering what had happened before the tournament. He had already missed the Jerry Pate Intercollegiate in Birmingham, Alabama, in late October because of chickenpox and then sprained his ankle while playing tackle football in the Oklahoma snow with his teammates the Saturday before the team left for Tucson.

Not that it showed. Cox, wearing an ankle brace, helped Oklahoma State land in a first-place tie with the Texas and Arizona teams in the field after the second round.

As the third round got under way on another cool morning, Trip felt more pressure to play well to ensure Oklahoma State's team victory than he did to win the individual title. He didn't know a golf team could be this close-knit when he first arrived from Arizona State. He and Cox were best friends. Tidland and Bratton were best friends. The twosomes competed against each other during practice rounds and in the endless games of spades they played in the van, on planes, and in their hotel rooms.

Westerberg was the odd man out but fit in perfectly with the group at large. Everybody looked out for him and had done so since he first arrived. Westerberg arrived as a foreigner in a strange land, barely able to speak the language. His teammates made him feel welcome and at home.

In some ways, Tidland and Bratton and Trip and Cox were opposites, but whenever they and Westerberg arrived at Holder's house to pile into the van for the airport, they were in lockstep, and they knew that if they played well, they could not be beaten.

Trip shot lower scores during the summer because he played much more conservatively when playing team golf. When he was wearing Oklahoma State colors, he knew his score was part of a larger goal. Instead of trying a bold shot that might result in an eagle opportunity, he would lay it up and knock it on the green and try to make a birdie the old-fashioned way. That way, he could virtually guarantee a par and take a damaging double bogey out of play.

Trip knew Oklahoma State had the best five guys in whatever tournament they were playing, despite others who thought Stanford was superior. As long as he didn't do anything stupid, and his teammates played similarly, they would have a chance to win every tournament they entered.

Trip approached the third and final round the way he had every other during his college career, and although he coveted team titles most of all, there was satisfaction in knowing that the individual title was within his grasp.

That was his thought as he teed off on the penultimate hole of the first tournament of the spring season.

He came through. His approach to the par-4 seventeenth landed within 2 feet. He made the birdie putt and was even for the day and 5 under for the tournament. On eighteen, he hit another solid drive, and for the second time in as many holes, a well-placed iron gave him a birdie opportunity, this one from 10 feet.

When the birdie putt fell for a final-round 70, it wasn't joy or satisfaction or relief that Trip felt so much as validation. His fifty-four-hole total of 6-under 207 won him the individual title by 1 stroke.

Winning his first collegiate tournament justified his decision to leave his brother. It also made the guilt he'd carried with him for the past fifty-four holes dissipate.

Trip dedicated the win to Hank and his recovery.

Ernie had wondered if Trip's first college tournament win would ever come.

It worried him that his oldest son hadn't won an individual title during his first two-plus years of collegiate golf. In some ways, it validated his fears about professional golf. If a player like Trip couldn't win college tournaments, how would he ever expect to win on the PGA Tour?

Ernie had watched a lot of good young players fail on the PGA Tour, and the last thing he wanted was for Trip to follow in their path, which is why he had been encouraging his son to consider remaining an amateur.

"In the pros," he often told Trip, "many are called; few are chosen."

He knew Trip was already as accomplished a ball striker as most tour players, but it worried him that it didn't always translate into low scores.

Some players played poorly and still scored, which is an important skill to possess on the daily grind that is the PGA Tour. Trip, on the other hand, seemed to always shoot the worst score he could have, even when that score was a 66. When Trip's ability to score caught up with his physical talent, Ernie knew, the possibilities were unlimited, but thus far that hadn't happened.

By Ernie's calculation, Trip needed to win six or seven individual collegiate titles if he were to try something as difficult as professional golf. The first victory was out of the way. There was still time, if he chose that dream. Trip had the rest of the spring season and his entire senior year remaining. Maybe this was the beginning of a hot streak that would convince them both that Trip had what it took to succeed on the PGA Tour.

Trip and his teammates piled into the van for the ride to the airport. The team felt a deep satisfaction. A trip that started on such a solemn note ended with another team title. As a team, Oklahoma State blistered Randolph Park, finishing 11 under, 2 strokes ahead of second-place Texas.

Bratton had matched Trip's 70, and the defending champion finished even par after three rounds, good enough for a share of fifteenth place. Chris Tidland finished the third round at even par and the tournament in a tie for twenty-third. Leif Westerberg had turned in Oklahoma State's lowest third-round score, a two-under 69, which meant Cox's final round of 73 would not count toward the team total. Cox's preparation was hindered because of his ankle injury, which made his three-round total of 3 over easier to stomach.

Holder was there. He'd flown to Tucson after making sure Hank had everything he needed and was being watched closely by his teammates. The coach sensed his team's satisfaction as he drove the van from the course to the airport.

"You guys think you're pretty good, don't you?" Holder said, goading them.

The fact was, they did feel good. The weather had prevented them from preparing the way they should. Cox had a twisted ankle and Trip a heavy heart, but they still managed to win the first tournament of the spring season.

It seemed like a solid first step toward accomplishing their ultimate goal.

"Yeah, we've done all right," Trip shot back. Trip wasn't intimidated by Holder, who, like Ernie, often intimidated others. It was Trip's role to stand up to their coach. In this case, he knew Holder was trying to push their buttons. "We've won four of the six tournaments we've entered."

Holder scoffed.

"You might have won this tournament, but the only two that matter are conference and the Big One," Holder shot back, referring, of course, to the NCAA Championships.

When they reached the airport, Holder watched his players pack their clubs and duffel bags into the plane's cargo hold until there wasn't enough room in the small compartment to cram one more tee or ball marker.

The first-place trophy they had just won still sat on the tarmac. Holder sensed his players' dilemma as they looked at the trophy and then at the packed luggage compartment and back again.

"Leave it," Holder said, waving his hand dismissively, before turning to board the plane. "It's not the one we're after anyway."

# 8

## Aloha

*Waikoloa and Kaneohe, Hawaii*
*February 22–24, 1995*

THE FIRST INDICATION that Tiger Woods's freshman year was not sprinkled with gold dust came on the night of Wednesday, November 30, 1994, at 11:10 P.M., in the dark parking lot outside Stern Hall on the Stanford campus.

Tiger parked his car in the lot near his dorm room in Larkin Hall after attending a charity function. Some local golfers from nearby country clubs had a dinner, and honored Tiger, and raised money to benefit the underprivileged community of East Palo Alto and its youth golfers. Tiger agreed to attend and was ending a satisfying evening walking through the parking lot when an unidentified man grabbed him from behind and held a knife to Tiger's throat.

The man called Tiger by his name and asked for his wallet. Tiger told him he'd left the wallet in the car, and after the man patted down Tiger to look for the wallet, he stole a gold chain from around Tiger's neck. He also took Tiger's watch, then used the handle of the knife to knock Tiger to the ground. He fled.

Tiger was not injured. After he called the police, he then phoned home and told Earl: "Hey, Dad, remember how I had a slight overbite? Well, my teeth are lined up perfect now."

The joke was a way for the freshman to defuse tension, but for the Woods family, the incident was a reminder of the dark side of fame. Just three years earlier, when Tiger played in the L.A. Open, there had been death threats with racial slurs attached, and now an assailant who called him by his name had mugged Tiger on the seemingly idyllic Stanford campus. Stanford police estimated that the campus averaged one to two robberies per year.

Tiger issued a statement through Stanford trying to downplay the incident.

"I was not beaten, and I was not injured," he said. "I immediately reported the robbery to the police and I did not seek medical treatment. My jaw was just sore, so I took some aspirin.

"People get mugged every day, and mine was just an isolated incident. I just want to move on from this, bury this in the past. I just want to get through my finals, enjoy a great Christmas, and then come back."

It may have been an isolated incident, but it did serve as a harbinger of sorts for a Stanford team that was heading into the winter and spring seasons suddenly not as infallible as it once thought. Tiger's freshman year took another step back when he had arthroscopic surgery to remove two benign cysts in his left knee, an unusual occurrence for a world-class nineteen-year-old athlete. Although the procedure didn't cause him to miss any golf, it did indicate that the seemingly indestructible and elastic body of Tiger did have its tipping point. His teammates, in fact, wondered aloud to each other and sometimes to Tiger's face about the many times he said he was sick or ailing or hurt. An article that year had quoted a Stanford weight room supervisor as saying Tiger was the strongest athlete "pound for pound" on campus, but his teammates wondered with a needling tone how the strongest athlete on campus could get so dinged up so often. Privately, some of his teammates thought he thrived on personal drama, the better to cast himself into some adversity, the better to summon his fighting spirit. Michael Jordan, Tiger's identified idol, often did the same thing on the basketball court.

On a larger scale, the team had to sit all winter on the idea of the remote possibility that Oklahoma State might be just as good as Stanford. The dramatic loss to the Cowboys at Hilton Head stung, but there remained among the Stanford team—especially from the three most confident players, Woods, Begay, and Martin—a feeling that they were the best team in the country. Oklahoma State would have to do a lot more damage to Stanford's psyche to register on this crew. Stanford was still ranked number one; Oklahoma State still ranked number two.

With that mindset the team boarded the airplane at San Francisco International bound for Hawaii in February of 1995, to first play the Taylor Made/Big Island Intercollegiate at Kings' Golf Club in Waikoloa, then hop to Oahu for the John Burns Intercollegiate, played at the Marine Corps base in Kaneohe. The ten-day stay in Hawaii would be a highlight for any college student, but for the Stanford players it meant heavy consultations with professors before the trip to get assignments. Stanford wouldn't do much in the way of luaus or surfing. Wally Goodwin had a tough enough time convincing the administration to let the team take so much time off school. A pledge had to be made to make sure the Stanford kids would be hitting the books, not the beach—although some of them would wind up combining the two, getting their studying and reading in at the beach. The good news was that Stanford was used to this stuff. Already the team had traveled to Japan in October for the Topy Cup, and already Tiger had jetted to Versailles for the World Amateur Team Championships.

The two Hawaii tournaments would provide a great sense of the college golf landscape with the NCAA Championships just three months away. Oklahoma State was playing in both tournaments, as were number-three-ranked UNLV, number-seven-ranked Arizona State, and number-ten-ranked Arkansas, among others.

Moreover, the start of the spring season meant the grind would begin until Tiger made his debut at the Masters, just six weeks away. Lest anyone forget, though, that he was still a freshman, the team continued to make Tiger sleep on rollaway beds or sleeping bags and always take the worst accommodations. He handled it with grace, and when they got to Hawaii, Tiger goofily jumped up and down on his cot over the fact that the team was in Hawaii, reminding everyone that he was still just nineteen years old and a kid at heart. Earl and Tida Woods would make this trip to Hawaii, too, their first road trip of Tiger's freshman year.

It would be an intense run of golf, with Stanford entered in nine tournaments over the next fifteen weeks. For Tiger, including the Masters, it would be ten in fifteen weeks. Goodwin and the rest of the team hoped he would hold up and deliver what they all expected would be theirs at the end of the year—a second consecutive national championship.

The Hawaii trip was the most anticipated of the year for the Cowboys. Oklahoma State players would miss seven days of classes, which was reason enough to want to go, and the main reason why Holder wouldn't take a player who was struggling with his grades. Holder considered the chance to spend nearly two weeks in Hawaii during the heart of an Oklahoma winter a perk for his players, and he treated it as such. They rented condos instead of staying in hotels. They spent as much time on the beach as they did on the course. They dined at the best restaurants.

In the middle of this paradise, however, Kris Cox wished he were anywhere else.

On the 396-yard, par-4 eighth hole at the Kings' Course in Waikoloa, Cox examined his ball in the middle of the fairway and then looked up, ignoring the river of ancient black lava to his left, to judge the distance to the green. The hole was downwind, a driver-wedge hole, and that's how he had played it.

But when he reached into his bag, he felt suddenly frantic, sick. It couldn't be. He looked into his bag again, more carefully this time, before putting his hands on his hips and looking up at the waving palm trees and the towering volcanoes in the distance, unbelieving.

He had two sand wedges.

He was in trouble, that much he knew. Big trouble.

There were two points Holder always emphasized during tournaments, especially to Cox, who had earned a reputation for overlooking such details: Count your clubs before your round so as not to incur a penalty for having more than fourteen clubs in your bag, and make sure your scorecard is correct before you sign it so as not to be disqualified from the tournament.

Holder was constantly harping about the smallest things, like not taking up too much space in the parking lot when they were loading or unloading the van during a tournament. He had seen players absent-mindedly set their clubs down and wander off, only to watch a van run over their bags, snapping their shafts.

Kris didn't know what to do. "I've got fifteen clubs in my bag," he told his playing partners, who winced, feeling his pain.

Located on the sunny Kohala Coast of Hawaii's Big Island, the 7,074-yard, par-72 Kings' Course is built over and around a lava flow and is framed by tropical flowers and palm trees. Designed by Tom Weiskopf and Jay Morrish, the links-style course provided a lush tropical setting for the first meeting between Oklahoma State and Stanford since Chris Tidland's birdie putt on the eighteenth hole at Hilton Head.

*Golf Week* was the arbiter of college rankings, and the magazine had ranked the Cardinal and the Cowboys one and two since the beginning of the season. If Stanford or Oklahoma State wanted to leave an impression on the other team's psyche, now was the time to do it.

The tournament's shotgun start had sent Kris off on the seventh hole. He had yet to complete his second hole and already he had made a mistake that could be the difference in whether the Cardinal or the Cowboys won the team title.

Kris looked in his bag again. He knew what had happened. He and his best friend had identical black bags with *Oklahoma State* on the side in orange script. They had identical orange, black, and white head covers. Trip must have accidentally put his wedge in Kris's bag before they left the range.

Cox would be assessed a 2-stroke penalty for every hole he played with the extra club. Two holes equaled 4 strokes. He hadn't even finished the second hole of the 108 holes the Cowboys were scheduled to play in the next ten days and he was stuck with the equivalent of the quadruple bogey. Even worse, Trip was somewhere on the course without one of his most important clubs.

Ernie Kuehne called Holder "Cobra" because nobody knew when he was going to strike. Kris had learned that firsthand. His coach had been lying in wait when he arrived at a meeting during his freshman year.

"You're late," Holder told him.

"By my watch, I'm seven minutes early," Kris responded proudly, holding out his wrist so Holder could see his timepiece.

"Your problem," Holder said, looking him right in the eye, "is that you're on Kris Cox time when you need to be on Mike Holder time. You think you're seven minutes early but in reality you're three minutes late."

Kris's punishment had been early-morning workouts. From that point on he had learned to be on Holder time, which was real time minus ten minutes. Holder was a stickler for details but was always there when his players needed him most.

Cox learned that early in his freshman year. He drove some friends to a local bar, where he had enough drinks to know that driving was not an option. He was walking home when Stillwater police arrested him.

The desk sergeant at the police station told Cox he could be released only to someone who was twenty-one or older. The only people he knew over twenty-one were his older teammates, but he'd been in school only a few weeks and wasn't carrying their phone numbers.

"What are you doing here all the way from Louisiana?" the sergeant asked, examining his driver's license.

"I play golf," Kris told him.

"I know Mike Holder," the sergeant said, reaching for the phone. "I'll call him."

Cox had been attracted to OSU in part because of the program's history, and he was about to make some of his own. He was on the brink of the shortest career of any Oklahoma State golfer in history, or so he thought.

He was wondering if the coach at the University of Southwest

Louisiana in Lafayette, his hometown, had a scholarship left when he heard Holder's voice.

"What did he do?"

Kris could hear Holder's questions but not the officer's mumbled responses.

"Did he get in a fight?"

"Was he driving?"

Kris heard the arresting officer's reply for the first time. "No, he was walking home," came the sheepish answer.

"This is a crock of shit," he heard Holder say.

Kris figured there would still be hell to pay once they got to the van, but Holder put his arm around him as they left the police station.

"You made one bad decision and one good decision," Holder told him. "Drinking was a bad decision. Not driving was a good decision."

"Yes, sir," was all Kris could think to say.

Kris waited for more but there was only silence. In fact, much to his relief, Holder didn't mention the incident again for months. That was when Kris learned that the bigger the problem, the more sensitive Holder could be.

It had been the same with Hank.

After the accident, Hank did a lot of talking, soul-searching. He admitted he had broken down and cried in the ambulance. He was afraid he had killed somebody.

The looks on Holder's and Trip's faces when they bailed him out of jail made a lasting impression as well. That's when Hank realized that what he was doing to himself was also impacting his friends and family, which he had never before considered. That's when he decided that if he couldn't quit drinking for himself, he would for them.

With Holder's help, Hank had decided to check himself into an alcohol rehabilitation center. The problem was, the center they had chosen in Minnesota wouldn't have an opening for two weeks. Holder stayed with Hank night and day. He had never felt a bigger sense of relief than when he put Hank on the plane to Minneapolis because he knew his role in this unfolding drama was finished. A member of the rehabilitation staff would greet Hank's flight.

Holder had shepherded Hank through the most crucial two weeks of his life. Friends and family had rallied around Hank as well. Tiger and Earl Woods had called to offer their encouragement. But it was Holder who had been in the trenches with Hank, for which the Kuehnes would be forever grateful.

"Mike Holder saved Hank Kuehne's life," Ernie Kuehne would forever claim.

Holder could be counted on during such defining moments. Kris knew that. He also knew that the top of his head might blow off when he found out that Kris was carrying two wedges in his bag.

Trip had counted his clubs before his round, had realized his wedge was missing. He knew it was probably in Kris's bag, but his friend was two holes away, which meant all he could do was make his 9-iron pull double duty.

When Holder caught up to Kris on the par-3 eleventh, Kris handed the wedge to him. "You might want to give this to Trip," he said matter-of-factly.

Holder's bottom lip quivered when he became suddenly angry, like a toddler on the brink of a tantrum. In this case, Holder's lip quiver measured on the Richter scale.

Cox knew that the only way he could begin to make up for his gaffe was to not compound the problem by coming undone on the course, and he was relieved to finish the first round at even par—officially a 76 after counting his 4-stroke penalty, 2 strokes for each hole he played with the extra club. Leif had also turned in a 76, which meant one of the two bloated 76s would count toward the Cowboys' aggregate total.

Trip, fresh off his first tournament win at the Ping/Arizona Invitational eleven days before, fired a team-low 2-under 70. Tidland finished at even par.

The Kings' Course may have looked inviting, Alan knew, but its links-style layout was further authenticated by ever-present trade winds. Alan had finished three rounds at 4 over when he won his first collegiate tournament on the same course in 1992. The wind was as big a factor in 1995, leaving even the signature drivable par-4 fifth hole exposed and vulnerable, yet the Cowboys were unable to take advantage.

Stanford was still the nation's number-one-ranked collegiate team and was playing the part. Casey Martin and Arizona State's Chris Hanell were tied with the first-round lead after firing 66s. Tiger Woods was tied for second a stroke back. Notah Begay and Steve Burdick shot 73s. Will Yanagisawa's 77 was thrown out.

The Cowboys, meanwhile, hadn't been dominated the way Stanford dominated them in the first round of the Big Island Intercollegiate Tournament since the fall's Ping Preview at the Scarlet Course. They were in eighth place, 13 strokes behind first-place Stanford, when Holder accosted them afterward.

When Holder was preparing his team for a tournament at Karsten Creek, he put as much pressure on players as he could. When they went on the road to compete, he did everything he could to take that pressure away.

Holder was a different person on the road. More relaxed, more fun to be around, Holder acted more like one of the guys instead of their lord and master. He took them to movies and amusement parks. Holder liked fine food, and while some teams, including Stanford, sometimes ate at less expensive restaurants to save money, Holder always insisted on high-end dining establishments, and his players looked forward to the long, satisfying meals.

He wanted his players to practice hard while preparing for a tournament at home, but he didn't want them spending hours on the range on the road. His experience told him that if you didn't bring your game with you to a tournament, you weren't likely to find it once you arrived.

Holder's road philosophy was never more evident than when the team was in Hawaii. The Cowboys arrived at the course early to warm up, but once they were off the course, the Oklahoma State contingent hustled back to their condos for a change of clothes and went directly to the beach, where they would spend the afternoon soaking up the sun and riding the waves.

Holder often chuckled at other coaches whose response to a poor round was to make the team practice instead of going to the beach, but that's exactly how he responded to the Cowboys' miserable first round at the Taylor Made/Big Island Intercollegiate. The sun and surf could wait. He sent them back out to the range, where they hit ball after ball onto the petrified lava flow.

Holder dealt with Kris's failure to count his clubs briefly, directly: "You're going to have to work this off," he said. Kris nodded, knowing exactly what that meant, dreading it. When they got back to Stillwater, for five straight mornings, starting at 6:00 A.M., he would spend a half-hour on Holder's stair machine, which would be set at the fastest setting—level ten.

The extra practice session in Hawaii seemed to work, because his team came roaring back in the second round. Kuehne turned in a second-round 68 to vault him into third place in the individual standings, 2 strokes behind Woods, who followed up his opening-round 67 with a 3-under 69, and 4 shots behind Hanell. Bratton also carded a 68. Tidland and Leif turned in 73s, and Cox's 74 was not counted.

This time it was Stanford's turn to blow up. Martin's second-round 79 counted when Burdick turned in an 80. Begay finished 1 over, and Yanagisawa finished even as Stanford tumbled into second place with a combined score of 572 after two rounds. ASU was 2 strokes better and had vaulted into the lead. Two strokes behind Stanford were Oklahoma State and Texas Christian.

When Stanford arrived in Hawaii, the last thing Goodwin expected was to have any of his players struggle. He had about as low-maintenance a group as could be imagined: Notah Begay, the fiery and passionate senior; Casey Martin, grounded in his faith and in his remarkable ability to overcome his disability; Steve Burdick, like Martin rooted in his faith and thought by his teammates to be the most consistent ball striker on the team; Will Yanagisawa, the self-starter who carved his own path; and, of course, Tiger Woods, the greatest junior player in the history of the game.

But something was beginning to emerge after two rounds of golf on the Big Island. His guys weren't playing very well.

Burdick, Martin, and Yanagisawa had turned in rounds of 80,

79, and 77 in the first two rounds of play. It got worse in the third round when Burdick chased his 80 with a 79. At least Martin had shot the excellent 66, and at least both he and Yanagisawa bounced back with 72s in the final round of the Big Island, but still—it was a less than stellar performance from some seniors in a tournament that offered a chance to fire a shot at Oklahoma State. Goodwin wasn't going to get too worried. There was another tournament in two days' time in Oahu, but the development was worth monitoring, at the least.

Tiger, meanwhile, fired a final-round 71, which tied him with ASU's Hanell at 9-under-par 207, necessitating a playoff for the medalist title.

Tiger seemed poised to claim the third individual tournament title of his freshman season when the playoff began on the 501-yard eighteenth hole, a par 5 laid out along the edge of a lava plateau. Hanell avoided the deep pot bunkers guarding the green with his approach before burying his 15-foot birdie try. Then he watched as Woods missed a 5-footer that would have sent the playoff to a second hole. Just like that, Tiger was beaten in a one-on-one showdown.

It didn't happen often, and it was big enough news for *USA Today* to toss a headline on it two days later. The development was enough to give ASU players a little fodder, and some of them were playing a practice round with Casey Martin when they began doubting Tiger's otherworldliness. ASU had its own Tiger, after all. The legend of Phil Mickelson, who won three NCAA individual titles at ASU in 1989, 1990, and 1992, was large in Tempe. Martin knew better. He'd seen too many mind-blowing things from Tiger.

"There's no way Tiger's better than Phil was," one of them said to Martin.

"I'll tell you what," Martin said. "This is no knock on Phil, but Tiger's a freshman, and he's better than Phil is now . . . and Phil's on tour."

The sincerity in Martin's tone convinced the Sun Devils players.

Meanwhile, Oklahoma State's Cox never recovered from the one-too-many-clubs incident. His third-round 75 put him at 9 over after fifty-four holes. A tournament that began for him with a 4-stroke penalty ended with him tied for sixty-first.

Fortunately for him, his teammates were dialed in.

Trip's 73 was the only Oklahoma State score above par, and it was still good enough for Trip to continue the momentum that began in Tucson. He finished tied for fourth with Bratton, who shot a clutch final-round 69. Tidland's 68 vaulted him into a tie for sixth, and Westerberg's clutch 71 put him in a tie for eighth.

Four of Oklahoma State's top five finished in the top ten, propelling them to the team championship by 1 stroke over surprising TCU and 4 strokes over the team they knew would be their measuring stick for the rest of the season, Stanford. The Cardinal finished third. Outside of Tiger's first-place tie, Casey Martin's tie-19th was the only top-twenty finish, and that was built on the strength of his first-round 66. Begay finished tie-25th, and more alarmingly, Yanagisawa finished tie-41st and Burdick finished tie-97th.

It was the third time in five head-to-head meetings that Oklahoma State had prevailed over Stanford, but the Cardinal wouldn't have to wait long for their chance to square the rivalry. In two days, the teams were scheduled to meet again at the John Burns Intercollegiate in Oahu. It would be the second-to-last time the two teams would meet until the NCAA Championships in Columbus. Stanford took the island-hopping flight, hoping for a better showing. Burdick, especially, landed in Oahu wondering if his game would come back in time to help his team. Deep inside, he wasn't sure it would.

The Klipper Golf Course at the Marine base in Kaneohe sits at the tip of Oahu's Mokapu Peninsula. The Ko'olau Mountains frame the front nine, and the back nine winds along a beach that regularly offers six- to eight-foot breakers.

It was early morning, and the Oklahoma State golf team was in its rented van, Holder behind the wheel, on their way to an early-morning practice round when they passed Marines jogging in tight formation.

"Just think, Leif," Holder said, pointing to the soldiers, a smile spreading across his face. "Those guys could wipe out your whole country."

It had taken time for Leif to get comfortable with Holder, time for him to understand, as he did now, that his coach was just needling him, having some fun.

His first year in America had been one of adjustments. It wasn't being away from home that was strange. Leif had attended a boarding school outside Stockholm with several other elite golfers for three years. Living in the United States wasn't a foreign concept, either. His older brother, Robert, was studying and playing golf at the University of Charleston. But not even the American westerns he had watched could prepare him for Oklahoma.

The landscape itself had been a shock, the remote, desolate plains radically different from the lush green of his hometown of Upplands Väsby, north of Stockholm. He knew he had entered cowboy country, but he didn't realize to what extent.

Leif was familiar with Pistol Pete, Oklahoma State's mustachioed, ten-gallon-hat-wearin', six-gun-totin' mascot, a caricature believed to have been based on a drawing of legendary former deputy United States marshal Frank Eaton. But he never expected to see students wearing cowboy hats and boots to school. He found it curious that male students were allowed to bring spit cups to class to dispose of tobacco juice. Not only was the Pistol Pete logo omnipresent at sporting events, but look-alikes were everywhere.

His golf experience was different from anything he had experienced, as well. His first day in Stillwater had been a grueling, sunburn-inducing day of laying sod on the eighteenth fairway at Karsten Creek. His first official team meeting of the 1993–94 season followed a few days later, which was something he would never forget.

Holder was furious. His team's twelfth-place finish at Nicholasville, by far the lowest finish at the NCAA Championships for any Holder team, ruined his entire summer. There were several new faces on the team, and Holder wanted to hammer his point home: What the team had done at nationals the year before would not be repeated. Holder promised things would be different during Leif's freshman season, and he hadn't yet determined whether the players responsible for the dismal finish would even be allowed to qualify for the first tournament of the season.

Leif knew Oklahoma State's poor performance at nationals the previous spring couldn't be pinned on him, but the meeting had been a shock. Who was this guy? Leif had played soccer and hockey at a young age. He started playing golf when he was nine. He had had a lot of coaches in his young life, but none that remotely resembled the one he had now.

He was thankful to be embraced by his new teammates. He quietly went about his business. He practiced a lot, showed up on time, and worked out to develop his six-foot-three, 190-pound frame.

He played some of his best golf during the first semester of his freshman year and was gracious and even apologetic on the course, even when he was defeating teammates in qualifying rounds.

Leif's game was typically European. Nick Faldo was his idol. Although he spent a lot of time breaking down the technical elements of his swing, he was a natural ball striker, not incredibly long but solid and straight.

His biggest obstacle during his first semester in Stillwater had nothing to do with golf. He had crossed the Atlantic with only a rudimentary knowledge of English. Many of the first slang words he learned were of the four-letter variety, which also endeared him to his teammates, who never tired of listening to him swear in his thick Swedish accent.

With the help of his teammates, he had largely overcome the language barrier by his second semester, when he posted a 3.8 GPA, which impressed his new head coach. Holder had few problems with players who showed up on time, went to class, and practiced hard. Leif did all three, and his new life settled into a comfortable routine before Holder surprised him again.

Leif had never been to Hawaii before and was looking forward to visiting the islands for the first time as a freshman, but he never expected to see Holder at the airport in Oklahoma City with boogie boards under his arm.

Holder bought the boards in 1991. By that time, boogie boarding at the beach after tournament rounds had become a team tradition. Holder had rented boards for his team year after year. Finally, he bought three.

It was another way to get his players' minds off golf. The last thing he wanted after a good or bad round was to have his players sit around and think about it. Having them pound range balls after the first round was an exception.

The truth was, Holder loved playing in the surf as much as his players did. For them, it was fun. For him, it was a competition. He didn't ride the waves as much as try to force them to succumb.

"There he goes again," one companion once said, observing him time and again diving into the blue-green mountains rising from the Pacific shoreline, "trying to whip the waves."

The surf wasn't the only thing Holder tried to make conform. It was in Hawaii where Leif first learned that if he was going to play for Mike Holder he would have to make some changes.

Leif got down on himself when he was playing poorly, and it was evident in his body language. Trip had the same problem. It was during the 1994 Hawaii trip that Holder told both his first-year players that if he saw a long face or droopy shoulders again, if he saw them express their disappointment or disgust after another errant shot, he would "sit your asses in Stillwater."

Westerberg never had a coach address the topic of body language before, had no idea he had done anything wrong, but Holder was adamant.

Holder could usually tell how an opposing player had played his last few holes by observing his droopy shoulders. It drove him crazy. How did moping about your last shot help you hit your next shot? His players were representing Oklahoma State University, and he didn't want them making jackasses of themselves by slamming clubs into their bags or acting glum.

There was a third and more practical reason why Holder made Trip's and Leif's body language a point of emphasis. Players who broke a club or were guilty of some other misconduct could be assessed a 2-stroke penalty.

Holder believed a player should look the same when he walked off the eighteenth green regardless of whether he had just shot a 65 or an 85. He didn't want his players experiencing emotional swings. You played better if you remained relaxed and focused on the next shot, not the last. A degree of detachment was required to play at your highest level.

Leif did his best to correct this behavior, as did Trip. But when Leif missed a 20-foot putt that appeared destined for the bottom of the cup at a tournament in Texas two weeks after returning from Hawaii in the spring of 1994, he let his putter fall on the green. He didn't throw it or slam it. He merely dropped it before looking at the sky in disbelief.

Holder confronted Leif on the ensuing tee box, getting in his face and letting him know that the dropped putter had not gone unnoticed.

Leif thought the storm cloud had blown over. He was playing as well as he ever had and qualified for the Morris Williams Intercollegiate tournament in Austin, Texas, but when Holder announced which five players would be traveling to that tournament, Leif was not among them.

"I told you if you ever did that again I was going to sit your ass in Stillwater, and that's exactly what I'm going to do," Holder explained.

Leif thought Holder had forgotten about the incident. Obviously, he hadn't. Leif didn't make the same mistake again and had to admit, almost a year later, as Holder parked the van in the Klipper Course's parking lot, that he had become a better player because of it.

For twelve holes, the Klipper Golf Course meanders over Oahu's Mokapu Peninsula no more spectacularly than a humble muni. The ocean is within earshot but shielded from view by dunes, the fairways dotted with kiawe, ironwood, and palm trees.

The twelfth green ushers players toward the roar of North Beach, a popular surfing destination, and the scenic 465-yard, par-4 thirteenth, one of the most spectacular ocean holes in golf, a visual feast that was former president Dwight D. Eisenhower's personal favorite when he visited Oahu in the 1950s.

Nestled between ancient Hawaiian dunes and the mesmerizing roll of the surf, the thirteenth tee has a view that stretches a mile down the coast past Pyramid Rock, Kaneohe Bay, and the distant Koʻolau Mountains.

Chris Tidland wasn't there to soak up the scene. He had qualified for the Los Angeles Open, a tournament he had attended annually growing up, for a second straight year. Greg Robertson, a redshirt freshman from the New Mexico Military Institute, would take his place.

It was common in college golf for players to miss collegiate tournaments to compete elsewhere. Bratton went through the same qualifying process to compete in the Phoenix Open. Kuehne had earned a spot in the Masters field by finishing second to Tiger Woods at the U.S. Amateur, and Holder wasn't going to prevent him from spending the week among the azaleas and dogwoods at Augusta National. Kuehne hoped to receive sponsor's exemptions to the upcoming Byron Nelson and the Colonial, which he planned to use as a warm-up to the NCAAs.

Every college player wants to prove he has what it takes to eventually compete on the PGA Tour. Kuehne still wasn't sure what he was going to do with his future. The stock market and life on tour were equally alluring, but he wasn't going to eliminate the option of turning professional. What better way to learn what that life might be like than competing against actual pros on PGA Tour–caliber courses?

Players like Chris, Alan, and Trip learned the fine line between success and failure on tour, and their occasional absence helped up-and-coming players like Robertson gain valuable experience, even if it gave the Cowboys a competitive disadvantage heading into their second-to-last regular-season matchup against Stanford.

Robertson's father was a former college football player and long-time high school coach, his mom a high school golf coach who had led her girls to four straight state championships. Greg's younger sister, JoJo, was a promising junior golfer in her own right. He was a two-time New Mexico state champion, but his bloodlines and previous experience could not fully prepare him for his indoctrination into the Stanford–Oklahoma State rivalry.

Robertson was flustered on the tee, and this was only for a practice round. He may have been a redshirt freshman playing in his first collegiate tournament, but he was aware of the rivalry, was aware that Tiger Woods, Notah Begay, Casey Martin, and the rest of the Stanford five had gathered around the second tee box, where the Cowboys would tee off for the shotgun start.

Alan, Kris, Trip, and Leif hit rockets down the middle of the fairway and were chatting with Stanford players when it was Robertson's turn. He teed his ball and took a practice swing before taking the club back and executing a textbook swing, right down to the perfect follow-through. The problem was, his ball had fallen off the tee on his downswing. Despite his impressive swing, his ball had traveled exactly one and three-quarters inches—straight down.

Alan, Trip, Kris, Leif, and Stanford's players were laughing hysterically while Robertson stared at his ball on the ground, embarrassed.

"Did he just whiff?" Holder asked, prompting more laughter.

Robertson's nerves weren't much steadier when the John Burns Intercollegiate got under way the next morning. His opening-round 77 made two things abundantly clear: Tidland, the steady senior who was playing in the Los Angeles Open, would be missed, and the four other members of Oklahoma State's starting five would have little room for error if they hoped to beat the Cardinal.

But Stanford had its own problems. Inexplicably, Tiger shot 75, his worst round as a collegian thus far. Begay, intent on finishing his senior season strong before launching the tour career he so firmly believed in, was up to the task and shot 69. The rest of the team was in some sort of sun-induced haze. Martin shot 74, Yanagisawa 76, and Burdick again brought up the rear with a 77.

What was wrong with Burdick? Neither Goodwin nor Burdick was anywhere near panic, but it wasn't a good start to the spring season; Burdick posted 80-79-77 in his last three rounds. He'd played well just before the winter break, tying for fourteenth at

220 · THE LAST PUTT

Shoal Creek, and then tying for third at Hilton Head, including rounds of 68 and 70. Everybody on the team admired the purity of Burdick's ball striking. He was levelheaded enough and talented enough that he envisioned a future on the PGA Tour, and it wasn't wishful thinking. One thing did concern Goodwin, and that was Burdick's decision to switch his golf clubs in the fall. For all his life, Burdick had played Pings, but he made a bold decision to switch to Mizuno forged irons. The move was part of his plan to elevate his game, playing clubs the PGA Tour boys played, but Goodwin wondered if the new golf clubs were adversely affecting his game. Burdick didn't think so. He just told himself it had been a long, wet winter, and his game was rusty.

Meanwhile, on the Oklahoma State front, another poor practice round proved golden for Bratton. The worse Alan played in the practice round, it seemed, the better he played when the tournament began. It had been that way throughout his career. Alan scattering balls all over the course during the practice round had become such a pre-tournament tradition that the rare occasions when he did play well were interpreted as a sign that his game would crumble once the tournament was officially under way.

In this case, his poor performance foreshadowed a first-round 69 that put him in a three-way tie with Begay and Arizona's Tim Beans.

All those hours spent boogie boarding agreed with the Cowboys, as Trip turned in a 71, Kris a 72, and Leif a 74, landing Oklahoma State in a first-place tie with Arizona after day one. Stanford was tied for fourth, 8 shots back.

A phone call to his mother, Valerie, was the cure for what ailed Cox's game in the Big Island Intercollegiate. Holder had voluminous knowledge on the subject of the golf swing, but Valerie Cox remained Kris's most effective swing coach, even when she was half a world away. She was sympathetic to his club-counting gaffe, offering support, as always, but after he finished 9 over in the Big Island Intercollegiate, it wasn't her support that Kris needed most.

He needed her advice.

She knew what she was talking about. It was in her blood.

Valerie's father, Oree Marsalis, was introduced to the game as a caddy in Shreveport, Louisiana, in the 1920s and eventually became one of the top amateurs in the Southeast, competing against some of the biggest names in golf, including three-time Masters champion Sam Snead. He designed the Barksdale Air Force Base golf course after joining the military in 1933 and served as its first pro. He defeated future U.S. Open champion Tommy Bolt in the Ark-La-Tex Amateur in 1935 and organized local LPGA events.

Oree's three daughters remained active in the golf community into adulthood, as did the entire family. Whenever the extended family got together, they played golf. Cox grew up assuming it was the same for every family.

He and Valerie disagreed on a lot of things, as mothers and sons can do, but they never disagreed on how best to fix what was wrong with his game. The reason for that was simple: Her advice was always spot-on.

All three Marsalis girls were accomplished junior players, but there weren't many opportunities for girls to compete in the 1950s and early 1960s. Oree made sure his girls played in regional and even national competitions whenever possible, but he wasn't always able to afford to send them to the two national tournaments the AJGA sponsored for girls every summer.

Valerie, Pam, and Debbie Marsalis could usually be found at Querbes Park Golf Course near downtown Shreveport. For the Marsalis girls and the gang of boys they played with, Querbes's tight, tree-lined fairways and postage-stamp greens were their personal playground.

The seventh, eighth, and ninth holes were nearest the clubhouse, and they would play them over and over again in the gloaming, when they had the course to themselves except for the mosquitoes and cicadas. You had to know your game to find your ball in the dark, which was the objective. Anybody who still had her ball when the club pro, a family friend, shone his flashlight to guide them back to the pro shop would be declared the winner.

Oree spent as much time on the driving range, or "Idiot Hill" as he called it. Oree was available to anybody and everybody. He spent hours working with his daughters, telling them to imagine that they were 150 yards from the hole, and that a huge tree branch hung over the bunker that guarded the front edge of the green. The girls would dutifully tell him what club they would use and where and how hard they would hit it before executing the shot. Then he would dream up some other scenario and they would start all over again.

Valerie met Elmo, Cox's father, on the driving range at Querbes. They played a lot of golf early in their marriage. Kris was two weeks overdue when Valerie, tired of resting, played eighteen holes. As an infant, Cox, an only child, spent as much time in a golf cart as he did in a baby carriage.

Valerie and Elmo played every Saturday. As Kris got older, Valerie bought him a set of youth clubs and let him play when they got close to the green.

Oree took his grandson out to a lighted par-3 course after work, where they played until the course closed down for the night. At a young age Kris became proficient enough to play with his grandfather and his grandfather's friends in their weekly game. "Don't tell your grandmother," Oree would whisper while slipping Kris his share of the winnings after a successful round.

When it became clear that Cox was a gifted young player, Valerie made sure he had the opportunities to play tournament golf that were mostly unavailable to women of her generation.

Cox's respect for his mother grew along with his exposure to competitive junior golf. He was eating lunch with several other players after an AJGA tournament round when the father of one of the participants charged into the room and hurled a sandwich he had purchased from a vending machine at his son. "You don't deserve a real lunch after the round you just played," he said. Valerie, on the other hand, was always encouraging, stressing sportsmanship above all else. She wouldn't tolerate Kris losing his temper. Playing a bad round was part of the game. She always knew what to say, especially after a subpar round. Usually, it was something like "You want to go to the water park?"

Valerie had heard how intimidating and aloof Holder could be and did not want Kris to attend Oklahoma State. No way her son was going to play for Mike Holder. She wanted Kris to go to Stanford, but when he scored 1050 on his SAT, 150 points below the required score for admittance, he picked OSU. She respected his choice and did her best to hide her displeasure.

But she slowly came to trust and respect Holder, as most parents do. Still, she remained a central figure in Cox's career, helping him work out the kinks over the phone when she didn't travel to tournaments to watch him from the gallery.

It was Valerie who was most responsible for her son emerging as a key member of Oklahoma State's national-championship-contending team.

Cox was floundering during his sophomore year in the spring of 1993. He was frustrated with Holder and struggling to make the starting lineup. Valerie confronted her son on the twelfth hole of the golf course across the street from the home she and Elmo had recently bought after relocating to San Antonio.

"What are you afraid of?" she asked him.

"What are you talking about?" Cox wanted to know.

"Why are you so afraid to succeed?"

"You're crazy," Cox shot back, angrily.

"You're the only one holding yourself back," she said.

Kris got mad. Valerie got mad. It wasn't until the spring semester that he cooled down and fully understood what she meant and what his struggles and doubt during the fall semester had really been about.

He had the tools. He had had the instruction. It was time to quit worrying about the possibility of failure. It was time to go play.

That's what he had been doing ever since, and that's what he did on the first nine holes of the second round of the John Burns. Cox and Westerberg made the turn at 3 under, Bratton and Kuehne were both minus 2, and even Robertson, playing for Tidland, was 1 under.

The Cowboys' composite score was 10 under with nine holes to play. Despite an array of poor play on the back nine, OSU finished

224 · THE LAST PUTT

the second round with a more than respectable aggregate score of minus 1, which had them looking down at the rest of the field for the second straight day.

Instead of falling farther behind, Wally Goodwin's team made a bold move, picking up 5 shots on the Cowboys to move into a second-place tie with Arizona and New Mexico.

As would become a trademark throughout his career, Tiger would follow a poor round with a stellar round. He was almost constitutionally incapable of stringing together two poor rounds, so he followed his 75 with a tidy 68, the lowest score of the day. Martin bounced back with a 72 and Yanagisawa with a 71. More important, Begay followed his 69 with a 71 to hold the thirty-six-hole lead, a 1-stroke edge over Cox and two others.

That was the good news. What was not so good was Burdick's 75. In five rounds in Hawaii, Burdick had yet to shoot even par or better.

Still, the Cardinal were 3 shots back and within striking distance.

So, here they were again, Stanford and Oklahoma State slugging it out for the team title. It was increasingly clear with each passing tournament that these two teams were the class of college golf.

Surveying the leaderboard, Goodwin knew what had been obvious since the Ping Preview at the Scarlet Course. "It's us and them," he admitted, if only to himself.

If Stanford or Oklahoma State wanted to send a message to the other team, the time was now. A Stanford win would even the regular-season rivalry before the teams met for the final time during the regular season at the Sun Devil Intercollegiate in Tempe, Arizona, in mid-April. An Oklahoma State victory would be their third straight against Stanford and would ensure that they would capture the season series, which would be especially impressive without Tidland.

The Cowboys teed off at 7:30 the next morning in a steady light rain. The first green was already saturated around the cup and the rain steadily worsened. Through seven holes, OSU was 1 over. Stanford was making the turn at plus 2 when the weather became too much of a factor. Play was suspended at 10:30 A.M.

Just when it appeared that nothing could get between the Cardinal and the Cowboys, Mother Nature sent both teams back to their neutral corners. The rain showed no indications of lessening a half-hour later, and tournament officials canceled the final round. Scores would revert to the thirty-six-hole total, and champions would be assessed from there.

And like that, Oklahoma State had a tournament victory—albeit an incomplete one.

Stanford had to chew on a frustrating second-place finish, with the feeling of not having gotten their true shot. The cancellation of the final round, however, meant Begay was individual champion.

It was Oklahoma State's fourth straight tournament victory, the first time a Holder-coached team had accomplished that feat since 1987. The Cowboys' rare run of dominance included six tournament wins in eight chances.

It wouldn't be the last time Mother Nature intervened between the Cardinal and the Cowboys. Nor would it be the last time they saw each other. They'd stayed at the same hotel complex all week and by now were far too familiar with each other.

As bags were zipped up and packed, and as the teams bade farewell to the Aloha State, Casey Martin didn't want to let the moment pass. He was beginning to get a little miffed that the defending national champs couldn't seem to gain an edge on Oklahoma State. They all knew each other well, from junior golf through their college days, so Martin was mostly joking when he told OSU's players, "We'll settle this later on; we'll see you guys at the Sun Devil." The Sun Devil was the last time Oklahoma State and Stanford would play in the same tournament before the NCAAs. If it qualified as "smack talk" in golf, it was lighthearted. But Holder detected something else—a Stanford team with something on their minds. "They're keeping an eye on us all the time," he told his players. "They are the defending champions, but whether they want to acknowledge it or not, they feel like we're the team to beat."

# 9

## Rough Spring

*Masters*
*Augusta, Georgia*
*April 3–9, 1995*

NOBODY PLANNED on the spring of 1995 unfolding so awkwardly for the Cardinal. Rather, it promised golden days: Tiger would play in his first Masters, Notah and Casey would finish their five-year journey together, and seniors Burdick and Yanagisawa would help the team take aim at another national title.

When the team got back from Hawaii, there was a brief reacquaintance with the campus, and then another tournament in a busy spring: the Duck Invitational at Eugene (Oregon) Country Club in early March, a sort of homecoming for Martin, who grew up defying expectations at Eugene C.C., his family's home club. It would be a fun trip, as King and Melinda Martin opened their home to the team, as did neighbors on the Martins' street. Casey and Notah, naturally, would stay at the Martin home, and they took in the freshman, too. Of course, Tiger was sent upstairs, to the family loft, where there was no bed, only a small desk. They made him sleep in a sleeping bag, too. The kid may have been only six weeks away from playing at Augusta National, but Martin and Begay wanted to flex whatever remaining power they had as seniors over a freshman. Tiger flexed back, in his own way. Each night they stayed at the Martin home, he would spend long sessions on the family phone talking about swing mechanics with Butch Harmon, his high-profile swing coach, who was based in Houston. Always, his teammates noted, Tiger was focused on getting better.

Stanford not only won the sixteen-team tournament, but Begay pulled a fast one on his buddy who grew up at Eugene C.C. With rounds of 70 and 68, Begay won the individual title in the thirty-six-hole tournament. It was his second consecutive tournament win. Begay was humming.

Two other things of note from the Duck Invitational: Again, Burdick failed to break par, posting a 75 and a 73 to finish tied for fourteenth. And Yanagisawa did not make the trip, owing to a major school project he needed to finish. Instead, Jerry Chang played for Stanford and shot 80-74 to finish tie-45th.

Chang was an intriguing player for Goodwin. He'd proved his worth as a walk-on from Westlake Village, California, for Goodwin in 1993, the year Begay and Martin redshirted. That year, Burdick and Chang were Goodwin's main guns, but Chang, a quiet and studious sort, faded back out of the starting five when Begay and Martin returned from their redshirt years. When Burdick got off to a sluggish start to his spring, however, Goodwin began to take a closer look at Chang's game. It would bear watching as the NCAAs approached.

For Yanagisawa to miss the Duck Invitational for academic reasons was not a big deal for Goodwin or the team. He was open with Goodwin and his teammates about his challenge to carve his academic place at Stanford.

When Yanagisawa transferred from Irvine in the winter of 1993, the adjustment was not an easy one. To play Division I golf for Irvine was one thing; to do it within the competitive academic climate of Stanford was another. Yanagisawa would only recognize it a year later, but he put himself under enormous pressure right away. He wanted to fit in with his teammates but knew he was the "new guy" and hadn't been on the same journeys as Begay, Martin, or Burdick. He hadn't been recruited by Stanford, didn't have that same sheen as the others. Although he shot 64 in his first practice session with the team, he was a redshirt and didn't bond as tightly as if he were on the traveling team. On top of that, he felt pressure to succeed academically, to make sure the admissions department hadn't made a mistake.

It didn't help that his first roommate, a mechanical engineering major, was not only a great student but an odd duck, to boot. A standard weeknight included the roommate lighting a marijuana joint around 10:00 P.M. on the dorm roof, then descending to his room, where around 1:00 A.M. he would attack a fluid dynamics upper-division problem, the sort of problem that takes some a week to solve. Yanagisawa's roomie would solve it by 3:00 A.M. He'd celebrate by lighting up another joint and call Domino's with the same order: pepperoni, jalapeños, and extra cheese. To top off the vibe, he'd darken the room and play house and trance music at high volume.

Yanagisawa had a little trouble relating to that scene.

He'd work twice as hard—minus the joint, pizza, and trance music—and not match his roommate's grades, which were never lower than an A minus. His confidence took a hit, and his mood worsened. He would sometimes drive off into the hills west of campus, just wanting or needing to be alone. By the end of his first two quarters at Stanford, Goodwin knew there was something wrong with Yanagisawa. He suggested Yanagisawa seek the counsel of doctors, and they confirmed what both Goodwin and Yanagisawa thought: He was clinically depressed.

Ever since he was a boy taking instruction in the back of his parents' Long Beach golf shop, Yanagisawa was someone who absorbed learning. So, when the Stanford doctors told him how to combat depression and meet it head-on, he complied. He worked at being less hard on himself and at accepting things. After the summer of '93, Yanagisawa returned to campus feeling refreshed, more confident, and more ready for the challenges of Stanford.

Clearly, his teammates treated him more as an equal. Begay was one of the first at Stanford to wear wraparound Oakleys, a very mid-nineties look. He liked to wear amber-shaded glasses, for reasons both aesthetic and athletic. He thought they were cool, and they helped his vision. Yanagisawa wanted to join the party, too. He requested some Oakleys, only he asked for clear lenses. When he put them on and then actually played wearing them, Begay broke up laughing.

"You look like a chemist!" he laughed. "Where's your Bunsen burner?"

To get needled by Begay was a mark that you were one of the boys. It all played out in Yanagisawa's excellent junior year, and in that epic final round at Stonebridge at the '94 NCAAs. He wasn't just making it at Stanford; he was an All-American—and he was named Stanford's 1994 Pac-10 Male Athlete of the Year.

Now, in the spring of 1995, he was confident enough to miss a tournament for schoolwork and would rejoin the team at their next tournament in Los Angeles.

The schedule was fast and furious, but so far, so good for Stanford. With Yanagisawa back in the starting five, the Cardinal won its second consecutive tournament when it captured the sixteen-team Cleveland Golf/Southwestern Intercollegiate hosted by USC at North Ranch Country Club in Westlake Village.

Tournament organizers hyped Tiger's return to Southern California in the newspapers and predicted galleries in the thousands, but L.A. lived up to its image as a blasé sports town. Fewer than one hundred fans—Earl and Tida Woods among them, making the hour-plus drive from Orange County—followed Tiger as he finished, shooting rounds of 75-72-72. In three consecutive tournaments now Tiger had posted a 75, which was unusual.

Between the mugging in late November, the arthroscopic surgery in the winter to remove the cysts, and his relatively mediocre play, some were right to wonder if the kid was entirely healthy. But with Tiger, Goodwin figured, it's all relative. The freshman had not finished lower than a tie for ninth in any of his eight starts this year, and he'd won two and lost a playoff for a third, so alarm bells weren't ringing.

The same couldn't be said for Burdick, who again was Stanford's lowest finisher with rounds of 77-76-74. The senior, an All-American two years ago, hadn't shot lower than 73 in all ten competitive rounds of 1995. Burdick knew he was dragging the team down. It began in Hawaii, when he was nagged by thoughts that the Cardinal maybe weren't as unstoppable as he thought, watching Oklahoma State up close in the islands.

Personally, he found himself edging toward self-doubt.

Goodwin always thought that of all his excellent seniors, Steve Burdick possessed the best skill set to make it in golf over the long haul. Burdick's pretty, rhythmic swing was one reason. The bigger reason was Burdick's mind. He was always calm, always in control. His metronomic ball striking was a product of a steady focus and concentration. He may not have owned the most newsworthy background story—just a supertalented kid who played golf at his father's knee at a young age in the rural Northern California community of Graeagle Meadows—but he had all the tools to be a successful pro player.

Burdick thought so, too. By his senior year, he'd accomplished a lot: national champion with the '94 team, first-team All-Pac-10 in his sophomore year of 1993, when he won two individual titles, the Husky Invitational and the Southwestern Intercollegiate. He also made third-team All-American in '93, when he competed at NCAAs as an individual. That was the year Notah and Casey redshirted, so Burdick and Jerry Chang carried much of the load for an overmatched Stanford team. Burdick was the best player on the team that year, and by his senior year he had the respect of his fellow seniors as the most consistent ball striker on the team.

The only consistency in his spring thus far, though, had to do with his own negative thoughts.

A quick turnaround saw Stanford board a flight for Atlanta, where Georgia Tech and its All-American, college golf's number-two-ranked player, Stewart Cink, awaited. The Cardinal were set to play in the fifteen-team Carpet Capital Classic at the Farm in Dalton, Georgia, hosted by Tech. But first, an exhibition had been set up between Tech and Stanford, a one-day match-play format at Druid Hills Golf Club in Atlanta, before the teams traveled on to play in the tournament. The match was billed as a college golf exhibition between two powerhouse schools, but really it was a chance for Atlanta golf fans to see Tiger in person the week before the Masters; secondarily, it was a chance for Cink, a decorated player, to match up against college golf's most famous player on his home turf. Georgia Tech coach Puggy Blackmon and Goodwin were friends, and they arranged the one-day match for fun and competition, even though Stanford would be traveling almost straight from Los Angeles.

Blackmon's Yellow Jackets were ranked number six in the country, but he knew the arrival of Stanford meant college golf royalty was on its way.

"This might be the best team I've seen in college golf since I've been coaching," Blackmon said. "Potentially, they've got five first- and second-team All-Americans. You've basically got two teams that are dominant in college golf this year—Oklahoma State and Stanford. Then there are the rest of us."

Advance publicity and the Masters tie-in led to a surge of interest in the exhibition, and some fifteen hundred fans lined the first fairway to watch Tiger and Cink tee off. Tiger got the added benefit of a Fulton County sheriff walking with him all day, for crowd control.

Again, though, Tiger didn't turn in a star performance. Cink, motivated by his home turf and gunning for Woods all the way, beat the freshman, 3 and 2, with a dazzling display, including six birdies and a 66. Tiger was gracious afterward, calling Cink's performance a "buzz saw," and dismissed any notions of jet lag—the team hadn't arrived at their hotel until 3:00 A.M.—or an unfamiliar golf course. Cink was a quiet and modest player but did serve notice for the upcoming NCAA Championships when he said after the match, "Even though Tiger's gotten a lot of publicity, there are other players out there that are good."

At the next day's Carpet Capital Classic, Woods again shot 75 in the first round—the fourth consecutive college tournament in which he posted a 75. This time, a bogey on seventeen and a double on eighteen undid him, and he blew past reporters to hit balls on the range until he figured out his swing.

His length off the tee, however, remained an attraction. On the

566-yard ninth hole at the Farm, again playing with Cink, Tiger launched his drive an estimated 50 yards past that of Cink, who himself was a bomber in college. Tiger's ensuing 3-wood landed greenside, and the people in the gallery, many of whom were members of the club, were suitably awed by the rare occurrence of driver–3-wood reaching the hole.

The end of fifty-four holes dealt Stanford another ding to its confidence: Riding a second-round 65, Cink won the individual title and led Georgia Tech to the team title. Tiger again finished second to Cink, this time after roaring back with a 69 in the second round and a 72 in the third, but Stanford's supporting cast did not play well.

Burdick went 76-76-78 to continue his downward spiral.

Goodwin and the team packed up to fly back to California but left behind two team members: Tiger, who would make the two-hour drive to Augusta; and Notah, who was tagging along as Tiger's guest. The rest of the Stanford team flew back, wondering just what had happened to their unbeatable aura.

Goodwin, meanwhile, was wondering if he had to make a lineup change.

Tiger Woods arrived on the grounds of Augusta National as a nineteen-year-old college freshman with typically big dreams: to win the 1995 Masters. It was entirely in Tiger's mind to have 1994 champion Jose Maria Olazabal slip the green jacket over the skinny shoulders of the kid from Cypress, California.

He told his teammates as much in the months leading up to the tournament. He took his invitation so seriously, he practiced putting on the lacquered hardwood floors of Stanford's Maples Pavilion, where the men's and women's basketball teams played, the better to approximate the lightning-fast greens of Augusta National. Tiger kept up his practice on the road, too. When Stanford traveled, he'd find the slickest surface in any hotel area—sometimes in the lobby—and practice putting there. His teammates would tease him, and Tiger took the needling but always maintained he was practicing because he was heading there on a business trip. Burdick, in particular, rolled his eyes at the grandiosity of the statements. But he envied Tiger's confidence. Burdick began thinking to himself that maybe he needed the same kind of hubris to lift his game, only he couldn't seem to find it.

Perhaps Tiger's mediocre—for him—spring season thus far could be attributed to his singular focus on playing the Masters. He earned the invitation by rallying for the now famous improbable win over Trip Kuehne at the U.S. Amateur at Sawgrass the previous August, and when interviewed by journalists from all over the world—Europe, Australia, the United States—he repeated what he told his teammates: He wanted to win.

When the world's best players arrived amid the dogwood and azaleas, Tiger got a vote of confidence from another of Butch Harmon's pupils. Greg Norman, the world's best player, told the media he thought Tiger had the talent to win. Norman was always kind to Tiger, confident enough in his own skills to welcome the arrival of another star and not feel overtly threatened.

If he was going to have a memorable Masters, it got off to a quick start: Tiger's practice-round partner on Monday was none other than Nick Faldo. Faldo was a five-time major champion in the spring of 1995, including the 1989 and 1990 Masters. Famously impressed with himself and few others, Faldo witnessed Tiger's length off the tee up close and was forced after his practice round to feed the media opinions of the wunderkind. Particularly of interest was Augusta National's famous par-5 fifteenth hole, where Faldo smoked a drive 275 yards, dead center, only to see Tiger airmail him with a 330-yard drive. That Tiger then used a 9-iron to 15 feet and made the eagle putt had the media all atwitter, considering that even the great Jack Nicklaus routinely hit mid-iron into fifteen, even in his prime. Cornered in the grillroom after his round, Faldo offered: "His shoulders are impressively quick; that's where he gets his power. He's young, and he has great elasticity. He's just a very talented kid; let's leave it at that."

The media were forced to get Faldo's opinions because Tiger, in an early misstep, ignored the media after his Monday practice round. He knew he had a Tuesday press conference set up, so he didn't think he needed to talk on Monday. Veteran scribes frowned upon the kid's insouciance, and Tiger received some knocks in the next day's papers. It continued on Tuesday when Tiger, in the opinion of some, didn't show proper reverence for the Masters. He told the media that Magnolia Lane was a shorter drive than he expected and the clubhouse smaller than he thought. He spoke of the cramped quarters at the Crow's Nest, the tiny living accommodations for the amateurs who were playing their first Masters. Some thought he was being unappreciative, showing a lack of respect for the august tournament that was the Masters. To Tiger, he was just giving his first impressions.

Outwardly, he didn't seem to care what anybody else thought. Inwardly, he was treasuring the moment. Trip Kuehne knew that.

The old combatants from Sawgrass weren't there to reprise old battles or, with the NCAA Championships just seven weeks away, engage in bluster about the brewing Stanford–Oklahoma State rivalry. The Masters would be a respite from all that. They would use the opportunity to rekindle old friendships. As painful as Sawgrass was for Kuehne, the fact was, the Woods family and the Kuehne family had a ton of history. Earl and Ernie had watched their junior players grow up in AJGA events, and the boys had bonded through the years. Tiger phoned Hank Kuehne in Stillwater after learning of the accident that had almost cost him his life. He continued to call, offering support to Hank as he began the long process of rehabilitation.

Eight months after Sawgrass, they would share this moment — the fulfillment of every amateur golfer's dream. They knew playing in the Masters for the first time would be like nothing else they had experienced. They anticipated the wonder, but nothing could have prepared them for the reality.

Tiger arrived Sunday at dusk and quickly grabbed his putter and some balls and went directly to the putting green to test the greens, see how they compared to Maples Pavilion. Trip arrived Monday, and he and Tiger bunked in the thirty-by-forty-foot room atop the clubhouse with the other amateurs. For Tiger, the unglamorous sleep accommodations recalled hitting the futon on the floor on his

Stanford recruiting trip. This place was a little different, though. All over the Crow's Nest were books and photos and sketches of great Masters moments. Plus, they could climb a ladder to an eleven-foot-by-eleven-foot cupola, from which they could view the grounds. There was also a sitting area with a game table, a sofa, chairs, a TV, and a telephone.

Tiger and Trip played cards at night and on one adventurous evening, in the tradition of most amateurs who have stayed at the Crow's Nest, snuck down into the Champions Room. If the Masters was golf's most exclusive invitation, the Champions Room was truly for members only. To get a locker in the Champions Room, one only need do one thing: win the Masters. Trip and Tiger were inside the tiny room, gazing at the lockers for Nicklaus and Palmer, Player and Ballesteros. They were surprised to find a computer in the room and joked with each other that they didn't figure "old" players like Masters champs would use a computer. They checked out the stats and scorecards of past champions and took a deep whiff of the entire aromatic scene.

For Trip, the idea of playing at Bobby Jones's home was powerful.

Jones remained the paragon of American amateur golf, a sensational champion who never turned pro. Unlike many of his peers, Kuehne wasn't sure he wanted the travel and grind of a professional golf life. The idea of playing top-flight amateur golf while pursuing a business career appealed to him, and the memory of Jones's accomplishments, driven home to Trip at Augusta National, were inspirational.

If it surprised outsiders to see Sawgrass's famous combatants laughing, joking, and hanging around, they didn't know Trip and Tiger. The two even took time to hook up for a practice round after lunch on Monday, following Tiger's morning eighteen with Faldo. They played for the handsome sum of $5, and in an unfortunate—for Kuehne—reprise of Sawgrass, Tiger ground out a par and closed out Trip on the eighteenth hole for the sawbuck, and for bragging rights—again.

On the Wednesday night before the boys were to play in the '95

Masters, Earl Woods and Jay Brunza visited the Crow's Nest. Kuehne didn't have to be told. He vacated, to leave the three alone. When he returned to the Crow's Nest, he likened Tiger's look to a look Michael Jordan might have before scoring fifty points. Trip knew the look. It was a different side of Tiger, the "coldness" that Earl coached into him. Trip always knew that when the round was over, though, the friendly Tiger would return.

When Thursday morning came, Kuehne succumbed to the difficulty and the pressure, shooting 79-76 to miss the cut.

For Tiger, the golf went well. He didn't win, but with rounds of 72-72-77-72 he was low amateur and made his first cut at a PGA Tour event after going 0 for 7 as a high schooler playing tour events on sponsor's exemptions. He finished tied for forty-first and left a bigger impression by landing atop the statistical leaderboard as longest off the tee in the entire field. "I need binoculars," said Olazabal, who played with Tiger in the first two rounds, "to see where he hit the ball."

His farewell press conference went much better than his first. Calling to mind the letter he wrote to Wally Goodwin in the spring of 1989, Tiger told the media he'd written a letter to Augusta National Golf Club. He read it aloud to them:

> Please accept my sincere thanks for providing me the opportunity to experience the most wonderful week of my life. It was Fantasyland and Disney World wrapped into one.
>
> I was treated like a gentleman throughout my stay, and I trust I responded in kind. The "Crow's Nest" will always remain in my heart, and your magnificent golf course will provide a continuing challenge throughout my amateur and professional career.
>
> I've accomplished much more here and learned even more. Your tournament will always hold a special spot in my heart as the place where I made my first PGA cut, and at a major yet! It is here that I left my youth behind and became a man. For that I will be eternally in your debt.
>
> With warmest regards and deepest appreciation, I remain,
> Sincerely,
> Tiger Woods

He added one more thing to a reporter in private before he left. "You know," he said, "this place is perfect for me."

Before he left the grounds, Tiger was asked how he would handle the mental transition from Augusta National to the obscurity of college golf, how he would handle, essentially, going from Broadway to off-Broadway.

"Playing college golf is not quite the same as playing Augusta," he said. "College golf is fine for me, though. I have a lot of friends out there. It's going to be a blast playing with my teammates again, traveling with the team."

Saying those words was one thing. Leaving Augusta in such a rush—he said he planned to attend a history class at 9:00 A.M. on Monday—was another. If there was such a thing as day-after-Christmas blues in golf, Tiger was a prime candidate.

Here is where Goodwin had a decision to make. Cognizant that Tiger had played in three tournaments in three weeks, the third being the draining spectacle that was the Masters, he could have left Tiger at home when the Stanford team was set to fly to Tempe, Arizona, to play in the ASU Thunderbird Intercollegiate at Arizona State's Karsten Golf Course. He actually thought about it, too. But something else was gnawing at the coach. The NCAA Championships were just six weeks away, and Stanford had lost its mental edge over Oklahoma State. The Thunderbird was the last gathering of top talent before the NCAA Championships. The Cowboys would be there, and Goodwin knew it was a chance for the Cardinal to wrest back some of the psychological edge and momentum before they all met again in Columbus.

Holder felt all along that Goodwin and his team were preoccupied with Oklahoma State, and Goodwin was about to prove him right. Goodwin was caught up in the rivalry. Even though it was a debatable decision, he decided to bring Tiger to Tempe, where tournament officials were already hard at work preparing to accommodate him. Gallery ropes were strung for the first time in the event's twenty-three years. Marshals would accompany Tiger's group in an attempt to control the crowds.

There was the requisite press conference for Tiger in Tempe before the event began, but there were other concerns, too. Burdick still hadn't found his game, and Yanagisawa and Martin, too, were having mediocre springs. Only Begay seemed truly sharp, and it showed when he bounced back from an opening-round 75 to shoot scores of 70 and 71 and finish tied for sixth individually. But fatigue caught up to Tiger when he followed rounds of 70 and 71 with a 79, his worst round as a collegian. Goodwin feared he'd worn out his star freshman and still had Stanford's marquee event of the spring—the Stanford U.S. Intercollegiate hosted by Stanford, where Tiger would make his home debut—the very next week.

Moreover, Martin (72-79-77) tied for fifty-eighth, Yanagisawa (79-73-77) tied for sixty-fourth, and Burdick, again, brought up the rear, sandwiching a second-round 72 with rounds of 79 and 81. The good news was, in the second round, Burdick shot level par for the first time all spring. The bad news was, he'd followed it with an 81. Poetically, it left him in a tie-81st in the field.

Worse, Oklahoma State—again—finished ahead of Stanford. Neither team won, though. That honor went to Arkansas, which was looking more and more like a national title contender. Host ASU finished second, and then Holder's Cowboys third.

Stanford, tired and losing steam, finished sixth.

Notably, it was the first time neither Stanford nor Oklahoma State won a tournament when both had entered. Previously, Stanford had won two; Oklahoma State, four. That either team had won six of the seven joint tournaments entered was more than just a statement on the rivalry—it was a statement about their joint dominance of the sport's landscape, which was rare indeed.

Casey Martin thought when the two teams left Hawaii that the Thunderbird would be a great chance to land a blow to OSU. Stanford would be in the swing of spring, the tournament would be held at a Pac-10 venue, and Stanford was too good, too talented, to be denied three times by the same team. After seeing the result in Tempe, Martin told himself: *OK, then. No more talking.*

If there was good news for Stanford, it was that the Cowboys, for the first time in four months, looked more vulnerable than they had since the Preview.

Holder's team had been building confidence and chemistry that are rare in college golf—or any sport, for that matter. Riding that, they posted a run of dominance that made those who considered Stanford the superior team rethink their assessments.

From the Golf World Intercollegiate in Hilton Head, South Carolina, the previous November, through the Golf Digest Invitational at the TPC at the Woodlands in Texas in March, the Cowboys won five straight tournaments and appeared poised to break the record of seven straight wins set by the 1987 Oklahoma State team that featured E. J. Pfister and Brian Watts. The five-win streak ended when the Cowboys fell to sixth at the Morris Williams Intercollegiate in Austin, Texas, and tied for second at the twelve-team Ping/American Invitational at MacGregor Downs in Cary, North Carolina, the following week.

They arrived in Tempe hoping to pick up their eighth team title of the season, which would position them to break the school record of ten tournament titles in a season.

The tournament called for the Cowboys to play thirty-six holes on the opening day, and they ran out of gas late in their second round, finishing in the dark after ten-plus hours on the golf course. Once again, the Karsten Course's closing holes—the sixteenth in particular—played a role in Oklahoma State's demise. Trip finished with a triple bogey on fifteen and a quadruple on sixteen. Kris was 3 under on the fifteenth tee box and finished 1 over. Leif doubled eighteen. Alan finished the last three holes at plus 4 as Holder's team staggered toward the clubhouse.

A third round played in extremely windy conditions made it difficult for either Stanford or Oklahoma State to make up ground. Neither team was able to win the tournament, but the Cowboys held serve by finishing ahead of the Cardinal in the overall standings.

From Stanford's point of view, Goodwin's plan backfired. Whatever momentum they hoped to gain by winning the tournament—or at least finishing ahead of Oklahoma State—evaporated in the desert heat, and Goodwin couldn't escape the feeling that his number-one player might have benefited more by not playing at all.

· · ·

The Stanford U.S. Intercollegiate, set for the following week at Stanford, was more than just Tiger's fifth tournament in five weeks. It was Tiger's homecoming.

He'd been at Stanford seven months now and had yet to play an event in the Bay Area. The only golf fans in Northern California who had a chance to see Tiger play were his teammates, who played practice rounds with him at Stanford Golf Course, or the members of the various private clubs in the area Stanford would use for practice.

So, for Tiger to play at Stanford, in front of fans, in live competition, figured to be a highlight. The rest of his life at Stanford had all fallen into place nicely. He loved the classes, the campus, the stimulation he got from other students. He even briefly pledged Sigma Chi fraternity before school and golf proved too much for him and he dropped out. Encouraged by his guardian angel Begay—or guardian devil, as the joke might go—Tiger still went to the parties, though. He seemed to enjoy them immensely, but not as much as his teammates enjoyed watching him hit the dance floor. Many were the times Casey Martin and the crew would see Tiger begin to dance, then jockey for position on a staircase, the better to get an aerial view of the kinetic pyrotechnics, which were unanimously judged to be both hilarious and horrifying at the same time. One nickname for Tiger was "Dynamite," because he resembled a man blowing up TNT. The boys roared in laughter. Any chance they had to get one over on the best amateur player in the world, they took the opportunity.

The word was out that the great Tiger Woods, the U.S. Amateur champion, fresh off the Masters, was set to play for Stanford at the Intercollegiate April 21–23. Goodwin had seen enough of the media interest in Tiger at every tournament that year, and figured in the added attraction of the Masters, when he went to the athletic department to warn them of something they'd never thought of: a crowd at a college golf tournament. Normally, a college golf tournament played out in front of girlfriends and family members. Goodwin wanted staffed supervision for parking and crowd control. The athletic department's response boiled down to, essentially,

"Yeah, sure, let's wait and see." When Goodwin got a call at his office from a youth group in underprivileged East Palo Alto, saying a group of a hundred kids wanted passes to come see Tiger play, Goodwin hung up the phone and said to Sara Hallock, his aide, "We're going to have a problem with the crowds this year."

Game day came—and so did the people. Hundreds of them poured into the golf course area, which was a problem, as the parking lot at Stanford Golf Course held room for about seventy-five cars. It quickly got out of control, and Goodwin collared Hallock and the sports information director, Gary Migdol, to funnel cars into a field adjacent to the second fairway. They were making it up as they went along. As the crowds found Tiger and followed him, the three of them had to hold up yellow rope, the better to create space between the freshman and his adoring fans.

Round one went fine. Tiger shot 73, and Begay, as was his wont, stole the show with an opening 66. Casey was good, too, shooting 68. Even Burdick shot 72. The only misstep came from Yanagisawa, who shot 76, but that score was dropped and Stanford was off to a roaring start to its own tournament.

The trouble came on day two. With even more fans pouring into Stanford to see the kid—some estimates were as high as two thousand—Tiger felt a pain rip through his right shoulder on his opening tee shot of the day.

Five consecutive weeks of competitive golf had finally exacted their tariff. Tiger had strained his rotator cuff.

Goodwin could tell something was wrong with him. So could Hallock, when Tiger kept asking for Tylenol, and she gave him two on the tenth tee. Ten is an uphill par 4 that starts by the Stanford clubhouse. It's a natural gathering point for spectators, near the parking lot, too. Goodwin walked up to his freshman after his tee shot.

"How's it going?" he asked.

"Not too good," Tiger answered.

Goodwin walked with him up the hill on ten, and after Tiger turned around to play the downhill, short par-4 eleventh, he approached Goodwin.

"Coach," he said, "I can't play anymore. I've got to withdraw."

Goodwin didn't waste any time. He grabbed Tiger by the arm and sneaked him through the bushes before the twelfth tee. Twelve is a signature hole at Stanford; the longest par 4 on the course, at 473 yards, it also features two massive oak trees in the center of the fairway that cause all sorts of decision-making quandaries. It would be fun to watch Tiger play the hole, most fans thought. The crowd waiting on twelve . . . just kept waiting.

Many of the dismayed fans did what unsatisfied customers do — they simply left. It didn't matter that the tournament was still going on, that there were twenty-seven college golf teams still playing, that teams as talented as Arizona State and Cal and Tulsa and Pepperdine were trying to ply their craft. About 80 percent of the fans split the scene, streaming across the ninth fairway and the seventh fairway as they walked to their cars. The rest of the players were irate at the exodus. They had to stop their games to allow for spectators to stroll across their fairways. Some of the players even fired golf balls in anger in the direction of the patrons.

If there was a metaphor for the downside of the Tiger Phenomenon, it was that scene: His star power attracted fans who ignored the greater notion of the game just to see Tiger.

After he withdrew from the tournament, he showed up in the final round to encourage his teammates. He watched Yanagisawa play the par-5 seventh hole and saw him struggle. He walked to Yanagisawa on the fairway. He asked if everything was OK and gave Will a pat on the back and some words of encouragement. When Yanagisawa stitched together a final-round 70, Tiger greeted him with a hug at the end of the round.

"I'm proud of you," he said.

Yanagisawa thought it an odd thing for a teammate to say, until later when he thought of it. Those were the same words with which Earl Woods used to greet Tiger after every round, good or bad. Yanagisawa felt touched by the gesture.

The Intercollegiate did end on a happy note for Stanford. Martin's pair of 69s in the final two rounds netted him a 10-under 206, and his first individual title of his senior year, on his home course.

Begay overcame a second-round 75 to shoot 69 in the third round and finish third, continuing his excellent spring. Yanagisawa threw up a pair of 70s to finish tie-15th. And even though Burdick shot 72 in the first and third rounds, his second-round 80 again was a red flag in Goodwin's mind.

With the Pac-10 Championships in Richland, Washington, set for the next week, and the West Regionals three weeks later, Goodwin was facing some decisions.

First, he would have to accept the very real possibility that Tiger Woods would miss the Pac-10s because of his rotator cuff injury. More profoundly, Goodwin was wondering something he never thought he would have to wonder.

He was wondering if Steve Burdick's spot in the starting five was hurting the Stanford golf team.

While the Cardinal lineup was in flux, the Cowboys' was set in stone. The grind of weekly qualifying was gone. Holder and everybody else who followed college golf knew exactly who Oklahoma State's best players were. Alan Bratton, Chris Tidland, Trip Kuehne, Kris Cox, and Leif Westerberg had been the Cowboys' starting five for most of the past two seasons, and their dominance changed many of the preseason opinions about whether Stanford or Oklahoma State was the best team in the country.

Based largely on their back-to-back wins over Stanford in Hawaii and their five straight tournament titles, the Cowboys emerged as the number-one team in the nation in the latest *Golf World* poll. Stanford was second.

Before the season started, several media outlets had speculated that Stanford had not only the best team during the 1994–95 season, but perhaps the best of all time. A *Sports Illustrated* article published in the wake of the ASU Thunderbird Intercollegiate correctly pointed out that Holder's team now featured three of the top five players in college golf. Bratton, who had one tie for first and five other top-five finishes and a 71.58 scoring average, was ranked second in the National Player of the Year standings, behind Georgia Tech's Stewart Cink. Chris Tidland, who had not been ranked among the top fifty players in the country in the magazine's previous poll, now ranked fourth, one spot behind Woods, who was ranked number one heading into his first college season based largely on his U.S. Amateur title. Trip Kuehne was fifth.

The article went on to speculate that perhaps Oklahoma State, and not Stanford, could end up being considered the greatest in the history of college golf, and while such publicity was flattering, Oklahoma State players knew those words would forever haunt them unless they could back it up at nationals.

But first came the Big Eight Championships at Prairie Dunes in Hutchinson, Kansas, where Holder would attempt to win his twentieth Big Eight Conference crown. Only former Kansas basketball coach Phog Allen, who had won twenty-four conference titles, had won more Big Eight titles in any sport than Holder.

Winning the conference tournament was always a top priority for Holder, and his teams typically responded by dominating the field, but the Cowboys' grip on the conference had been slipping in recent years. Archrival Oklahoma had finished ahead of Oklahoma State for the first time in 1992. The Cowboys barely nipped Kansas by 1 stroke in 1993, and by 5 in '94.

The ninth-ranked Sooners appeared to be Oklahoma State's most formidable opponent in the 1995 Big Eight tournament, but Tidland and Bratton quickly put that notion to rest. The two seniors—and the two players most aware of the program's history of dominating conference opponents—turned in three stellar rounds to finish in a three-way tie for first and lead the Cowboys to a 22-shot lead over Kansas.

Alan and Chris had often talked about facing off in a playoff with an individual title on the line, and now here they were, at the end of highly decorated collegiate careers and at the top of their games, heading to the first playoff hole to fulfill yet another goal together. Just then, tournament officials informed them that a Big Eight rule prohibited playoffs between individuals. The three-way tie would remain a three-way tie.

It was the second time in five tournaments Bratton was denied the opportunity to compete in a playoff against a teammate. He and Kuehne finished tied for first at the Golf Digest Invitational at the Woodlands in Texas. Both Texas natives had friends and family in the gallery, and Trip had joked about how he would finally have a chance to avenge his loss to Alan in a playoff in the Texas 4A high school tournament in 1989. But Holder prevented it.

Based on Holder's experience, there were no winners when teammates faced each other in playoffs. It could be a miserable experience and often led to uninspired play, as Kuehne and Cox had proved during their rushed, uneven semifinal round at the U.S. Amateur at Sawgrass the previous August.

The Cowboys finished a disappointing fourth at the Maxwell Intercollegiate in Ardmore, Oklahoma—where Holder had attended high school—in the last warm-up before the NCAA Central Regionals at Bentwater Country Club in Montgomery, Texas.

The regional tournament was always anticlimactic for the Cowboys, who always had much more to lose than they had to gain. Winning, which they hadn't done since 1990, was nice, but surviving the cut to become one of the ten teams from their region to advance to the NCAA Championships was essential. One disastrous weekend, and their national title hopes would end before they even arrived at the Scarlet Course.

Survive they did, finishing 5 strokes behind first-place Oklahoma, thanks largely to another sterling performance by Bratton. The co–Player of the Year from 1994 was making a bid to become Player of the Year in 1995. He finished with a fifty-four-hole total of 211, cementing his place among the pre-tournament favorites heading into Columbus.

Leif Westerberg finished a surprising sixth and Kris Cox twenty-fourth, while Chris Tidland and Trip Kuehne finished in a tie for thirty-sixth.

In the final analysis, all that had been settled during the spring and fall seasons was that Stanford and Oklahoma State had flip-flopped atop the national rankings.

Now, the stage was finally set for what could become the most-hyped NCAA Championship in history.

Now all the Cowboys had to do was what they had been unable

to do the year before—beat Stanford in the only tournament that mattered.

Because Steve Burdick was so well liked by his teammates, his woes were painful for the entire team.

He was particularly close to Casey, since Casey had hosted him on his recruiting trip. They went to a Stanford football game and then spent the Saturday night doing what Burdick would laughingly call *such* a Stanford thing: They joined some Stanford students in trying to make hot-air balloons. The students used balsa wood, dry-cleaning bags, candles, and staples to create mini hot-air balloons. One makeshift hot-air balloon got caught in a tree and they panicked, thinking they were going to burn down a dorm. Thankfully, they didn't.

Those laughs seemed a long time ago when Burdick had his nightmarish spring of 1995. After practices, or after tournaments, he would spend time alone and try to figure out what was happening. It was a downward spiral he couldn't stop. He questioned everything about his swing and would be embarrassed that he'd gone from an All-American to a guy who couldn't break 80. Worse, he felt he was hurting the team. The defending champs had high expectations, and his poor play was dragging them down. That pressure added to his woes and maybe made him play even worse.

His stroke average was 76.3 for the spring, a full 3 strokes worse than his fall average of 73.2. When Burdick thought about it on its deepest level, he came face-to-face with his worst fears: Tiger's presence intimidated him.

Burdick always thought he'd make it on the PGA Tour, but when he practiced with Tiger, he was blown away by how much better Tiger was. What really killed Burdick was that Tiger had all that talent and was the best player Burdick had ever seen, and he'd gone 0 for 7 in PGA Tour events to that point. Then, when he did make a cut at the Masters, he finished tie-41st. Burdick would think: *If he can't crack the cut line, or the top forty when he does, what does that mean for me?*

Burdick searched for solutions. He tried to muscle up off the tee and compete with Tiger's distance in practice rounds. This caused Burdick to change his swing and felt futile. He couldn't hit it as far as Tiger. Worse, it caused him to stand over the ball with fear. And when he did play decently, like the 72 at the Stanford U.S. Intercollegiate? He would go to sleep thinking the score was an exception, and that he was bound to shoot 80 the next day. More often than not, he did.

Burdick didn't know if his mental problems begat his physical problems, or vice versa. It was a chicken-and-egg of the worst sort.

At the Pac-10s, it all bottomed out. Tiger didn't go because of the injury, and Jerry Chang was sent in his place. The team was flailing, and only Yanagisawa, who had a knack for playing well at big events, finished in the top ten, with a tie for sixth. Chang actually played quite well, with two rounds of 72 helping him to a tie-20th. But Begay finished tie-25th, including finishing rounds of 75 and 76; and Martin finished tie-35th, never shooting lower than 74. Worst of all, Burdick shot rounds of 78-74-77-80 to finish tie-53rd, last on the team. Stanford finished a dismal eighth out of ten teams, their worst Pac-10 finish in Goodwin's tenure outside of 1993, when Begay and Martin redshirted. They would qualify for the NCAA West Regionals, based on their season-long performance, but Burdick had a sick feeling in his stomach that he might not be part of the team anymore.

He confided as much in Martin.

"That might be my last tournament at Stanford," Burdick told him.

"What are you talking about?" Martin said. "No way."

Mostly, Martin didn't want to believe it. He and Begay so enjoyed Burdick as a fellow senior and teammate and always admired how he radiated positivity. To watch him struggle with his game and still try to comport himself with dignity alternately tore up his teammates and increased their admiration for him.

But when the team got back to Stanford, Goodwin asked Burdick to come to his office. He suggested they move next door, to the small locker room in the Stanford clubhouse, where they sat on a bench. They sat there for a moment, the coach who was always so relentlessly positive, the grandfatherly figure in Burdick's life, and the young man who was watching his dream slip away.

"Stevie boy, I love you to death," Goodwin said in that soft, familiar rasp. "But you've been struggling, and you know it."

Burdick nodded his head.

"I'm taking Jerry to Regionals," Goodwin said.

It felt like a punch in Burdick's gut.

Worse, he knew he couldn't argue his case. He didn't have a case. He did try to fight, though.

"Can I get a chance to qualify?" Burdick said.

Goodwin, unlike most college golf coaches, didn't subscribe much to the qualifying process. True to his nature, he ran a program light on structure and always went with his top five players in his opinion, and by their play, not forcing them to qualify on a weekly basis in practice rounds.

Goodwin shook his head.

Burdick sat on the bench thinking about it all. He was one of Stanford's most experienced players. He'd played in every tournament since his freshman year. He'd been an All-American, won a national championship. And now, he wouldn't have the chance to defend the title.

Burdick left Goodwin in the clubhouse and got into his car. He took a drive west of Highway 280, to the Portola Valley, where California's foothills roll toward the Pacific. He drove to a vista point that overlooked Stanford, "that beautiful campus," he called it.

He prayed in his car and read his Bible. Eventually, Burdick turned the ignition on his car and drove back to campus.

Gary and Jacki Burdick had purchased plane tickets for the NCAA Championships in Columbus. They were to watch their outstanding son finish up a stellar golf career at a school that made them so proud and watch him defend a national championship. Burdick had to phone them and to tell his father, his swing coach and first golf partner, that he'd lost his spot on the team. When his father answered, and when Burdick had to say the words, he couldn't stop the tears.

On the morning of May 18, 1995, Goodwin burst into a hotel room in Albuquerque, New Mexico, to see Tiger Woods and Casey Martin in bed, curled up and sick as dogs.

This was a problem. The NCAA West Regionals first round was that morning, and 40 percent of Goodwin's starting five were sweaty, pale, and out of it. Stanford needed to post at least four scores in the day's play or be disqualified as a team. If both Tiger and Casey withdrew from the first round, the unthinkable would happen—Stanford would not advance to the NCAA Championships. The dream scenario of Stanford becoming the first team from the West Coast to repeat as champs since their Cardinal forebears had in 1938–39 hung in the balance.

It wasn't a good sign when neither Tiger nor Casey had shown up for the team breakfast, and when Goodwin phoned their room, Casey had answered, sounding like a dying man.

The culprit had to be the previous evening's dinner. Goodwin had taken the team to a southwestern barbecue restaurant. Tiger and Casey sat near each other and ordered the same thing: ribs.

The meal finished, the Stanford team headed back to the hotel, where Tiger and Casey were rooming together. The next morning would be round one, and the boys would need to be on their game, so they retired early, to rest.

That is, until Casey shot up in bed at midnight, feeling furiously sick.

Waves of nausea crushed him, and it took mighty strength to fight off throwing up. Soon Tiger shot up in the bed next to him. He dashed for the bathroom and got sick.

"Are you OK?" Martin grunted to Woods in the darkness.

"No, I feel terrible," Tiger answered.

"I do, too," Martin could barely muster, before he, too, bolted out of bed and barreled his way to the bathroom, where he got sick, repeatedly.

It was about 1:00 A.M. Their tee times were merely hours away. And both players were out of it.

The early-morning hours continued with each player trading trips to the bathroom, violently ill with what they could only presume was the scourge of food poisoning.

Goodwin stood in that hotel room, staring at two sick golfers, covers pulled high on their beds, neither one looking as if he could lift a golf club. He couldn't believe it. Normally an empathetic sort, Goodwin didn't have any time for taking it easy. He needed one of them to play.

"Can one of you do it?" he implored. "I need you. It doesn't even matter how you play. Just play."

"Sorry, Coach," Martin grunted, "I don't think I can do it."

Goodwin left the room and came back, one more time. He looked at Tiger.

"I will play," Tiger said, hoarse. "I feel awful and I'm going to suck . . . but I will play."

For all the times his teammates teased Tiger Woods for being a drama queen, for feeling more injuries than the average player, and for always being the sick guy, his performance in the first round of the 1995 NCAA West Regionals is always the ultimate counterargument. Having dry heaves throughout the round, and lying on the grass between shots, Tiger shot 72. The team was able to hand in four cards for the first round: Begay's 71, Yanagisawa's 74, Chang's 78, and Tiger's 72.

Martin was healthy enough to play in the second round, and Stanford finished the Regionals with a sixth-place finish. It wasn't what they were aiming for when they landed in Albuquerque, but with the top ten teams qualifying, it was enough to get them to the NCAA Championships.

The defending national champions would, indeed, defend after all.

# 10

## Showdown at the Scarlet Course

*Columbus, Ohio*
*May 29–June 1, 1995*

THOUSANDS OF COLLEGE golfers had read the words engraved on the plaque that hung on the outside wall of the pro shop at the Scarlet Course in Columbus, Ohio. It told them they were about to step onto hallowed ground.

The Scarlet Course was college golf's equivalent of Notre Dame Stadium or Pauley Pavilion, and, like the U.S. Open at Pebble Beach or the British Open at St. Andrews, playing the NCAA Championships here was the ideal coupling of an elite event playing out on the most ideal stage.

Those who didn't understand the significance of the Scarlet Course as host of the NCAA Championships need only stop and gape at the plaque:

> The Ohio State University Golf Courses, the collegiate home
> of Jack Nicklaus, the greatest golfer to ever play the game.

The Scarlet Course was the last golf course designed by the legendary Alister MacKenzie before his death. MacKenzie's life works included Augusta National and Cypress Point, commonly considered two of the finest courses on the planet. His work in Columbus, while less famous, was still praiseworthy. Seven thousand one hundred and nine yards of sensible golf lay ahead, a subtle test of contoured greens and tree-lined doglegs that not only made up a classic, traditional golf course layout, but also made sure the Scarlet Course was rated as the finest collegiate golf facility in the country by *Golf Digest*.

Now, it was the backdrop where Oklahoma State, now ranked number one in the nation, and Stanford, the defending champions and ranked number two, would meet for the final time during the 1995 season.

Seven other national championships played out at the Scarlet, more than at any other site. If history was a guide, the showdown ahead was inevitable.

The first championship was held at Scarlet in 1941 and was won by Stanford. The most recent at Scarlet was in 1987, won by Oklahoma State.

In between, the Scarlet Course had hosted plenty of drama, much of it played out by future PGA Tour stars.

In 1970, Houston's John Mahaffey chipped in on the sixteenth hole to out-duel Wake Forest's Lanny Wadkins for the individual title. Five years later, a power-packed trio of Wake Forest's Jay Haas, his teammate Curtis Strange, and Alabama's Jerry Pate played as a threesome until Haas won the NCAA title by 1 stroke. And in 1980, Utah State's Jay Don Blake birdied the fourth extra hole to defeat amateur legend Hal Sutton of Centenary.

The team champion that year was Oklahoma State, coached by a thirty-one-year-old Holder. It was already his third national title as the Cowboys' coach. He came to Columbus in 1995 searching for his seventh.

The long-anticipated public-private showdown between Oklahoma State and Stanford was billed by *Golf World* as "College Golf's Version of the Game of the Century." The pre-tournament buzz gave the long-overlooked championship its most visibility since Texas's Ben Crenshaw was gunning for his third straight individual title in Stillwater in 1972, the championship overseen by Holder's predecessor, Labron Harris, at OSU.

The teams would be easy to find in Columbus. One of the subtle joys of college golf is its unique pageantry of colors. Whereas a PGA Tour event is littered with corporate sponsorships on golf bags, shirts, and caps, a college golf event is sponsor-free. Teams are identified by a standard as old as American college sports itself: school colors.

The colors announced the teams, like plumage. Holder's boys arrived with the traditional orange or black polo shirts and golf bags, set off by black pants or black shorts. Goodwin's crew was notable for their, yes, Cardinal red golf bags and Cardinal red polo shirts. A walk across the practice range revealed all the other teams splashing their colors: the fire-engine red of the Houston Cougars, the maroon and gold of the USC Trojans, the familiar burnt orange of the Texas Longhorns. It was like the old Panasonic commercial joked: "If these colors aren't right, perhaps your TV set needs adjusting."

If college golf was low-wattage on the national sports scene, it wasn't because of a lack of history. Ninety-seven other national championships had been held, and the tournament had evolved since 1897. In its early days, the trophy exchanged hands among elite Ivy League schools like Yale, Harvard, and Princeton. It wasn't until Tulane's Fred Lamprecht won back-to-back individual titles in 1925 and 1926 that another region of the country was heard from. College golf's western schools broke through when Stanford won the 1939 title. Years later, the sport would see its first true dynasty. Dave Williams built a monster at Houston and would turn into the John Wooden of his sport, winning sixteen national titles.

The newest dynasty was Holder's. But those who followed college golf knew that Stanford and Oklahoma State weren't the only teams capable of winning a national championship. Some were predicting that Texas, the national runner-up the previous year, would make good on its talent, led by star Harrison Frazar. Arizona, with future PGA Tour mainstays Rory Sabbatini and Ted Purdy, was a factor. So was Florida, with senior Chris Couch. Georgia Tech had one of the best players in the field, medalist contender Stewart Cink. Arizona State was the Pac-10 champion and flush with confidence after badly outplaying Stanford at the Pac-10s.

Yet, as true as all that might be, Oklahoma State and Stanford provided the sexiest story line, and ESPN knew it. The network built a broadcast tower near the eighteenth green, a reminder to the players that this championship was different. It would play out on national television, with all the fanfare, even the possibility of TV analyst Ben Wright's sometimes caustic commentary passing judgment on their fates.

It all resulted in a larger national press corps than usual, and a different buzz. ESPN even came up with its war cry for the telecast's opening: "SHOWDOWN AT THE SCARLET COURSE."

There was tension, as every competitor found his own motivation. As gracious a presence as Wally Goodwin was, even he felt a bit slighted from a year earlier. "The way I look at last year, we won the NCAA tournament, but we did not win the national championship," he said. "If you look at what happened all year, and the voting, Oklahoma State was national champion because they were voted number one."

Oklahoma State didn't see it that way. No Cowboy took solace in finishing atop the *Golf World* season-ending poll. To them, the national championship was lost at Stonebridge when Stanford posted the lowest team score. The Cowboys had finished a disappointing fifth. At Columbus, Holder would publicly pay respect to a Stanford team that won five tournaments and finished second in five others.

"Everybody knows they're still the best team in the country," Holder told *Golf World*, even though his team had won eight tournaments for the second straight year.

In saying that, Holder was being conscious of a tenet he always preached to his players: Respect your opponent. He felt differently on the inside. While he may have wanted the media to believe that Stanford was the best team in the country, he was convinced his team was superior.

Praising Stanford was one way Holder took pressure off his team. In the past, he believed, his intensity had cost his team as many national championships as it had claimed. He knew now was the time to let his players play.

He took the team to Six Flags in Dallas on the way home from the NCAA Central Regionals, which Bratton won while Oklahoma State had finished second. He had grown attached to Bratton and Tidland and found himself thinking of ways to make their final championship special.

"You seniors are going to go out in style," he told them before they left for Columbus. "Nothing you can do this week will upset me. Let's go to a course we love, in a town we love, watch some movies, and enjoy the week."

He never mentioned the dubious distinction that possibly awaited Alan and Chris if they failed on their quest to win a title. He didn't have to.

"He's worked so hard," Holder told a reporter when asked about Bratton. "He's done everything you could want a boy to do. It would be nice for him to experience what it's like to win a national championship.

"But if he doesn't, I'm not going to think any less of him. I think sometimes people place way too much importance on this tournament . . . me included."

Oklahoma State and Stanford hadn't squared off since the Thunderbird Intercollegiate at Arizona State six weeks earlier. Incredibly, after seven head-to-head meetings spanning the fall and spring seasons, Oklahoma State's Cowboys had struck the golf ball 6,650 times. Stanford's Cardinal had struck it 6,651.

The final tally wasn't nearly as close in the team competition, however. Five times out of seven, the Cowboys had finished in front of Stanford. OSU's scoring average was 71.97; Stanford's, 72.70. But Oklahoma State's slim edge would be meaningless once the first round in Columbus began.

"If you can't win the tournament," Kris Cox acknowledged, "that voids it."

The two favorites would not have the only say in who would win the team title. The Scarlet Course was a player in this drama, too. Holder called it a "graduate test" for a champion and said he wouldn't mind if every NCAA championship were held at the graceful old track. It was by far his favorite of all the NCAA sites he'd seen in his twenty-seven years as a player and coach.

"The primary factor in this whole scenario is going to be the Scarlet Course," Holder predicted.

The NCAA paid the USGA a stipend to run its ultimate tournament. Hence, the man in charge of setting up the golf course was Tom Meeks, the USGA director of rules and competition. Meeks would gain fame for years to come for his punitive U.S. Open set-ups, and his work at the Scarlet Course was no different. Rough grew to a burly three inches, and if any of these college kids hit undisciplined tee shots, a heavy toll would be exacted. Host coach Jim Brown of Ohio State surmised that the rough might be difficult on players from the West and the South, who weren't used to midwestern layouts.

"You've got to walk single file down some of these fairways," Goodwin concurred.

MacKenzie courses were famous for defending par at the green. The old Scotsman didn't trick up his golf courses, preferring to emphasize second shots into greens and expert strategy in attacking pins. His greens could be friendly, or they could be cruel, depending on how you thought through your approach shots. This week at Columbus, however, Meeks had mowed the greens tight, running to a PGA Tour–like 10 on the Stimpmeter, a device used to measure the speed of the putting green, and the putting surfaces emphasized every nuance.

"We're trying to make it the Open of NCAA golf," said Jim Brown, coach of the host Ohio State Buckeyes. "This week, you better hit the ball straight."

Holder built a dynasty recruiting and coaching disciplined ball strikers. If they kept it in the fairway, nobody was better in the country. If they strayed into the Scarlet Course rough, however, trouble lurked. Stanford featured the better troubleshooters. Woods and Begay, in particular, were famous in college golf for their ability to create something out of nothing. And if anybody on OSU's side knew about the miraculous recovery skills of Tiger, it was Trip Kuehne. So did his father, Ernie, who was reminded upon his arrival in Columbus that the story lines this week ran deeper than just Oklahoma State versus Stanford.

As if he needed reminding.

Ernie was as fired up for the NCAA Championships as he had been for any tournament in which his children had participated. Winning an NCAA team title had long been Trip's primary goal. It was a big factor in his giving up his scholarship to ASU to walk on at OSU.

The next four days would offer Trip his best chance, as it would offer Bratton and Tidland their last chances. That it was Tiger—and, by extension, Stanford—standing in the way was a rich bit of story line for the Kuehnes.

Ernie was greeted by a reminder of the obstacle as he pulled into the parking lot of the Columbus, Ohio, hotel where he would stay for the duration of the week.

There was Earl Woods, hat pulled low, headphones on, standing as still and stoic as a cigar-store Indian. Earl and Ernie's eyes locked in a long, intense glare before Earl threw down his cigarette and walked to the opposite side of the parking lot.

Tiger's defeat of Trip at the U.S. Amateur the previous summer was still seared into Ernie's near-photographic memory. Trip outplayed Tiger in that tournament, at least in Ernie's mind. Ernie had never seen a player strike as many errant shots and still win as Tiger did that day. How many players can hit a 3-wood 250 yards out of trouble to an island green—as Tiger did on sixteen—and get away with it? How many players could hit as many bad shots as Tiger had that day, find his ball, and still have a lie that allowed him to execute one miraculous recovery shot after another?

Ernie couldn't deny Tiger's skill. It was obvious. But there was also no denying that Tiger, in Ernie's estimation, was the luckiest athlete alive. It had always been that way. Tiger's skill and an incredible series of unlikely events had been equally responsible for Tiger winning three U.S. Junior Amateurs and making the comeback against Trip at Sawgrass.

Ernie was hoping this would be the week Tiger's luck would finally run out.

Ernie and Earl had a complex relationship. Ernie knew that Earl and Tiger had not been welcome at many of the courses that hosted elite AJGA events. It wasn't as if Tiger wasn't allowed to participate. He was. But Ernie had witnessed the subtle racism that made Earl and Tiger feel like outsiders. He reached out to Earl and Tiger, making sure they were accepted by the Kuehne clan and welcome in their home.

They had been frequent houseguests through the years, Tiger playing basketball with Trip, Hank, and Kelli. Pam even hung a stocking with Tiger's name on it from the mantel in their hotel room when both families found themselves at a tournament in Florida one Christmas.

Ernie and Earl enjoyed meals together, served on prestigious AJGA boards together, and watched their children splash together in numerous hotel swimming pools. Tiger and Hank had become closer than ever in the time since Tiger's win over Trip at the U.S. Amateur, but there would be no polite exchange of pleasantries between Earl and Ernie this week.

They were amateur golf's alpha-dog dads, and their backs were up and their teeth bared. The glare they exchanged in the parking lot was the equivalent of them marking their territory. They both knew what was at stake. If things went according to plan, and everyone assumed that they would, Tiger and Trip would once again be competing for a title both players, and both fathers, dearly coveted.

The message was clear, if not spoken, and their understanding complete. They were longtime friends and occasionally, as they would be this week, fierce rivals. Earl and Ernie would keep their distance during the next four days.

The Cardinal and the Cowboys wouldn't have that luxury. The teams were grouped together—along with Texas—for the first thirty-six holes. The NCAA pairings committee paired teams according to seedings, and the three leading contenders for the national championship would slug it out on the same tee boxes for the first two days.

So, Jerry Chang, promoted to the starting lineup just two weeks earlier, shook hands with Leif Westerberg, the Swede, and they played together. Will Yanagisawa, the hero of the '94 NCAAs, teed it up with Kris Cox, whose grandfather, Oree, and mother, Valerie, were proudly watching. Casey Martin, at the end of five memorable years at Stanford, had the Golden Boy, Trip Kuehne, in his three-some. Playing in the final group, as the teams' number-one players, were the seniors Notah Begay and Alan Bratton, the two unques-tioned team leaders.

And then there was the penultimate group: Tiger and Chris Tidland.

Chris knew the deal. Their shared Southern California back-ground—and the Western Am, the previous summer—meant he'd played against Tiger before, and his experience, coupled with the pre-tournament buzz, told him to expect a big gallery.

His expectations were met. One of the Scarlet Course's trade-marks was low-slung, split-rail wooden fences surrounding the tee boxes. When Tidland arrived to tee off, he found a gallery layers deep behind the fence. Access is intimate at college golf tourna-ments, and the energy and presence of those who came to see Tiger created a buzz no other playing group had to deal with.

Writers leaned on Tiger's presence for pre-tournament stories. He was an easy write, and the media used the opportunity to craft more of the legend. One scribe sat at the tenth tee during a prac-tice round and watched Tiger tee off, alongside Chang and Yanagi-sawa. Though the morning dew was heavy, Tiger launched a 295-yard drive. Yanagisawa found himself 50 yards behind Tiger. So did Chang.

"I killed mine," Chang said, shaking his head.

"I killed mine, too," Yanagisawa said.

"I could beat him," Chang said, "if I had a tornado behind me."

Holder fed the media beast, too.

"He's the best of all time," Holder said that week. "His record backs it up. There has never been a player at this stage of his career who has done what Tiger Woods has done. He's a phenom, and I said that from the first time I saw him when he was thirteen years old."

Comparisons to all-time college greats ran rampant. At Nicklaus's college home, there was talk of the Golden Bear, who had already won the 1959 U.S. Amateur when he won the 1961 NCAA individual title as a bomber off the tee—not unlike Tiger—and a cold-blooded assassin on the greens—again, not unlike Tiger. Since Jack, Ben Crenshaw's Texas career (three individual NCAA titles) and Phil Mickelson's Arizona State career (three individual NCAA titles) became the collegiate gold standard. Some thought the Stanford freshman was bound to top them.

"I came along in the Crenshaw era," said Florida coach Buddy Alexander, himself a former U.S. Amateur champion and Tiger victim from Sawgrass. "And I saw Mickelson a few years later, and all three of these guys are terrifically long, but Tiger is the longest. And Tiger is an outstanding putter, too, which is an underrated part of his game."

So, they came to the Scarlet Course, by the hundreds, to see Tiger. They stared at the freshman at the first tee box, almost boring holes through him. They studied his walk, his golf bag, his body, his mannerisms. Tiger, used to it all at the tender age of nineteen, had his thousand-yard stare down. Clad in navy shorts, white golf shoes, a white polo shirt, and a two-toned, red and white Stanford golf hat, he gave them nothing. He never glanced at the gallery, instead just practicing his usual concentration tricks: shutting his eyes and visualizing a golf shot, or focusing his gaze down the fairway of the hole, oblivious to the gawkers.

Everybody knew Tiger's tee time, except for the man whom many considered to be the most knowledgeable coach in college golf.

Holder assumed Tiger was playing number one for Stanford and would tee off later in the day. Instead, Notah Begay was number one, as he had been all year.

When Holder saw Tiger, he thought, *He's sure early for his tee time.*

Holder was puzzled when Tiger pulled a club from his bag.

"Tiger, are you playing in this group?" Holder asked.

"Yep," Tiger replied, his focus never wavering.

"Well, I get a bonus," Holder said. "I didn't expect that."

Tidland had never played well at nationals, finishing tied for seventy-fourth as a redshirt freshman and tied for twenty-eighth as a sophomore. Worse, he was convinced that his 11-over finish, good for a tie for sixty-seventh, had cost his team the national championship at Stonebridge the previous year.

The feeling of inferiority he had felt since his freshman year was still pronounced. No question, he'd been a key contributor for Oklahoma State for four years, but still, he felt he had something to prove. Nobody felt the pressure of the expectations that come with playing golf at OSU more than he did.

Holder tried to improve Tidland's ability to handle pressure by putting more pressure on him, as he had done at Palmetto Dunes. But as the NCAA tournament approached, Holder took a different tack.

He wouldn't let Tidland practice as much as he ordinarily might, instead encouraging Chris and Leif Westerberg to drive to Fort Worth, Texas, and take in the Colonial tournament for a day. He spent a lot of time with Chris in the weeks leading up to the NCAA Championships, letting him know that he was going to help him through the tournament that had become Tidland's personal nemesis.

"This is your last one," Holder told him again and again. "Have fun. You've had a great year, a great career. Enjoy this."

What relaxed Chris more than anything was Holder's plan to walk with Tidland during each of the four rounds. Having Holder with him and being paired with Tiger, his old friend and rival from Southern California, was both comfortable and exciting, making the first two rounds a leisurely stroll for Tidland.

Despite the large gallery, he was as relaxed as ever, thanks largely to Holder, who knew exactly what buttons to push. Between shots, Holder talked about anything except Tidland's round. He talked about how the Cowboy alums like Bob Tway, Scott Verplank, Bob May, and David Edwards following them in the gallery would play in that week's PGA Tour stop, the nearby Memorial. With OSU basketball coach Eddie Sutton also in the gallery, they talked about basketball, and how Bryant "Big Country" Reeves had led the Cowboys to the Final Four that spring. The coach and player talked about *Braveheart*, the Mel Gibson movie they had watched earlier in the week and all loved. They talked about where they would eat that night, Holder even promising Chris he could pick the restaurant if he had a good round.

The carefree conversations ended when Chris approached his shot. That's when Holder helped him focus intently on the task ahead—the next shot. Then they would be off walking again, talking about whatever popped into their minds.

Chris had two phenomenal rounds. He controlled his golf ball as well as his emotions. The lack of length that had been a handicap earlier in his career was now a strength. Chris was sneaky long, and during the first thirty-six holes he kept his ball in the fairway, then used the short game that had always been his greatest asset to chip the ball close. Nearly every putt he had was makable during the first two rounds.

After thirty-six holes, Chris had easily outplayed Woods by 7 strokes while posting back-to-back 69s, tying him for the individual lead at the halfway point with Auburn's Chip Spratlin. A beaming Holder, collared by ESPN, bragged about his senior's performance. His gambit to walk with Tidland had paid out in spades.

"I had the pleasure of watching him play all thirty-six, and he played very well," Holder said. "He hit the ball and took advantage of opportunities. I'm not surprised. He's probably going to be a first-team All-American, and he's been an All-American before."

Holder then got to the heart of the matter.

"It's just good to see him play the way he's capable of playing in a national championship," Holder said. "He really hasn't up until now. I've always known that he could."

That Tidland was 7 strokes clear of the great Woods spoke loudly. To be sure, Tidland and Holder witnessed moments of Tiger-esque brilliance, 300-plus-yard drives and long irons that had the height of 9-irons, making the crowd gasp. But, as was the case for most of Tiger's jinxed spring season, he was also loose, his shots not always finding their targets. The up-and-down nature of his first round included four birdies (the good) and five bogeys (the bad). His famous competitive streak flared, drawing a warning from tournament officials after he slammed his wedge into his golf bag in anger on just his third hole of the tournament. Tiger had hooked his drive, and his punched wedge fell into a greenside bunker. He was ticked and slammed the club. It broke. The great Tiger Woods was on probation for the next seventy holes and would draw a 2-stroke penalty if he acted out again.

His putting was erratic, as if he couldn't find a comfortable speed on the green, and a few three-putts spilled out of his game. Tidland watched as Tiger failed to get up and down in spots he usually would—but he also watched as Tiger then hit a shot nobody else in the field could hit.

It wasn't as if Tiger was playing that poorly. With Woods, it's all relative. His talent was so immense that even while not playing to his standards, he was still hanging around the top of the individual leaderboard. Though 7 strokes separated him from the individual lead, his first-round 73 was decent, and he was slightly better in Thursday's second round. An example: The par-5 fourteenth, at 489 yards, was the easiest par 5 on the course. But Woods got long and bombed his second shot over the green. Walking with his own double-strapped golf bag—there are no caddies in NCAA golf—Woods arrived at the green and had to have a fan point out his golf ball. He sized up his bad lie, then flopped it to 2 feet. Birdie. He came home in 34 and would sign for a 72.

Tiger was among the lucky ones. He finished his second round.

It hadn't been easy. On their second hole of their second round, on Thursday at 8:32 A.M., the first day of June, play was stopped. A midwestern thunderstorm was barreling in, and golfers were rushed off the course. Golf is a sport, naturally, played in the elements—except one: lightning. Any threat of lightning stops a competitive golf tournament, no questions asked. As epic and historic as the Scarlet Course was as a host, it brought with it the unavoidable climate of Ohio in late spring.

So it was that the players at the 1995 NCAA Championships headed for safety on that Thursday morning. The rain accompanying the thunderstorm was massive. It deluged the Scarlet Course and, in doing so, changed the lay of the land. The course was waterlogged. Tee shots got no roll. Putts slowed down.

"The greens are like spinach," said Ohio State coach Jim Brown.

The weatherman was now on the leaderboard, and the storms meant teams were now playing their rounds in varying conditions. Those who teed off later played an entirely different Scarlet Course from those who played before the storm. Not only that; lightning storms are a unique beast. Players from the middle of the country grew up with them. Players from California or the West Coast, like Tiger Woods, Casey Martin, Will Yanagisawa, and Jerry Chang, did not. Goodwin fretted about this detail.

The players wouldn't return until 11:50 A.M., a delay of three hours, eighteen minutes, and the whole day turned into a madcap attempt to finish before sunset. It was important, since Thursday was Cut Day. Fifteen of the thirty teams would go home, while fifteen would advance.

It wouldn't get done. Darkness engulfed the grounds, and the second round was halted at 8:43 P.M., with nine teams and seven threesomes yet to complete their rounds.

To explain the scoring at a college golf event is to explain organized chaos. Five players from each team play the golf course, but only the top four scores in every round count toward the team's aggregate total. The highest score is tossed out. So, how to figure out who's winning? The 1995 NCAA Championships featured on-course scoreboards for the first time, but the information displayed was, at best, incomplete or, at worst, inaccurate. It wasn't until all the players had finished their rounds and the scores could be tallied that participants knew precisely where they stood in the team and individual competitions.

That teams did not finish their rounds meant it was all an unfinished story. Title contenders like USC left the course without completing their round. Vagueness ruled the day.

Still, some story lines were discernible.

Of the teams that had finished, Goodwin's boys were handling their business. After round one, Begay's 70 was the best on the team.

He was continuing his blistering-hot spring and rising to the fore, as was his trademark at the biggest moments. Martin and Yanagisawa slogged their way to 75s on Wednesday, one of which was dropped because Chang came through with a very clutch 71. In the second round, Tiger's 72 was a team best, and Jerry Chang's 76 was dropped. Begay led the team at the halfway point, 1 stroke ahead of Tiger after his Thursday 74. The defending champions were consistent enough to be leading after two rounds—Yanagisawa and Martin again matched scores, this time with 73s—but Goodwin felt a little uneasy in noting that none of his players had yet to post a round in the 60s. One thing about Stanford's golf team: With Tiger capable of spectacular stuff at any time, and with Begay and Yanagisawa's NCAA pedigree from a year earlier, there was always the potential of a scintillating score. So far at the Scarlet Course, there was nothing scintillating.

And yet—first place.

After the second round, Goodwin sounded a small note of concern. He noted that the media scrutiny with Tiger on the team meant it had been an exhausting year. At times during the season, Goodwin's players would complain to the coach after rounds. They were hungry and wanted to eat, but Goodwin would have to wait for reporters to finish with Tiger before the team van could leave. Famously even-keeled, Goodwin once snapped at a reporter who asked for two minutes with Tiger that "two minutes turns into twenty minutes."

The Stanford coach sounded as if his team was, perhaps, fatigued. So was he. On top of it all, Arizona State sophomore Chris Hanell reminded reporters, "They're the ones with the pressure."

"There are many more pluses to it than minuses," Goodwin said of the onus to repeat. "The minuses, depending on whether I've had a lot of sleep, are either big or little . . . it's been an amazing year, with all the events that happened, starting way back in October. Our kids are pulling through, considering the pressing business of the last several months."

He didn't sound entirely convincing.

Two rounds of NCAA golf were mostly in the books, and Stanford had thirty-six holes to make the long-awaited dream a reality. It had been three years since Begay and Martin willingly redshirted to play one memorable year with Tiger on their team, to form what they hoped would be the best college golf team in history. They were halfway home.

Oh, and there was the little matter of the team in second place, just 2 strokes back. It was the Oklahoma State Cowboys.

Before the tournament, Mike Holder told his team nothing they could do during the week could upset him. It took the coach all of two rounds to render that prediction false. After Thursday's play, he gathered his team beneath a towering leafy tree by the eighteenth green and let them know, in true Holder fashion, that their focus was less than he expected.

In the first round, Tidland was the only Oklahoma State player to play steadily. Although he didn't know it, the senior held his erratic teammates together on the front nine. He was stunned to learn from a spectator on Thursday that even though he was 1 under, Oklahoma State's aggregate score through the first nine holes of the tournament was 8 over. This made him all the more determined to squeeze as many strokes out of his game as possible. His teammates were struggling.

Even Holder was unaware that Bratton, Kuehne, Cox, and Westerberg were spraying the ball all over the course and scrambling to make pars or, more often, bogeys. Holder's focus was entirely on helping Chris navigate his ball around the course in the fewest strokes possible.

It wasn't until after Tidland had finished his first round that Holder was told by reporters the Cowboys had put the wheels back on. After a disastrous front nine, Bratton, Kuehne, Cox, and Westerberg played the back nine in 5 under to pull themselves back toward contention.

"I would have been out there having heart palpitations if I did know," Holder joked with reporters. "I would have needed my dad's nitroglycerin pills."

Kuehne had led the back-nine charge, coming home in 2-under

34 to finish an even-par 72. He was equally oblivious to the plight of his teammates.

"If I would have been watching, I would have been scared," he said. "You can't win this tournament on the first day but you can sure lose it. But everybody hung in there and hit some good shots on the back nine."

After thirty-six holes, Holder wasn't panicking. His team was only 2 shots back, after all. And he wasn't intent on repeating the reaming he had given his team after the second round at Nicholasville two years prior. But nobody, with the exception of Tidland, was playing well. It was time to refocus, Holder-style.

"What's wrong with you guys?" he asked under the tree. "I just spent two rounds watching a guy make it look easy. Why are you making it look so hard?"

Cox's play may have best exemplified Oklahoma State's plight during the first two rounds. He was playing horribly in the first round but managed two birdies on the back to post a first-round total of 75. It was more of the same in the second round until he holed out from 105 yards for birdie on the 379-yard, dogleg-left sixteenth hole. The bit of fortune and skill saved a 73 in his second round.

Cox gave David Edwards full credit for the birdie on sixteen and its ensuing confidence boost. The former Cowboy had been helping Oklahoma State golfers lock in their yardages with their wedges in the weeks leading up to the NCAA tournament. It was those lessons, Cox knew, that helped make sixteen the turning point of his second round and, he hoped, his tournament.

It was what Cox did after the second round that annoyed Holder. The coach never wanted his players giving their teammates a play-by-play of their round. "Save me the play-by-play," he would often say. "Just give me your score." And yet, Holder overheard Cox giving Tidland a hole-by-hole description of his round.

He didn't want his players scoreboard watching, didn't want them gossiping with other players or each other about where they stood in the team or individual standings. He always preached the same message: Your concern about what opponents and teammates are doing only emerges after your golf ball lands in the bottom of the cup on the last hole of the last day.

The only important shot was the next shot, even if the next shot wouldn't take place until his players teed off for the third round the following morning.

Holder believed in this philosophy so completely that he had the following advice printed on the backs of the permanent yardage books each of his players carried:

- In competition, concentrate on the next shot. Do not let the gallery, scoreboard, opponent, teammates, or score influence your play.

- If you assume that:

  Things are going well, they may not be.
  Things are not going well, they may be.
  You are beaten, you may not be.
  You have won, you may not have.

- Never underestimate your opponent or the golf course. When you lose respect for them, you have lost respect for yourself.

- Avoid complaining about anything (pace of play, course conditions, weather, food, practice conditions, etc.). Just be thankful that you are competing and concentrate on doing your best.

- Never make excuses.

Holder chastised Cox, then turned his attention to Trip. Kuehne had followed his back-nine charge on Wednesday's 72 by giving away 3 strokes in his Thursday round of 75. That's when the coach noticed Westerberg.

The Swede carded a 78 in the first round, and Holder's response was to assign assistant coach Bruce Heppler to shadow the sophomore all over the course. Drawing comfort from Heppler's presence, Westerberg improved with a second-round 75, but now here

Westerberg was, with Holder preaching the importance of mental focus, staring blankly into space.

It set Holder off. He couldn't help it. His explosion was brief and intense before Holder quickly composed himself.

Alan was waiting. He was Oklahoma State's number-one player and was being outperformed by everyone but Westerberg through the first two rounds. A *Sports Illustrated* photograph of Alan standing in the rough and under a tree looking for a ball hadn't yet been published, but it accurately described the first two rounds of his final NCAA tournament.

And yet, Holder wasn't concerned about his steadiest player's uninspiring start. Bratton had proved he could deliver in the biggest tournament on college golf's schedule the previous year by finishing second overall, sharing NCAA co–Player of the Year honors with Texas's Justin Leonard. Holder knew Bratton would consistently deliver, and when he didn't, it was a surprise. Even after Bratton was just as erratic while turning in scores of 75-76 in the first two rounds, Holder knew he would make his presence felt.

From Alan's perspective, he felt he deserved the wave of criticism that he expected Holder to unleash at any moment, and Holder's belittling tactics always motivated him. That's why he was so surprised when Holder said nothing of the sort.

"I'm not worried about you," he told Alan. "You're too good. If we roll you around this course two more times you're going to do OK."

The co-leader, Tidland, was the one Cowboy the media wanted after the second round. After the tree meeting broke up, he spoke with reporters.

Tidland's sights were set firmly on winning the team championship, just as they were for his four teammates. He had won three tournaments in his career, including his victory at the Golf World Intercollegiate at Palmetto Dunes earlier in the season. He tied for first at the Big Eight Championships but never dreamed of being the medalist at the NCAA Championships.

All the pre-tournament focus had been on Tiger Woods, yet here he was, someone who his own coach doubted could play at Oklahoma State, 7 strokes clear of Woods and tied for the lead. *Golf World* had not even named him among the top players in college golf seven months before.

Even in the team-first atmosphere fostered by Holder and Goodwin, the prestige of the NCAA individual title was large. This is where the legends roamed. Nicklaus, Harvie Ward, Hale Irwin won it. Crenshaw, Verplank, and Justin Leonard won it. Like Crenshaw, Mickelson won three. It was widely considered the toughest amateur stroke-play event in the country, and if a player won it, he raised his profile considerably. The confidence gained could pave the road to the PGA Tour, and once there, the name recognition could only help things like potential endorsement deals.

If everybody anointed Tiger Woods as the sure favorite to win the individual title, nobody anointed Tidland's co-leader. His name was Chip Spratlin, and he played at Auburn, a walk-on with zero college wins to his credit. Spratlin's prep work for Columbus was hardly auspicious. He fired an anonymous 74-75-77 to finish sixty-third at the East Regionals at Yale and never played as Auburn's number-one player.

"I'm sure people will be surprised if I win it," Tidland said. "I'll be surprised if I'm the medalist, too."

As the horn blew at 8:43 P.M. to signal the close of the second day's stop-and-start proceedings, at least Stanford and Oklahoma State knew their day was done. Not so lucky were teams like USC, Florida State, and New Mexico. They were among the nine schools still on the course and would have to return early on Friday to finish the second round. It felt like going uphill. The lucky teams that finished would get a good night's rest and feel as if they were ahead of the game. Moreover, some big schools were on the move on the day the field was cut in half, from thirty teams to fifteen.

If the field would be cut in half by Friday morning's close of the second round, little clarity would come with it. In the gathering dusk, as Holder and the Cowboys left the course, as Goodwin and Stanford retired to a team dinner, as the soggy Scarlet Course slept overnight and tried to dry out, the only thing certain was the uncertainty. The weather was now a factor, the golf course would only grow longer and wetter as the weekend approached, and the most prophetic words were spoken by a freshman.

"There are thirty-six holes left," Tiger said. "That's a lot of time. Anything can happen in thirty-six holes."

# 11

## Believe in Destiny

*Columbus, Ohio*
*June 2–3, 1995*

PERHAPS THE BIGGEST change from the first thirty-six holes to Friday's third round was Holder's potentially disastrous decision to change his itinerary. The coach's strategy to walk with Tidland had been wildly successful for thirty-six holes, as Chris was tied for the individual lead with Chip Spratlin of Auburn, at 6-under 138 after the second round.

Then Holder got greedy.

He decided to walk the third round with Trip Kuehne, whose rounds of 72-75 to open the NCAAs made him the second most efficient player on the Cowboys that week. Kuehne had a history of playing well in the third round of the NCAA tournament. His third-round 65 at Stonebridge the year before was Oklahoma's lowest individual round of the tournament.

Holder thought he could help Trip go low, which would benefit the team's cause. He was also confident in Chris's frame of mind.

But the gambit backfired in two ways: One, Kuehne never found his game, posting a 3-over 75 in the third round; and two, Tidland's confidence began to waver without Holder by his side.

It's hard to quantify how much help a golf coach gives his player by walking eighteen holes with him. Holder virtually pioneered the concept of walking with players, first offering advice on par 3s and then walking an entire round with them.

Stanford players, meanwhile, considered the concept of Goodwin walking eighteen holes with them almost unimaginable. Their coach was cut from an entirely different piece of cloth. Players would joke about Goodwin popping up from behind scoreboards on a par 3, giving a few of his sotto-voce bromides—"Hey, boy, how you doin', boy? Get me a few pars and we'll be OK . . . see you in a little bit!" they can imitate in that grandfatherly tone—and then being on his way. Some players estimated Goodwin never walked one entire hole with them, tee to green, in their Stanford careers, let alone a round. Not that they felt Goodwin was neglectful. They liked his structure: Trusting the players to accomplish things on their own, he gave them just enough freedom that they felt in control.

Without Holder walking with him and distracting him between shots, Tidland had more time to think. Thinking, sometimes, is a problem in golf. It was during these downtimes that it dawned on Tidland that he was actually in position to win the individual title at the NCAA tournament. As he contemplated the magnitude of that accomplishment, his control began to wane.

He made his first bogey of the tournament early in the third round. *Whoa,* he thought to himself, *what was that?* He felt his swing quicken and found himself more timid on putts. In short, his confidence was leaking. Salvation came when he holed a shot from the fairway for an eagle on twelve to get back to even par. By the time he made bogey on eighteen to finish his round, he was relieved to have shot a respectable 72. But it was 3 shots worse than his first- and second-round 69s.

Negotiating the course wasn't as easy as it had been. Doubt hadn't crept into his thinking during the first two rounds. Holder hadn't allowed it. Now, it was lurking.

His 72 gave Auburn's Spratlin some breathing room in the race for the individual title, as Spratlin took a 2-shot lead with a third-round 70.

Holder regretted the decision the moment he saw Chris's scorecard. He knew he would walk with Chris again in the fourth round. He just hoped, prayed, that his decision wouldn't end up costing Chris the individual title.

What made Holder even more miffed was that Oklahoma State was losing ground in the team standings.

The wet weather had continued, and strong winds had blown all day. In the ESPN booth, Englishman Ben Wright called the conditions "unconscionably vile." While just miles away the big-money PGA Tour players were playing the Memorial under "lift, clean, and place" conditions, the college kids were playing the ball down, mud splotches be damned.

It should have been Oklahoma State's kind of day. But they couldn't take advantage. They were behind, they were the ones who needed to make a move if they were going to claim Holder's seventh national title, but they failed to do much of anything but hang in there.

Bratton shot a team-best 69, which he considered the greatest tournament round of his career, not because it was his lowest score—he had shot thirty-three rounds in the 60s during the past four years, many of them lower than 69—but because he had been unable to sustain any type of rhythm during the round. He didn't feel in control of his swing, in control of his ball, and that he had somehow managed to finish his round 3 under, he knew, was nothing short of miraculous.

Kris Cox was the only other Oklahoma State player to join Bratton in breaking par, with a 71.

Westerberg, again, was struggling and shot 76—the third consecutive day he shot 75 or higher. And Trip's 75 wasn't just a rough day; it was more evidence that Holder's strategy had backfired in round three.

Worse, teams ahead of them moved into position, poised to win the national championship. Even USC passed Oklahoma State, when Chad Wright shot 67 to move the Trojans to an aggregate 5 over, 1 stroke better than the Cowboys.

And if Oklahoma State had USC to deal with, there was the matter of the two teams tied atop the leaderboard after fifty-four holes: Texas and . . . yes, Stanford.

The Longhorns improved 14 shots from their second-round to-tal. They and the Cardinal were locked at 3-over 867, 2 clear of USC, 3 clear of Oklahoma State. The 'Horns received a brilliant round from Harrison Frazar, who finished the front nine with a score of 4-under 32, totaling fourteen greens hit in regulation, five birdies, and no bogeys en route to a 67.

That the Longhorns were tied with Stanford meant many ob-servers felt as if the 1995 NCAAs might be a reprise of the 1994 NCAAs, with Stanford and Texas as the two most relevant schools.

"There are a lot of teams that can win it tomorrow," Texas coach Jimmy Clayton said. "I've never seen this tournament this close."

Clayton knew all about Stanford, and the pain of Stonebridge was still fresh in Texas's mind. If Stanford was the team filled with experienced talent, and coached by their trusting adviser in Good-win, Friday's third round was an example of all the Cardinal had to offer. Though no player went outrageously low, like Begay's 62 or Yanagisawa's 64 from the '94 championship, the fact that Tiger and Martin each shot 70 meant the team had a baseline to draw on, clutch play when it was needed most. At various points during the third round, Stanford's lead over Oklahoma State was as much as 9 strokes, and observers were suitably impressed.

"The Cardinal issued a statement," said ESPN's Ron Franklin in the broadcast booth, "and showed their great depth."

Concurred Wright: "Depth is the story. And they've got such pride in their performance. No one is going to make a really high score."

Stanford wore khaki shorts and white polo shirts with red col-lars in the third round. The short pants revealed Martin's ailing leg, wrapped tight in a bandage. Wright marveled. "He's a study in cour-age," Wright said, "how he's plodded around here in the mud flats."

On the par-4 eighteenth hole, Martin's ninth of the day, he made a nearly 100-foot putt for a birdie, going out in 34.

Tiger, meanwhile, was crafting his best round of the championships. In Wright's words, he still hadn't put on the "afterburners," but Woods's springtime, with the injuries and illness, wasn't an "afterburner" spring. It was a grinder college spring for Tiger, as evidenced by some of the scrambling he did in Columbus. On the par-5 fourteenth, he hit a wildly errant drive but recovered with an approach that found the green—and made par. Similarly, on the par-4 fifteenth, he missed the green from the fairway into a bunker but got up and down for par.

And on the short, birdie-able par-4 sixteenth, Tiger hit iron off the tee and hit a 4-iron in, but left it short. He ran his chip about 10 feet past—only to bury the comebacker for another par, giving a low-energy fist pump to announce his pleasure with the proceedings. Like Martin, Tiger went out in 34, but there were no fireworks.

"Aesthetically, he's not been the best, but he's right there," said Franklin.

Added Wright: "That's the test of the great player. To play ordinarily, and still produce a great score, that's the thoroughbred."

Tiger didn't feel like a thoroughbred. He felt like an also-ran. Truth told, there was a lot of external pressure not only for him to help Stanford win the team championship, but for him to win the individual championship, too. Close observers of Stanford began to wonder if all that came with being Tiger in the past year—winning the U.S. Amateur, flying to France, entering college, leaving home, getting mugged, having surgery, playing in the Masters, and straining a rotator cuff—was adding up to a fatigued Tiger who was less than stellar on the golf course. In Tiger's mind, he hadn't done anything of note since Sawgrass. Sure, he made the cut at Augusta National. Remember, though, his game plan going in: He wanted to win the Masters.

"I'm a little bummed I didn't shoot a lower score," said Tiger, whose 73-72-70 start at the Scarlet Course meant he was improving each day. "I hit a lot of good shots, but I didn't make many putts for birdie."

A hulking figure was following Tiger's round, a bulky man wearing headphones and smoking a cigar. The man had a jacket tied around his waist and binoculars around his neck, and he carried

an umbrella to combat Ohio's rain. Earl Woods always cut a notable figure. Curiously, after Tiger's par save on sixteen, Earl dropped
back a hole to watch Notah Begay play a few holes. Why would he
leave his son?

"Well, I've watched Tiger for years," Earl said. "And quite frankly,
sometimes it gets very boring. And I'm a team player, so I wanted
to give Notah some support."

Boring? Watching Tiger?

"Well, I've seen him hit almost every shot he has, and I know
what he's going to do in advance of him doing it," Earl Woods said.
"So I just let him do it because he's the best person out there to
handle it and I don't get upset or uptight. Sometimes, I just want to
see what the other guys are doing."

What the other guys were doing was surviving. Begay didn't find
a rhythm in the second round, shooting 74, and he was on his way
to another round of 2 over when his second shot at eighteen sailed
high and long, off a tent, and into a precarious position above the
hole, to a downhill green and a tucked pin.

In the gallery, Earl Woods assessed the scene.

"We'll be lucky to make bogey here," he told Begay's father.

Instead, Begay did what he'd done all his life: find a creative solution in the short game. After careful assessment, he hit a high, arc-
ing flop shot that landed about three-quarters of the way to the flag
and trickled down to 2 feet. It would be a kick-in par for a 73.

Earl Woods was ecstatic.

"Jesus Christ!" he said. "What a fantastic shot!"

It was a happy ending, yes, but Begay's father noticed the deeper
story: His son was getting into a lot of trouble around the Scarlet Course, loose with his irons, wild off the tee. He didn't have his
game. It was only through the miraculous recovery shots that he
was able to start 70-74-73.

Who knows how much worse it would have been in the wet
conditions if Goodwin hadn't had a brainstorm? Begay played the
round of golf with, of all things, a pallbearer's glove. With conditions so wet and slippery, Goodwin bought pallbearer's gloves for
the team, because of their adhesive nature. They cost Goodwin

about two bucks per pair and were an example of the fun and creativity the old coach could show at times.

"I've never heard of it, in all my time," Ben Wright said. "It strikes me that Stanford has a genius for their coach."

Stanford's coach was smart enough to know that Friday was a good day for his team, but that four teams within 3 shots of the title in a team golf event was a precarious situation, at best.

"This is the tightest tournament I've ever seen, NCAAs or any other event," Goodwin said. "This is remarkable . . . if you're an athlete, this is the position you want to be in."

Stanford was in an envious position. The defending national champions were fifty-four holes into their quest for a repeat and tied for the lead. If Stanford carried a fifteenth club in the bag, it was confidence. The players didn't even have to say it. When they retired for a team dinner that night at a local restaurant, they looked around the table at one another. Notah Begay . . . Casey Martin . . . Will Yanagisawa . . . each had won a national championship, each had come through when the stakes were highest. Jerry Chang was the newcomer, but he blended in nicely with his workmanlike game and agreeable personality. And then there was Tiger. There wasn't a player on the Stanford team who felt unsure or uneasy about his position.

Before he left the Scarlet Course, Goodwin told reporters the same.

"I'm sure there is [confidence]," Goodwin said. "They've played really well, and we're going to be very tough to beat."

The host coach, Jim Brown of Ohio State, felt the same way.

"Their team is so solid, one through five," Brown said. "They look at Tiger and know the score he's going to shoot, so that gives the other guys a comfort factor. And I think that's key for them. They're one of the teams I picked.

"Them, and Oklahoma State."

One other factor was at work as the third round closed on Friday evening: The Stanford–Oklahoma State rivalry was firing up on the eve of the college golf season's final day.

Oklahoma State players, as well as players from other teams, had been asked countless questions about Tiger Woods and Stanford throughout the week by a media corps seemingly obsessed with the Cardinal freshman and his teammates' bid to win back-to-back national titles.

The result wasn't exactly resentment. Every player in the field understood how good Woods was, and the college game could only benefit from the extra attention he brought. Few appreciated Woods's ability more than Holder, but the incessant questions about what had become an all-too-predictable theme also caused weariness and irritation.

Holder's frustrations bubbled over during post-round interviews.

"I don't know where it all started, but the media seemed to pick up on it and that's all they wanted to talk about," Holder said when asked about a budding feud between Oklahoma State and Stanford.

As the questions about Stanford kept coming, Holder became more and more irritated.

"If somebody just goes out to watch Stanford play [Saturday]," Holder said, "they might miss the tournament."

When asked if Stanford had replaced tradition-rich Oklahoma State as the team to beat, Holder shot back: "Why would we look at them? I think they think a lot more about us than we do about them."

Stanford tried to remain above the fray.

"I honestly haven't been in a tournament this whole year where I worried about them," Begay said of Oklahoma State.

Said Tiger, echoing Begay's sentiments: "They are not the ones. We can't just limit it to Oklahoma State. Hopefully, we can beat whoever is in contention."

Goodwin stressed that it was a friendly rivalry, which was more accurate than not. Oklahoma State and Stanford players often visited or exchanged playful trash talk on the practice range and in the clubhouse before and after tournaments. But Holder took exception to the comparisons between his program and Stanford's, pointing out the differences in the teams' schedules.

"You can look back at the number of top-twenty-five teams we've played," Holder said. "We've played a much more difficult schedule than they have."

To Holder's ears, the tenor of the post-round press conferences made it seem as if the final round would be a Stanford coronation more than a legitimate competition. Holder had been playing or coaching at the NCAA Championships for a quarter-century and knew better. The first three rounds of the tournament meant little as long as teams and individuals remained within striking distance during the final round.

The NCAA tournament, he knew from experience, was won or lost on the final day.

There were times during the week when even he admitted that things didn't seem to be going the Cowboys' way. The harder they tried, it seemed, the worse they played. But he was still confident that he had the superior team and that his Cowboys would eventually triumph. It was a belief that his players shared, and it was reinforced when Trip Kuehne got back to his hotel room later that night and found two anonymous notes on and under his door.

One read: "If you don't believe you can do it you never will. Believe in yourselves. Believe in destiny."

The second message was condensed and it, too, was unsigned. "Believe in destiny," it read.

Kuehne took them off the door and studied them.

And the Cowboys went to bed, if not to sleep, believing it.


On Saturday morning, June 3, 1995, Chris Tidland looked at the omelet on his plate, then at the stack of blueberry pancakes and back again.

Oklahoma State had come to the same Bob Evans restaurant at the same time every morning since the team had arrived in Columbus. It was Holder's way of attempting to establish a routine during a tournament week. For Tidland, the routine included the same fare every morning.

He cleaned his plate before the first round but ate less each subsequent day, the nerves associated with contending for the individual title and Oklahoma State vying for the team championship robbing him of his appetite until all he could do was try to force down a few bites.

He looked around the table and noticed that his teammates weren't eating much either. Today, they all knew, everything they had worked for since the first time they had picked up a club would be on the line.

Tidland had been in lots of pressure-packed situations, but none with such an overwhelming sense of finality. He was about to play the fourth round of the NCAA Championships, which meant this would be the final round of his college career. The only thing that gave him comfort was knowing that Holder would be once again by his side.

Two shots back and in contention for a national championship, Tidland was exceeding his wildest expectations. But the number-one goal of everyone at the table remained winning the team title. Oklahoma State was in fourth place, 3 shots behind Stanford and Texas, which meant Tidland and his teammates could ill afford to give strokes back to the Scarlet Course today.

Earlier in the week, Stanford players had similarly gathered around a table in a Columbus eatery when the talk turned to life and its many twists and turns. Chang said something that hung in the air.

"Life is full of regrets," he said.

For some reason, Will Yanagisawa found himself thinking of Chang's words when he went to sleep on Friday night and woke up Saturday morning. He made a list of positive swing thoughts, and mental keys to his game, and reviewed them as if they were a final exam. One thought controlled him: He didn't want to have any regrets in his final round as a collegian.

Heck, if history repeated itself, Yanagisawa might be the little big man again.

As teams arrived at the Scarlet Course for the final round, weather reports were grim. As if the whole week hadn't been a gray slugfest, more thunderstorms were predicted for Saturday. This presented a significant problem, since the NCAA did not allow the competition to bleed into Sunday. Eighteen holes would have to be played, even if it meant clearing the teams off the course more than once for lightning warnings. Potentially, Saturday could be the longest day of all.

Still, the morning started promisingly enough under blue, sunny skies. Players could see their shadows on the greens, and it was so warm some players were wearing short pants. Oklahoma State topped off their black shorts with "Cowboy" orange polo shirts. The shirts were unmistakable. If you weren't sure an Oklahoma State player was playing the golf hole, all you needed to do was look about 450 yards back at the tee box. If you saw a shock of orange, it was an Oklahoma State player coming your way.

Stanford opted for Cardinal polo shirts and khaki slacks. It had been a decade since Dave Williams coached Houston to back-to-back team titles in 1984 and 1985, and a decade before that since the Jay Haas–Curtis Strange Wake Forest teams won back-to-back titles in 1974 and 1975. Stanford was the only team west of Texas to have ever done it as a team, and that was back in 1938–39. Now was their time to add to the lore or, as Earl Woods might say, to let the legend grow.

If Friday night brought Holder's competitive ire to the forefront when asked about Stanford's repeat chances, ESPN's opening montage on Saturday would have frosted him had he seen it. Across the black TV screen appeared the words THE DEFENDERS, with footage of returning champs Notah Begay, Casey Martin, and Will Yanagisawa, described by Franklin as "poised and ready" to repeat. Next came the words THE NEWCOMER with footage of Jerry Chang. And then, of course, came the words THE FRESHMAN.

Franklin called Woods a "living legend" for the second day in a row and said Tiger's addition might cap off "possibly the best college golf team ever . . . Stanford's answer to the Dream Team." Nary a word about Oklahoma State, or even Texas, which was tied with Stanford.

Tiger moved the needle, even if it meant ignoring other worthy teams. In Oklahoma State's case, not everyone was still convinced they were worthy.

In college golf, as in professional tournaments, the teams play in reverse order of success. The teams furthest from the front go off first, and the players furthest from the lead go off first for each team. That meant Oklahoma State would tee off before Stanford, and Chris Tidland would be the final player on the course for the Cowboys. Stanford would be last off, along with Texas and USC. And Tiger, who had the lowest fifty-four-hole score of any Stanford player, would be the last player on the course for the Cardinal.

It did not begin according to plan for Oklahoma State. Instead of moving closer to co-leaders Stanford and Texas, they started going the other way. With a game plan to blitz the board early with birdies—the better to get inside Stanford's head—Oklahoma State didn't execute.

Kris Cox started poorly. It was during a long, sleepless night that Cox began to finally understand what it meant to play team golf. He had been too nervous to sleep, and as he stared at the ceiling in his hotel room, he realized that he was more consumed with playing well to help Chris and Alan win an NCAA title than he was with playing well for himself. He wasn't overly religious and was surprised when he found himself praying: "Give us the strength to handle whatever might come our way tomorrow."

He was unable to shake the nerves the next morning, and it showed when he bogeyed the first hole. *Here we go again,* he thought as he moved on to the second hole. *Here we had a great season, but if we don't turn things around quickly it will end with the same disappointment as last year.*

Bratton, playing the number-one hole behind Cox, was making a mess of the 430-yard par 4. The dogleg right calls for a cut tee shot, but Bratton got quick and duck-hooked his ball underneath a tree with branches that extended to the ground. He had to chip out to the practice range and made a double-bogey 6. Between Cox and Bratton, Oklahoma State lost 3 shots before Stanford even teed off.

Bratton needed something good to happen. The old phrase "there's a lot of golf left" sounds better when you don't double the first hole of your final collegiate round, so Bratton was desperate. He got to the par-5 fourth hole and hit an excellent tee shot. Walking to his ball, he looked to the side of the fairway and saw, of all things, a dead bird. This was a very good sign indeed.

Bratton had a running gag with his old high school coach, Danny Hayes, who had been following him at nationals all week. It had started when Alan was playing for Hayes at A&M Consolidated High in College Station, Texas. If Hayes found a feather anywhere on a golf course, he'd put it in his hat, a sign to Bratton that a birdie was forthcoming. More often than not, Bratton felt, he would deliver.

"Hey, if a feather is worth a birdie, what's a dead bird worth?" Bratton shouted to Hayes.

He answered his own question with a gorgeous 4-wood from the fairway to 12 feet. After rolling home an eagle putt, he smiled at his former high school coach. He was back to even par. Maybe there was some magic in Alan Bratton's golf bag on this day, after all.

When he made par on holes five through ten, he was beginning to think so. But on number eleven, Bratton got aggressive with a birdie putt. He ran it past the hole and wouldn't make the sizable comebacker. An injurious bogey meant the Cowboys lost another stroke to par.

The Cowboys were bleeding strokes. Stanford was on the golf course now and racking up pars. Tidland lost 2 shots to par early, falling further behind Bratton. All Holder's game planning, all his motivational tactics, going to see *Braveheart,* Trip's belief in "destiny"—none of it was adding up. This day was shaping up like Stonebridge all over again.

Stanford, meanwhile, was relying on their vast experience and cool heads. No Cardinal player was giving it away as the morning wore on. Woods and Begay parred their way through the front nine. Time was on Stanford's side. Time was Oklahoma State's enemy, and they needed some serious mojo. Up ahead at number eleven, Trip got some.

The "believe in destiny" notes that had been left at Trip's door the night before had been unsigned, but Trip had a pretty good idea who was responsible. Ron Balicki had been covering college golf for *Golf Week* since 1983 and had become a respected and well-liked figure in the sport, although nobody wanted him to pick his team to win the NCAA Championship.

Before every NCAA tournament, Balicki wrote a column predicting which team would win the team title. Not once had his prediction been correct, which meant he was always the object of much good-natured ribbing among players and coaches. His inability to pick a winner was eventually dubbed the "Wrong Ron Curse." Whichever unlucky team he did pick was doomed.

Holder's wife, Robbie, had warned Balicki not to pick the Cowboys and therefore scuttle her husband's chances of winning a seventh national championship. The families of other Oklahoma State players had pleaded with "Wrong Ron" to pick any team other than the Cowboys.

Undaunted, Balicki, after studying the field, sat down to write, tongue planted firmly in cheek: "Who will it be?" he concluded. "Although I know once I get to Columbus I will face the wrath of Robbie Holder and the threats—you don't think they'd really do those things, do you?—of their families and followers, I'm going with the Cowboys of Oklahoma State."

"You gotta believe!" Balicki wrote while playfully attempting to debunk the idea of a "Wrong Ron Curse." Those exact words had been written on one of the two notes that Trip had found.

And it was no coincidence that Balicki also happened to be staying at the same hotel as Oklahoma State. His room was right across the hall from Trip's.

The curious "destiny" note had a different impact on Trip than it had on everyone else. Chris, Alan, and Leif thought that it was nice that someone cared enough to leave the note but knew it wouldn't help them hit a single shot the next day. Trip, on the other hand, had taken the message to heart, so sure that it was a sign that Oklahoma State would mount a final-round charge that would lift them to a victory, he actually wrote the words *believe in destiny* on his ball before he teed off.

And now there was finally some evidence that destiny was indeed involved. Trip airmailed the eleventh green, his ball landing in a grove of cedar trees. He inspected his lie and realized he had no shot. He had just resigned himself to taking an unplayable lie when he noticed a rules official from the USGA nearby. Kuehne remembered him from the Ping Preview in the fall, and they made eye contact. The rules official told Kuehne that if he could take a stance, even if it meant bending branches back, he could play the ball as it lay.

Ernie had instilled in him a strong sense of right and wrong on and off the course, which had been reinforced by Holder, who believed in honor and integrity on the course above all else. That's why Trip had been so upset when he thought Stanford's Notah Begay should have taken a penalty stroke after addressing his ball during the Ping Preview the previous fall. Now, on eleven, in the final round, he wanted to make absolutely sure what he was doing was legal, so Trip asked him again: He could get into the branches, push them away, and hit his ball? Yes, said the rules official.

Kuehne couldn't believe his luck. He was ready to take an unplayable and perhaps make double bogey. Instead, he got up and down for a vital par. Emboldened, he birdied the next hole.

Finally, or so it seemed, things were turning the Cowboys' way.

And then the siren sounded.

The dreaded sound indicated lightning was near and play would be halted. The clouds suggested this would be the worst storm yet.

Lightning turned the skies above the Scarlet Course into a giant and dangerous strobe light. Bratton had just teed off on the fifteenth hole and huddled in a shelter nearby with Robbie Holder, his mother, Lyle Myrta, and his girlfriend, Gretchen. Heppler, Holder's assistant coach, sought refuge in the cart barn. Mike Holder was in another on-course shelter when he witnessed a lightning strike of terrifying force.

At 12:18 local time, players were pulled from the course. The NCAA Championships were, once again, on hold.

One of the reasons why college golf failed to generate much of a following—despite the explosion of interest in golf in the 1990s—was that it was virtually impossible for a spectator to know what was happening on the course.

Electronic scoreboards, a fairly new invention at golf events, had been erected on the Scarlet Course for the championships. But the scoreboards had been so unreliable all week, in part because of power outages resulting from thunderstorms and partly because they were woefully behind, few players and spectators gave them more than a casual glance. The electronic scoreboards may have lent the NCAA tournament a bigtime tournament feel, but they were little more than props.

Oklahoma State players knew they hadn't been playing well and that they had given up ground. They were unsure of where exactly they stood in the team competition as they trudged toward the shelter of the clubhouse.

Holder, who had been walking with Tidland, sent his assistant Bruce Heppler, who had been walking with Leif Westerberg, to get lunch for the team. Holder knew his players hadn't eaten much for breakfast and he wanted to keep their energy up. The way it was raining now, and with forecasts calling for another band of thunderstorms to pass over the Scarlet Course later that afternoon, he knew this had the potential to turn into a long day.

He didn't ask his players where they stood or what they had shot. He didn't want them scoreboard watching and he wouldn't do it himself. He had made that a point of emphasis after Oklahoma State had finished a distant fifth behind Stanford at the NCAA Championships at Stonebridge the year before.

He had written a list of key points in his crabbed handwriting in the notebook where he meticulously kept records of every round shot by every individual on every team in every tournament in which Oklahoma State played.

He had written "Will not be denied" at the top of the list. Below it was written "Only worry or pay attention to yourself," and beneath that were other specific points such as "No scoreboard watching" and "No player companion watching" that he vowed to stress during the 1995 season. Any information about OSU's place in the team standings, or Tidland's place in the individual race, was useless, to his mind. There would be time to count strokes when their rounds were done.

Truthfully, the coach welcomed the rain delay. To him, it was a momentum breaker to Oklahoma State's advantage. It gave him a chance to refocus his players before sending them back onto the course. It also meant that players competing for teams ahead of them in the team standings could lose their focus.

"This is good," Holder told Heppler when he returned. "This will make them think about it."

Holder couldn't prevent his players from hearing tidbits of information that filtered through the clubhouse, locker room, caddy shacks, and on-course shelters where stranded players, parents, followers, coaches, and rules officials waited out the storm. With nothing else to do, conversations naturally revolved around what was beginning to unfold on the course, the results trickling in like ballots on election night.

The 1995 NCAA Championships had turned into a two-team race. The surprise was that neither of those teams was Oklahoma State.

The Cardinal and the Longhorns were dead even at 3 over through nine holes, the same scores with which they began the final day. Arizona State was 8 strokes back through sixteen holes. USC, playing alongside Stanford and Texas, was also 8 strokes back, through nine holes.

And 8 strokes back through thirteen holes were the Cowboys of Oklahoma State. As lightning cracked and a heavy, angry rain lashed the Scarlet Course, it seemed an impossible deficit. Had "Wrong Ron" struck again?

Stanford was making its way around the golf course with a supreme belief that the 1995 NCAA Championship was theirs for the taking. If some mistook their belief for a sense of entitlement, so be it. The Cardinal knew they were good, knew they had done this before, and knew they had Tiger Woods as their last player on the golf course.

Goodwin wasn't nervous. He kept the same game plan for the final round as he had kept since he got the job in 1987. The right players had been recruited, and Goodwin gave them just the proper amount of "atta boys" and mostly left them alone. Begay and Martin, in particular, knew everything was set up for another Stanford triumph.

Perhaps the only thing that would derail the thought would be something unexpected, and truth told, none of them was overly excited that a weather delay arrived at 12:18 P.M.

If there was one thing Stanford didn't need, it was a halt to the action. Just before the weather siren sounded, Begay found his golf ball in a dead spot off the ninth green. He had no shot. All the seemingly impossible golf shots Begay practiced for five years at Stanford led him to believe that, sometimes, the seemingly impossible was possible. He chipped in for birdie to make the turn with a head of steam.

Tiger had just holed out on number nine and was even par for the day. Stanford wasn't entirely sure where it stood, owing to the ineffective scoreboards. The Cardinal were fairly sure it was a two-horse race between themselves and Texas. One thing Notah Begay noticed when he did glance at the pages of the electronic board. Oklahoma State wasn't even on the first page of the leaderboard when the weather delay rocked the Scarlet Course.

Seeking a dry spot inside the locker room, the Cardinal scurried for shelter. The locker room was a mess. Ping standup golf bags littered the room, fighting for space with umbrellas and drying rain gear. The air smelled of wet socks and wet grass. Stanford's five tried to find their own little nook in the locker room and did, a faraway spot with some benches.

Tiger stretched out on a bench and shut his eyes. His teammates didn't know if he was sleeping or meditating, so they didn't bother him. Martin, Begay, Yanagisawa, and Chang spent the time drying out their gear and catching up with other teams. Naturally, they wanted to know how other schools were doing. Through word of mouth, Stanford sussed out that the Cardinal were in a pretty good spot on the leaderboard.

What more could they ask? Only nine holes remained, if only they could get out of the locker room and back on the Scarlet Course.

Finally, two hours and twenty-five minutes later, the lightning storm passed. Word spread that golf might resume at 2:45 P.M., and the best players in college golf would face the challenge of trying to return to the moment.

Not Begay, though. True to form, he didn't feel any nerves. He felt, if anything, cocky. That's why he was so surprised and impressed that Tiger opened his eyes from his ruminative state and addressed his elder teammates.

"Guys," Tiger said, "it's time to get your focus back. Concentrate on that. Get your minds right."

Begay found himself caught up in Tiger's words. He was the senior, but it was the freshman who was delivering the wisdom. For Begay, "focus" wasn't as important as, say, "kicking ass," as Begay liked to put it.

*He's right*, Begay thought to himself. *Get your mind right.*

Players headed to the range to get a couple of swings in when the weather cleared and tournament officials prepared to restart play. Tidland had been thankful for the delay. His round had been shaky and he still felt out of sorts. He hoped he'd find whatever he was missing on the practice range.

"Well, Tiddy," Holder said, using Tidland's nickname. "This will be the last time I'll ever get to watch you warm up."

Holder had said the same thing when they were warming up earlier. Then, those same words had only made the sense of finality that Chris felt before playing the first hole of his final collegiate round more profound. Now they had the opposite effect. Tidland laughed.

The players returned to the exact spots where their balls lay when play was suspended at 12:18 P.M.

Tiger went to the tenth tee, a 416-yard par 4 with a slight dogleg left, and stretched out his Achilles tendons and quads. Bratton walked out to his ball in the right rough on the par-4 fifteenth, near where his ball rested in the right rough, and took several practice swings in the wet grass. Will Yanagisawa went to the twelfth fairway with a short iron in for his third shot on the par 5. Leif Westerberg went to the seventeenth tee, the 207-yard par 3 abutted by the traffic of Kenny Road. Chris Tidland went to his ball in the fairway of the par-5 fourteenth, with a short iron to the green for his third. Jerry Chang headed to the thirteenth hole, a downhill par 3 with water in front of the green. Wally Goodwin went with him. Casey Martin went to the twelfth tee, just behind Yanagisawa.

The sky, so blue in the morning, was now gray and foreboding. The golf course was now a soggy, rough-hewn trudge.

Yanagisawa found this out shortly. His third shot at twelve hit the green, and when he tapped in for his par, he removed his golf ball from a veritable lake inside the cup. His ball was soaked, his hand was soaked, and he had to shake off the water and dry his ball before marching to thirteen.

Bratton, meanwhile, was the first to make a move.

Out of the wet rough, he sent his second shot on number fifteen to the left of the green, into a bunker. From there, though, he carved a bunker shot to 24 inches, a tap-in par. The consistency of the bunkers had changed from the rain, and Bratton took advantage. It was a good par, and Bratton had a purpose to his stride as he headed for the short par-4 sixteenth, the water squishing beneath his cleats.

During the rain delay, Tidland learned he was 4 shots behind Auburn's Spratlin. It was not ideal, but not an insurmountable deficit. He had a 20-footer for birdie on the par-5 fourteenth but missed by 6 inches. Tidland tapped in for his par just as another thunderclap sounded in the distance.

Every player, coach, parent, and spectator knew what that meant. More lightning, another band of thundershowers, more rain on the way . . . and another delay was in the offing.

Heppler was with Westerberg on the eighteenth green when his well-struck 10-foot putt lipped out, stopping so close to the edge that the ball appeared to be suspended over the hole. He and Heppler kept watching it, expecting the ball to disappear. When it didn't, Heppler glanced up at the brooding thunderheads.

"Run up there and tap it in," he told Westerberg, who had a plane to catch. "The horn is going to blow."

Westerberg was booked on a 4:45 P.M. flight to England, where he would play in the British Amateur the next week. He was excited. The Amateur Championship, as it's called in Britain, had once been considered one of golf's four "majors." It was no longer as prestigious as it was when Bobby Jones captured the title during his "Grand Slam" run in 1930, but it remained Europe's major amateur championship, as prestigious as the U.S. Amateur in America.

Holder had given Westerberg his blessing to book a late-afternoon flight from Columbus to London. Westerberg had made sure to give himself ample time to play the final round of his sophomore season before heading to the airport.

He never considered the possibility of a weather delay. Or two.

Westerberg hustled across the green. The moment his putter struck the ball, the ball plopping into the cup to complete a final-round 72, his best round of the tournament by 3 strokes, the siren sounded once again, as if on cue.

Heppler looked at his watch. It was 3:10. It had been just twenty-five minutes since play had resumed.

Another . . . weather . . . delay.

Bratton couldn't believe it. He had already parred fifteen with a tap-in. His birdie on sixteen had pulled Oklahoma State a stroke closer before he hit his best shot of the tournament and one of the best shots of his college career on the par-3 seventeenth.

The next-to-last hole on the Scarlet Course featured 207 yards of uphill incline with two bunkers guarding either side of the green. A shot that strayed too far left went out of bounds. The severe green discouraged players from aiming for the flagstick. Most preferred to land short for an easier, uphill putt. The hole would finish four rounds as the fourth-toughest overall. Saturday's pin position—back and right—only made the hole more of a riddle. This par 3 was not playing like a potential birdie hole. The seventeenth waited like a killer in the mist.

Bratton's irons had been leaking right anyway, so he decided to try it. He hit his 4-iron perfectly. Spectators on the eighteenth green could hear the gasp when the ball landed on the green and began tracking toward the hole. They could hear an even louder groan when it lipped out and ran 6 feet behind the cup.

That's when Bratton heard the siren's song. He shook his head in disbelief. He was finally playing great golf, and now he had to sit on a 6-footer for birdie on the second-to-last hole of the national championships.

He walked to the green and marked his ball and then walked over to talk to his mom, who had dropped him off at the scruffy Texas A&M course in the mornings and hauled him to regional tournaments during the summers.

Alan had always been a competitive but humble kid. "I don't need to toot my horn," he used to say. "My mother does it for me." Lyle Myrta had always been unable to conceal her pride when it came to Alan's accomplishments. She was the one who phoned the newspapers with his tournament results, clipped the articles, and carefully mounted them in scrapbooks. "These are your last two holes of college golf," she told her son when he came near.

They had come a long way together since Alan was introduced to the game when he took a club to the forehead that required five stitches after walking into his brother's backswing. Alan hugged her, not knowing that approximately 600 yards away near the eighteenth green, fate was intervening once again.

"What do I do?" Westerberg asked Heppler.

Thanks to Heppler, Westerberg had finished his round. He was free to leave. Barring a playoff, which had never occurred in the ninety-eight-year history of the NCAA tournament, he was through for the day, had done all he could to help Oklahoma State's cause. Kuehne, Cox, Bratton, and Tidland were still out on the course, bunched over the last four holes. It was in their hands now.

"I don't know," Heppler answered as they ran for the clubhouse. "I'll ask Coach."

In the brief time the players were on the course, Texas actually picked up a 2-shot lead over Stanford. So there it was: the Longhorns, burning to avenge the '94 pain of Stonebridge, one step closer, at 4 under overall. Stanford, at 2 under, was in second. Oklahoma State, running out of time, was at 5 over, well back of the contenders.

Goodwin was, as ever, even-keeled. He'd grown up in Ohio and coached in the Buckeye State later in life also. This wasn't his first June thunderstorm.

"This is kind of scary," he said, "because when these storms come across Ohio like this, they come in a hurry and you've got to scramble."

He acknowledged something his players were beginning to feel, also: These delays were slowing Stanford's coronation.

"It's very difficult to come back," Goodwin said. "You sit around for an hour and a half, and then they've got to get their minds going again. They were playing so hard. Then they have to go out and hit some golf balls, then concentrate on their first shot. They play—what, four or five shots?—and then here comes the whistle again. It's a difficult situation, but everybody's in the same boat."

He was asked about the leaderboard.

"If the boys have had experience with thunderstorms, it helps," Goodwin said. "Of course, a lot of our guys are from California, and we don't have lightning out there, so we haven't had this experience."

During the first weather delay, bolts of lightning hit near the clubhouse. Goodwin noted that his players were almost in awe of it and asked about it.

"It was pretty exciting for some of the guys," he said.

Goodwin, it should be noted, was wearing a red polo shirt—and a bolo tie. "Coach Red" was in full bloom.

Back in the locker room, players reassembled for their crowded dance again: finding a place for the Ping standup bags, spreading wet umbrellas, shaking out dripping rain gear, retreating to a nook or a bench to rest, relax, detach. The 1995 NCAA Championships were turning into one long day of purgatory.

In the locker room for the second rain delay, Casey Martin felt weary. The on-again, off-again day felt chaotic. Tiger again lay on a bench and closed his eyes. Yanagisawa took note of his surroundings. He noticed Arizona's Ted Purdy walking around the locker room, collecting autographs on NCAA T-shirts for his nephews. He noticed something else, too. He noticed Leif Westerberg packing his bags and leaving the golf course.

Holder hadn't hesitated. In his mind, there was no debate. Playing in the British Amateur was a big deal. He had given Westerberg permission to make his travel plans and he wasn't going to change his mind on the unlikely prospect of Oklahoma State rallying on the last few holes and forcing a playoff.

Besides, Westerberg's family had made a hefty investment in the trip. Flying from Columbus to London, Holder knew, wasn't cheap.

"I promised you could go, so go," Holder said.

"What if we get in a playoff?" Westerberg asked.

"You get in that taxi and go to the airport and get on that plane," Holder told him. "If we get in a playoff we'll take care of it. We'll have four players."

Leif had been part of this group for two years, had traveled all over the country competing with his older teammates. He had developed a relationship with them all and cared about them deeply. The feelings were mutual. Trip would never forget the first time they met, when they were laying sod at Karsten Creek and the fair-skinned Swede was getting fried in the Oklahoma sun. Despite not growing up with American football, Westerberg had been one of the most enthusiastic and fearless participants in their snow football games.

He admired Alan's quiet calmness and his work ethic. He had a special relationship with Chris, who spent a lot of time with him on the range, breaking down his swing and working on his mechanics. Westerberg didn't have a car in Stillwater. He had relied on his teammates for rides for the past two years, which would end when he returned to Stillwater for the fall semester of his junior year. Tidland had told him that he was leaving his 1986 Volkswagen Golf for Leif to use the next two years.

Now there was not even time to say goodbye. Leif's teammates were still walking in from their respective holes when he climbed into a cab for the airport. It felt strange. Leaving a tournament they had worked so hard to prepare for when the individual and team titles were still unresolved was no ordinary event, but this was not an ordinary day. He wasn't ready to concede defeat despite his team's sizable deficit. It wasn't as if he could pat himself on the back for his role in Oklahoma State's long-awaited national championship when they were 9 strokes down, either.

As the cab, windshield wipers squeaking, drove down Tremont Avenue, there was only one thing he was certain of: His role in this unfolding drama had concluded.

"What about a playoff?" Cox asked Holder as the taxi pulled away.

"We'll cross that bridge when we come to it," Holder said.

Heppler questioned the wisdom of Holder's decision.

"We're nine back," Holder explained. "If we get in a playoff with our four on their five I'll take it. I'll trade nine shots for the chance to play them four on five."

Tidland couldn't believe it. He was more nervous than he had been all day. He knew what would be at stake while playing the few remaining holes. Making up a 9-shot lead was daunting. If they were going to make a move, they would have to do it soon. They were running out of holes to play.

Westerberg was their fifth-best player. More often than not, his score was the one that was kicked out during tournament competition. But he had finished in the top ten five times during his freshman and sophomore seasons and had proved himself to be a clutch player. The even-par round he had just concluded demonstrated it.

Besides, if they were somehow able to rally to force a playoff, it would be nice to know that Leif was there to cover you up if you made a triple bogey.

"We can beat them with four," Trip said, as if reading Chris's mind.

Maybe it was the "destiny" messages he found, or Holder's belief that the rain delays were to the Cowboys' advantage because they made Texas and Stanford sit on their sizable lead, but Trip felt suddenly upbeat. He and Leif were the ones most likely to get down on themselves on the course, to beat themselves up mentally when things weren't going well. But now, when things looked as grim as they had looked since late in the first round at Stonebridge the year before, Trip, for reasons not even he could explain, felt a sudden burst of confidence.

"Believe in destiny," Trip told his teammates.

The second band of thunderstorms had passed, and the all-clear signal was given. The tournament was about to lurch ahead one more time. They would head back to the range for another quick practice session before heading back onto the course one last time.

Earlier in the day, Trip had wondered whether this would be his final round of college golf as well. He was only a junior, but he had already earned his bachelor's degree and had accomplished what no student-athlete in Oklahoma State history had accomplished when he was named the university's top student. Balancing his brilliance in golf and in academics had always been his strength, and the awards kept coming. He had also been named the national recipient of the Ben Hogan Award given annually for athletic and academic excellence.

He was OSU's best-known golfer after finishing runner-up to Woods at the U.S. Amateur, playing in the Masters and two other pro events. He could easily turn professional and sign a lucrative endorsement deal.

Whether to turn pro or follow Ernie's advice and remain an amateur was still a riddle he couldn't solve. He still wasn't sure what his future would hold, whether he should play golf for a living or embrace his other love and earn his living from the stock market. But it was the present that concerned him now.

When Holder was out of earshot, he gathered his teammates around him. He couldn't remember the last time he was so positive that something good, perhaps even miraculous, was about to happen.

Leif had missed two makable birdie putts on seventeen and eighteen but had still finished with a solid score. The team was excited to hear about Alan's birdie. Trip had made birdie on seventeen. Cox was a streaky player who everybody knew was capable of getting hot. Chris had played the best golf of any of them during the first three rounds.

They all knew exactly where they would go to restart their rounds. Trip would begin in the rough a wedge short of the eighteenth green. Bratton had a 6-footer for his second straight birdie on seventeen. Cox had skanked his second shot into a bunker after a perfect tee shot on fifteen. Tidland had just tapped in for par on fourteen and would tee off on fifteen.

"Here's what we're going to do," Trip said breathlessly. "I'm going to birdie eighteen. Cox is going to make a couple birdies. Bratton is going to birdie seventeen and eighteen, and Chris is going to get at least two birdies on his way in."

He added one more thing.

"Believe in destiny," he said. "We can do this. We're gonna win this thing."

# 12

## Destiny

*Columbus, Ohio*
*June 3, 1995*

OUT THEY WALKED, taut, to face the swamped Scarlet Course. It was nearing 4:00 P.M. and her finishing holes would determine everything.

Stanford and Texas headed to holes ten through fourteen, where players' games were frozen in time during the rain delay. Oklahoma State, meanwhile, saw all of its players taking on the final four holes, the only holes left for the Cowboys to make something of their final tournament together.

In their favor: Holes fifteen, sixteen, and eighteen statistically were playing as three of the easier holes that week. Seventeen, everybody knew, was a bear and played fourth-toughest of the Scarlet's eighteen during the course of the tournament.

But weather was wreaking havoc on the statistics. With casual water all over the course from the vicious thunderstorms, holes would play differently in the final two hours before sunset. Eighteen, in particular, would play tougher. Of course, an added factor in eighteen's difficulty was the fact that college kids were playing the final hole of the NCAAs on the final day, with all its attendant pressures. How each player handled the slower greens, the soggy fairways, the squishy lies, and the changed conditions would be a new variable. Bunkers featured massive pools of water. There were small lakes of casual water on greens. The golf course was borderline unplayable, is what it was, but the NCAAs needed to finish, and they needed to finish today, so the tournament slogged on.

The Scarlet Course takes a hard right turn in its final quartet of holes. The par-4 fifteenth, at 428 yards, is one of the most difficult on the golf course given its dogleg left, its trees left, and its fairway bunkers in the right side of the landing area, running parallel to McCoy Road. A par on fifteen was considered as good as gold, according to MacKenzie's original design. Players then took the ninety-degree turn to holes sixteen and seventeen, along Kenny Road. Sixteen, a sharp dogleg left, was a birdie-able hole, despite a water hazard left, trees on the right, and the most severe green on the course. MacKenzie cut players a break with a relatively short distance of 379 yards.

From there, players headed to seventeen, alongside the passing traffic of Kenny Road. They'd have to block out the noise and visual of passing cars to hit a tee shot of 207 yards and take on that uphill incline to that severe green.

And from there, the short walk to eighteen tee, and the Scarlet's finishing hole, a classic dogleg left that approaches the stone clubhouse, the safe haven that featured the plaque honoring Jack Nicklaus's legacy. The first two days, the college kids took a good bite out of eighteen. In the final two days, eighteen was biting back.

Alan didn't have time to think about eighteen. He stood on seventeen green in a state of suspended animation, feeling good about a birdie on sixteen and a near ace on seventeen. But his team trailed Stanford and Texas, and he had to do something about it—right now, in the encroaching gloaming of a June afternoon in Columbus.

He had more than enough time to study the line while waiting for the other two players in his threesome to join him on the green. The putt was straightforward enough. The biggest unknown was how the saturated green would react to the latest dousing of water. How much slower would the green be?

The Oklahoma State fans who had followed Alan to the seventeenth green erupted when he rolled the 6-footer in for birdie. He hadn't played as well as he wanted to during his final NCAA Championship, but he was feeling confident. He had just made back-to-back birdies, which was just what the Cowboys needed if they were going to make things interesting.

As he walked to the eighteenth green, his mood improved even more. A second cheer from the eighteenth green filled the air and told him that Trip had made good on his promise by making birdie on eighteen. Two holes, two birdies. With no room left for error, that's the kind of efficiency the Cowboys desperately needed.

Trip had guaranteed a birdie on eighteen, knowing it necessitated a gamble. To fire at the flag meant he risked missing the green to the left and short-siding himself, bringing bogey into play. But to make birdie he would have to take an aggressive line at the flag with all the inherent risks. He took a deep breath, dead aim, and watched as his ball rolled to within 5 feet of the pin.

As he studied his 5-footer, he heard the reaction to Alan's birdie on seventeen. He knew exactly what it meant.

He buried the birdie putt to finish with a final-round 73. Now, all that was left for Trip Kuehne to do was watch and wait.

Most players hit 3-woods or irons on the eighteenth hole to avoid driving the ball through the fairway on a par-4, 414-yard finishing hole. Alan pulled his driver and did what he didn't want to do: He drove his ball through the fairway.

His second shot was complicated by one of the many signature maple trees that line the fairway, but he compensated with another clutch shot that left him on the front of the green, 36 feet from the cup.

The eighteenth green, like much of the course, was partially submerged. Alan's ball was in standing water. The rules allowed him to move it in either direction as long as it was equidistant to the hole. He took the drop and surveyed his chances from his new lie.

Alan was a good short putter, as reliable within 10 feet as anyone on Oklahoma State's team. He was not a great lag putter. Normally, he would leave this putt 3 or 4 feet short for a tap-in par. In this case par wasn't good enough.

*Be aggressive with this one,* he told himself after painstakingly reading the green and lining up the putt. And that's just what he did. But he was too aggressive, or so he feared, as he watched his ball speed toward the hole.

His heart sank. He had hammered the putt, and while his line was true, the ball was moving too fast. He was sure it was going to roll 4 or 5 feet past the hole. Instead, it hit the back of the cup, bounced up, and plopped dead center into the bottom of the cup.

Alan pumped his fist and smiled as the crowd around the green erupted with cheers. Added to the one he made before the last rain delay, he ended his college career with three straight birdies for a final round of 2-under 70.

Thus far, the prediction Trip made before he and his Oklahoma State teammates headed back to the course after the second rain delay had come true. He birdied eighteen and Alan birdied seventeen and eighteen, making up 3 quick strokes on par and bringing Oklahoma State 3 strokes closer to a Stanford team that was still negotiating the final few holes.

Trip and Alan had done all they could do. Now it was up to the other half of the Cowboys' remaining foursome—Kris Cox and Chris Tidland.

Cox's bunker shot landed within 7 feet on fifteen, and he made the putt for par before hammering his tee shot on the par-4, 379-yard sixteenth. Wedge in hand, he was standing over his second shot when he suddenly backed off.

Ernie Kuehne, meanwhile, was on the move. He scooted from the eighteenth green after his son's birdie to pick up Cox on sixteen.

Ernie had started doing what Oklahoma State players playfully called his "duck walk" after Alan almost holed his tee shot on seventeen before the second rain delay. It was a most positive sign.

Ernie is a short man with a powerful build whom Trip and his teammates referred to as "Big E." He knew virtually everybody on the course from his many years on the AJGA circuit. He was a power broker, a kingmaker. Numerous college coaches sought his opinion before offering scholarships to high school players. If Ernie Kuehne thought you were worthy of a scholarship, all he had to do was pick up the phone and call a coach, and one would be forthcoming.

Ernie used all his contacts to cull information when he was on the course. He had been all over the grounds during each of the four rounds, a walking scoreboard collecting and exchanging information with reporters, coaches, and anybody else who wanted to know where his son's team stood against the field. When the news was good, and he was rushing from hole to hole to follow the action, his shuffling gait would quicken, his right foot stepping farther to the right, his left farther to the left, lending him the appearance of a waddling duck.

"Look at Big E's walk," Trip had said when he noticed his father hustling to the seventeenth green to watch Alan attempt his birdie putt. "Something must be up."

Kevin Casas was a Kuehne family friend who was covering the tournament for the *Dallas Morning News*. Casas was a twenty-two-year-old cub reporter and golf fanatic who knew many of the Oklahoma State, Texas, and Stanford players. He was so desperate to cover the so-called Showdown at the Scarlet Course that he begged his sports editor for the assignment, even offering to cover his own expenses.

Casas's mom worked for Southwest Airlines, which meant free airfare, if only they could find a way to get him to Columbus at the last minute. He hopped a plane from Dallas to Little Rock, Arkansas, where he boarded a flight to Chicago before flying the final leg of his journey to Columbus.

Casas had one problem. The *Morning News* was paying him $100 per day to cover the event, but the only hotel room he could find cost four times that amount per night.

"How much you payin'?" Ernie had asked him.

"Four hundred," Casas replied.

"She-it," Ernie spat. "Stay with me."

Casas took Ernie up on the offer and had been glad for it until he was awakened at 3:00 A.M. on Saturday to see Ernie, a chronic insomniac who slept fitfully, in the nude, hovering over his rollaway bed.

"Think the Cowboys can win tomorrow?" he asked.

Oklahoma State's 3-stroke deficit after the third round did little to shake Ernie Kuehne's belief that the Cowboys would beat Stanford and win the 1995 NCAA tournament. He was pumped, ready to take on anybody who didn't think OSU had the fortitude to pull out a come-from-behind victory.

Ernie answered his own question before the groggy Casas had a chance to reply.

"I think they have a chance. If the Cowboys can put the pressure on early in the round, Stanford might fall apart coming down the stretch . . ."

Ernie went on and on, never allowing Casas to address the question that he had awakened him to answer. Casas was grateful. He didn't want to tell Ernie what he really thought. He thought Texas was going to spoil the season-long rivalry between Oklahoma State and Stanford and avenge their collapse from the year before. Casas finally drifted off to sleep, thinking, *Old man, you're crazy. The Cowboys don't have a chance in hell of winning the tournament tomorrow.*

Now Ernie was standing near the sixteenth green watching Kris give himself a little pep talk before attempting a shot that could continue the comeback that Ernie had felt certain would happen.

Kris knew the wedge he held and the yardage to the hole were an ideal match. Taking a deep breath and a practice swing, he measured the distance to the hole one more time, envisioning the shot in his mind. He knew this was a great opportunity for him to hit one close and give himself a birdie opportunity. He remembered Valerie's advice: "Take it straight back." He addressed the ball, took another deep breath, and stood over his ball for several seconds before drawing his club back . . .

Ernie Kuehne smiled when the ball landed a foot from the hole.

Kris had just made Oklahoma State's fourth birdie since the second rain delay ended. If Stanford was playing par golf, their lead had been whittled to 5 strokes. If they were playing above par . . . well . . .

Seventeen was a tough enough hole, made more so when Kris

pulled a 3-iron 60 feet wide of the flagstick and ran the putt 12 feet past. He faced the prospect of giving back a stroke when Oklahoma State didn't have that luxury.

He made the comebacker for par.

Kris had never been so nervous as when he walked to the eighteenth green, but his nerves wouldn't impact his swing. He followed up a perfect 3-wood off the tee with a 9-iron to within 8 feet to give himself a shot at becoming the third straight Cowboy to birdie the Scarlet Course's finishing hole.

By the time he reached the green, he could hardly draw the putter back. As the Oklahoma State fans ringing the green watched breathlessly, the ball scooted past the hole, and the Cowboys' momentum was momentarily broken.

Kris was grieving his missed putt and Oklahoma State's lost stroke when he signed his scorecard, making his final round of 1-under 71 official.

Valerie and Oree had been in Columbus all week. Oree, eighty-two, couldn't spend an entire day walking the course as he once had. Instead, he and Valerie retired to a short balcony overlooking the eighteenth green. Kris walked over and accepted hugs and encouraging words from the two people most responsible for him being in this position, before joining Alan and Trip Kuehne behind the green to wait for Chris to come in.

Alan and Trip Kuehne were wearing their "rally caps" backward. Kris turned his black Oklahoma State Final Four hat around, too, hoping that he hadn't killed the rally that they desperately needed to continue.

On seventeen, Chris handled the tough par 3 with a tee shot to the green and a two-putt for par. He, like his best friend, Alan, chose a driver off the tee on eighteen but kept it in the fairway, putting him in range for a short iron to the green. It was 7-iron distance for Chris, and he hit it perfectly.

"That's the best swing you've put on it all day," Arizona's Ted Purdy remarked after Chris's approach landed 3 feet from the cup.

Chris didn't know where he stood in the individual standings. Spratlin was still on the course. He didn't know whether his disappointing final-round 74 would count toward Oklahoma State's aggregate daily total when he tapped in for birdie on eighteen, but a tap-in birdie wasn't a bad way to end his college career.

Chris, who Holder initially didn't think had enough game to play at Oklahoma State, ended his final round of college golf in contention for the NCAA individual championship and with a chance—however faint—of winning the team title. No matter what *Golf World*'s ranking said, he was clearly established as one of the top collegians in the country.

Before he signed his scorecard, he walked over and asked Alan what he'd shot. He was pleasantly surprised to hear his friend had shot 70. He assumed Alan had finished with a 1-over 73. His eyebrow rose again when he learned of Trip's 73 and Kris's 71. Both scores were several strokes lower than he expected.

Chris knew Leif had shot even par, and that he himself had turned in the highest score of the five, and therefore, despite being in contention for medalist honors, his final-round score would be tossed out. Any disappointment he may have felt was trumped by a sudden sense of opportunity.

After all five Cowboy scores were officially recorded, Holder could only fall back on his superstitions and began rubbing the buckeye in his pocket. He had picked up his good-luck charm when his Cowboys won the national title at the Scarlet Course in 1980. Although it would seem out of character, Holder was always cooking up charms. A ticket dangled from his belt loop even though he had been issued a coach's badge. That tradition was born years before when security personnel didn't recognize him and made him buy a ticket to coach his own team at the NCAA Championships. The Cowboys won that year. He had bought a ticket ever since.

Now, his team might not need luck. He had thought that if his Cowboys came in at even par they would have a chance. When they finished the last three holes at 5 under par to finish the final round with an aggregate score of 2-under 286, he had a good feeling. Win or lose, their late birdie binge had made what seemed like an unlikely national title at the beginning of the day a possibility, however remote.

Now all they could do was wait and hope that Stanford stumbled coming in.

"Let's go stand behind the eighteenth green and watch these guys come in," Holder told them. "You never know what's going to happen."

When Oklahoma State finished, the angry Ohio skies calmed. There was a glimmer of late-afternoon sun fighting through the gray, enough to cast shadows on the green. Stanford, though, didn't feel entirely comfortable with the weather. Goodwin sensed that his California kids were keeping half an eye on the sky, fearing another round of those unfamiliar and unsettling lightning storms.

And yet, Stanford took to the back nine still feeling that familiar confidence of being maybe the greatest college golf team in history. For Notah, Casey, and Will, there was a rush of adrenaline they'd felt the year before at Stonebridge. It was a good feeling. The last time they felt it, they'd won the national championship. This time, they had the feeling again—and they had Tiger Woods as the last Stanford man on the course.

The first Stanford player to head for home was Will Yanagisawa. The '94 hero hadn't played to his liking in the first three rounds, but true to his history, he was stitching together an excellent eighteen holes on the final day. Maybe there was some magic in his blade—after all, he was using Tiger Woods's backup putter, just to change his luck. It worked when he rolled in a 6-footer for a good par on seventeen. Yanagisawa was 2 under for the round and had a gut instinct that Stanford was pulling away from Texas. The short walk from seventeen green to eighteen tee passed a leaderboard, and sure enough, Stanford was in the lead. Texas was in second.

Yanagisawa noticed two other things: One, Oklahoma State was miles behind. Two, the scoreboard was woefully out of date.

So, he told himself: *Just make a four on eighteen, and see what happens.*

He safely drove the fairway on eighteen and liked the feeling.

Just then, a spectator approached him. It was the father of Texas player Robbie Skinner, who was playing with Yanagisawa. Skinner's father had walked the entire round and chose this time, of all times, to offer a curious salutation.

"Congratulations, Will," Mr. Skinner said, "on another national championship for Stanford."

Yanagisawa couldn't believe his ears. His first thought was that there was a ton of golf left, and the congratulations were beyond premature. His second thought: If anybody doesn't need any tempting right now, it's the golf gods. Already, Stanford had performed this stop-and-start dance of weather delays that was making the day weird enough.

As if on cue, Yanagisawa turned the dogleg to face the eighteenth green. He noticed something—a shock of orange behind the green. It was Cowboy orange, which meant Oklahoma State's players were gathered behind the green. There would be no reason to gather unless the Cowboys felt they had a chance.

*Hmm,* Yanagisawa thought. *They must have finished well.*

But to stand behind the green like that was still an unusual move. Yanagisawa chalked it up as a very Holder thing to do. Were the Cowboys trying to intimidate Stanford? Was it an attempt to rattle the Cardinal?

An answer came on Yanagisawa's next swing. He came over his 4-iron and pulled it left, way left, and his ball hit off the scoring tent. He laid two far off the green, and when he tried to flop a 60-degree wedge, the conditions became a factor. The wet rough snagged his clubface, and his third shot came up short of the green. It would take a miracle up and down just to save bogey.

*OK,* Yanagisawa told himself, *don't give it all away here.*

From a more difficult lie than his first, he gouged a flop shot to 9 feet. Then, calling on the short-game training he'd practiced since his days in the back of his parents' golf shop in Long Beach, he rolled home the 9-footer for a 5. It was a good bogey, and though Yanagisawa shot a fine 71, he'd wonder if the bogey would come back to haunt Stanford. He went to sign his card, then wait for Jerry Chang, Casey Martin, Notah Begay, and Tiger Woods.

Chang was next, but it wasn't to be for the newcomer. He came home in 2-over 74, his second-worst round of the championships. Greenside, Oklahoma State was beginning to feel something, a turning of the tide, a sense that things might be, just maybe, going their way.

Next up for Stanford was Casey Martin. Though Martin came to the eighteenth tee box 2 over for the round, he still felt a rush. This was where he loved to be, with big things riding on a final hole. Ever since his strong finish as a freshman at the 1991 NCAAs, he'd enjoyed these year-end surges of adrenaline, and it showed when he roped a drive over the corner of the dogleg. Casey Martin was always long off the tee, and in his final college golf hole, he was once again.

Casey still didn't have any accurate information as to where the leaderboard stood. He assumed his team was playing well, nobody was imploding, and with Notah and Tiger behind him, matters were in excellent hands. He had a short iron into eighteen and had a decent chance for birdie. It stayed decent when he knocked his 9-iron to 10 feet.

Casey, too, noticed the Oklahoma State players hanging around the eighteenth green and knew that Holder's boys had to be up to their old tricks in some fashion. He thought to himself: *Oklahoma State? Really? Wow. OK, then . . . Oklahoma State.*

And then Casey Martin . . . missed his 10-foot birdie try.

He would tap in for a par and a 74, matching Chang's score.

Goodwin, by now greenside at eighteen, began to put together the numbers. Oklahoma State was in with 1,156 strokes, 4 over par. Stanford, unfortunately, was beginning to creep back toward that number.

And now here came Notah Begay and all that he represented. The man who had brazenly shot 62 a year ago to lead Stanford to that coveted national title was on eighteen tee box with a chance to be the hero again.

Except one thing was different. This time, Notah Begay was limping home, bleeding strokes all over the back nine in a damaging run of golf.

It started at fifteen, where Notah arrived 2 under for the day. Standing at fifteen tee, Notah was the portrait of senior mettle, coming through huge for his team.

But he missed the green, couldn't get up and down, and made bogey on the par-4 hole.

With all the action bunched on the final few holes, word was beginning to travel through the Scarlet Course. Stanford was beginning to wobble.

"The big Indian just made bogey," Ernie Kuehne announced to the Cowboys greenside on eighteen when he heard Notah Begay gave a stroke back on fifteen.

Back in Palo Alto, Goodwin's assistant Sara Hallock was following the scores on the Internet. Online was the only source of information, after ESPN's window of broadcast time had closed. Incredibly, after all the hype and all the attention showered on Tiger, golf fans would not be able to see the conclusion of the championships. ESPN went off the air after the second rain delay, at 4:00 P.M. Eastern. Now it was past 6:00 P.M. Eastern and the only word came via the slow dial-up modem on Goodwin's office computer. When the page for Notah's scorecard finally refreshed, she grimaced. Notah repeated his sin from fifteen, missed the green again, and bogeyed the short, birdie-able sixteenth hole.

He arrived at seventeen needing a few things: a bandage to stop the bleeding and some information, too. Where did Stanford stand overall?

The last he'd known before the end of the second rain delay, Texas had a 2-stroke lead. But that information seemed stale, out of date. Word was, the Longhorns were giving back strokes, and Stanford might have the lead. In fact, one greenside observer passed on some bad information: Stanford was either tied for the lead or had fallen behind.

Fallen behind? Say what? Where was the proper score? The scoreboards were down. Had Oklahoma State, as somebody suggested, made a move? Or not?

If Stanford held a 1-shot lead, as Begay hoped, he'd play it safe on seventeen: aim for the fat of the green, take his two-putt par, and move to eighteen to close out the national championship.

But if Stanford was now behind by a stroke? Somewhere in his gut, Begay felt he had to make birdie on seventeen.

It wouldn't be the conventional play. Not only was seventeen a bear, but the pin position, tucked back right, meant that going for the flag would involve the risk of landing in the greenside bunker right, short-sided.

Begay didn't have a choice, in his mind. He needed a birdie to help his team. He aggressively teed it up and fired at the pin.

Sure enough, his tee shot landed in the bunker, short-sided.

The short-game wizard who spent all those winters practicing in the New Mexico cold while preparing for a career he believed would net major championships had almost no shot from there.

No way could he make par. His out would roll past the flag, downslope, and he'd have a long two-putt for bogey—his third consecutive.

Greenside at eighteen, the details of Begay's travails continued to trickle in, lending the Cowboys hope that their late-round birdie blitz would be enough. Yanagisawa and Chang stood watch, along with Goodwin. Casey Martin went in to sign his scorecard.

When Begay arrived at eighteen tee, a familiar feeling of comfort and confidence overcame him. Despite a triple-header of bogeys, he knew he was going to play eighteen well, and that Stanford was going to win the national championship again. It was, he thought to himself, Stanford's tournament to win. Always was, always would be.

It nearly unfolded that way when Begay roped a 3-wood to the middle of the fairway. He walked to his ball and eyed the eighteenth green, with its growing gallery of interested observers. He didn't know if it was a sixth sense, but he had the distinct impression he needed to make birdie for Stanford to win this thing. Nobody had told him anything, and the lack of scoreboard communication made the final round seem strangely mute as far as breaking news. Still feeling relaxed, he pulled 8-iron. Remembering his three keys from his boyhood days in New Mexico—grip, posture, alignment—he enacted that awkward, effective swing of his. His golf ball tracked, right at the flag. It landed with a comforting thud on the waterlogged eighteenth green, just 3½ feet above the hole.

The math was becoming more and more clear. With more scores trickling in, Holder and the Cowboys were realizing they were gaining ground. Texas was fading and up to 8 over as a team. With Begay's three-headed bogey monster on fifteen, sixteen, and seventeen, the Cowboys now knew they had pulled dead even with Stanford in the aggregate total at a collective 4 over par. It was incredible, but true. Oklahoma State's surge and Stanford's combination of stalls and stumbles meant the national title was now, officially, up for grabs between the two best teams in the land, and the two teams who felt they deserved it most.

But Begay's cold-blooded approach on eighteen changed any optimism. The brilliant second shot left Stanford in control. Surely, Oklahoma State's players knew that Begay, a deadly putter, would bury this 42-inch putt and their stunning comeback would come up short. Stanford—or at least Goodwin, Yanagisawa, and Chang—knew it, too. Casey hadn't left the scorer's trailer yet.

Goodwin had a decision to make. Should he call his senior over and tell him exactly the stakes? So many things raced through the coach's mind: Notah's personality, Notah's focus, Notah's experience. He thought quickly of that high school basketball player he saw that winter night in 1990 in Albuquerque, the one with the fire in his eyes that always warmed Goodwin's coaching heart. He decided to stay put. He knew Notah Begay would compete to the very end.

As Begay sized up the putt, he knew it broke left to right. If Notah's belief in ambidextrous putting was firm, the putt called for him to putt left-handed. Thing was, his left-handed putting stroke that day was betraying him. He practiced the putt left-handed, then, curiously, backed off and stood over the putt—right-handed. His father knew exactly what was happening. Even though the putt called for a left-handed stroke, he knew his son didn't believe in the lefty stroke. He would fall back on what was working that day and putt right-handed.

A few feet away, the Cowboys looked at each other, as if saying, "What is he doing?"

They sensed he was tentative.

And then Begay struck the putt. It never had a chance.

He shoved it past the hole, the break sliding away from his right-handed stroke.

He gave a slight hitch to his belt loop, walked past the hole to the ball, tapped it in for par, and picked it up.

A par on eighteen. A final-round 73.

Stanford and Oklahoma State were tied at 4 over par.

Holder knew Begay was going to miss the putt, was convinced something like this would happen since the scoring controversy at the Ping Preview, when Trip thought Notah should have taken a penalty stroke when his ball rolled into a bunker after he addressed it. He looked at Trip now, and they shared a knowing smile: "What goes around comes around," Holder said.

At that precise moment, Casey Martin walked out of the scorer's trailer. He still didn't know which team was leading the championship. He saw Begay's putt slide past. *Oh, no,* he thought. *That might have been big.*

The only player left on the course for Stanford was Tiger.

The freshman was so far removed from the action, he had no idea what had transpired in front of him. When he hit his tee shot safely off the eighteenth tee box, he walked to the fairway thinking his first year as a collegian would end as a member of a national championship team. Strangely, though, he noticed a figure approaching him. As Tiger arrived at his ball, Notah Begay walked out to him.

From Begay's perspective, Tiger could only benefit from a visit. In Notah's mind, here was the greatest amateur player in history, with a chance to win his school a title with a birdie. To Notah, Tiger would want to hear the situation, would want to know exactly what he needed to do.

"Par gets us in a playoff," Begay said. "Birdie wins it."

Tiger buckled in shock.

"What?" he said.

After all the rain, after all the lightning, after all the hype, the TV coverage, the reams of words written about Stanford and Oklahoma State, the Cowboys were in with 1,156 strokes. With Tiger's ball sitting in the fairway, Stanford stood at 1,153 strokes.

Having a player on the golf course who, time and again in his career, summoned up greatness, Stanford felt big things were possible. For Oklahoma State, excitement had been replaced by a profound feeling of dread.

Just ask Trip Kuehne what Tiger Woods could do.

Tiger's short iron into eighteen took flight—and landed 18 feet short of the pin.

It all came down to this: Tiger Woods, 18 feet, for the national championship. Nine months earlier, Trip had seen the sort of magic that followed Tiger in situations like this. That was in Sawgrass, and the Havermeyer Trophy in Tiger's California home spoke to how these things usually turned out for Tiger.

The color drained from Trip's face. Destiny be damned. He had a horrible feeling about this.

Trip's goal had never been to capture a U.S. Amateur, which didn't make his loss to Tiger at Sawgrass any easier to digest. But he had made winning an NCAA team title his goal since he was a junior player. To lose both the most prestigious individual amateur title and his most coveted collegiate team title to his friend and rival in the same year was almost too much to take.

But there remained one wild card in all this: the water on the greens from those relentless Ohio storms. Just how much water had soaked into those greens couldn't be quantified.

And so Tiger drew back his putter and struck a true putt that tracked . . . and tracked . . . and tracked . . . and fell one revolution short.

Tiger's golf ball was 3 inches shy of glory.

His Stanford teammates were stunned. They never imagined it.

Oklahoma State never imagined it, either, and a wave of relief rolled over them; their hearts started beating again. They knew what to do. They knew exactly what this meant. As soon as Tiger tapped in for par, and a team total of 1,156 strokes, 4 over par as a team, Stanford's players stood motionless. While the Cardinal tried to make sense of it all, the Cowboys picked up their golf bags and headed straight to the practice range, to prepare for the first-ever sudden-death playoff in the ninety-eight-year history of the NCAA Golf Championships.

Leif Westerberg settled into his seat on the plane that would take him on the first leg of his journey from Columbus to England. He buckled his seat belt and used the phone in the seatback in front of him to make a quick phone call before takeoff.

Before he left the course he had procured the phone number of the pro shop so he could call to find out who had won the NCAA tournament. Basically, he wanted to confirm Stanford's second straight victory. Or perhaps Texas had caught them. Or USC. He didn't consider the possibility of Oklahoma State winning, or being tied with Stanford. Nine strokes was a lot of ground to make up, and when he left the course his teammates were running out of holes.

He just hoped his two missed birdie opportunities on seventeen and eighteen hadn't proved to be the difference.

"I was wondering if you could tell me who won nationals?" Westerberg asked politely when the pro shop attendant answered the phone.

As soon as he heard the words "It's going to a playoff right now," he felt his body turn cold. Despite having mentally discounted his team's chances only moments ago, he knew exactly what the clubhouse attendant would say next.

"It's between OSU and Stanford. And guess what?" Westerberg heard the voice say as he held the plane's phone to his ear, his face frozen in an expression of disbelief. "Oklahoma State is missing a guy."

"No shit," he snapped. "I'm that guy."

Westerberg panicked. The door of the plane was closed. Could he still get off? He had to get back to the course, back to his teammates, who shouldn't have to play a playoff for the national championship a man down.

He didn't know the rules. Would Oklahoma State be allowed to participate in the playoff without the full complement of players? The attendant hadn't said when the playoff was scheduled to start. If he did get off the plane and race back to the course, would he arrive in time?

He unbuckled his seat belt and was considering charging up the aisle toward the door when he remembered that he had checked his clubs. Even if he was allowed to deplane, how could he get his clubs out of the belly of the plane?

The plane started taxiing. He gripped the armrests, the veins in his arms bulging. It was too late.

What was he doing here? He wasn't supposed to be on this plane. He was supposed to be on the Scarlet Course. He was supposed to be helping his teammates win a national championship.

Instead, he was on a plane, taxiing down a runway.

Wally Goodwin had no idea how the playoff would be formatted.

He wasn't alone. NCAA golf history had never had a sudden-death playoff before. Players were confused. Parents and girlfriends were confused. Where did the players go? How would the players be grouped? And how would the departure of Westerberg affect the formatting?

To Goodwin's ears, USGA rules official Tom Meeks sounded a little confused, too.

The way Goodwin understood it, because Westerberg was gone, Oklahoma State would send its number four and number three players out—Kris and Trip—in a foursome with Stanford's number five and number four, Chang and Yanagisawa. That would leave a final fivesome of both teams' numbers one and two players—Alan and Chris for Oklahoma State, Tiger and Notah for Stanford, plus Stanford's number three player, Casey.

The one man on the golf course who wasn't confused was Holder. He had long served on the NCAA's golf committee, and one of the committee's duties was to review and amend the rule book every year. He and other committee members reviewed and revised rules for team and individual playoffs annually. Holder's team had been involved in a somewhat similar playoff during the 1993 NCAA tournament in Nicholasville, Kentucky, when the Cowboys took advantage of a playoff to avoid missing the cut for the first time in the program's history.

Stanford won the coin toss, which meant that they had the option of A or B position in the NCAA's sudden-death playoff procedure. Goodwin chose the A position, which Goodwin thought meant he would send two players out in the first group. What it really meant, according to the rules, was that his third, fourth, and fifth players, as designated before the tournament began, would tee off in the first group with Oklahoma State's fourth and fifth players. Since the Cowboys didn't have a fifth player, Kris, who had been so nervous during the final holes of regulation that he had to back away from a routine wedge and missed a makable birdie attempt on eighteen, would be alone in the first group with Chang, Yanagisawa, and Martin.

It also meant, Holder knew, that his first, second, and third players—Alan, Chris, and Trip—would go out in the second group with Tiger and Notah.

In Holder's mind, that meant Stanford would have a distinct advantage. Holder's experience told him that it was preferable to have as many players as possible in the first group because they would be under less pressure. Players in the second group are under more pressure because they are aware of what has taken place in front of them. If an opposing player makes birdie, for example, they may feel obligated to offset that score with a birdie of their own. If a teammate in the first group hits a poor shot, his teammate in the second group may be more inclined to take a risk to make up for it.

A counter to that argument would be that Oklahoma State was making out better in the deal. They'd have three big guns in the final fivesome, and Stanford just two. In this theory, Oklahoma State's final players on the course would know exactly what they had to do to win and would take strength from having two other teammates in their group.

Had it been up to Holder, he would have sent all four of his players off in the first group. Instead, Stanford would post three scores to Oklahoma State's one, which Holder felt would put a lot of pressure on the Cowboys in the second group.

Goodwin preferred the opposite strategy. He wanted a numerical advantage in the second group. He wanted clutch players like Notah, Tiger, and Casey to know what they had to do before they teed off.

One thing Holder was sure of: Having Kris alone in the first group was a major disadvantage for the Cowboys. He didn't regret letting Westerberg go, even though Westerberg's presence would have made it feel like more of a fair fight. Kris was so nervous that he had to concentrate on his breathing as he missed routine 3-foot putts on the practice green. Holder didn't waste time worrying about it. He just concentrated on getting Kris in the right frame of mind to play the hole because his score, he knew, would set the tone for Chris, Alan, and Trip in the next group.

The last thing he wanted was for Chris, Alan, and Trip to tee off thinking they had to make a birdie because Kris had made a double bogey.

While Goodwin tried to gather his team and his wits after the baffling turn of events unfolded, and Meeks attempted to lay out the format, Alan Bratton felt a wave of regret.

Two weeks before, at the NCAA Regionals at Bentwater Country Club in Montgomery, Texas, Alan and his teammates had watched a playoff between Texas Christian and Northwestern to determine which team would finish tenth in the Regionals and therefore gain a berth to the NCAA tournament.

The first Northwestern player hit his drive out of bounds.

"Geez, I'd hate to be that guy," Alan said as the next Northwestern player prepared to tee off. "He knows his score is going to count."

Alan was on the practice green, rolling in three straight long putts, wishing he hadn't said that now that he and his teammates were in the exact same situation without Westerberg. He hoped Kuehne, Chris, and Kris weren't thinking about that, too.

"Being a man down is to our advantage," Holder told his players moments later, knowing it didn't matter if it was true, only that they believed it. "We know our scores are going to count and they don't."

Holder then told them something his players never expected.

Second place was never good enough for Oklahoma State's coach. He was never satisfied until the national championship was secured. It had been that way since 1977, since the painful personal memory of nemesis Houston winning a national championship he believed belonged to his Cowboys. But despite how demanding he had been, and how much he had driven this group to fulfill what he believed was its destiny by winning a national championship, he wanted them to know that whatever happened in the playoff would not change his opinion of this team and what they had already accomplished that day.

Their rally to force the playoff was, in his estimation, an even greater clutch performance than that of the 1991 team who rallied from 3 down before the last round and 2 down at the turn. That team had fired a composite 287 on the final day to win. This team had started the day 3 down before seeing the deficit balloon to 8 and had shot a 286—through two rain delays, no less.

"It doesn't matter what the outcome of the playoff is," Holder told them. "This is the greatest clutch performance I've ever had from a team in twenty-two years of coaching. Win, lose, or draw, that was the best I've ever seen a team play, because we didn't have our best stuff all week. And especially today, we were all over the golf course. But you guys hung in there and hung tough and made a lot of birdies coming in. I'm just speechless."

But when the first playoff group gathered on the eighteenth tee box, the emotion was gone. Holder was all business. For everyone else, however, confusion settled in.

Casey Martin took the tee box with Chang and Yanagisawa, but only Kris showed up for Oklahoma State.

"Why is he going out by himself?" Martin said, pointing to Kris. "They need to have two golfers out here in this group."

As far as Holder, standing on the tee box, and his players were concerned, there was no confusion as to the format.

"My positions are filled," he said. "Play on."

"That's not how this was explained to me," Casey said to Meeks.

"It's right there in the handbook," Holder interjected.

Goodwin, though, wasn't there to engage. He'd taken a position by the eighteenth green, inadvertently putting his players in a position to fend for themselves. For all of Goodwin's tenure, his laissez-faire philosophy, his trusting of the bright and self-sufficient Stanford kids, had worked. In this particular instance, it didn't.

Meeks tried to put his foot down.

"Oh, yes, you did agree to this," he said.

Martin didn't think anybody was being deceitful, but he was under the impression that two Oklahoma State players would play in the first group, and he didn't put it past Holder to try to pull a fast one. The whole thing felt . . . inaccurate. That was the word he came up with. If Stanford won the toss, why did Oklahoma State get more players in the last group? Shouldn't the Cowboys send two players out in the first and second groups?

Kris, as the only Oklahoma State player in that foursome, wondered why Martin was making a big deal. He had other issues. He had just dealt with the possibility that his missed putt on eighteen in regulation cost the Cowboys a national championship. In the time between his missed putt and the ultimate conclusion, Kris wrestled with the notion that he'd let his friends down, especially seniors Chris and Alan. He had been given a reprieve by Stanford's meltdown, but he was more nervous than ever.

He didn't want to go ask Valerie and Oree for advice. He didn't want to take any more practice swings, and most of all, now that they were standing on the tee box, he didn't want to debate the playoff format. The only thing he wanted to do was rid himself of the nervous nausea he felt, and the only way to do that, he knew, was for everybody to shut up so he could go play.

Win or lose, he wanted to get this playoff over with.

The gallery that crowded around eighteen included a growing list of famous faces, most of whom were pulling for the Cowboys.

Former OSU golfers David Edwards, Scott Verplank, Bob Tway, and Bob May had once again driven to Columbus from Dublin, Ohio, where they were participating in the Memorial at Muirfield Village. But they weren't the only recognizable faces in the crowd rooting for OSU. The loyalty former OSU players felt toward Holder was evident when E. J. Pfister, the NCAA medalist in 1988, also arrived. OSU basketball coach Eddie Sutton, the hero of the previous Final Four, was also on hand.

Stanford did not have the same alumni legacy and had to make do with close friends and family hoping the Cardinal could repeat as champions.

Ernie Kuehne didn't think they were going to.

"What do you think?" a reporter asked Ernie.

"Tiger ain't got that look in his eye today," Ernie said.

Chang, Yanagisawa, Martin, and Kris all hit their tee shots safely in the fairway. Kris walked off the eighteenth tee box, relieved that the playoff was finally under way. Holder marched up the fairway with Kris. He didn't want Oklahoma State's lone player in the group to feel alone.

Casey was first to hit in. Again, with a 9-iron, and again, he made it count. The ball strike was pure, and his golf ball landed 10 feet from the cup.

Kris was next. The delighted screams from OSU faithful began virtually the moment the ball left his club. Carrying Oklahoma State's fortunes on his back, he made a nice pass at it, and the rest of the gallery understood that the OSU cheers weren't premature when it landed in virtually the same place as his approach in regulation and rolled 8 feet from the cup.

Stanford supporters followed with low murmurs when Jerry Chang and Will Yanagisawa sent their second shots flying over the green.

Advantage Oklahoma State.

Chang chunked his third shot and two-putted for bogey. Yanagisawa chipped to within 15 feet. Again, he'd put pressure on his put-

ter. It had come through on seventeen in regulation and to save bogey on eighteen in regulation. If he had missed either of those two
putts, Stanford's collapse would have been complete—they'd have
missed the playoff entirely.

Once more, the littlest Cardinal stood tall. He buried the long
putt for par. Stanford's fans greenside finally had a reason to cheer.

Casey was next. He lined up his 10-footer, carefully reading his
line. Here was a chance to make the putt he knew would give Stanford the momentum it needed to wrest this championship away
from Oklahoma State and make the Cardinal back-to-back champions. It would mean so much on so many levels—his years of
overcoming his disability, a natural climax to five years with Notah
at Stanford, and the ultimate validation that their joint decision to
redshirt and wait for Tiger was worth it.

He missed the putt. Pushed it right. Casey Martin had to settle
for a tap-in par.

Three Stanford players, and no birdies in the bunch. Two pars
and a bogey. Ever since the last rain delay, the Cardinal were a mess.
It felt too much like the entire spring season, which had started so
unsatisfactorily in Hawaii and now was careening toward the ultimate disappointment.

Still, Tiger and Notah were on the course. Stanford still had its
chance.

Any momentary disappointment Chris felt about finishing tied
for second with Purdy for the NCAA individual title—1 stroke behind Auburn's Chip Spratlin—quickly dissipated when it became
apparent that the team title would be determined in a playoff. Now,
his and Alan's last chance had come down to this: one hole for the
NCAA Championship, one hole to avoid being remembered as
Holder's first class not to win a NCAA title.

Chris, like Tiger and Notah, hit a picture-perfect tee shot down
the middle of the fairway. Now it was Alan's turn, and he was so
jittery he could barely get his ball on the tee. His ball was teed too
high but he was afraid to re-tee it; his hands were shaking so much
he was afraid it would fall off and cost him a stroke.

He regretted it as soon as he hooked his drive. It wasn't a disastrous shot—the eighteenth was a dogleg left, after all—but he hadn't put it where he wanted, either.

Now, Notah, Tiger, Chris, Trip, and Alan were standing by their drives, the drama playing out on the green in front of them partially obscured from view.

They heard the cheers when Kris hit his second shot and exchanged glances. Everybody knew what it meant: He had hit it close.

Trip's, Chris's, and Alan's smiles faded when yet another roar erupted from the fans circling the green. The Oklahoma State players all thought the same thing: They assumed Yanagisawa had birdied, too, but the cheers were actually a reaction to his making the 15-footer for par.

Trip, Chris, and Alan could see the portion of the green where Kris stood over his birdie putt. They watched him line it up, watched him take his practice strokes before stepping over the ball. Then they watched as he backed off the putt and started over. From their vantage point, they didn't realize that their teammate was shaking so much that he had to abandon his stance to regain his composure.

"Uh-oh, that's not a good sign," Chris told Kuehne as they watched Kris back away from a putt, just as he'd done earlier.

Alan, standing several yards away, thought, *That's unusual.*

Then, they heard the crowd roar. It was a sudden and warm noise to Cowboy ears, the kind of thing that can happen when pressure at a golf course builds into nearly unbearable silence—only to be broken and relieved by the cheer of accomplishment.

Kris Cox made his birdie putt.

He erased his memory of the miss on eighteen and, as the lone Cowboy in the first foursome, put Oklahoma State in the red.

The scoreboard: Oklahoma State, 1 under par.

Stanford, assuming Chang's bogey would be tossed out, even par.

Holder hugged Kris greenside, knowing how much making that putt meant not only to him but to Oklahoma State's chances. Kris had battled his nerves through two rain delays and over the final dramatic holes of regulation. He had mourned the missed putt on eighteen, terrified that it would cost the Cowboys the national title. He had been sent off in the first group of the playoff with three Stanford players, and he had responded in the grandest fashion possible.

"What a putt," an emotional Holder whispered to a misty-eyed Kris as they embraced. "You're going to remember that putt for the rest of your life."

Ernie Kuehne leaned in to Kris.

"Your grandpa almost fell off the balcony when you made that putt," Ernie said.

Kris turned and smiled and waved at Valerie and Oree on the balcony. He had never seen them look so happy. He went over and jumped up on the railing to give them both as much of a hug as the balcony railing would allow, sharing the moment with his mom and grandpa.

Kris hopped down and retreated greenside to watch the rest of the playoff unfold.

Alan, Chris, and Trip Kuehne assumed the playoff was tied. They still believed the cheer following Yanagisawa's putt meant he'd birdied the hole, too. In their minds, the scoring was all even because Chang's bogey would likely be Stanford's high score and therefore thrown out.

Tiger hit his approach to virtually the identical location he had during regulation—18 feet from the pin. The Cowboy players felt another wave of dread. There was no way he was going to miss from less than 20 feet twice in the same spot. Not with this much at stake.

Notah prompted yet another roar from the Stanford contingent when his second shot landed 12 feet from the flag. Tiger and Notah, friends since junior golf, bonded for years as the nonwhite players in an overwhelmingly white sport, were throwing some haymakers in the name of Stanford University.

Trip's and Chris's answers were not stellar. Both hit their approaches onto the front right edge of the green, about 45 feet from the hole, which was located on the back left.

Alan's drive had landed in casual water. Mother Nature's looming role in the proceedings continued. He had to ask for, and get, a drop in the fairway.

Trip and Chris felt confident about Alan. Tiger Woods may have been the best amateur in the world, and he may have had more ability than anybody they had ever seen, but in their opinion Alan Bratton was the best collegiate golfer in the field. After all, he made three straight birdies to end regulation and force this playoff.

Now he had a wedge in his hand. Chris and Trip liked their chances.

Alan felt the eyes upon him. He would usually hit a 9-iron from here, but it was easier to hit a 9-iron fat in these soggy conditions. He might chunk this shot if he hit a 9-iron soft. Besides, he was pumped up. He wanted to hit something hard.

He struck the ball solidly, but it came up short and spun back to almost the same spot where he had placed his ball after it landed in a puddle on the eighteenth green earlier. This one, it looked to Alan, would be even longer than his dramatic flourish on eighteen in regulation.

"At least I know the line," he told himself as he threw his bag over his shoulder and walked toward the green.

Alan's shot hadn't been as close as Chris and Trip had hoped. Now a colder reality was sinking in. Notah and Tiger had 12- and 18-footers for birdie. That meant Chris or Trip would need to make at least one of their much longer putts to keep pace, and Alan might have to drop another long one, as well.

Perhaps the championship was now swinging back to Stanford. Maybe their deeply held confidence was going to bear fruit after all. If both Tiger and Notah made their putts, which was highly possible, Stanford would be 2 under par. That meant one of Alan, Trip, or Chris would have to make his putt just to tie.

The shortest of their putts was 38 feet. It was not a likely situation.

Advantage Stanford.

Chris putted first and, as could be expected, with wet greens and a long putt, left it 3 feet short. The crowd groaned. He marked his ball and walked carefully away, waiting to see what Trip could do.

When Trip left his birdie attempt 3 feet short, the tables had turned.

The best Trip and Chris could do was save par, and Alan was lining up a 38-footer prayer for birdie. Chances were, Notah and Tiger would make at least one birdie, which meant they would remain deadlocked after Chang's score was discarded. If that were the case, they would all return to the eighteenth tee box to play the hole again. If Woods and Begay both made their birdie putts, Stanford would win.

Alan was away. He knew the line, felt comfortable over the putt. *Don't hit it as hard as you did the last time,* he told himself.

He didn't. The speed . . . the line . . .

Dead-solid perfect.

Holder knew the ball would find the hole from the moment it left Alan's blade. He had watched his senior drain three long putts on the practice range before the playoff. Alan marched confidently after his ball and pumped his fist as it rattled into the hole. The crowd erupted.

Alan had finished his career by making birdie on four consecutive holes to complete one of the greatest clutch performances in the history of the NCAA tournament. By doing so, he knew, the Cowboys were now 2 under as a team. It was simple math. As Alan bent down to retrieve his ball, he knew Tiger and Notah both had to make their putts to just tie Oklahoma State.

Destiny, indeed.

For so long, Tiger and Notah had been linked, especially since the day of Tiger's recruiting trip, when Notah pulled him into Goodwin's office and told him Stanford didn't need him to be a national champion. Notah loomed large in Tiger's freshman year, from the prank of making him carry the luggage, to the friendship bonded over three quarters of school and eight months of college golf practice rounds, travel, hotel rooms, and meals out. They'd become good friends and would stay so the rest of their lives.

But at this moment, it was about golf, and it was about coming through when their team needed them most, and if there were any two players in college golf capable of making these putts to extend the playoff, it was these two.

Tiger was away. He needed to make his putt to even make Notah's putt relevant. Everybody watched, in stony silence. Woods took forever to line up his putt. He stalked it. Walked behind the hole. Crouched. It was over a minute now.

Trip could barely breathe. The memories of Sawgrass were choking him. Holder had watched and admired Woods since he was thirteen years old, standing at driving ranges watching the prodigy hit buckets of balls, hoping that he could somehow convince Tiger to wear Cowboy orange. Goodwin watched, remembering the Letter, and Tiger smiling broadly, that famous smile, when he committed to Stanford that day in Earl and Tida's house, over a pizza.

And when Tiger brought his putter back, most everybody thought its path would lead to another chapter in the legend.

Until it rolled and rolled closer to the hole . . . and . . . stopped.

Short.

Again.

Tiger's reaction was swift: He whipped his hat and putter to the ground in disgust. Shock waves rippled through the crowd, which was half gasping, half cheering. Greenside, Casey, Will, and Jerry couldn't believe it. To see Tiger leave a clutch putt short once was an event. To have it happen twice, on the same hole, in the same early evening, with the same thing—an NCAA championship—at stake? Unthinkable.

Incredibly, there was still a chance Stanford could win.

Notah would need to make birdie, and Chris and Trip would have to miss short par putts to prevent an Oklahoma State victory.

With all the momentum in the world sliding away from Stanford and toward Oklahoma State, and with the Stanford team riding an unfortunate tsunami of missed clutch putts, Notah missed again.

Five Stanford golfers were done with the eighteenth hole in the playoff, and their aggregate score was even par.

Two Oklahoma State players were done with the eighteenth hole

328 · THE LAST PUTT

in the playoff, and thanks to Alan's and Kris's birdies, their aggregate score was 2 under par.

Incredibly, there was still confusion, as there had been all tournament, about the scoring. Chris did not yet know that Yanagisawa had made only par, not birdie. Trip had only just figured it out. Understanding that the Cowboys had a 2-stroke lead, he had all the energy and confidence imaginable. He marched up to his ball, gave it a quick look, and banged it into the hole for par.

Chris, who still assumed that Oklahoma State needed to make both putts to win the long-coveted national championship, was dumbfounded by Trip's carefree attitude toward the biggest putt of his collegiate career.

*What are you doing?* he thought as Trip's putt plopped into the hole. *We need to take our time, here. What's the rush?*

Kuehne plucked the ball from the cup, marched off the green, and hugged Alan, which annoyed Chris even more. *Hey, guys,* he thought to himself. *I could miss this easily.*

His teammates were assuming he would safely two-putt from 2 feet to win the tournament. What he didn't yet realize was that OSU's edge was 2 strokes and not 1. Chris had battled the pressure of performing at the NCAA tournament his entire career, and until this year the pressure had crushed him. Now here he was, feeling the pressure again even though he had two chances to bag a 2-footer. In some ways, it was funny, and they would laugh about it for years afterward. On a tumultuous day wracked by lightning and thunder and delays and confusion, there was something poetic about the fact that the last golfer on the course didn't know what the correct score was.

Trip and Alan were mystified when Chris lined up the 2-footer as if it were an 18-footer. They had never seen anybody take more time over such a short putt, each second prolonging a celebration that was four years in the making. It wasn't until later when they asked him why he took so long.

"We had a two-stroke lead?" Chris replied. "Why didn't anybody tell me?"

Chris finally tapped in, and a wet, agonizing, endless day had reached an unbelievable conclusion. Oklahoma State 2 under par, Stanford par in the first playoff in nearly a century of NCAA championship competition.

The four Cowboys embraced in a team hug in the soft evening light. Chris and Trip still held their putters in their hands, and the collision of the bodies in the group hug made their caps fall off.

Meanwhile, stunned Stanford players looked on in silence, utterly baffled. It was theirs. It was always theirs. They thought they were the best and always knew, just knew, things would go their way. And then, suddenly, it wasn't theirs.

Holder, the "Great Stone Face" himself, disappeared into a grove of trees, trying to hide the tears that streaked his face. He would later tell reporters what he had told his team before the playoff began: This was the greatest example of clutch golf he'd ever seen.

He was relieved his decision not to walk with Chris during the third round had not cost his Cowboys the team championship, although he would always maintain his belief that his miscue had prevented Chris from becoming the sixth Oklahoma State player to claim the individual title.

Joy was mixed with relief for Alan Bratton and Chris Tidland, who had finally accomplished what they had come to Stillwater to do—win a national championship. More important, the best friends and career roommates achieved all this together.

Alan, long plagued by feelings of inferiority, knew he had left an indelible mark on perhaps the greatest golf program in the land. He and Chris had felt like underdogs from the first moment they stepped on campus but would soon join a short list of Oklahoma State's four-time All-Americans.

Chris accepted congratulations from Bob May, the person most responsible for convincing Holder to allow him to come to OSU, a person who knew what this moment meant. May, too, had only narrowly escaped the same fate he had just dodged—becoming a member of the first class under Holder to graduate without winning a national title.

Trip Kuehne's story was one of redemption. The most painful event of his life, the loss to Tiger at Sawgrass, was now avenged.

That it occurred during an unforgettable season that included his appearance in the Masters field and the near death of his brother in a car accident made it all the more emotional.

This would be as close to closure as Trip Kuehne would ever get.

Trip hugged Ernie, who had been with him at Sawgrass and who had never been prouder.

Kris Cox waved to his mother and grandfather on the balcony, saw the pride in their faces, the tears in their eyes.

Leif hung up the airplane phone after making another call and leaned back in his seat, a warm feeling of relief and satisfaction overwhelming him. Had his teammates lost in the playoff he would never have forgiven himself. The British passenger sitting next to him had sympathized with his plight, and when Leif told him that his team had won the playoff, had captured the NCAA Championship, the gentleman ordered a mini-bottle of champagne from a passing flight attendant. When the bubbly arrived, he offered a toast, he and Leif clinking plastic cups at thirty-five thousand feet.

Meanwhile, as the Oklahoma State celebration continued, the pro shop attendant delivered a message from Leif to Alan, Chris, Trip, and Kris. "Congratulations to the Cowboys," it read. "I'm going to have a huge drink to celebrate."

Stanford could only watch in disbelief. For years, the plan was to win the 1995 NCAA Championship. The plan, the "Great Experiment," came up short. It ended in emptiness in a playoff on this weird, endless gray day of midwestern thunder and lightning. They felt a long way from the gentle caress of Stanford's familiar California sun.

For Notah, Casey, and Will, the sensation felt bizarre. A year earlier, they were the ones backslapping and laughing and hugging. A year earlier, they were the national champions, the surprise team. Now, a year later, "Next Year's Team" hadn't even done what last year's team had. Last year felt so carefree and easy. This year, in truth, had felt harder, with the media scrutiny and the expectations.

Back home on the Stanford campus, Steve Burdick watched online as the results were posted. He felt sick and empty. What if his game hadn't collapsed? Maybe, just maybe, he would have made up the stroke they needed to repeat. He wanted to be in only one place—with his teammates.

In Columbus, the Stanford players stood with great calm and composure to watch Oklahoma State's celebration. Goodwin took a good look at his team. Nobody threw anything or swore or pouted. They took the aching pain as competitors, as the kind of kids Wally Goodwin always wanted on his team. He felt a rush of pride at their demeanor and wondered where he'd seen it before. It struck him. Last year at Stonebridge, Stanford won that championship trophy, he'd thought, with equanimity and grace. In defeat, he felt his team was radiating the same emotions. He was happy with them.

They watched the hugs and the tears from the players in Cowboy orange. Each one of the Stanford players could think only one thing: What if? What if either of Casey's putts had fallen on eighteen? What if either of Tiger's putts had fallen on eighteen? What if Notah had made the short putt on eighteen in regulation? In truth, they knew golf was a fickle mistress. And in truth, they liked every one of Oklahoma State's players. They'd grown up playing against Chris and Alan, against Trip and Kris. There had been junior tournaments as preteens, there had been U.S. Junior Amateurs, there had been road trips and play time in hotel swimming pools; there had been lunches and dinners; there had been college events through the years; there had even been a U.S. Amateur at Sawgrass that nobody would ever forget. Deep down, the Stanford players knew Mike Holder's teams would always fight to the end. A part of them felt pride for Oklahoma State and appreciation for their fantastic rally. It was, they knew in truth, one hell of a comeback.

In golf, each of them, Tiger, Notah, Casey, Will, and Jerry, since he was young, had been taught to deal with defeat and to offer a handshake of congratulations on the final green when defeat did come, when the final putt did fall. It was part of the game. This was their time to offer those congratulations—in the June midwestern dusk, at the Scarlet Course, at the site of the greatest NCAA Championship in the history of the sport.

# Epilogue

Fifteen years later, the 1995 NCAA Championship not only is remembered for the drama it produced but still resonates because the cast of characters who created that drama would go on to profoundly change the face of the sport.

And to this day, Notah Begay still teases his friend Tiger Woods.

"You know what?" he likes to say, a wicked grin on his face. "We were better without you."

That Stanford didn't win the 1995 NCAA Championship with Tiger after winning it the year before without him remains one of the oddities of the school's sporting history, but it's a stubborn fact. Leave it to Begay, the prankster, to still needle the world's greatest player about it.

After leaving the Scarlet Course that night of Oklahoma State's triumph, Wally Goodwin took the Stanford team to a restaurant. He observed them throughout the meal, and again as they flew home to California, and marveled at their equanimity. Despite the pain and thoughts of all the missed opportunities—what if either Tiger's or Notah's last putt had fallen?—he still says, to this day, he was as proud of his team's grace in defeat as he had been in their 1994 triumph.

Stanford wouldn't win the 1996 NCAA Championship, either, in Tiger's sophomore year, and their fourth-place finish would be the best team finish for Goodwin since 1995 before his eventual retirement in 2000.

Tiger, however, did win the individual national championship in 1996, joining the likes of Jack Nicklaus and Phil Mickelson as an NCAA medalist.

It was a precursor to an enormous change in Tiger's life—and in the history of American sports. Three months later, after winning a record third consecutive U.S. Amateur at Pumpkin Ridge in Oregon—like so many of his other triumphs, it featured a huge comeback over Steve Scott and many of his signature fist pumps—he turned pro.

Though Earl and Tida Woods always paid lip service to the idea of their son finishing his Stanford education, the obvious riches that awaited him were too strong a lure.

Tiger soon became the PGA Tour's Golden Goose, a one-man force of nature and with TV ratings the likes of which his sport had never seen—bigger than Palmer, bigger than Nicklaus.

Woods's accomplishments are now legendary, and he is arguably the world's most recognizable athlete. He has been the world's number-one-ranked golfer for more weeks than any other player in history. In 2009, *Forbes* magazine named Tiger the world's richest athlete for the eighth consecutive year.

In 2004, Tiger married the former Elin Nordegren and the couple welcomed two children: a daughter, Sam Alexis, and a son, Charlie. In the spring of 2006, Earl Woods died at the age of seventy-four from cancer. Two months later, Tiger won the British Open at Hoylake, his eleventh major championship. His sights were set on toppling Jack Nicklaus's all-time record of eighteen—the same mark taped to his childhood bedroom wall.

But Tiger suspended his pursuit on December 11, 2009, in the wake of a growing scandal involving his admitted infidelity, saying he would take an "indefinite leave" from golf. As of March 2010, his total stood at fourteen major championships.

Tiger wasn't the only member of the Stanford team to break barriers.

Begay would graduate from Stanford with an economics degree and earn his PGA Tour card in 1998. He became the first Native American to win on tour since Rod Curl in 1974, and the first Native American to play in the Masters. Begay did Curl one better, becoming only the third player in history to win two events in each of his first two years on tour. When Begay made the 2000 Presidents Cup team for the United States, he paired with Tiger in all four team matches.

After he reached as high as number nineteen in the world rankings, a series of back injuries interrupted his career from December of 2000 through much of the decade. Eschewing surgery for rigorous exercise and stretching, Begay earned his PGA Tour card for the 2009 season at Q-School.

Still remembering his roots in New Mexico, he runs the Notah Begay III Foundation, which delivers sustainable programs for Native American youths (www.nb3foundation.org). He lives in Dallas with his wife, Apryl, and their two children.

Casey Martin's influence reached an even higher level.

After graduating with a degree in economics, Martin played on the Nike Tour—including a win in 1998—before eventually earning his PGA Tour card for the 2000 season. Though his golf career included highlights such as a tie-23rd at the 1998 U.S. Open, Martin's leg deteriorated and affected his play.

He famously sued the PGA Tour for his right to use a golf cart during play, and in 2001 the case *PGA Tour, Inc. v. Martin* went to the Supreme Court of the United States. In a seven-to-two decision, the court ruled that walking is not a fundamental part of the game, and Martin had the right to a cart.

As his leg continued to plague him, Martin never regained full-time PGA Tour playing status after 2000, but he remains a hero to disabled athletes aspiring to compete in golf.

In 2006, he was named head golf coach at the University of Oregon in his hometown of Eugene, in many ways a dream job for the lifelong Duck fan.

Some Stanford players from the 1994–95 team still chase the golf adventure. Will Yanagisawa, the transfer from UC Irvine who fulfilled his dream of a Stanford diploma when he graduated in 1995 with a degree in psychology, is still based in his hometown of Long Beach, California, and has spent the past fifteen years playing pro golf tours in Canada, Japan, and Asia.

Steve Burdick dealt with his disappointment from the spring of 1995 by remaining an amateur until after the 1996 U.S. Amateur, then trying Q-School in the fall of '96. After failing to make it past the first stage, Burdick switched gears and began work with the College Golf Fellowship, a faith-based nonprofit organization that offers spiritual support and encouragement for college golfers and coaches nationwide, acting as chaplain. Burdick and his wife, Jenelle, live in his hometown of Rocklin, California, with their two children.

And Jerry Chang remains a member of Tiger's inner circle of friends, after playing on the 1996 Stanford team that finished fourth at nationals. He now works in the financial industry, based in his hometown of Los Angeles. Of all the Stanford team members, Chang and Begay remain closest to Tiger, and gave the induction speeches when Tiger was enshrined in the Stanford Athletic Hall of Fame on November 20, 2009 — one week before he crashed his Cadillac Escalade into a fire hydrant and tree near his Orlando home, setting in motion the events that led to his indefinite leave from the game.

The coach at the helm of it all still, amazingly, at age eighty-three, coaches golf.

Though a career from 1987 to 2000 at Stanford, including the national championship and two Pac-10 Coach of the Year awards, might seem enough, Goodwin had one surprise left.

In 2003, Goodwin came out of retirement to coach at the University of Northern Colorado at age seventy-six and helped guide the Bears to the 2007 NCAA Division I Independent Championship. Goodwin's influence is still felt at Stanford, where a backup player on the 1994–95 team, Conrad Ray, is now head coach. Ray follows Goodwin's game plan of top-notch recruiting and won the school's first national championship since the 1994 season when he skippered the Cardinal to the title in 2007.

Goodwin now serves as coach emeritus at Northern Colorado and splits his time between Colorado and the Rafter Y Ranch in Wyoming with his wife, Nan. They have two adult children and four grandchildren. The couple returns to Stanford every December to see old friends and catch a few basketball games, one of Goodwin's first loves.

On the Oklahoma State side, Mike Holder had bigger things in store than merely revolutionizing the coaching of college golf.

Holder would go on to help his alma mater in a much more significant way. In 2005, after thirty-two years as Oklahoma State golf coach, during which time he produced nine national titles and 110 All-Americans, Holder was promoted to vice president of athletic programs and director of intercollegiate athletics at Oklahoma State.

While using many of the skills he honed while raising money for Karsten Creek, Holder has been instrumental in raising hundreds of millions of dollars, the majority of which was donated by T. Boone Pickens, Holder's close friend and longtime supporter of his golf program.

The influx of cash is being used to upgrade the school's athletics facilities and create an OSU athletics village. The athletics program has also enjoyed unprecedented success since Holder became athletics director. In many ways, it's not a stretch to say that in recent years the athletics department and the entire university have been drafting off the success of the golf program.

Holder won only half as many NCAA championships as Houston's Dave Williams, but he may have had a greater impact. His influence on the college game remains immense. Many of the concepts he pioneered have become standard practice. Meanwhile, the beat goes on at OSU. Holder's handpicked successor, Mike McGraw, led the Cowboys to the program's tenth national title in 2006, one year before Stanford won its seventh.

Alan Bratton played professionally from 1995 to 2000, competing on the Asian Tour in 1996–97, the PGA Tour in 1999, and the Nationwide Tour in 2000. After spending three years as a player development manager for Ping, Bratton returned to Oklahoma State, where he, like Martin, is helping shape the lives of a new generation of golfers as associate head coach for the men's and women's programs. Bratton and his wife, Gretchen, have three children.

Chris Tidland was a member of the PGA Tour in 2001, 2007, and 2010 and the Nationwide Tour in 1996, 1999, 2002–6, 2008, and 2009. He has won two professional tournaments but still calls winning the 1995 NCAA Championship his greatest thrill in golf. He and wife, Amy, his next-door neighbor when they were growing up, have two children and live in Stillwater near the Brattons. Chris and Alan remain best friends and practice partners at Karsten Creek.

Valerie Cox, Kris's mother, died unexpectedly of a heart ailment three weeks after watching her son help Oklahoma State win the 1995 NCAA golf tournament. Kris was devastated. He said he could not have overcome his grief if not for his teammates, three of whom served as pallbearers. Cox has played professionally on various tours, including the PGA Tour, since 1996. Kris and his wife, Beth, have three children and reside in Dallas.

Trip Kuehne returned to Oklahoma State as a senior only to find out that the camaraderie he felt during the 1995 season could not be replicated. He ended his collegiate career as a three-time All-American, was named to the Big Eight's All-Academic team three times, and was an academic All-American twice. Shortly after Oklahoma State's come-from-behind victory at the Scarlet Course, Kuehne became the first Oklahoma State athlete to also be named the school's top student.

In retrospect, Trip's loss to Tiger in the 1994 U.S. Amateur proved to be a pivotal moment not only in Woods's celebrated career but also in Kuehne's. "Two lives changed that day," he now admits. Partly as the result of that experience, where for the first time his best wasn't good enough, Trip resisted the temptation, not to mention the riches, of the PGA Tour. He did so not for a lack of talent but because he didn't want to turn the sport he loved into a profession. In so doing, the "Can't Miss Kid" from Texas's first family of golf resurrected the image of Bobby Jones and the spirit of the gentleman amateur.

One of Trip's goals was to win the USGA title that Woods had denied him, especially after sister Kelli won the U.S. Women's Amateur in 1995 and '96 and brother Hank won the 1998 U.S. Amateur (with Trip caddying for him). He accomplished his goal by winning the 2007 U.S. Mid-Amateur championship, after which he announced he would retire from competitive golf after the 2008 Masters. Ernie not only predicted that Trip would win his long-awaited USGA title before the Mid-Am began but was with him the entire way, carrying his bag, just as he had during the U.S. Amateur loss to Tiger thirteen years before. Trip's Mid-Am title made the Kuehnes the first family in golf history to have three members win USGA titles.

"I want people to realize that you don't have to turn professional if you're an All-American," Trip said upon retirement. "There are other things out there. You can get a good-paying job, you can enjoy the game of golf and play because you love the game."

Trip lives with his wife and son in suburban Dallas, where he runs an investment management company.

Hank Kuehne transferred to SMU, where he became a three-time All-American. He and Trip never achieved their goal of winning the NCAA Championship together, but any disappointment vanished when Trip used the lessons he'd learned against Woods in 1994 to help Hank win the nation's top amateur title in 1998. Hank has played professionally on various tours, including the PGA Tour, where he twice tied for second, until a back injury stalled his career in 2007. In 2003, he won the tour's driving distance title, besting John Daly, who had won eight straight titles. Hank has not had a drink since his 1995 car accident.

Kelli Kuehne has played on the LPGA Tour since 1998 and has been a spokesperson for diabetes awareness.

Leif Westerberg has played on Challenge and/or European tours since 1997 while living in his hometown of Upplands Väsby, Sweden, with his longtime partner, Katharina Sjöblom.

As Oklahoma State players left the course after the playoff ended in 1995, they realized something they had overlooked in the emotional aftermath of the program's seventh national championship. They were famished, especially Tidland, who had been so nervous that he had been unable to get much down all day. At the end of what many players described as the longest day of their lives, the team descended on a chain restaurant, where girlfriends, parents, and boosters joined them for a celebration.

Alan and Chris, who were of legal age, ordered beers, wondering how Holder would react. Much to their surprise, instead of chewing them out, he said nothing.

It made for one more lasting memory.

As the Stanford players and Oklahoma State players handled their defeat and victory at different restaurants in Columbus that night, a sense of finality hung over the scene. A new day would come tomorrow, and the players would set out on their own divergent paths. And yet their bonds as friends and teammates remain strong, even all these years after the last putt was stroked.

# Appendix

1995 NCAA Golf Championship
Scarlet Course, Ohio State University
*May 31–June 3*

PAR: 72
YARDAGE: 7,109
BOLD = Daily leader
UNDERLINE = Daily low round
*t* = Tied for position in individual standings

## Official Team Finish (Top 5)

1. OKLAHOMA STATE UNIVERSITY 291 292 287 **286** —1,156
   *t-2*   Chris Tidland: 69 **69** 72 74—284
   *t-17*  Alan Bratton: 75 76 69 70—290
   *t-17*  Kris Cox: 75 73 71 71—290
   *t-39*  Trip Kuehne: 72 75 75 73—295
   *t-63*  Leif Westerberg: 78 75 76 72—301

2. STANFORD UNIVERSITY 289 **292 286** 289 —1,156
   *t-5*  Tiger Woods: 73 72 70 71—286
  *t-17* Notah Begay: 70 74 73 73—290
  *t-24* Casey Martin: 75 73 70 74—292
  *t-35* Jerry Chang: 71 76 73 74—294
  *t-39* William Yanagisawa: 75 73 76 71—295

3. UNIVERSITY OF TEXAS 289 296 **282** 290 —1,157
  *t-11* Jeff Fahrenbruch: 72 73 72 71—288
  *t-14* Harrison Frazar: 71 79 67 72—289
  *t-24* Marcus Jones: 71 71 72 78—292
  *t-52* Robby Skinner: 75 79 71 73—298
  *t-52* Brad Elder: 75 73 76 74—298

4. ARIZONA STATE UNIVERSITY **288** 300 289 287—1,164
  *t-5*  Joey Snyder: 71 74 69 72—286
  *t-8*  Scott Johnson: 72 72 74 69—287
  *t-47* Christopher Hanell: 69 78 76 73—296
  *57*  Larry Barber: 77 77 72 73—299
  *t-63* Todd Demsey: 76 77 74 74—301

5. UNIVERSITY OF SOUTHERN CALIFORNIA 295 293 **281** 296—1,165
  *t-5*  Chad Wright: 71 73 67 75—286
  *t-24* Roger Tambellini: 75 72 73 72—292
  *t-35* Justin Boatman: 76 72 72 74—294
  *t-49* Chris Johnson: 74 76 69 78—297
  *74*  Cory Okuna: 75 84 74 75—308

## Individual Finishers (Top 20)

  *1*  Chip Spratlin, Auburn: <u>67</u> 71 70 75–283
  *t-2* Ted Purdy, Arizona: 74 70 70 70—284
  *t-2* Chris Tidland, Oklahoma State: 69 **69** 72 74—284
  *4*  Chris Wollman, Ohio State: 70 73 71 71—285
  *t-5* Tiger Woods, Stanford: 73 72 70 71—286

*t-5* Joey Snyder, Arizona State: 71 74 69 72—286

*t-5* Chad Wright, USC: 71 73 67 75—286

*t-8* Scott Johnson, Arizona State: 72 72 74 69—287

*t-8* Garrett Willis, East Tennessee State: 72 70 76 69—287

*t-8* Dennis Hillman, Tulsa: 73 68 75 71—287

*t-11* Jeff Fahrenbruch, Texas: 72 73 72 71—288

*t-11* Charlie Wi, California: 70 73 74 71—288

*t-11* Scott Rowe, Northwestern: 71 70 75 72—288

*t-14* Harrison Frazar, Texas: 71 79 67 72—289

*t-14* Ken Staton, Florida State: 68 75 73 73—289

*t-14* Garrett Larson, California: 72 72 71 74—289

*t-17* Alan Bratton, Oklahoma State: 75 76 69 70—290

*t-17* Kris Cox, Oklahoma State: 75 73 71 71—290

*t-17* Didier deVooght, Ohio State: 75 71 72 72—290

*t-17* Notah Begay, Stanford: 70 74 73 73—290

# Acknowledgments

Accurately estimating the length of a putt is one of the most difficult things a sports journalist does. For laughs, nothing beats a congregation of scribes putting their heads and notebooks together after witnessing a big putt at a big event. "OK, how long did you have it? Was it an eight-footer? Ten? Wait . . . you had it at fifteen feet? OK, let's start over . . ."

Estimating the length of a putt that occurred nearly fifteen years ago is exponentially more difficult, which is why we are indebted to all those who helped us reach into the past and bring this college golf season to life.

"If I knew it was going to be so historic," Begay told us with a laugh, "I would have taken better notes."

We'd like to thank the sports information departments at Stanford and Oklahoma State as well as the folks at *Golf Digest* for allowing us to tap into their archives for the 1994–95 season.

Pete McDaniel's preview of the 1995 NCAA tournament and his game story in *Golf World* were invaluable, as were the many stories produced by *Golf Week*'s Ron Balicki and writers at the *Daily Oklahoman* and *Tulsa World*.

Kevin Casas covered the tournament for the *Dallas Morning News* and was such a treasure trove of information that we started calling him "Deep Throat" after Woodward and Bernstein's anonymous Watergate source.

Despite repeated requests, Tiger Woods did not grant us an interview for this book, which we regret. His agent, Mark Steinberg, was always prompt to reply and courteous, but the answer was always the same. Jerry Chang, one of Tiger's best friends, was similarly elusive and did not respond to numerous inquiries.

Every other member of the Stanford and Oklahoma State teams cooperated, and we would like to thank them most of all. From Stanford: Notah Begay III, Casey Martin, Will Yanagisawa, and Steve Burdick—take a bow. From Oklahoma State: Alan Bratton, Chris Tidland, Trip Kuehne, Kris Cox, and Leif Westerberg—you, too. Your journeys were our stories.

Other former Stanford and Oklahoma State players aided our research into the history of both programs. On the Stanford side, particular thanks to Grant Spaeth, Mark Freeland, Christian Cevaer, Brad Lanning, Dave Flemming, and Sara Sanders for illuminating the Stanford experience. From an Oklahoma State perspective, Grier Jones, Mark Hayes, Mike McGraw, and Greg Robertson filled in many gaps.

Parents, relatives, classmates, and friends all helped tell the stories, too. Thanks to Mark Soltau, Jaime Diaz, and Rudy Duran for helping us to understand Tiger better. A huge credit goes to John Strege's *Tiger,* which painstakingly documented Tiger's youth and proved a great resource. Special thanks to Melinda Martin, Casey's mom, for the DVD and for returning $5 through the mail when she thought we overpaid for the price of shipping. Now that's a mom for you.

Not only is Mike Holder the foremost authority on Oklahoma State golf, but he keeps detailed notes on every tournament in which his team competes, complete with weather conditions and round-by-round results for every participant. His notes were invaluable as we pieced together the 1994–95 season. He also answered numerous questions and verified a hundred facts via e-mail without once seeking a restraining order. Thanks, Coach.

Wally Goodwin, despite living in Colorado and Wyoming, made sure his trips to California to visit Stanford included long sit-downs on multiple occasions and was beyond generous with his time and memory. Your players were right, Wally. You're a good man.

His successor, Conrad Ray, and his assistant coach, Sam Puryear, never failed to make their archives available or answer the most repetitive questions at the most inconvenient times, and they did so with grace and good humor—displaying a command that shows why Ray led the Cardinal to the 2007 national championship, just as his coach did for the school in 1994. Good luck to Sam in East Lansing.

ESPN's footage of the 1994 and 1995 NCAA Championships gave us a window into the event itself. Thanks to Amy Tidland for unearthing video from Stillwater's local news coverage. Her husband didn't even know she'd kept it.

Dan Hayes graciously hosted us at his home in Venice, California, as did Pat Harmon at his office in Naperville, Illinois. The Lantern in downtown Naperville and Kinder's Meats in Pleasant Hill, California, provided much-needed fuel.

Thanks to Susan Canavan, Meagan Stacey, and Lisa Glover at Houghton Mifflin Harcourt for their belief in this project and for all their hard work. Barbara Wood caught us flatfooted with her sparkling copyediting. Special thanks to our wives and children for putting up with their grumpy and often exhausted husbands and fathers while this book was being written, especially in the final, frantic days after Brian's laptop was stolen and two-plus chapters had to be reproduced in ten days. Note to all readers: Back up your data. And save all your notes. Thankfully, Brian did at least one of the two.

Finally, special thanks to Greg Dinkin and Frank Scatoni at Venture Literary. It was, after all, their idea.

# Index

Price, Nick, 24
Purdy, Ted, 137, 253, 294, 322, 342

Quinney, Jeff, 95

Racism
  and Shoal Creek Country Club,
    83–85
  and Tiger, 38, 203, 258
Ralston, John, 93
Rantanen, Mikko, 168
Ray, Conrad, 42, 52, 95, 144, 165, 171, 336
Red River Classic, 113
Rice, Condoleeza, 48
Riley, Chris, 46, 79–80, 140
Roberts, George, 52
Robertson, Greg, 218, 223
Robertson, JoJo, 218
Rogers, Bill, 69
Rosburg, Bob, 17, 24, 93

Sabbatini, Rory, 253
Sanders, Sara, 49
Sargent, Tom, 38, 39, 124
Sawgrass. See TPC Sawgrass course;
    U.S. Amateur (1994)
Scarlet Course, Ohio State University,
    1, 5–6, 54, 62, 71, 251–52, 255–56,
    259, 300, 306, 341
Schutte, Warren, 41
Schwab, Charles, 52
Scott, Steve, 333
Seaver, Charlie, 92
Sellinger, Art, 177
Shoal Creek Country Club, 83–85,
    110–12, 113–14
Silveira, Larry, 94
Simpson, Scott, 94
Single, Doug, 87, 90, 91
Sjöblom, Katharina, 338
Skinner, Robbie, 307
Smith, Sherman, 75

Snavely, Ted, 46
Snoop Dogg, 103
Solheim, John, 75
Solheim, Karsten, 74, 75, 76–77
Southern California Amateur, 46
Southern California/French Junior
    Cup, 40
Southwestern Intercollegiate, 96
Spaeth, C. Grant, 50, 93
Spratlin, Chip, 262, 270, 272, 273, 291,
    305, 322, 342
Stadler, Craig, 94
Standup golf bags, 75
Stanford University, 2, 5, 38
  Athletic Hall of Fame, 335
  Tiger as student at, 24, 29–31, 83
    (see also Woods, Tiger, AT
    STANFORD)
  mugging incident, 202–3
  recruitment of, 20, 38–39, 40–45
  U.S. Intercollegiate at, 238, 240–43
  and Woods family, 34, 41, 63, 139, 333
  Yanagisawa feels pressure of, 2
    27–28
  GOLF TEAM OF, 92–94
  Daly on, 112
  diversity on, 84, 169
  at Golf World Intercollegiate, 141,
    142, 143
  and Goodwin, 86–87, 89–92, 94, 99,
    101 (see also Goodwin, Wally)
  and "Great Experiment" of Begay
    and Martin (redshirting), 41,
    148, 174, 230, 266
  Hawaii trip of, 204–5, 210, 211–12,
    213, 219–20, 224, 225
  at Jerry Pate Intercollegiate, 83,
    84–85, 111, 112
  in 1991 NCAA Championships, 148
  in 1992 NCAA Championships, 148
  as 1994 NCAA Championships
    winner, 61–62, 110, 116, 332

Wadkins, Lanny, 252
Waldorf, Duffy, 94
WallyGolf, 99
Walsh, Bill, 47–48, 75, 76
Ward, Harvie, 270
Watson, Ray, 93
Watson, Tom, 4, 93, 94
Watts, Brian, 71, 239
Weiskopf, Tom, 206
Wentworth, Kevin, 72, 132–33, 134
Westerberg, Leif, 59, 61, 64, 65, 77–78,
        114, 138, 197, 198, 200, 211, 213,
        213–14, 220, 223, 239, 243, 245,
        258–59, 261, 266, 268–69, 274,
        285, 287, 290, 291–92, 293,
        295–96, 296, 297, 306, 315–16,
        318, 330, 338, 341
Westerberg, Robert, 214
Western Amateur, 46, 59, 140, 143, 259
West Regionals, 243
Williams, Dave, 4, 56, 68, 69, 71–72,
        253, 282, 336
Willie, Louis J., 84
Willingham, Tyrone, 48
Wilson, Mark, 19–20, 22
Winek, John, 121, 122
Winters, George (uncle of Chris
        Tidland), 130–31
Woods, Earl, 10–11, 32
    death of, 333
    ethnicity of, 37
    in Hawaii, 205
    and Ernie Kuehne, 9–10, 186,
        257–58
    and Hank Kuehne, 209
    and Kelli Kuehne story, 177
    and Kuehne family, 234
    and 1994 U.S. Amateur, 13, 24, 28
    at 1995 Masters, 235–36
    and 1995 NCAA Championships,
        257, 276
    and Southwestern Intercollegiate,
        229

    and Stanford, 41, 44, 47, 139, 333
        and Heppler's call, 63
    Tiger encouraged by, 242
    and Tiger's upbringing, 19, 22–23,
        25, 33, 34–35, 36, 236
Woods, Charlie, 333
Woods, Elin (wife), 333
Woods, Sam Alexis, 333
Woods, Tida (Kultida), 23, 32, 32–33,
        33, 34, 36, 37, 41, 43, 205, 229, 333
Woods, Tiger (Eldrick), 1, 8–9, 18, 211,
        333–34
    as basketball player, 144
    and "Big I" (1989), 36, 42, 64, 102
    at British Open (2006), 333
    childhood and upbringing of, 32–37
        psychological conditioning, 11,
        22–23, 34
    ethnicity of, 37–38
    golf game of, 259–60
        Holder on, 63, 64
        length off tee, 231–32, 236
        swing, 5, 35–36, 64
        troubleshooting, 256
    and high school graduation, 40, 45
    and Holder, 40, 62–64, 64, 259, 279
    "indefinite leave" from golf, 334, 335
    infidelity of, 333
    and Hank Kuehne, 177, 209, 234,
        258
    and Trip Kuehne, 3, 24–28, 187, 233,
        256, 258, 314, 329–30
    and Kuehne family, 258
    and lightning in tournaments, 264
    marriage and family of, 333
    as "nonpracticing Buddhist," 172
    in Northeast Amateur (1994), 139
    and origin of "Eldrick," 35
    and origin of "Tiger," 32
    personal characteristics of
        competitiveness, 34
        confidence, 204, 233
        discipline, 33–34